Adventure Planner

... in the Golden
Triangle, Thailand

SAILING IN HA LONG BAY

LEFT *The Nam Ou
River, Laos*

RIGHT *Bus stop,
Attapu, Laos*

RACING DOG RIVER RAPIDS, NORTHERN SUMATRA

THE GREAT BOROBUDUR, CENTRAL JAVA

OF SIPADAN, NORTHWEST SABAH

NORTHWEST SABAH

THE TARSIERS OF TANGKOKO

MANADO'S CORAL PARADISE

LEFT *Coral
reef, Bunaken,
Indonesia*

AMONG THE WRECKS OF CORON, WEST PHILIPPINES

Frommer's®

ADVENTURE GUIDES

SOUTHEAST ASIA

ADVENTURE GUIDES

SOUTHEAST ASIA

Edited, designed and produced by AA Publishing
© The Automobile Association 2000
Maps © The Automobile Association 2000
Coloured maps: Cartographic Dept, The Automobile Association.
Black and white maps: Advanced Illustration, Congleton, Cheshire.

Published by AA Publishing,
a trading name of Automobile Association Developments Limited.

Published in the United States by:
IDG Books Worldwide, Inc.
An International Data Group Company
919 E. Hillsdale Blvd., Suite 400
Foster City, CA 94404

Frommer's is a registered trademark of Arthur Frommer.
Used under license.

ISBN 0-02-863709-7

Find us online at www.frommers.com

Colour separation by Chroma Graphics, Singapore.
Printed and bound in Hong Kong by Dai Nippon.

PREVIOUS PAGE Luang Prabang, Northern Laos.
INSET Rope bridge, Sabah, Borneo.

CONTENTS

Introduction 7
About the Authors 8
How to Use this Book 9
Regional Map 10
Practical Matters 12
When to Go – Adventure Planner 14
Travelling Safe 16

THAILAND • MYANMAR 18–81
A Trek to the Northern Hill Tribes 20–29
A Motorbiking Odyssey 30–39
Kayaking and Climbing at Phang Nga 40–49
Cycling in Isaan 50–57
Riding the E&O Express 58–65
Learning to Dive in Phuket 66–73
Steaming up to Mandalay 74–81

VIETNAM • CAMBODIA • LAOS 82–137
Smooth Sailing in Ha Long Bay 84–91
Northwest Vietnam by Jeep 92–99
Nam Ou River Voyage 100–109
Slowboat on the Mekong 110–119
Cambodia's Angkor Wat 120–129
Exploring the Bolovens Plateau 130–137

MALAYSIA 138–157
Malaysia's Jungle Railway 140–147
Island-Hopping around Langkawi 148–157

SUMATRA • JAVA 158–177
Racing Dog River Rapids 160–177
The Great Borobudur 170–177

BORNEO • SULAWESI 178–233
Life with the Iban 180–187
On the Headhunters' Trail 188–197
The Coral Wall of Sipadan 198–207
Climbing Mount Kinabalu 208–215
The Tarsiers of Tangkoko 216–223
Manado's Coral Paradise 224–233

PHILIPPINES 234–256
Meeting the T'boli People 236–247
Among the Wrecks of Coron 248–256

Contacts 257–289
Activities A–Z 290–311
Index and Gazetteer 312–319
Acknowledgements 320

INTRODUCTION

The exotic mysteries of Southeast Asia have attracted adventurous travellers for centuries. It encompasses a huge area of lush forests, active volcanoes, ancient caves and crystal seas which vie with each other to create a sumptuous landscape. Such variety gave birth to many and varied cultures. Once thriving cities are now mysterious ruins overrun by prolific jungle, but the peoples of Southeast Asia have adapted to many changes and a lively modern culture flourishes. Towns and cities, bustling with industry and commerce while still retaining their traditional identity, sit alongside areas hardly influenced by the outside world. To understand a region it is best to get in among it—paddling down the Mekong River or jeeping through the jungles of Dien Bien Phu, you are hot on the heels of a Hollywood vision, but sea canoeing around Halong Bay, motorcycling around the Golden Triangle, wreck diving off the Philippines—these adventures go far beyond the media myths. And then there is "culture," a word which hardly does justice to the fantastic ruin of Angkor Wat or the rich anthropology of Borneo. For travellers who are not content with life near a beach and a bar, this adventure guide to Southeast Asia is the perfect introduction to a refreshingly different way of exploring the world.

RIGHT Hat Tham Phra Nang Beach, Southern Thailand
ABOVE Feeding the orangutans at Sepilok, Sabah, Borneo

About the Authors

BEN DAVIES

Ben Davies is a well-known travel writer and photographer who has written and photographed in almost every country in Asia. He is an associate editor for *Asiamoney* and has contributed to newspapers and magazines ranging from the *International Herald Tribune* to *Vogue Singapore* and the *Phnom Penh Post*. Since moving to Asia ten years ago, he has written and photographed books on Thailand, Indonesia and the Philippines. His latest, *Isaan— Forgotten Provinces of Thailand* is a photographic book for Luna Publications.

JILL GOCHER

Australian photojournalist Jill Gocher has spent much of her life travelling, starting forty-something years ago as a "military brat." She writes exclusively about travel and culture, concentrating on Southeast Asia. She is the author of three books published by Times Publishing of Singapore. *Ciberon* is about the eponymous, small Javanese Sultanate; the other two are large-format illustrated books: *Indonesia, the Last Paradise*, and *Australia—the Land Downunder*. In addition, she has contributed both words and pictures to hundreds of books, magazines, and travel guides.

Jill is the editor of *Swesone*, the small inflight magazine of the Myanmar airline, Yangon Airways. While luxury travel has its charms, she is happiest when away from the modern world, spending time in less complex environments, tuning in to ancient rhythms.

SAM HART

Researcher and compiler of the "Blue Pages," Sam Hart has worked as a freelance journalist since 1996, writing in the U.K. for *The Guardian*, the *Young Telegraph*, the *Big Issue*, and *Nursing Times*. She has also worked as a T.V. researcher and a radio journalist. After travelling extensively in Southeast Asia, she is now a staff reporter on the *Big Issue* and teaches English as a foreign language to Kurdish refugees.

CHRISTOPHER KNOWLES

Christopher Knowles used to travel the world as a tour guide, specializing in journeys by train across Europe, the Soviet Union, the Silk Road, Mongolia and China. The author of books on Shanghai, China, Japan, Moscow and St. Petersburg, Tuscany, and the English Cotswolds, he also runs a company specializing in walking vacations.

SIMON RICHMOND

Simon Richmond's first brush with adventure was on the Big Dipper roller-coaster in his hometown of Blackpool, England. He's been in search of the same adrenalin rush ever since. Now based in Sydney, Australia, he's worked as a journalist in London and Tokyo. His features have been published in many U.K. newspapers, the *Sydney Morning Herald*, *The Australian* and *Australian Financial Review*. He now

spends most of his time travelling and writing guidebooks for the AA, Lonely Planet and Rough Guides.

How to Use this Book

The book is divided into three distinct sections:

This comprises the introductory material and some general practical advice to guide you on your travels. We have included an introduction to the writing team. Our authors come from all walks of life and cover a wide age range. What they do have in common, though, is a spirit of adventure and a wealth of travel experience.

The map on pages 10–11 shows the areas covered, and is colour-coded to highlight the regional divides. The 25 adventures are numbered for reference; the contents page will guide you straight to the relevant page numbers.

Pages 12–13 and 16–17 offer practical advice from experienced travellers, complementing information given later.

The seasonal calendar on pages 14–15 gives a guide to the optimum time to visit the areas covered in the adventures. However, many factors may affect when you might like to go, and greater details of climate patterns and their effect on activities are given at the end of each chapter. When arranging your trip always seek advice about the conditions you are likely to encounter from a tour operator or country tourist information office.

The main section of the book contains 25 adventures, chosen to give you a taste of a wide range of activities in a variety of places— some familiar, others not. The first page of each adventure carries a practical information box that gives you an idea of what to expect, plus a grade, numbered according to the relative difficulty of the activity or the level of skill required.

Going it Alone—Each adventure ends with a page of dedicated practical advice for planning that specific adventure yourself. This information should be used in conjunction with the "Blue Pages" at the end of the book (see below).

Any prices mentioned in the book are given in US$ and were the approximate prices current at the time of the trip. Due to variations in inflation and exchange rates these are only meant as guidelines to give an idea of comparative cost.

1 Challenge Rating: If you have even thought about booking the trip, you will manage

2 Not too difficult but you may need some basic skills

3 You will need to be fit, with lots of stamina and may need specialist qualifications

4 You need to be fit and determined—not for the faint-hearted*

5 This is for the serious adventurer—physically and mentally challenging!*

Sometimes only part of the trip is very hard and there may be an easier option

★ **Comfort rating:** Indicates the degree of hardship you can expect, where 1 is comfort-able and 3 is uncomfortable. This category not only covers accommodation, but also factors such as climate and other conditions that may affect your journey.

⚔ **Specialist equipment:** Advice on any equipment needed for the journey, covering specialist items like diving gear, and also clothing and photographic gear.

"Blue Pages"—*Contacts* and *A–Z of Activities*—begin with selected contacts specific to the 25 main adventures. Here you'll find names referred to in the main stories, including tour operators, with addresses and contact numbers.

The A–Z lists a wide range of the best activities available in the region, with general information and full contact details of outfits and organizations to help you plan your journey. Finally, the book ends with a comprehensive index and gazetteer.

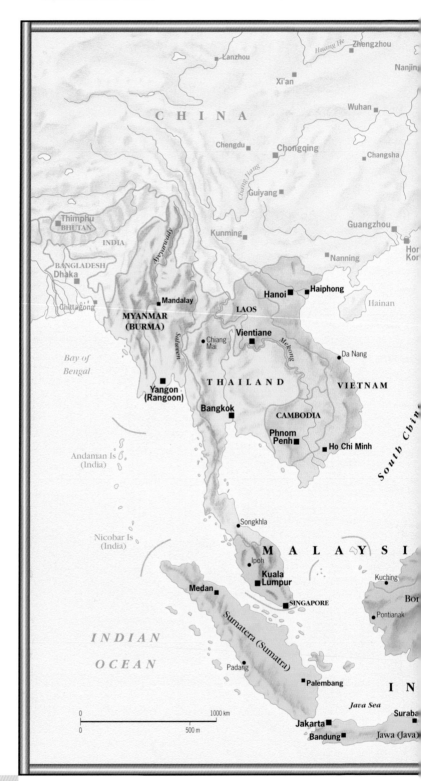

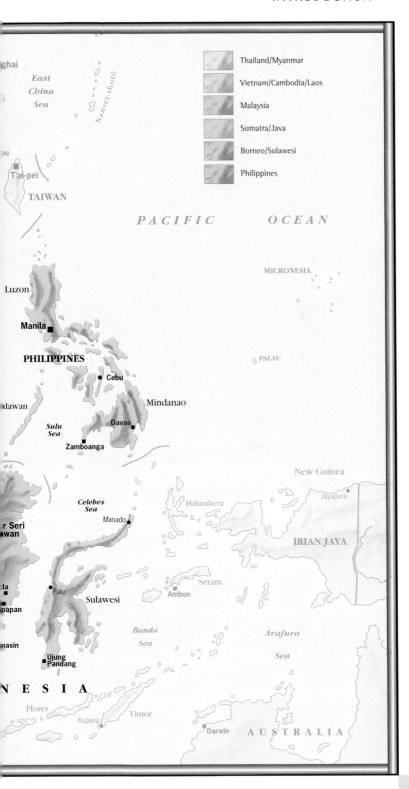

Thailand/Myanmar

Vietnam/Cambodia/Laos

Malaysia

Sumatra/Java

Borneo/Sulawesi

Philippines

Practical Matters

PREPARATION

To get the best out of your adventure holiday it's worth taking time to plan carefully. Research the areas you are interested in and use the "Blue Pages" to help you find a suitable tour operator. Think about when you will be travelling and what type of activities will be involved. Make sure your chosen tour operator knows the region well and can offer advice and alternative arrangements in case of unforeseen circumstances.

LANGUAGE AND CUSTOMS

Many of the languages spoken in the countries and regions covered will be unfamiliar to visitors. Where there are many local languages or the area is remote, it may prove difficult to communicate. However, there is often a widely used language in any area (such as English or French) of which many locals will have some knowledge. It is generally appreciated if visitors attempt a few words and a phrase book or mini-dictionary will be useful. Try to learn something of the local customs and etiquette to minimize the risk of causing offence through inappropriate gestures, body language, or dress.

MOST COMMON LOCAL LANGUAGES

Cambodia:	Khmer
Indonesia:	Bahasa Indonesian, Dutch, English plus 250 dialects
Laos:	Lao, French, Vietnamese, Meo
Malaysia:	Bahasa Malay; English, Chinese, Iban and Tamil widely spoken
Myanmar:	Myanmar (Burmese); also local minority languages and some English
Philippines:	English, Filipino, Cebuano
Thailand:	Thai; English, locally also Chinese, Lao, Khmer, Malay
Vietnam:	Vietnamese, French, English

TRAVEL DOCUMENTS

Make sure you have a full, valid passport and that it is valid for much longer than your stay. Check with the embassy or consulate of the countries you might be visiting about visa requirements. These can vary enormously and can change rapidly. If you intend travelling across borders, make sure you have all the relevant documents. Before you go, check the political situation for potential problems, (see below) especially in disputed areas, and try to find out local information before you travel to remoter areas.

CONTACTS:

U.S. State Department
Website: travel.state.gov/travel_warnings.html
Travel warnings and consular information.

Foreign and Commonwealth Office, U.K.
Tel: 020 727 01500
Website: www.fco.gov.uk
Travellers' advice line for information about potential political risks around the world.

HEALTH MATTERS

Many of the countries covered here are developing areas with relatively basic medical facilities. Check with your doctor or travel clinic and allow plenty of time for any necessary vaccinations. Record your vaccinations on an International Health Certificate and carry it with you.

CONTACTS:

World Health Organization
Website: www.who.ch/
For the latest information on health matters around the world.

U.S. Centers for Disease Control
Tel: (888) 232-3228; faxback: (888) 232-3229
Website: www.cdc.gov
Telephone and fax hotlines offering the latest health information and advice on vaccinations.

LOCAL CURRENCIES

CAMBODIA:	**Riel consisting of 100 sen**
INDONESIA:	**Rupiah (Rp) = 100 sen**
LAOS:	**New Kip (K) = 100 cents**
MALAYSIA:	**Ringgit (Malaysian dollar/M$) = 100 sen**
MYANMAR:	**Kyat = 100 pyas**
PHILIPPINES:	**Philippine peso = 100 centavos**
THAILAND:	**Baht = 100 satangs**
VIETNAM:	**New Dông (coins not used)**

CURRENCY

The safest way to carry currency is by traveller's cheques, preferably in US$, which are readily accepted in most places. Local currencies rates can fluctuate. Carry your money concealed in a money belt and avoid carrying all your valuables and money in the same place.

Please note: Any prices given in this book are in US$ and were the approximate prices current at the time of the trip. Due to variations in inflation and exchange rates these are only guidelines.

INSURANCE

Always make sure you have comprehensive travel and medical insurance before you travel. Check the policy carefully and ensure those arranging the insurance are aware you will be taking part in "dangerous" activities. Most standard insurances do not cover you for activities such as scuba diving, climbing, canoeing e.t.c.— the very type of activities you may tackle.

AT THE BORDER

Local import/export laws vary and you should seek the advice of consuls, border officials or carriers to ensure you are not contravening them. If buying souvenirs, bear in mind that there are universally strict laws against importing items made from some animals, obscene material, offensive weapons and narcotics. Some countries require additional documentation for prescription drugs and in others, alcohol is strictly controlled. Never take risks and always pack your own luggage.

TIME DIFFERENCES

	London, noon = 0 hours (Greenwich Mean Time)	New York Noon local time	San Francisico Noon local time
CAMBODIA	+7 HOURS	+12 HOURS	+15 HOURS
VIETNAM	+7 HOURS	+12 HOURS	+15 HOURS
LAOS	+7 HOURS	+12 HOURS	+15 HOURS
THAILAND	+7 HOURS	+12 HOURS	+15 HOURS
INDONESIA: Sumatra, Java, W & Central Kalimantan, Bangka, Billiton, Madura	+7 HOURS	+12 HOURS	+15 HOURS
INDONESIA: Bali, Flores, S & E Kalimantan, Sulawesi, Sumbawa,Timor	+8 HOURS	+13 HOURS	+16 HOURS
INDONESIA: Aru, Irian Jaya, Kai, the Moluccas, Tanimbar Malaysia	+ 9 HOURS	+14 HOURS	+17 HOURS
MALAYSIA: Peninsular Malaysia, Sarawak, Sabah	+ 8 HOURS	+13 HOURS	+16 HOURS
MYANMAR (BURMA):	+6.5 HOURS	+11.5 HOURS	+14.5 HOURS
PHILIPPINES:	+8 HOURS	+13 HOURS	+16 HOURS

No account has been taken of daylight saving time

When to Go

OCTOBER	NOVEMBER	DECEMBER	JANUARY	FEBRUARY	MARCH

THAILAND

A Trek To the Northern Hill Tribes

A Motorbiking Odyssey, Northern Thailand

Kayaking and Climbing in Phang Nga, Southern Thailand

Cycling in Isaan, Northeast Thailand

Riding the E&O Express, Singapore to Bangkok

Learning to Dive in Phuket, Southwest Thailand

MYANMAR

Steaming up to Mandalay, on the Ayeyarwady River

VIETNAM

RIGHT Hmong women, Vietnam

Northwest Vietnam by Jeep

LAOS

Nam Ou River Voyage, North Laos

Slowboat on the Mekong, Southern Laos

Exploring the Bolovens Plateau, Southern Laos

CAMBODIA

Cambodia's Angkor Wat, Northern Cambodia

MALAYSIA

Malaysia's Jungle Railway, East Coast

Island-Hopping around Langkawi, Northwest Coast

SUMATRA

LEFT Mount Sinabung, northern Sumatra

JAVA

BORNEO

Life with the Iban, Southern Sarawak

On the Headhunters' Trail, Northeast Sarawak

The Coral Wal

Climbing Mount Kinabal

SULAWESI

PHILIPPINES

Meeting the T'boli People, South Philippine

Adventure Planner

APRIL	MAY	JUNE	JULY	AUGUST	SEPTEMBER

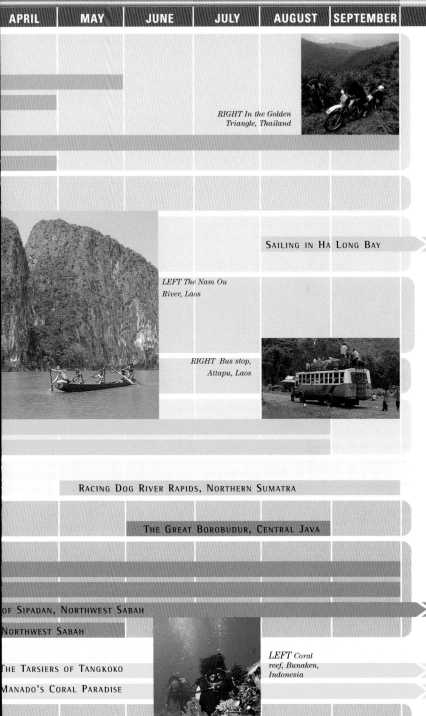

RIGHT *In the Golden Triangle, Thailand*

SAILING IN HA LONG BAY

LEFT *The Nam Ou River, Laos*

RIGHT *Bus stop, Attapu, Laos*

RACING DOG RIVER RAPIDS, NORTHERN SUMATRA

THE GREAT BOROBUDUR, CENTRAL JAVA

OF SIPADAN, NORTHWEST SABAH

NORTHWEST SABAH

THE TARSIERS OF TANGKOKO

MANADO'S CORAL PARADISE

LEFT *Coral reef, Bunaken, Indonesia*

AMONG THE WRECKS OF CORON, WEST PHILIPPINES

Travelling Safe

What To Do Before You Go

Confirm in advance of departure as many flights or voyages, and as much accommodation, as possible.

If you have only a limited time available, arrange your "adventures" in advance—some destinations restrict the number of visitors allowed in a particular period. A planned and packaged itinerary, though perhaps more expensive, may prove a wise investment.

❑ Photocopy all important documents and carry them separately from the originals. Keep a copy at home.

❑ Do not pack essential items in your suitcase—carry them in hand luggage.

❑ Give a copy of your itinerary and any contact numbers you have to friends or relatives.

❑ Research thoroughly the places you are visiting to ensure that you are adequately aware of the conditions that await you.

❑ Choose the right seasons.
In some countries election times are best avoided, while public holidays may make travelling difficult.

❑ Check whether you need a visa.

❑ Check with a doctor about vaccinations or prophylactics that may be necessary for the area you are visiting, and obtain an International Health Certificate with your vaccinations recorded on it.

❑ Purchase travel insurance, ensuring it covers your proposed activities—most standard insurances do not include adventure activities.

What To Take

A soft bag is much better than a hard-frame suitcase. Make sure you have a way of securing the bag, such as a lock or a strap. Pack fewer clothes than you think

---

THE FOLLOWING WILL MAKE ANY TRAVELLING EXPERIENCE MORE COMFORTABLE:

❑ A torch/flashlight and spare batteries.

❑ A first-aid kit to include rehydration tablets and insect repellent. Effective suncream/block. Diarrhoea treatment, antihistamines, aspirin.

❑ Water bottle

❑ Waterproof bag for valuable items

❑ An umbrella

❑ Passport and spare passport photographs

❑ A supply of books to read and/or short-wave radio

❑ A folding walking stick for mountain descents

---

you will need, and more photographic film. If you do not want to be bothered with washing clothes, laundry services can be cheaply and easily obtained in most of the places featured in this book. It is always better to take film than to have to buy it locally. A spare camera battery is also recommended.

Take the RIGHT clothes. It may be sweltering on the coast, but if you are climbing a mountain, it will be very cold at the top. Shorts may be fine on the beach but not in a mosque. Footwear is especially important if you are tackling contrasting adventures, for example sandals for island hopping but boots for hiking. And don't forget your bathing suit.

Money

Take US$ travellers cheques and a separate supply of American dollar bills. Don't forget to take note of the numbers. Most major credit cards are widely accepted (although some countries favour one over another), but this cannot be relied on in remoter areas.

What To Avoid

Although you should consider taking a course of anti-malaria tablets, it is better to avoid being bitten by mosquitoes in the first place. Cover all exposed flesh in a good insect repellent.

Avoid offending local sensibilities, whatever your own opinions. Liberal views and open debate may be acceptable at home, but in some countries discussion of religion and politics can be touchy subjects and possibly illegal.

If you are planning to go scuba-diving, or take part in some other instructor-led activity, don't automatically go for the cheapest options unless you are very experienced and competent to judge. A reputable operator may cost more to use, but it may save your life.

Avoid taking things for granted. Local people often presume you know about local conditions or else trivialise or exaggerate possible dangers or irritations, so don't be embarrassed to ask questions.

It is best to be careful about what you eat and drink. Water anywhere may be contaminated so always drink bottled water and avoid ice in drinks, no matter how hot it is. Only eat cooked food and, remember, washing food is only helpful if the water used is pure.

Drugs

Do not, under any circumstance, be tempted by offers of drugs—traffickers can face the death penalty. Do not ever carry anything for anyone else, no matter how apparently innocent the request.

PERSONAL SAFETY

Theft

Take only what you really need when out and about—leave as much as possible in a safe at your accommodation. In countries where mugging is a real threat, it is as well to carry a little cash to give away if necessary. Unfortunately, those countries where street theft is a problem, may expect you to carry ID—make a reduced copy of your passport, include a proper passport photograph and enclose the whole thing in a plastic wallet.

Beggars, Sellers and Confidence Tricksters

Difficult though it may be, think twice before you give money to beggars. Sometimes it is a ploy—before long you are surrounded by a sleeve tugging crowd, from among which one member leaps out and snatches your camera or money. Persistent sellers are a nuisance but if you can avoid looking them in the eye and learn the local words for "no thank you" you will find them less troublesome. As for confidence tricksters, do not be taken in by flattery and be deeply suspicious of bargains.

Violence

As a foreigner, you are unlikely to be affected by violent crime. In cities, ask locally if there are areas that are best avoided.

Travelling Alone

The two main things for individuals are to let people know where you are travelling and to carry an absolute minimum of luggage—there will be no one else to watch over it.

Women

It is a tiresome truism that Western women travelling alone may be considered of easy virtue, if only because in some countries women rarely venture anywhere alone. Ignore, with as much dignity as possible, the unwelcome attentions that may come your way. Dress with consideration for local customs (especially completely covering arms and legs in Muslim countries or in remote areas). Note that although most toiletries will be available in major towns, they may not be elsewhere.

EAMING UP TO MANDALAY 74–81

1 THE NORTHERN HILL TRIBES 20–29

2 A MOTORBIKING ODYSSEY 30–39

4 CYCLING IN ISAAN 50–57

5 RIDING THE E&O EXPRESS 58–65

6 DIVING IN PHUKET 66–73

3 KAYAKING AT PHANG NGA 40–49

Map labels: Myitkyina, Bhamo, **MYANMAR (BURMA)**, Lashio, Monywa, **Mandalay**, Taung-gyi, Sittwe, Meiktila, Pyinmana, Pyè, Henzada, Chiang Mai, Lampang, Phitsanulok, Bago, Pathein, **Yangon (Rangoon)**, Mawlamyine, Nakhon Sawan, Khon Kaen, Udon Thani, **THAILAND**, Dawei, Nakhon Ratchasima, Ubon Ratchathani, **Bangkok**, Mergui, *Gulf of Thailand*, Surat Thani, Nakhon Si Thammarat, Phuket, Hat Yai, Songkhla, **MALAYSIA**, **SINGAPORE**

0 — 400 km
0 — 200 m

THAILAND·
MYANMAR

Thailand has deservedly earned a reputation as one of Southeast Asia's great travel destinations. It offers four distinct regions: the south, with its sunswept beaches and islands; the mountainous north, home of hill tribes and the legendary Golden Triangle; the bountiful central plains called the rice bowl of Asia; and the arid northeast, known as Isaan, famed for its Khmer ruins and mighty Mekong River. Amidst all this diversity, Thailand's unifying strengths are its Buddhist religion, its monarchy, and stable democratic system. Everywhere, you will find charming people known for their *mai pen rai* (no worries) attitude to life. By contrast, poverty and politics mean a less easy life for the delightful people of neighbouring Myanmar, formerly Burma, three-quarters of whom live in the valley of the fabled Ayeyarwady River that forms the country's backbone. Take the steamboat up to Mandalay for an insight into this little-known, yet beautiful and exotic country.

Thailand's northern hills at Mae Hong Son, "City of Mists"

THAILAND

A Trek to the Northern Hill Tribes

by Ben Davies

The hill tribes, or chao khao, *of northern Thailand live in the lush mountain region along the border with Myanmar (Burma), where they worship the spirits and have traditionally cultivated opium. I spent three days trekking to their villages, river rafting and elephant riding to gain an insight into this fascinating people.*

In the northern reaches of Thailand, precipitous mountains and spectacular wooded valleys form the backdrop to some of the kingdom's most enchanting and enigmatic peoples. The hill tribes, or *chao khao* as they are officially known, comprise nine groups (the major ones are the Karen, Lahu, Lisu, Akha, Hmong, and Yao). Numbering around 500,000, they originally migrated from Tibet, Burma, and southern China, settling on the elevated slopes of Thailand during the late 19th and early 20th centuries.

These days, trekking agencies have sprung up in all the major towns, offering a veritable smorgasbord of hilltribe tours. But for adventurers who want to get off the beaten track, there are still plenty of opportunities both to visit the ethnic peoples and go rafting, caving, cycling, and elephant riding.

My journey had begun a day earlier with a gruelling five-hour bus journey from **Chiang Mai** (see page 32) through grand mountain scenery to the town of **Pai**, in the far northwest. Although it's possible to trek closer to Chiang Mai or **Chiang Rai**, the hilltribe villages there tend to attract large numbers of tourists; further afield, you are generally rewarded with a more intimate experience.

In Pai, I signed up for a three-day group tour at one of the many small trekking agencies that crowd around the market on **Rangsiyanun Street**. The following morning, in the company of an unemployed American family therapist and a 25-year-old yachting fanatic from Hawaii, I head off in a pick-up truck in the direction of Soppong. After stopping at a small Lisu village to collect our young guide and his Lahu interpreter, we finally draw to a halt by the side of the road and follow our guide up into the trees towards the hilltribe people.

3 Most treks involve walking for between three and four hours a day, depending on the type of group you join and the precise route you take. For something less taxing, it's possible to hire your own guide or even to travel part of the way by motorbike.

★★ If you enjoy creature comforts, the only real option is to book an organized trip through the Lisu Lodge, 50km (30 miles) from Chiang Mai (see Contacts), which offers its own bamboo cottage set in beautiful mountain scenery. Otherwise, expect to sleep in the hilltribe villages, in extremely basic bamboo huts with mattresses spread out on the floor. Simple hotels and guest houses can be found in the towns of Pai and Soppong, and luxurious hotels in Mae Hong Son, Chiang Mai, and Chiang Rai.

✗ Bring at least double the amount of camera film that you think you may need. Sun hats, sun cream, and walking shoes are a prerequisite, along with waterproofs if you plan to travel in the monsoon season.

HILLTRIBE LEGENDS

The people of the Yao tribe have a legend. They believe that the first man was the offspring of a dog named Pan Kou, who defeated a cruel tyrant and for his reward was given the hand of a Chinese princess.

In northern Thailand, there are plenty of other legends that have been handed down from one hilltribe generation to the next. Amongst the Karen, who are one of the oldest of the hilltribe people in the region, a popular belief holds that if a villager is sick, the spirit, or *pi*, responsible for the illness must be divined by examining grains of rice. Once the offending spirit has been identified, the people will entice it into a basket with offerings of spicy chicken before slamming the lid shut on it and then burying the basket in the forest.

Animism also plays a major role amongst other hill tribes. The Akha have traditionally worshipped the sun and the moon, whilst the Hmong, who are the second largest tribal group in the North, worship the spirit of the sky, who they believe created the world.

Don't expect to be the first tourists to discover these people, however. Many are used to seeing foreigners. Their traditionally colourful costumes are fast giving way to jeans and T-shirts. But a trek into the northern hills is more

than just a chance to see the hill tribes. It is also an adventure, a walk through beautiful countryside, and, if it is done in the right company, an opportunity to experience a totally different way of life.

VISITING THE LAHU

The village of **Pa Mon Nok** lies high up on the hillside at the end of a narrow path that winds its way up past clumps of bamboo and teak seedlings. It is a Red Lahu village of 30 families, with breathtaking views of the mountains beyond.

We have walked more than two hours from the main road to get here, huffing and puffing up the slopes, urged on by our guide, a Lahu tribesman from one of the surrounding villages.

Our guide leads us to a collection of flimsy-looking bamboo huts scattered around a muddy courtyard overrun by pigs, chickens, and horses. We climb a ladder into one of these simple habitations, from where a plume of smoke emerges. In the semi-darkness, it is just possible to make out a few pots and cooking utensils lit up by shafts of light filtering through the bamboo. Our guide speaks with one of the elders in the family. We are then invited to sit cross-legged around the hearth while our translator tells us about the traditions of the Lahu people.

Originally believed to be of Tibetan origin, the Lahu began to arrive in Thailand in the late 19th century. Today they number around 30,000, divided into four different sub-tribes; the Lahu Nni, or Red Lahu, similar to those in Pa Mon Nok, the Lahu Na or Black Lahu, as well as the Yellow Lahu and White Lahu. Poorer than the other tribes, these people practise shifting cultivation of crops, abandoning their land after a few years to clear new areas of forest. Traditionally, they have also been frenetic growers of the opium poppy.

But if the Lahu lack the wealth of the Karen and the bright clothes of the Lisu, they have earned the respect of the other hill tribes in numerous other ways. The Lahu are reputed to be the greatest

TRAVELLERS' TIPS

- ❏ Visiting a hilltribe village alone or without a guide can be risky.
- ❏ Wear light, comfortable clothing suitable for hiking.
- ❏ Take off your shoes before entering a house.
- ❏ Respect hilltribe beliefs and do not touch or photograph village shrines.
- ❏ Never hand out Western medicine unless you are qualified to do so.
- ❏ Avoid handing out money as a gift. Postcards, pens, or notebooks are a far better option.
- ❏ Always ask permission before photographing the people, and if they refuse, respect their wishes.
- ❏ Remember it's a criminal offence to smoke opium.

THAILAND

hunters amongst the hilltribe people. They are also renowned for their skill in pounding rice with giant wooden pestles, as well as their ability to transport water to their fields using an intricate system of bamboo aqueducts.

Eating *khao niau*, a type of sticky rice, together with chicken skin and sweet sausage brought by our guide, we share our food with the two women and a child, communicating self-consciously with smiles and signs before quietly taking our leave.

OFF THE BEATEN TRACK

From the village of Pa Mon Nok, we continue to the west, walking around the hillside and then up over the far side. In places, we are hemmed in by lush palm and evergreens. In other places, vast tracts of forest have been hewn away to make way for fields of corn and pumpkin, now bathed in soft afternoon light.

Trekking through such beautiful landscape is an experience that is almost akin to meditation. Here in the northern hills, surrounded by wild orchids, leaf

LEFT Elephant camps offer shows and rides through the forest
RIGHT Forest paths may be slippery in the rainy season
BELOW Rafting on the Pai River

THAILAND

ORCHIDS

There are more than 1,000 species of orchids growing in the wild in northern Thailand. Orchids were first cultivated in Siam by Prince Tivakornwongpravat over 100 years ago. Today the most famous varieties include the *Sirikit* (named after the present queen) and the *Vanda Caerulea*, which grows in high altitudes. If you do not get a chance to admire them on your trek, visit one of the orchid farms on the outskirts of Chiang Mai.

butterflies, and rich tropical vegetation, even the nearby town of Pai seems a million miles away.

It's late afternoon by the time we arrive at **Baan Pa Mon Nai**. This is a prosperous-looking Red Lahu village of about 50 families, set in a large clearing surrounded by trees. Like many villages in northern Thailand, Baan Pa Mon Nai is accessible by vehicle in the summer months. But now in the rainy season, the dirt road is impassable and walking is the only reliable means of transport.

We are taken to a simple hut in the upper part of the village. Inside, there is one spacious room with a bamboo floor and reed mats for sleeping—next to a smouldering fire. Down below, on the far side of the muddy yard, is a simple hut containing primitive water pumps and a large wrought-iron bowl for washing.

POPPIES AND OPIUM

At night in Baan Pa Mon Nai, the croaking of tree frogs and cicadas fills the air. A few pigs rummage in the dirt below the village houses. The only other sound is the far-off rhythmic crushing of a woman pounding corn in the yard.

Traditionally the northern hilltribe people have been prolific growers not only of corn and rice, but also of the opium poppy. Cultivated on the higher slopes at elevations above 1,500m (5,000 feet), opium is a highly profitable cash crop and relatively easy to grow. When the poppies are ready for harvesting, generally from early January to the end of March, the pods are cut, allowing the resin to leak out and congeal. The resulting gum is then scraped off and wrapped in dried poppy petals or banana leaves before it is either sold in raw form to Chinese middlemen or secretly taken to refineries and processed into heroin.

You are unlikely to come across fields of red and white opium poppies in northern Thailand, however. Instead, the people have been encouraged by the government—and especially the King—to turn to other cash crops, such as tomatoes or cabbages. In the North it is now far more common to see a bare-footed *chao khao* tribesman cultivating strawberries than opium.

The following morning dawns wet and misty. Once again we follow a network of slippery paths through the trees, passing Hmong or Karen people carrying giant baskets of wild mushrooms, which they will cook in huge cauldrons over a fire. Once an old man walks past clutching a rusty musket used to shoot wild birds. Finally, in the early afternoon, we reach the Karen village of **Baan Meung Phen**.

WHERE TO TREK

Chiang Mai and Chiang Rai may be the best-known trekking centres, but you will undoubtedly be rewarded if you travel further afield. There are several interesting and established trekking areas to the east, around Nan Province, while the hilltribe people to the west, around Pai, Soppong, and Mae Hong Son, have had considerably less exposure to tourists. There are also good opportunities for more luxurious trekking and "soft" adventure packages in the region around Tha Thon and Mae Malai. These be should booked in advance (see Contacts).

ON THE MENU

Don't expect five-course gastronomic spreads on your trek. Typically your guide will buy meat and vegetables from the market on the day that you leave and will prepare them at midday or in the evening, along with rice or noodles. Northern delicacies you may be fed include spicy minced pork known as *larb*, sweet sausage, and chicken skin. If you really can't live without Western-style snacks, bring them with you, but don't give them to the children as this encourages begging. Bottled water, hot tea, coffee, and beer are available in the larger villages.

TRIBAL VILLAGES

One of the most striking things about the Karen is their prodigious cotton-weaving skills. Like many hill tribes, these people use narrow looms, which they work by sitting on the floor with their legs outstretched. The results are a multitude of colourful garments—blouses, sarongs, and shirts—which they generally wear with a profusion of beads and bracelets.

Like the Suay people in northeast Thailand, the Karen are also renowned for their handling of elephants, a skill that goes back to the days when they inhabited the jungles of Burma. Above all, however, they are recognized for their skill in brewing liquor. In many villages, when a Karen bride gets married, her first priority after the wedding ceremony is to brew up a batch of extremely potent rice liquor for her in-laws.

At nightfall, bowls of boiled noodles served up with egg and rice are laid out in front of us. Afterwards, we sleep on mats laid out under a covered porch, separated from our hosts by a simple wicker screen.

TRAVELLING BY ELEPHANT

Early the next morning, after a swift breakfast of toast and coffee, three specially trained elephants and their mahouts (drivers) collect us from the village. Now the first thing to remember if you are about to climb on to an elephant is, don't panic. These beasts may weigh a tonne and be kings of the jungle, but they haven't been used for years as work animals without good reason. Elephants are among the most intelligent of animals, and the most sensitive. And even though they may live for up to 100 years, they rarely stumble.

Thailand's long association with elephants is firmly entrenched in history. The kingdom's most famous species was known as the white elephant, a breed so rare that any captured animal would be handed over to the king. With their white eyes and toenails, these albino animals acquired such mythical status that the king would employ special poets and chefs to entertain them in the palace grounds. One distinguished poet described the snoring of the white elephant as being like the sound of bells.

But history has a funny way of disappearing from your mind as you place one foot gingerly on the kneeling elephant's trunk before being hauled up by the mahout on to twin bamboo seats atop this mother of all beasts. When you are on an elephant, the whole world sways from side to side as though you were a tottering drunkard on a big night out. So high up are you from the ground that small slopes suddenly begin to resemble mountains.

From a clearing near the Karen village, the trail meanders alongside the river offering tantalizing views of the countryside. Countless butterflies with wings of white and yellow flutter past into the trees. Occasionally, giant geckos or water buffalo emerge out of the undergrowth, while sunbirds take flight at the sound of our approach. Orchids, too, grow in this part of the countryside, nestling behind clumps of bamboo.

THAILAND

25

ABOVE A Black Lahu village house and (INSET) a Red Lahu family in their bamboo hut, in the Soppong district
BELOW A woman of the long-necked Karen tribe, known as the Padang; the metal coils depress the collar bone

By the time we emerge from the forest, the sun is already high in the sky. Our mahouts strain to keep their animals from devouring every bush in their path. Finally, after two hours of riding, the elephants come to a halt, kneeling on the ground to allow us to climb off—and return to the solidity of the ground.

RIVER JOURNEY

If you go trekking in the monsoon season, keep your eyes open for one of

with enviable speed, clambering on to your ankles and sucking your blood until they are satiated and drop off. The only way to fight off these dreaded creatures is to wear long trousers and thick socks or, better still, to avoid trekking in the monsoon season.

Such is their notoriety, that the famous 19th-century French naturalist Henri Mouhot identified leeches and

nature's most disreputable creations. Leeches, the size of tiny caterpillars, come out with the rains and hang around in trees or along paths waiting for people like you or me. Once they have spotted their prey, they propel themselves along the ground

mosquitoes as being the greatest evils in the entire tropics. "Thousands of these cruel insects suck our blood night and day," he wrote in his book *Travels in Indochina*. "I would rather have to deal with the wild beasts of the forest."

In the heat of the midday sun, our group sets off once again, following a trail that leads down to the river bank, where a flimsy bamboo raft is waiting to transport us downstream. Before climbing on to your raft, make sure that you put your cameras and money into waterproof polythene bags, which can be hung from a bamboo post. You must then keep very still, with your weight evenly distributed to avoid toppling the raft.

Moving away from the bank, we drift down river for an hour and a half, propelled by the gentle current that takes us through a landscape of deforested hills and limestone crags. Now, in August, the water is low, and the raftsmen at the front and the rear desperately push us off rocks and over burbling rapids. But at the end of the rains, in September and October, this narrow stretch of river can be transformed into a fast-flowing torrent that will carry the raft to Tham Lawd in little more than 40 minutes.

CAVES AND FLYING SAUCERS

The town of **Soppong** is synonymous with two major tourist attractions: the

magnificent **Tham Lawd**, an 8-km (5-mile) drive north of town near the banks of the river; and the large number of Lisu villages that lie in the vicinity.

Tham Lawd, otherwise known as Cave Lod, is believed to be part of one of the largest cave networks in the whole of Southeast Asia, although only a small part of the cave is accessible. In this awesome cavern, the rocks take on strange and formidable shapes: an elephant's head here, a frog there, and even a flying saucer. Stalactites hang from the roof, which in some places is higher than any cathedral.

From the first cavern, we follow the steps up to a second cavern, in many ways even more impressive. From there, a third cavern looms out of the darkness, to be reached by a small raft that crosses the stream.

Sobered by the sheer scale of what we have seen, we emerge into the bright light of day. After three days, the adventure is over and our group goes its separate ways. The women return to Pai, while I take the staggeringly beautiful route west to **Mae Hong Son**, known as the "City of Mists" (see page 37).

BICYCLES AND KAYAKS

If you don't fancy the idea of just trekking amongst the hilltribe people, there are plenty of other adventure activities that can be included in your trip to northern Thailand. They range from cycling through the hills around Pai (often steep and winding, but very exhilarating), to motorbiking (see pages 30–39), kayaking, and travelling by four-wheel drive vehicle. Although many of these activities are arranged by travel agents, it is relatively simple to hire a bicycle or for that matter a four-wheel drive car in the major towns. Always check with the locals before heading off on your own, especially in sensitive border areas. You may want to sign up on a two-day white-water rafting trip along the Pai River (July–February) run by Thai Adventure (see Contacts).

ARTS AND CRAFTS

The hilltribe people offer an extraordinary range of fine handicrafts and costumes, from beautifully sewn Shan wallets to Hmong bags, Lisu tassels, and Akha jewellery, many of which you may find on sale. If you intend to buy these northern items, always try to purchase them from the villagers themselves—and remember to haggle. That way you can be sure that both you and the people who actually make the handicrafts get a fair price.

GOING IT ALONE

INTERNAL TRAVEL

From Bangkok there are frequent flights to Chiang Mai, Chiang Rai, and Mae Hong Son, from where you can catch regular buses along the tortuous mountain route to Pai (4–5 hours). Trains (with sleeping compartments) also run from Bangkok to Chiang Mai, taking about 11 hours. If you need to take a specific train or flight during peak season or at the time of a festival, make a reservation in advance.

WHEN TO GO

The best time to trek is from the end of October to the end of February. During these months the country-side is lush, the rivers full, and the weather cool, with temperatures ranging from 21°C (70°F) during the day to as low as 5°C (41°F) at night. Between early March and the end of May it is uncomfortably hot and much of the tropical vege-tation is reduced to brown stubble. Temperatures rise as high as 40°C (104°F), although the average is 30°C (86°F). The rainy season is between June and October (September is wettest), when trails can be slippery, leeches common.

ARRANGING A TREK

There is a wide range of tour operators in Chiang Mai, Chiang Rai, Mae Hong Son, and Pai, offering treks to the hilltribe villages that range from easy half-day visits to more strenuous 1-week treks. These days, there are also several oper-ators that combine trekking with mountain biking, white-water rafting, elephant riding, and any other form of "soft" adventure you care to dream of (see Contacts). Typically, prices will include accommodation and all forms of transportation as well as basic foods. Before agreeing to a particular trek, make sure that the guide who will accompany you to the villages speaks not only Thai and English, but at least one of the hill-tribe dialects. Check to see that you are dealing with a licensed agency. Finally, make sure that there will be a maximum of six or seven people in your group, so that your own adventure is not crowded out by others.

OFF ON YOUR OWN

You are strongly advised not to go trekking on your own or to arrive in hilltribe villages without a guide.

Robberies, although uncommon, are not unknown. Your inability to communicate with the people, together with your lack of understanding of their rituals, also threatens both your peace of mind and theirs.

HEALTH MATTERS

❑ To reduce your chances of sickness, make sure that you bring your own bottled water (two bot-tles per person per day as a rough guide).

❑ Peel or wash any fruit, and avoid eating uncooked vegetables.

❑ You should bring a small first-aid kit that includes antiseptic, plasters, and dysentery tablets.

❑ Inoculations against hepatitis and protection against malaria are recommended, but you should seek advice from your doctor before departure.

WHAT TO TAKE

❑ Warm clothes for November–February.
❑ Sensible walking boots.
❑ Sun hat and sun-screen.
❑ Plastic bag in which to keep things dry.
❑ Long trousers to wear at night (pro-tection against mos-quitoes).
❑ Insect repellent.
❑ Toiletries and tissue paper.
❑ A torch and matches.
❑ Small denomination notes to pay for drinks or handicrafts.
❑ A sleeping sheet (optional) to use in the hilltribe villages.

HILLTRIBE DANCES

It used to be common to see hilltribes dancing to celebrate the birthday of crop grandmother, the end of harvest time, or even the death of a villager. These days, the dances are more likely to be especially for tourists. The norm is to agree a price before proceedings begin. If you are not com-fortable with this, simply explain that you are tired after your hike or offer to sing to the village children in your own language. To see the full gamut of tribal dances, ask at the bigger hotels in Chiang Mai, Chiang Rai and Mae Hong Son.

THAILAND

A Motorbiking Odyssey

by Ben Davies

From the dramatic hills above Doi Ang Khang to the legendary opium-growing region around the Golden Triangle, this six-day circuit of northern Thailand offers some of the most exciting and spectacular motorbiking in the country—along with the thrill of being far from the crowds.

There can be few more magnificent places on Earth for a motorbiking adventure than beautiful northern Thailand. In this lush region, flanked to the west by Myanmar (Burma) and to the north and east by Laos, you will find spectacular mountains rising to 2,595m (8,515 feet) and abundant river valleys, enchanting waterfalls, and limestone gorges—as well as breathtaking views that can compare with almost anything in Southeast Asia.

Occupying almost a third of the country and bisected by a surprisingly good network of surfaced roads, the North even has its own unique history. Formerly known as Lanna ("Kingdom of a Million Rice Fields"), this was one of the cradles of Thai civilization. Founded in the 8th century by King Lao Cankaraja, Lanna flourished for more

ABOVE Rice fields near Mae Salong, an area where opium used to be the main crop
RIGHT Tough going off road

5 This circuit is recommended only for people with previous motorbiking experience. Unless you feel confident biking around hairpin bends and travelling through isolated parts of the country, you are strongly advised either to join an organized group (see Contacts) or to take the easier 3-day circuit from Chiang Mai to Mae Hong Song, Mae Sariang, and back to Chiang Mai.

★★ You will find a range of comfortable hotels and guest houses along the route. Make sure, however, that you get to your destination well before nightfall.
Simple hotels and guest houses can be found in the towns of Pai and Soppong, and luxurious hotels are available in Mae Hong Son, Chiang Mai, and Chiang Rai.

 250cc trailbikes are best for this 950-km (590-mile) journey. They can be rented from shops in either Chiang Mai or Chiang Rai (see Contacts). 125cc bikes are also widely available, but lack power on steep hills and overheat on long distances. Petrol stations are found in towns and bottles of fuel can be bought in shops in villages. In case of breakdown, contact the rental shop and ask them to arrange to have the motorbike taken back by truck.

THAILAND

than 500 years, with its capital in Chiang Mai. Only in 1796 was it finally annexed by Siam, marking the end of the greatest chapter of northern independence.

Although I had travelled to northern Thailand several times before and had even written guidebooks on the area, I wanted to revisit some of the furthest-flung corners of this ancient region. It was to do this that I arrived in the northern capital, **Chiang Mai**, one rainy July afternoon for the start of my motorbiking tour.

PREPARING FOR THE JOURNEY

In Chiang Mai it's almost as easy to rent a motorbike as it is to arrange a trip to the local orchid farm. You don't need to show a licence (although this is a legal requirement) and so long as you can start the engine and drive off without falling into the path of an oncoming vehicle, your motorbiking skills remain beyond question.

But if the rental shops around Tapae Gate (in the east of the city) take a generally cavalier attitude, under no circumstances should you fall into the same trap. Make sure that the bike is in perfect working order, check the brakes, the lights, the tyres, and the oil and find out what will happen if you either return the bike late or, by some misfortune, fail to return it at all.

Before leaving Chiang Mai, there are two sights that are worth a visit. On Highway 1006, 9km (5 miles) to the east of town, lies **Bor Sang**, a village that has

become world-renowned for its hand-painted umbrellas made from mulberry paper and presented in a rainbow of colours. And 16km (10 miles) to the northwest is the famous 14th-century temple of **Wat Doi Suthep**, built on a hill where one of King Keu Naone's most beloved white elephants died.

After overnighting in the Montri Hotel (next door to J.J. Bakery, which has the best ice-creams in town), I meet up with my intrepid motorbiking companion and teak expert Francis Middlehurst. Climbing on to our two gleaming Honda 250 motorbikes, we drive past the Chang Puak (White Elephant Gate) before taking the Northern Highway 107, signposted to Mae Rim and Chiang Dao.

LITTLE SWITZERLAND

Above the roar of motorbikes, the toot-ing of tuk-tuks (three-wheeled motor scooters), and the revving of vintage trucks, I am struck by two indisputable facts. Thai drivers are among the worst and most irresponsible on Earth (they happily overtake in the face of oncoming traffic), and they show absolutely no regard for the rules of the road (see box). The good news for experienced motorcyclists is that you will rapidly adapt and even get to enjoy this anarchic state of affairs. The bad news for beginners is that Thailand is not the place to learn.

From the outskirts of Chiang Mai, we head north on busy Highway 107, past an ugly sprawl of petrol stations,

RULES OF THE ROAD

As you drive along the winding roads of northern Thailand, there are some basic principles that you should always take to heart, including the sheer unpredictability of Thai drivers and their delightful disregard for the rules of the road. In Thailand, priority goes to the driver in the biggest vehicle. That means if a truck or car is overtaking in the middle of the road, it's your duty to get out of the way regardless of the rights or wrongs of the matter. Failure to get out of the way of oncoming traffic can lead to fatal accidents. So too can the deceptively sharp corners and sudden steep hills that are a constant feature of the northern route.

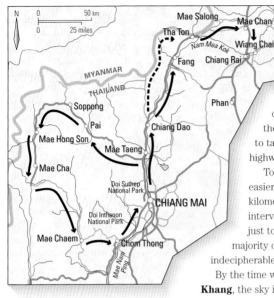

The motorbike circuit, centred on Chiang Mai

wandering along the road—in the unlikely event that one of these giants of the jungle should decide to take an amble along a highway.

To make the journey easier, the Thais have put kilometre stones at regular intervals along the road. But just to add a little spice, the majority of names are written in indecipherable Thai script.

By the time we reach **Doi Ang Khang**, the sky is black and the storm clouds unleash a steady downpour. Crawling along the narrow, winding road past wild horses and a mule train, we take a right turn on to Highway 1249 zigzagging down this steep mountain road for 20km (12 miles) before rejoining the main Highway 107.

SHANS AND BUDDHAS

In **Tha Ton**, there's a giant white Buddha on the hillside, distinguished by a large golden topknot. Reached by a narrow concrete path that begins a short distance beyond the bridge (you can go by motorbike), Wat Tha Ton offers glorious views of the ricefields below and the Kok River snaking its way into the distance.

factories, and housing developments. Soon, however, the traffic falls by the wayside, and the drab urban landscape gives way first to lush cattle-grazing pastures and further on to limestone cliffs clothed in lush vegetation.

A short distance beyond **Chiang Dao** (68km/42 miles), there is a choice of routes. The main route along Highway 107 continues north along a pleasant stretch of road to Tha Ton, 108km (67 miles) further. A longer, but far more exciting, option (you should bring a map or a guide) is to take Highway 1178 to the left, which leads up through the Shan hills into the rugged mountain area known by the locals as Little Switzerland.

While riding along this awesome stretch of road, which follows the Burmese border past Arunothai and Sinchai, we are introduced to some of Thailand's most inventive and entertaining road signs. Besides the inevitable zigzags and large trucks going up or down a hill to indicate a steep slope, there are signs of a man with a rock falling on his head—used to highlight the possibility of landslides. Further on, there's even a sign with an elephant

---

A SHORT CIRCUIT

For a shorter and easier motorbike circuit, follow the loop that takes you from Chiang Mai to Mae Taeng, Pai, Mae Hong Son, and Mae Sariang before coming round in a full circle to Chiang Mai. This should take a minimum of 3–4 days of motorbiking and will allow you to admire some of the most spectacular scenery in the kingdom.

Originally a Thai Yai or Shan village, Baan Tha Ton—as it is known to the locals—provides an ideal base from which to explore the surrounding region. We overnight in the Thaton Lodge, a delightful chalet-style hotel on the banks of the river. Its owner, Shane, a soft-spoken former Irish mercenary, arranges rafting and boating trips on the Kok River, as well as trekking to several ethnic minority communities.

Tha Ton has another claim to fame. It is recognized throughout the North for its culinary delicacies, including pork stomach soup and—for the really adventurous—*luu*, a salad made with pig's blood.

The following morning, after break-fasting on more mundane fare (eggs and bacon) on the pleasant hotel balcony overlooking the river, we climb back on to our bikes, following Highway 1089 for the spectacular trip to Mae Salong.

DRUGS AND DRIVING

One of the most remarkable things about a motorbiking trip through northern Thailand is the sheer quality of the roads. Not only are they in many cases tarmacked, but for the most part they

Stopping off in one of the hilltribe villages and (INSET) enjoying the hospitality that is typical of the northern region

even have neat white lines painted down the middle. For that, we have drugs to thank. In a bid to reduce opium cultivation, which was prolific in many remote parts of the region, the U.S. government and drug-enforcement agencies financed the building of roads in order to police the area better. Fortunately, traffic generally consists of a few speeding trucks or a trickle of water buffalo.

More significant than the quality of the road, however, is the fact that the 40-km (25-mile) stretch of highway from Tha Ton to **Mae Salong** (now renamed Santikhiri) traverses some of the most idyllic scenery in the North, passing rugged mountains and impossibly steep

valleys dotted with hilltribe villages (Lahu, Lisu, and Akha).

Mae Salong's history is as spectacular as its views. In 1949, after the communist victory in China, remnants of the Kuomintang army (KMT) under Tuan Shiw-Wen sought refuge first in Burma and later in this remote border area. In exchange for guarantees that they would oppose the spread of communism, the KMT were allowed to stay, financing their presence through opium cultivation and smuggling.

RIGHT A golden buddha at Wat Tha Ton. The climb to the shrine is rewarded with views over the pretty Kok River valley

Chinese influence is instantly recognizable in the architecture (look out for the garish spirit houses) as well as the Yunanese food (ask for rice noodles or *khanom jiin*). In the morning market you will even find such invigorating liquid sustenance as viper wine (supposedly an aphrodisiac) and snake's gallbladder liquor (it is believed to improve longevity).

BEYOND THE GOLDEN TRIANGLE

By the time we leave Mae Salong the sun is already high in the sky, bathing the countryside with a pleasing golden hue. Following Highway 1234, we continue along a steep, winding road that offers unparalleled views towards Burma and the area loosely termed the Golden Triangle.

It was a short distance to the east of Mae Salong that one of the great battles of the 1980s opium wars took place. On the morning of January 21, 1982, 800 border patrol police attacked the headquarters of drug kingpin Khun Sa, near the village of Baan Hin Taek, using mortars, machine guns, and helicopter gunships. Although Khun Sa and his 8,000-odd troops fought back with rocket missiles, they were eventually forced to retreat over the border into Burma, taking with them 200 mules loaded up with heroin.

Today the area is relatively quiet and untroubled. From Baan Hin Taek (now renamed Ban Thoed Thai), a network of dirt tracks leads up into the hills near the Burmese border. But the roads are steep and treacherous and should not be attempted without a guide.

A better option is to continue along the main road (Highway 1234) until you see a turning on the left signposted to Doi Tung. This mountain is highly revered for its 10th-century temple known as **Wat Phra That Doi Tung**, which is believed to hold part of the Buddha's left collar bone. So important is this reliquary (probably the earliest in the Lanna kingdom) that pilgrims come from all over the northern Thailand to bang on every bell in the temple in the hope that this will gain them merit. (You should leave an offering of 5–10 baht/a few cents).

From Doi Tung, we take the excellent highway past a terraced hillside to Mae Chan and Chiang Rai (48km/30 miles), where we check into the gloriously named Saen Poo Hotel, equipped with everything that a motorbiker could dream of, from a fridge to a TV and even a nightclub.

NORTHERN LEGEND

Legend has it that the city of **Chiang Rai** was founded on the spot where one of King Mengrai's favourite elephants halted on the banks of the Kok River, before circling three times and falling to its knees. The king took this as an auspicious sign and ordered that a great city be built along the banks of the river. But Mengrai's dutiful construction of Chiang Rai did not bring him the everlasting happiness he craved. In 1317, some 50 years after work on the city began, he was supposedly struck dead by lightning.

Chiang Rai's fame owes as much to its location near the infamous Golden Triangle as it does to its spurious historical claims. In recent times, dozens of trekking shops have sprung up around the Wangcome Hotel on Premwipak Road. They organize visits to surrounding hilltribe villages as well as boat trips to the popular elephant camp at Ban Ruammit (an hour down the Kok River).

There are a couple of temples worth seeing before you leave town. At **Wat Ngam Muang**, situated on a small hill overlooking the city and the river, you will find a brick monument containing the ashes of King Mengrai. Further to the east on Trairat Road is the royally acclaimed **Wat Phra Kaeo**, which houses one of the largest surviving bronze Buddhas from the Lanna period (13th–15th century).

After overnighting at the Saen Poo, we leave early the following morning, in order to cover the 300km (188 miles) to Pai (via Mae Taeng), a magnificent if demanding journey for which you should allow a minimum of six hours.

HIGHWAY SPIRITS

In the northern hills, the people have an unusual superstition. They believe that spirits, or *phi*, live on the roads and especially around hairpin bends, where they determine the fate of approaching vehicles. On really steep bends, you may well find spirit houses filled with flowers and even glasses of whisky donated by apprehensive villagers.

On the remarkably beautiful stretch of road from Mae Taeng to Pai and Mae Hong Son (Highway 1095), there are more than 150 hairpin bends. But you will also be treated to spectacular scenery of mountain forests and water-falls, as well as hilltribe villages and national parks.

Travelling along these snaking roads is a thrilling experience. One moment you may pass a hilltribe dweller wearing black leggings, silver earrings the size of billiard balls, and carrying a basket full of cabbages on her back, and the next a pick-up truck filled with monks in orange robes. Some encounters are of an even more peculiar nature. Twice we passed trucks with large elephants in the back—presumably being transported to the next trekking destination.

Arriving in the delightful town of **Pai** (see pages 20–9) set in a broad valley hemmed in by mountains, we spend the night at the Rim Pai Cottages, feasting on spicy *gaeng khia wan gai* (chicken curry) at one of the many restaurants near the market.

The following day, we continue our journey west along Highway 1095, another splendid road that leads past Soppong (take a right turn to see impressive Tham Lawd, otherwise known as Cave Lod) to Mae Hong Son, the City of Mists.

CITY OF MISTS

Situated in a lush valley ringed by densely wooded hills and mountains, this peaceful provincial capital makes the perfect spot to rest for a day, to explore the surrounding hilltribe villages or to visit the notorious long-necked tribe known as the Padang (arranged through local tour agents).

To see **Mae Hong Son** at its most beautiful, get up at dawn and wander out into the streets in the soft morning light, stopping at the tranquil Chong Kham Lake in the centre of town. Here, by the waterside, you will find two of Mae Hong Son's most famous Burmese-style temples: the 19th-century Wat Chong Klang with its distinctive white and gold *chedis* and, next door, the older Shan-style temple of Wat Chong

TRAVELLERS' TIPS

If you are renting a motorbike:

- ❑ Check tyres, oil, brakes, and lights before leaving.
- ❑ Arrange comprehensive insurance.
- ❑ When riding in groups, don't stay too close together (a 50-m/150-foot gap is ideal).
- ❑ Leave early in the morning and always plan to be at your final destination by 4pm so you can arrange accommodation before nightfall.
- ❑ For your own security, never drive on the roads at night.
- ❑ Avoid driving alone in rural areas.
- ❑ Wear a motorcycle helmet and proper shoes (never flip-flops).
- ❑ Wear trousers and long-sleeved shirts for protection.
- ❑ Get hold of the B & B map of northern Thailand that shows the latest route network.
- ❑ Remember traffic drives on the left-hand side of the road (normally).

Kham. Higher up on the mountainside (take the small road to the west of town), you will also find the wonderfully named Wat Phra That Doi Kong Mu, which offers resplendent views of the surrounding countryside.

After a day exploring the area around Mae Hong Son and the famous fish cave known as **Tham Pla** (17km/10 miles north), we continue on the last leg of our journey, driving down Highway 108 to Khun Yuam (70km/44 miles) before turning left on to Highway 1263.

BELOW On the road in Chiang Rai province: you will need a 250cc bike to cope with the steep hills of the North

This magnificent ride is a fitting end to our motorbiking odyssey, skirting the Mae Surin National Park past hilltribe villages (Hmong, Karen, and Shan) and virgin mountain territory. In places, the road is still under construction, but any obstacles are more than made up for by the superlative views.

Arriving in **Mae Cham**, an ugly little market town, we take Highway 1192 through the magnificent Doi Inthanon National Park (2,565m/8,415 feet) past a succession of mountain peaks, caves, and waterfalls (best in the rainy season) to **Chom Thong**. From here it's a 47-km (29-mile) ride on Highway 108 back to Chiang Mai and the end of our circuit.

GOING IT ALONE

INTERNAL TRAVEL

Chiang Mai, the northern capital, is served by frequent flights from Bangkok, as well as cheap and comfortable overnight sleeping trains (which take 11 hours). Less popular VIP buses take 10–12 hours on the same route. There is also an airport in Chiang Rai. If you wish to catch a specific flight or train in peak season or at the time of a major festival, you should book well in advance through a local or international travel agent.

WHEN TO GO

The best time to go motorbiking in northern Thailand is during the dry season, from the end of October to the end of May. From November to February the weather is cool and you may encounter early morning mist, while from March to May temperatures soar as high as 40°C (104°F). The rainy season is between June and October (September is wettest). At this time, roads can be slippery and occasionally extremely dangerous.

PLANNING

If this is your first visit to Thailand and you do not know the roads or the language, it may be worth joining a motorbiking tour group (see Contacts). That way you will not only learn about the local culture, but you may have a safer and more enjoyable trip.

FINDING A BIKE

Chiang Mai and Chiang Rai offer the best selection of motorcycles for rent. Honda 250cc trail bikes are ideal for the steep hills of the

North. Anything with less power will severely slow your progress up the slopes. Before renting a bike, make sure that everything is in full working order as you will be liable for any damage when the bike is returned. And be certain to arrange comprehensive insurance and use of a motorbike helmet through the rental shop (you will have to leave a deposit and your passport). Luggage can be strapped to the back of the bike using bungies. Petrol (*naman*; ask for *super*) is widely available at gas stations and village shops along the route. In case of breakdown, contact the motorbike rental shop.

ACCOMMODATION

There is no need to book hotels or guest houses in advance. There's a range of accommodation in all the major towns, but to guarantee a particular hotel in the high season, you should reserve in advance.

OFF ON YOUR OWN

Motorcycle touring in the North is easy to organize and fun to do, although you should always travel with a minimum of two people in case of breakdowns or accidents. Parts of the circuit described here are

extremely demanding and while experienced motorcyclists should have little problem with them, beginners would be wise to take an easier and shorter route.

WHAT TO TAKE

❑ International driving licence or permit.

❑ Address/phone number of motorbike rental shop.

❑ First-aid kit.

❑ Motorbiking gloves.

❑ Thai phrase book.

❑ Small denomination notes to pay for snacks or petrol.

❑ Plastic bags in which to keep things dry.

❑ Sunglasses, sunscreen.

❑ Toiletries and tissues.

HEALTH MATTERS

For motorbiking, be sure to bring a medical kit with plasters, bandages, antiseptic, plus more general items such as diarrhoea pills.

Before you leave home take out full medical insurance that will cover you if you have a motorcycle accident.

In the event of an emergency, contact any of the big hotels, which generally have access to English-speaking doctors, or telephone your embassy or consulate in Bangkok.

FESTIVALS OF THE NORTH

Northern Thailand is famous for its colourful and often exuberant festivals. The dates often vary from year to year, but two not to miss are Songkran (often known as the water festival), generally held in April, and Loi Krathong, held at the beginning of November. At other times of year, there are flower festivals, monk ordinations, temple fairs, beauty pageants— almost any sort of celebration you can think of.

THAILAND

Kayaking and Climbing at Phang Nga

by Simon Richmond

In southern Thailand, towering limestone rocks burst out of the jungles and coastal waters, forming a dramatic backdrop for kayaking tours around islands and through mangrove forests. I found they make for challenging climbs, too, at idyllic Railay beach.

Any port in a storm, they say, but the forbiddingly isolated and gloomy **Ko Thalu**—one of some 40 limestone islands and rocks that punctuate southern Thailand's Ao Phang Nga (Phang Nga Bay)—looks far from welcoming. On the second day of my three-day exploration of the bay by sea canoe and kayak, the persistently heavy rain has forced a change of plan and opened up an opportunity to view an even more extraordinary environment: a cave where swiftlet nests, used in the Chinese delicacy bird's-nest soup, are harvested.

In the mouth of the cave four or five swarthy men are resting on a seemingly precarious bamboo platform, strung high above the water on to a rock ledge. These are the *chao ley*, or sea gypsies, of the Andaman Sea. For weeks at a time they forage in the black recesses of the cave for the swiftlet nests, also known as "white gold" because of the exorbitant price this rare commodity commands. So much money is involved in their trade that the men take no chances and have a rifle ready to ward off unwelcome guests. Fortunately harvesting has finished, so the white-bearded leader grants our small group privileged access into the looming cavern.

In the dark it's impossible to see the swiftlets, but we can hear them as they navigate their way through the cave using the echoes created by the clicking sound of their call. Single torch beams illuminate thousands of tiny flies and the bamboo scaffolding that soars 50m (170 feet) or more to the roof of the cave. The harvesters shin up these teetering structures to reach the nests. These the birds make with saliva, which hardens into cream-coloured rubber shaped like a small bra cup.

The floor of the cave is a soft mass of bird dung and rotting bamboo (the

 4 The basic paddling strokes for kayaking are simple to learn, although manoeuvring through the narrow channels in the mangrove swamps can be tricky. Kayaking can be tiring, especially if you're paddling across open seas, but there's no hurry and the landscape is best appreciated by taking your time. Rock climbing requires a high degree of fitness, especially given the heat factor. However, many climbs are more about mastering technique and balance than simply using sheer brawn to haul yourself up.

★★ Expect sore limbs and slightly bruised and grazed knees from the rock climbing. Sun cream and hats are essential, and long trousers are worth considering if you want to provide some protection for your legs.

All kayaking equipment is provided; the only things you need bring are sun protection, swimming gear (including masks, snorkels, and fins for skin diving), and your own beers. The full range of climbing equipment is available for hire from several outlets in Railay, but if you're serious about the sport, it's a good idea to bring at least your own harness, chalk bag, and shoes (the ones for hire can be grubby and worn from the sand and constant use).

superstitious harvesters never remove old bamboo from the cave) seething with ugly red cockroaches. The additional litter of used torch batteries and empty energy-drink bottles indicate that modern conveniences have seeped into this medieval occupation.

Light floods in from another entrance to the cave, through which the swiftlets pass each day in their search for food. Around dusk so many birds are returning to their nests through this hole that it would be impossible to stand where we are now: on the spot where the *chaoy ley* sacrifice a buffalo carcass each year to appease the cave spirits' taste for blood.

KARSTS AND HONGS

The limestone islands and jungle outcrops—known as "karsts" (see box)—that typify Phang Nga and Krabi provinces are riddled with caves and passages. Where the roof of a cave chamber has collapsed, allowing sunlight to flood into the centre of the karst, hardy and unique plants—such as *pralahoo* and cycad palms—have found a home, creating tropical greenhouses. The Thais call these hidden oases *hongs*, or rooms. Many have floors at or below sea level and become lagoons at high tide, when the sea rushes in through the original entrance to the cave.

The best way of exploring the islands and their hongs is by kayak and canoe, this "soft," "green" approach being ideally suited to the delicate natural environment. If you're short of time, you can take one of the many day trips that run around the bay out of Phuket or Krabi, but expect to encounter congestion at the most popular islands, where several canoes will wait in line until the tide reaches the right level to sail through the passages to the hongs. A better option is to take a longer tour, such as the three- or six-day packages offered by SeaCanoe (the originator of this form of ecotourism and still the only

international standard sea-kayaking company in Thailand).

Unfortunately, the weather was not promising as I walked the rickety wooden pier at **Laem Phrao**, near the northern tip of Phuket, to board *Urida 1*, the floating base for my three-day trip around the islands and mangrove forests of Ao Phang Nga. I joined Kendrick, a doctor from Colorado, whose previous experience of kayaking was in the considerably less hospitable environment of Alaska.

On board we were outnumbered by the boat's staff: Jarearn, the enthusiastic lead guide, his mate Rambo (so called because he was an ex-soldier), Baht, the boat captain, Ian, the engineer, and Fon, the cook. Once introductions were out of the way, we set sail into the bay, where the rocks, some up to 400m (1,300 feet) tall, materialized out of the misty clouds in shades of grey and green, like images in a developing Polaroid photograph.

EXPLORING THE HONGS

The first lagoon we approached is one of the most famous, that within the island **Ko Hong**. For this first day of the trip, Jarearn would be paddling us into the

CREATING THE KARSTS

Formed over 30 million years ago, from the titanic crash between the shifting Indian subcontinent and mainland Asia, the limestone crags of Phang Nga and Krabi provinces are the eroded remnants of an ancient mountain range stretching from China to Borneo. Known as "karsts", these rocks have been sculpted into incredible shapes by centuries of monsoon rains and the rise and fall of the oceans. The term "karst" was first applied to the Karst, a limestone region on the Dalmatian coast of former Yugoslavia, and is now used for similar, widely scattered, areas all over the world.

hong in the *Sea Explorer* inflatable canoe. Entering a hong—usually through a narrow recess with jagged walls and overhung with stalactites—is a tricky business that requires skill and intimate knowledge of the prevailing conditions. The tidal water has to be at just the right level for safe access. Passengers may have to lie flat against the canoe where the cave roof practically scrapes their noses. It's all part of the experience, but anyone afraid of enclosed spaces will find it something of a trial.

Any anxiety suffered in the dark caves evaporates once you enter the lush, sunshine-flooded world of the hong, where sheer rock walls are draped in an abundance of trees and plants tenaciously clinging to every crevice and crack. In the face of such beauty, most

ABOVE Karsts in Phang Nga Bay, seen from the mouth of a cave, and (INSET) a kayaking party beneath the sheer limestone walls RIGHT The bamboo scaffolding erected inside one of the caves to reach the swiftlet nests that are used in bird's-nest soup

travellers fall silent naturally, but the boat guides will anyway ask you remain quiet so as to increase the chances of spotting wildlife. You're most likely to see birds, such as the oriental pied hornbill (*Anthracoceros albirostris*), little heron (*Butorides striatus*), and possibly even Brahminy kites (*Haliastur indus*) and white-bellied sea eagles (*Haliaeetus leucogaster*).

A different stratum of marine life reveals itself once the tide has dropped and the muddy floors of the hongs emerge from the sea: in the afternoon,

following a splendid lunch and an enforced siesta due to the onset of heavy rain, we venture on foot into another lagoon, where the mangrove trees stand revealed in all their glory, like weird, modernist sculptures. Around their arched roots, fiddler crabs, each with one outsized orange pincer, scuttle in and out of holes in the mud.

Because of its connection with James Bond (see page 44), **Ko Khao Phing Kan** is a much-visited island and its narrow beaches are plastered with tourists and gift stalls all through the day. By the time the *Urida 1* arrives at 5pm, however, most other visitors have left and we are free to admire the geological wonder of a huge, perfectly cleft rock and the mini-karst Ko Tapu ("Nail Island").

The day finishes with a paddle through the pungent **Bat Cave** (so called because of the giant fruit bats that live there) into another hong, dripping with verdant foliage and studded with spindly trees rising from tar-black rocks. This was the first hong discovered by John Grey, SeaCanoe's American founder, and was the inspiration for the sea-kayak tours.

In better weather the boat would have sailed into the sunset for one of the beaches, where we would have camped and enjoyed a barbecue. Instead, we return to the natural shelter provided by the cluster of islands around Ko Hong and remain on board for the night, sinking several beers with the delicious supper of soup, barbecued jack fish, chicken curry, vegetables, and rice.

THE BIG LAGOON

Day two is our first opportunity to try paddling for ourselves. After the briefest of instructions on how to paddle, our mini flotilla of yellow, moulded-plastic "sit-on-top" kayaks sets off into **Hong Yai**, or Big Lagoon, on the northeast side of the bay. This is not an enclosed paradise like the hongs in the middle of the islands, but a 2-km (1-mile) long inlet where mangroves nestle between sheer rock walls that are split horizontally by a series of ledges, each defining major shifts in the sea level over time.

Paddling slowly through such beautiful and unusual surroundings— even in the rain—it's clear why SeaCanoe warns its customers to bring more camera film than they think they'll need. The company provides dry bags, but if you're travelling in the monsoon season it's as well to carry your own. Alternatively, invest in a waterproof disposable camera.

The rains force us to make our unscheduled, but eye-opening, visit to the swiftlets' cave. Eventually, the weather lets up as we return to the support boat and head south to two small islands, around and between which we're going to be paddling. It's tougher work out in the open seas, but we get a chance to rest when Jerearn takes us to meet a group of fishermen sitting on the veranda of a traditional house built on stilts. They chat to us while they wait for the tide to turn.

The last port of call before we head for our evening's base—Long Beach Bungalows on Ko Yao Noi, one of the few inhabited islands in the bay—is an idyllic island with a beach of soft brown sugar sand set back between clumps of rugged rocks and fringed by swaying palms and scented bushes alive with butterflies.

MONKEYS IN THE MANGROVES

Phang Nga Bay has the largest expanse of mangrove forests in Thailand, and on our final day we embark on a 3-hour paddle through one of the most beautiful, at **Ao Thalan**, on the east side of Ao Phrang Nga. For the first hour we drift with the water's flow along a narrow channel that slices a towering karst into two. The only sound, save for the gentle lapping of water, is the incessant chirping of cicadas in the trees that shoot up

---

THE BOND CONNECTION

Thailand has designated Ao Phang Nga a National Marine Park and it's also a UNESCO World Natural Heritage Site. But if most travellers know anything about the bay, it's because of its starring role in two James Bond movies: *Tomorrow Never Dies* (doubling for Ha Long Bay in Vietnam—see pages 84–91) and *The Man with the Golden Gun*. Ko Khao Phing Kan, in the far north of the bay, is commonly known as James Bond Island, and figures on almost every tour.

from vertical rocks. A curious giant water monitor lizard (*Varanus salvator*) eyes us from its rocky perch before deciding to swim away.

Jerearn brings a basket of fruit for the locals: crab-eating macaques (*Macaca fascicularis*), also known as long-tailed macaques. Once we're into the maze-like channels of the mangroves Jerearn starts tapping the side of the kayak to attract their attention—but it's other day-tripping kayakers from Krabi that we encounter before the troop of monkeys. When the macaques do arrive, they quickly gobble up the bananas and disappear back into the tangle of mangroves.

Paddling in this environment allows you to try out some different techniques. The narrow passages between the mangroves sometimes mean that it's best to split the kayak paddle in two (there's a quick-release catch in the middle) and use the shortened oar for manoeuvring. Spinning the kayak around tight corners can also be achieved by switching abruptly from forward to backward strokes.

By midday, as we emerge from the mangrove forests into the open waters of the Klong River, I really feel I'm getting the hang of it. But after one more swim, followed by lunch, in a bay surrounded by picturesque islands, it's time to return to Phuket, where the final challenge is to wade through the shallows to the wooden jetty at Laem Phrao.

CLIMBING IN KRABI

My adventures amid Thailand's karsts were not yet at an end, however. The next day I skirt the bay by road, travelling towards the province of Krabi and its main town, also called **Krabi**. Once there, I immediately transfer to a long-tailed boat and head back out to sea towards Railay, a tiny beach resort on the Pra-Nang Peninsula (Laem Pra-Nang), Thailand's rock-climbing hotspot.

Although Pra-Nang is part of the mainland, there are no roads (and so no cars) and the only way to get to the peninsula is by boat. Approaching the dramatic limestone cliffs that frame **East Railay beach**, you feel as though you're arriving at some fabulous treasure island. It's also immediately clear why Railay's walls—the rock faces that are the climbing routes—command such respect among the international climbing community.

Lounging on the postcard-perfect, white sand beaches of West Railay and Ao Pra Nang remains the most popular activity in Railay, and at the height of the season, from December to January, it's common to find every bed in the village taken. However, rock climbing is fast catching up, attracting many amateurs and professionals from around the world as well as nurturing local talents, some of whom run the climbing outfits in the village and act as guides for visitors.

There are at least 30 different climbing areas around the peninsula, many with funky names such as Jurassic Park Wall, Escher World, and Sleeping Indian Cliff. The most popular are a couple at the south end of East Railay beach—One-Two-Three and Muai Thai—since they offer a good range of routes for all levels of climber and have easy access from the beach when the tide is out. In peak season, expect huge crowds here and long waits between climbs.

GOING UP THE WALL

Most outfits in Railay offer a three-day course, which will teach you the basics of climbing, and hire of all equipment. By the end of these courses you should have practised all the important rope and knot techniques, acted as a lead climber (the first person of a pair to go up a route), and learned to abseil. The important thing is that you trust your instructor and the equipment: check out both before starting any course.

I just wanted to get a taste for the sport, so Tex—one of Railay's most experienced climbing instructors and

THAILAND

the star performer in a fire-juggling show on the beach at night—advised me to start with a half-day, rather than a full-day, session. In any case, most beginners find their muscles begin to ache after a few hours' climbing and they don't learn much more in a full day than they do in either a morning or an afternoon.

My half-day session starts at 8am, when the temperature has yet to reach its sultry high and while the tide is out, allowing access to the One-Two-Three wall. After demonstrating the correct way to tie knots in the rope, Jack, my curly-headed guide, dabs his hands in his chalk bag and is off up the wall, wearing no shoes and climbing with the

dexterity of a monkey. I try to memorize his moves, but once I'm on the wall it takes all my concentration just to stop myself falling off.

Jack is below, shouting encouragement and telling me to look out for the chalk marks on the rocks that indicate where to put my hands. His other tips are to take my time, to look around for the best places to put my feet and hands before moving them, to try to relax, and to stop from time to time and

LEFT AND FAR LEFT Learning to rock climb at the One-Two-Three Wall on East Railay beach
BELOW As 007 saw it: a tourist boat makes its way past the limestone towers of Phang Nga Bay to "James Bond Island," Ko Khao Phing Kan

THAILAND

enjoy the view. I feel a tremendous sense of achievement when I reach the final bolt and know that now the only way is down.

BUDDHA'S FOOTPRINT

For those who want to climb to the heavens for a view of the rocks without slogging it out on one of Railay's climbing walls, there is another option, and I set off back to Krabi to take it. Be prepared, however: those who go in search of Buddha's footprint, atop a 600-m (2,000-feet) high karst, some 8km (5 miles) north of Krabi town, should expect a degree of suffering along the way.

The place to head for is Wat Tham Sua, or Tiger Cave Temple, so called because one rock in the compound has the look of a tiger's paw. Check out the main temple hall, built into the mouth of the cave and adorned with a giant pink statue of Buddha and a skeleton in a glass case (to remind people of the impermanence of life). You could then take the easy option and follow the circular walking route beyond the psychedelic tableaux of Kuan Yin, the Chinese goddess of mercy, and into a valley where the monks and nuns live in tiny wooden chalets (*kutis*) sheltering in the mouths of more caves.

I, however, take the route up to **Buddha's Footprint**, a mere 1,272 steps—and I soon regret bringing only one bottle of water. This is a serious climb, which zigzags agonizingly up the hill, offering no clear view of the summit until you're immediately below it. But the sweat, pounding heart, and shortness of breath are instantly forgotten when I reach the top and take in the magnificent 360-degree view of the surrounding countryside.

From this concreted perch I can see both the karsts out at sea and those inland, around which rivers meander in muddy, flowing ribbons. Rubber plantations are marked out in neat rows. It's the perfect panorama of southern Thailand, and what's more, looking down, I can indeed make out the shape of a human footprint in an exposed lump of limestone. Perhaps Buddha did stand on this spot, after all.

RAILAY'S CAVES AND LAGOONS

If you don't fancy rock climbing, you may like to explore the numerous caves around Railay. At the north end of East Railay beach, and easily accessible, is **Diamond Cave**, so called because of the glittering calcium deposits coating some of the rock formations. Legend has it that this is where two star-crossed lovers hid from angry relations. A walkway has been built through the cave and various features are illuminated, such as a waterfall and a spectacular chamber hung with many stalactites and stalagmites.

The peninsula's loveliest beach is **Ao Pra-Nang** (sometimes known as Hat Ham Par Nag), and it's also the location of the Princess Cave. More adventurous types may want to scramble up the rock behind the cave to discover the lush, hidden **Princess Lagoon**. Check with the local people for the best route, since finding the right path can be tricky and it's not recommended that you undertake the climb alone, especially in the rainy season when the mud can make it more dangerous. Also, make sure to wait for high tide, as it's a tidal lagoon.

THE PRINCESS CAVE

Inside the Princess Cave there is a shrine to an unfortunate princess who drowned off the bay in ancient times. The locals believe that the spirit of the princess lives in the cave, and from here controls their fates on the seas. Every full moon the local people bring offerings of flowers and fruits to the cave and a ceremony is held to ask for her blessing.

GOING IT ALONE

INTERNAL TRAVEL

The main international access point for Ao Phang Nga and Krabi is the island of Phuket, which has an airport on its northwest coast. There are also direct bus connections with Bangkok, but these take so much time that you're better off flying if you can afford it. Apart from the bus (see below) an alternative, relaxing way of crossing the bay from Phuket is to take a combination of ferries, first heading to Ko Phi Phi from Phuket town in the morning and from there taking the afternoon boat to Krabi. This trip can also be done in the opposite direction.

Travel agencies in Phuket town and Patong can arrange air-conditioned minibus trips to Krabi for around 300 baht ($8) one way. This 3-hour trip passes through the small town of Phang Nga, which is where you should get off if you want to explore the bay on an organized longtail boat trip; try Sayan Tour or Mr Kaen Tour, both at Phang Nga bus station. Half-day tours cost 200 baht ($5) per person for a minimum of four people, while a full-day tour, including lunch, costs 450 baht ($12). For a more stylish and expensive alternative, ask East West Siam about trips on their traditional Chinese junk.

WHEN TO GO

The best time of year is November to April. In monsoon months (summer) heavy rain can be a problem and the ground gets muddy. For Railay beach, note that accommodation is at a premium at the height of the season, December–January.

ARRANGING A KAYAKING TRIP

The best kayaking trips are offered by SeaCanoe. Day trips are around 2,500 baht ($70) per person, the 3-day expedition $550 and the 6-day expedition $990. If you have some experience of kayaking, you may want to take one of the more challenging 6-day expeditions, without the escort boat, which involve paddling 10–15km (6–9 miles) a day.

Another reputable company is Santana, which offers day trips around Ao Phang Nga from $85, 2-day trips from $170 and 3-day combined jungle trek and canoe trips in Khao Sok National Park from $260.

ARRANGING TO GO CLIMBING

Longtail boats depart all day from the main pier in Krabi for the 45-minute journey out to Laem Pra-Nang, all stopping at East Railay beach, from where West Railay beach is no more than a 5-minute walk across the narrow isthmus.

Stick with the longer-established climbing operations, such as Tex Climbing, near Coco House, King Climbers, behind Ya-Ya's, and Pra-Nang Rock, at the north end of East Railay beach.

Half-day to 3-day climbing courses, including hire of equipment, cost from 500 baht ($14) to 3,000 baht ($80). Rental equipment is available from all operations with a full set for two people (including harnesses, shoes, quickdraws, figure of eights, belay devices, rope, and chalk bags) from 500 baht ($14) for half a day and 800 baht ($20) for the day.

Intermediate and advanced climbers will want to get hold of the route guidebooks produced by either King Climbers or Pra-Nang Climbers; the former also include details for climbing on Ko Phi Phi.

WHAT TO TAKE

❏ Waterproof sunscreen.
❏ Swimming gear (including mask, snorkel, and fins).

HEALTH MATTERS

❏ Bring bottled water (two bottles per person per day), peel or wash any fruit, and avoid eating raw vegetables.
❏ Bring a small first-aid kit that includes antiseptic, plasters, and dysentery tablets.
❏ Inoculations against hepatitis and protection against malaria are recommended, but check with your doctor at least a month before leaving.
❏ Before you leave home, take out full medical insurance.

OTHER THINGS TO DO IN RAILAY

For non-climbers, Railay is also an excellent spot for snorkelling, diving, and kayaking. Phra Nang Divers is a PADI (Professional Association of Diving Instructors) centre offering the full range of dive courses, from a 4-day open-water course, to live-aboard dive safaris and local diving trips. Several of the chalets have kayaks for rent, so you can explore the bays around the peninsula.

THAILAND

THAILAND

Cycling in Isaan

by Ben Davies

In the northeast of Thailand, magnificent hills, idyllic rice-farming communities and the great Mekong River form the perfect backdrop for a 5-day (300-km/190-mile) cycling trip through some of the most scenic and remote countryside in the kingdom.

K nown as Isaan after the great Mon-Khmer kingdom that flourished in this region more than ten centuries ago, the northeast is one of the most glorious, but least visited, destinations in Thailand. Bordered to the north and east by Laos and to the west by the Phetchabun mountain range, it encompasses a landscape largely dominated by the sandy Korat Plateau. Countless rice-farming villages and rural communities are scattered along the banks of the Mekong River, framed by the spectacular mountains of Laos.

Isaan is renowned as much for its scenery as for its unique culture (largely influenced by neighbouring Laos), for its spicy food, and above all for the friendliness and *joie de vivre* of its 18 million

inhabitants, predominantly made up of poor farmers, many of whom have migrated from Laos and Cambodia.

It was to explore this beautiful region that I caught a train from Bangkok to **Nong Khai** (11 hours) and rented a mountain bike from Mut Mee Guest House, on the banks of the Mekong.

Before leaving Nong Khai, take an afternoon to visit the fine old French-Chinese architecture on Meechai Road, which runs parallel to the river, and the striking Brahmin temple of Wat Kaek, built by the famous Luang Puu (Venerable Grandfather). One more site is worth a visit: legend has it that when the famous gold statue inside Wat Po

RIGHT In Nong Khai people load their belongings on to a boat that will take them across the Mekong River to Laos
BELOW A tuk-tuk, so called because of the noise its two-stroke engine makes, awaits passengers

 To get the best out of your trip, you will require a reasonable level of fitness and the ability to cycle about 50km (30 miles) a day on predominantly tarmac roads (it's possible to complete the route more quickly). Highly recommended are tailor-made cycling tours (with a back-up van) that take you along the back roads, allowing you to experience the best of Isaan culture.

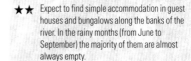 Expect to find simple accommodation in guest houses and bungalows along the banks of the river. In the rainy months (from June to September) the majority of them are almost always empty.

 Mountain-biking equipment is provided by organized tour groups (a minimum of two people is generally required). Cycles can also be rented from the Mut Mee Guest House in Nong Khai (reserve in advance) or can be brought up by train from Bangkok. If you are going it alone, bring spare inner tubes and repair kits, as you won't find repair shops along the way.

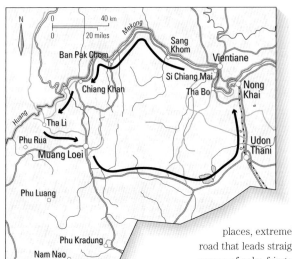

The Isaan tour follows the mighty Mekong part of the way

Chai (off Prajak Road) was being brought over the river from neighbouring Laos, the boat carrying it sank. But the image miraculously resurfaced and has since become the most revered statue in Nong Khai.

POTHOLES AND BANANAS

The following morning, decked out in a pair of slinky black cycling shorts (which I purchased in Nong Khai market), a luminous orange shirt (to attract the attention of oncoming traffic), and one of those rather incongruous plastic hats that look foolish but save lives, I pedal off self-consciously in the direction of Si Chiang Mai. To get to this town, you must ignore the spanking new Highway 2 (signposted to Udon Thani) and instead cycle west past the railway station and under the Friendship Bridge. (The bridge crosses the Mekong River to Laos, and many people combine their Isaan cycling trip with a visit to Laos.) Go under the bridge and follow an unsigned, pot-holed, and, in places, extremely uncomfortable road that leads straight on, past a rural cameo of palm-fringed villages and dusty markets, to **Tha Bo** (22 km/14 miles).

When you arrive in this town—famed for its bananas, vegetables, and other plants—you must take a right turn on to Highway 211. From here it's a pleasant ride down a straight tree-lined and well-surfaced road to **Si Chiang Mai** (13km/8 miles).

A short distance from the river on Rim Kong Road, there's a small guest house and basic hotel—and, near by, a charming Lao-style temple (Wat Hat Pratum). Best of all, there are rows of stalls along the river promenade where you can picnic on *somtam* (spicy mango salad) and *ghai yang* (barbecued chicken), two of Isaan's greatest culinary specialities, best eaten with *khao niau*, a type of glutinous rice. To eat it, roll the translucent grains into a ball and dip it into the pungent sauces that will have been placed in the middle of the table.

A MORE REWARDING EXPERIENCE

If you fancy experiencing the very best of Isaan countryside and culture, consider travelling in the company of an English-speaking cycling guide. Not only will a guide be able to give you insight into the local people and their culture, but generally he or she will also be able to organize transport and cycle hire, as well as providing all the necessary back-up. Most important of all, a guide who knows the area will take you down all the little back roads—and safely all the way back again (see Contacts).

TEMPLES AND WATERFALLS

If you want to reach Sangkhom by late afternoon, make sure that you leave Si Chiang Mai early. Although the distance is just 45km (28 miles), the second half of the journey involves some hefty hills, one of which is likely to take its toll on even the fittest cyclist.

The first stretch (Highway 211) runs alongside a flat landscape of glistening ricefields and fruit plantations. Soon, however, the route curves through low-slung hills, passing on the right the signpost for the peaceful meditation centre of Wat Hin Maek Peng, with its contemplation chambers built on gigantic boulders overlooking the river.

Near Sangkhom the scenery becomes more impressive. Climbing steeply through the hills, the route passes **Than Thong waterfall** on the right (spectacular only in the rainy season). It then sweeps down once again, offering panoramic views of the Mekong below, littered with giant rocks.

A short distance before Sangkhom, I take a small turning on the left that leads high up into the hills to a temple from where you look out on to the river snaking through the Isaan countryside. The best time to be here is in the early morning and at dusk. But, there's no alternative route down, so I have to backtrack to the main road, from where it's a further 2km (1¼ miles) to the delightful little village of Sangkhom, and the pleasant River Huts Bungalows.

WESTERN ROUTE

Sunrise viewed from the banks of the Mekong in **Sangkhom** is one of the great spectacles in Southeast Asia, especially if you have cycled for two days to see it. In a matter of minutes, the waters change from grey to orange and finally to the cloudy brown colour that is a trademark of this mighty river. Out of the mist, small fishing boats dart across the surface of the river, only to disappear, drifting over the invisible border with Laos. Apart from that, there is only the silence and the tropical scenery, framed by the mountains beyond.

Still overawed by the magnificence of the scenery, I remount my cycle and continue west along the river bank, where the locals are drying out bananas in the hazy morning sun. From Sangkhom, it takes less than an hour (14km/9 miles) to reach **Than Thip falls**, signposted a short distance to the left off the main road. Here a charming little waterfall is set in the middle of a banana grove with pools of cool mountain water tumbling down the hillside.

Beyond Than Thip, the route curves gently in and out of the hills. Occasionally, I stop for water or for *khway tiao nam* (noodle soup) in one of the small villages along the way, before continuing on to the sleepy little town of **Pak Chom**.

Here I check in at the Pak Chom Guest House, perched somewhat precariously on the banks of the river. I drink Beer Singh (the local brew) with a Swedish honeymooning couple before retiring to bed early, to be lulled to sleep by the presence of the Mekong just outside my bungalow.

RICE AND RAPIDS

In many respects the 41-km (25-mile) stretch of road from Pak Chom to Chiang Khan is one of the most scenic of

---

NATIONAL PARKS

Two of Thailand's most popular national parks can be found in Isaan. Phu Reua lies 50km (30 miles) southwest of Loei town on beautiful Highway 203. To get to Phu Kradung, you must follow Highway 201 for 82km (51 miles) south. It's a tough pedal to get to both of them, and be warned that Phu Kradung National Park is closed daily at 3pm to allow visitors to climb the mountainside (2–3 hours). It is also closed during the rainy season, from the end of June until early October.

THAILAND

the trip, climbing up and over low hills fringed by fields of rice and sweet corn.

In the paddies, farmers dressed in *paisins* (sarongs) and large straw hats are planting the rice crop. Typically, the rice seed is soaked overnight before being sewn into nursery beds. After a month, the seedlings will be uprooted and taken out to the paddy fields, where they are planted in rows and left for a further three months before being harvested by hand.

Leaving behind a line of rice farmers waving and shouting "*choc dee*" (good luck), and laughing at the sight of a lone foreigner on a bicycle, I continue my journey in the scorching midday heat along this narrow strip of tarmac.

A short distance before Chiang Khan, there's a right turn that is signposted past the temple of Wat Tha Kaek to the popular **Kaeng Kut Khu rapids**. This series of rapids can be crossed by boat after heavy rains (ask at the hotels in Chiang Khan). But when I see them, they are small and disappointing, the vast expanse of water barely disturbed by the treacherous currents below.

Returning to the main road, it's an easy 3-km (2-mile) cycle further west to **Chiang Khan**, spread seemingly interminably along the banks of the Mekong, against a backdrop of mountains.

MONKS AND MERIT

On the outskirts of Chiang Khan, there's a hillside temple reputed to contain a footprint of the Buddha. Every year, during the Lenten retreat of Khao Phansaa, tens of thousands of the Buddhist faithful descend on **Wat Pra Bhat** to burn incense, donate robes to the monks, and to make merit in the hope that they will gain a better position in the next life.

There are plenty more temples in this picturesque little town, where the monks file down the narrow streets at dawn. Off Chai Khong Road, you will find the ornate Lao-style temple of **Wat Mahathat**, which is the oldest in Chiang

Khan, dating back 300 years. Further to the east lies the earthy-coloured **Wat Tha Khaek**, peacefully situated

on the banks of the river a short distance from the rapids.

But there is more to Chiang Khan than its temples. It is a place to savour. Even if you have only an afternoon to spare, leave your bike in the hotel or guest house and wander down to the banks of the river, where the locals grow tomatoes, beans, and other vegetables. Then explore the little *sois* (side roads) and charming old wooden buildings off Chai Khong Road, or visit the customs house, where boats overloaded with cargo and local people criss-cross the river to Laos, just a few hundred metres away on the far bank of the Mekong.

BORDERLANDS

After a day spent wandering the streets and relaxing in the sprawling riverside restaurants, I climb back on my bike physically and mentally prepared for the last and most demanding leg of my journey through Isaan. From Chiang Khan, there are two routes to the provincial capital of Loei. The shorter one runs south for 50km (30 miles) down Highway 201 and can be cycled in a matter of hours. The longer and more demanding route follows a staggeringly beautiful but rarely used road as far as Ban Pak Huay, where you must stay the night before continuing to Loei.

I opt for the second route (Highway 2195), leaving at dawn to make sure that I reach my overnight stop by mid-afternoon. Soon the road climbs into the hills, leaving the town and the river far behind. Gradually, almost imperceptibly, the scenery changes, the ricefields and fruit plantations giving way to unculti-vated land and rugged cliffs. This is wild countryside where you are as likely to see water buffalo being herded down the middle of the road as you are to meet other vehicles.

TOP LEFT Plenty of room on top with public transport Isaan-style

RIGHT On the road—and making the most of the cooler part of the day
ABOVE Harvest time in the ricefields near Tha Li

It was near here that long-simmering border tensions between the Laotians and the Thais exploded at the end of 1987, culminating in a three-month border war. Nowadays the area is deceptively quiet, and unless you are familiar with this district, as I am, or have travelled extensively in Isaan, make sure that you cross in full daylight and preferably with a local guide.

It is late afternoon by the time I arrive in **Ban Pak Huay**, set on the banks of the Heung River. This charming village has a couple of very basic bungalows by the river (OTS Guest House). If there's nobody there, simply ask for Khun Oi, the remarkable lady who runs the place with the help of her son.

By the light of the moon, I bathe in the shallow waters of the Heung River, the pains of cycling soothed by the cool water and the visible excitement of this gentle, friendly community still unused to the sight of many foreigners. Less than 30m (100 feet) away, on the far bank of the river, a few lights glitter from over the border with Laos.

Siberia of the Northeast

My final day's cycle ride is a magnificent journey through one of Thailand's most striking provinces. **Loei** is known as the Siberia of the Northeast, and with good reason. In the winter months, from November to January, temperatures can fall as low as zero centigrade with thick mist covering the roads in the early morning. Conversely, during the hot season, from March to June, temperatures can soar as high as 40°C (104°F).

Loei Province boasts plenty of other distinctions. In February, it plays host to the annual Cotton Blossom Festival (featuring among other events a Miss Cotton Blossom Beauty Queen contest), while at the end of June the people of Dansai village celebrate the Phi Ta Khon festival (a fertility rite) by donning brightly coloured masks and processing down the main street sporting giant wooden phalluses.

From Ban Pak Huay, I follow an arrow-straight piece of road that cuts through ricefields as far as **Tha Li** (8km/5 miles), an old smuggling town reputed to house some of the most prodigious drinkers in the province. Shortly before entering the village, I take a left turn down Highway 2114, continuing along another fine stretch of road that curves through low hills overshadowed by the Khao Ngu and Khao Laem mountains.

On the final section of the route, there's one last side trip that's worth the effort. A left turn 11km (7 miles) from Loei will bring you to the famous meditation cave of **Tham Paa Phu**, with its temple and cells built into the cliff. From here, you must return to the main road before joining the big, busy dual carriageway to **Muang Loei** (literally Loei town), an ugly sprawling city that marks the end of the journey. Keen cyclists can continue to the national parks at **Phu Reua** or **Phu Kradung**— glorious mountain rides, but challenging for even the fittest cyclist.

But after all the exertions of my tour I prefer to take the easy route home, putting my bike on the roof of a *songthaew* (pick-up truck) and heading back to Nong Khai, just five hours and not an ounce of effort away.

FESTIVALS OF ISAAN

The people of Isaan believe that, to remind the Buddha that it is time for the annual monsoon, they must fire rockets up into the clouds. If you happen to be in the Northeast during May (Nong Khai or Loei are the best places), you may see these giant missiles hurtling through the sky propelled by up to 100kg (250 lb) of home-made explosives. Or if you arrive in July, you may find Isaan people making candles the size of houses to donate to the monks during Khao Phansaa, the Lenten season.

GOING IT ALONE

INTERNAL TRAVEL

There are regular trains (including a comfortable nightly sleeper) taking 11 hours to Nong Khai from Hualamphong Station in Bangkok. Bicycles can be placed in the rear wagon, but you should make arrangements at the station in advance. Less popular VIP buses take 10 hours on the same route. Regular air-conditioned and ordinary buses connect major towns and cities throughout the Northeast, and *songthaews* (pick-up trucks) serve the smaller local routes.

WHEN TO GO

The best time to cycle in northeast Thailand is between October and the end of February, when the skies are clear and temperatures average a pleasant 27°C (81°F). Be aware, however, that at night it can get extremely cold, with early morning mist. Between March and May, temperatures rise to a sweltering 40°C (104°F) with a high level of humidity. Cycling during the rainy months, from June to September, can be fun, especially if you are in a group, although roads may be slippery and at times extremely dangerous.

PLANNING

Most nationalities receive a 1-month tourist visa on arrival in Thailand, although you should enquire at the nearest Thai embassy for the latest information.

ARRANGING A BICYCLE

The recommended way to arrange a mountain bike in northeast Thailand is to contact one of the major cycle tour operators either in Chiang Khan or in Bangkok. If you are determined to undertake a solo tour, mountain bikes can be rented from Mut Mee Guest House in Nong Khai, although to avoid disappointment in high season (Nov–Feb), you should make arrangements well in advance of departure.

Before renting a bike, make sure that everything is in full working order as you will be liable for any damage when the bike is returned.

At present, there are no special requirements for tourists wishing to bring a bicycle into Thailand on the plane, although you should check the latest situation with the specific airline concerned.

ACCOMMODATION

Standard hotel accommodation can be found in Nong Khai and Loei. Elsewhere along the Mekong route, don't expect much in the way of luxury. Si Chiang Mai, Sangkhom, Pak Chom, and Chiang Khan have guest houses or pleasant bungalows overlooking the river. In Ban Pak Huay, there's one tiny set of bungalows.

RULES OF THE ROAD

❑ Traffic drives on the left-hand side (normally).
❑ The bigger vehicle gets priority.
❑ Beware of slippery roads after the rains.
❑ Never cycle in remote areas alone.
❑ Never cycle at night.
❑ You should wear reflective clothing and a plastic safety helmet.
❑ Gloves, sunglasses, and sun protection are vital.

HEALTH MATTERS

❑ Make sure you are fully acclimatized before you go cycling.
❑ Drink large quantities of water and bring rehydration salts.
❑ Carry a basic medical kit that includes plasters, anti-infection ointment, and diarrhoea tablets.
❑ Make sure you are fully up to date with tetanus and any other inoculations recommended by your doctor.
❑ Make sure you have full medical insurance.

TRAVELLERS' TIPS

❑ Cycle with a minimum of two people at all times as accidents and breakdowns are by no means uncommon.
❑ If you have a breakdown, rent a local *songthaew* (pick-up truck) to take you to the nearest city.
❑ Take an up-to-date map, a Thai dictionary, and a puncture repair kit. If you are going it alone, on your own bike, also take a spare inner tube.
❑ Leave early in the morning when it is still cool and make sure that you get to your destination by mid-afternoon.
❑ Those who resent pedalling, but wish to see the countryside, can hire a 100cc motor scooter. This can also prove a useful back-up if you are with a group of cyclists.

THAILAND

Riding the E&O Express

by Jill Gocher

The Eastern & Oriental Express, the luxury train that plies between Singapore and Bangkok, offers a ride into fantasy. En route, it makes two stops—one at Kachanaburi to visit the famous "Bridge on the River Kwai," and the second at Butterworth to explore the delights of Penang Island, "Pearl of the Orient."

E nsconced in the cushioned depths of a plush sofa in the observation lounge of the Eastern & Oriental Express, with a long gin and tonic clinking icily at my side, I ponder the many train journeys I have made. I reach the conclusion that as trains go, the E&O Express is right up there amongst the best. It is an adventure in luxury, a nostalgic re-creation of the early, gracious days of travel, when style and glamour were just part of the package.

The 46-hour journey from Bangkok to Singapore takes you through the verdant ricefields of southern Thailand and over the border into Malaysia, to traverse the entire length of the Malay

peninsula before crossing the Causeway to modern Singapore.

Singapore is a fitting terminal for a journey of stature, right at Asia's southernmost tip and just north of the Equator. Once, this modern city was a

1
This route requires nothing more than the ability to relax in luxury while enjoying elegant surroundings and fine cuisine.

★★
★
The cabins have been designed to provide optimum comfort within the narrow parameters of a train carriage.

Bring smart casual clothes for day-wear and an elegant ensemble for the evenings. As the brochure succinctly puts it, "dressing up is encouraged."

colonial headquarters—where planters from the wilds of Malaysia came for a little Rest and Recreation—and the first Asian stop on many a world tour. While much of its colonial graciousness and architecture has given way to concrete and towering skyscrapers in the great Asian race to development, Singapore does retain part of its heritage. Many of the well-known institutions, such as Raffles Hotel, have been renovated and remodelled with a lingering charm that can't be denied.

BELOW The sleek lines of the E&O. From the welcoming party at the station (LEFT), it's pampering all the way

THE JOURNEY BEGINS

The train can be boarded either in Bangkok or Singapore. My companion and I started the journey in Bangkok, after a far-too-short hiatus at the superb Oriental Hotel. This gracious old lady played her part in Bangkok's early trading days, and has been the city's premier hotel for over a century. Established in 1876, it became the social hub for the Bangkok élite and travelling Europeans. Today, it is charmingly redolent of a bygone era—a nostalgia-lover's delight.

We set off on the five-minute ride to the nearby Central Railway Station with plenty of time to make the 11am

THAILAND

deadline. In a city famous for its traffic jams, proximity to one's destination makes all the difference. After a few minutes in an air-conditioned waiting room, we are shepherded across the station to the train, which stands gleaming in all its green and silver livery.

The staff are on hand to settle everyone comfortably in as the train steams out of the station, then we head up to the dining car for brunch. Tables are set elegantly with fresh white linen; polished crystal wine glasses and silver cutlery gleam softly in the morning sun, while the wall lamps cast yellow light on the timber panelling of this salon on wheels. The slightly hypnotic rhythm of the swaying train adds to the feeling of relaxation and comfort.

As we glide out of the city, we feast on newly baked breads, freshly brewed Colombian coffee, and an ingenious goat cheese soufflé with salmon croutons, followed with medallions of pan-fried snow fish and accompaniments.

Generally, train journeys mean direct interaction with local cultures, offering close-up experiences of the flavours, sights, and sounds of a foreign country. Not so the E&O Express. Here, passengers are presented with a stylized, romanticized rendition of Asia. For tourists rather than passengers, the train is designed to provide luxury and comfort for the well-heeled in the most enjoyable manner possible.

Passengers are treated as honoured guests, and are greeted by Thai staff with a *wei* or bow. Service is polite and friendly. Female bar attendants dress in red *cheongsams* or traditional Thai outfits, while cabin attendants wear elegant Thai-inspired costumes.

MARVELLOUS MEALS

The journey is enlivened by light diversions. One night it is a Thai musical recital, the next, a Malay dance performance. A piano player performs nightly at the main bar and, for one afternoon, a talented Thai fortune-teller is available to reveal good things about your future.

Dining is considered to be one of the journey's special attractions—a culinary adventure where Thai, Malay, Burmese, and Indian flavours are discreetly introduced to the predominantly Western cuisine. Chef Kevin Cape has explored Eastern cooking styles and come up with creative dishes that earn him invitations to international culinary exhibitions.

A medallion of "scented cod" is bathed in a coriander and watercress bouillon, a hot fruit springroll offers a departure from the typical Chinese version, while a medallion of beef is accompanied by Malaysian-style almond and raisin *ketupat*, or rice cake, served on a nest of aubergine and cumin purée—all delicious and faintly exotic without being overwhelmingly foreign. A selection of French, Italian, Australian, German, and Californian wines presents enough variety to satisfy most tastes. The menus are changed regularly, enabling those who do the trip more than once to enjoy new tastes, and an à la carte menu is available for every meal.

MALAYSIA'S FAVOURITE ISLAND

Penang was founded by Captain Francis Light in 1786 following a deal made with the Sultan of Kedah, the first British colony in the Malacca Straits. Coins were fired into the dense jungle to encourage land clearing, and from then on the young colony grew swiftly. With the offer of free land for settlers, it attracted many immigrants, from India, Malaysia, Burma, Thailand, Java, Sumatra, and (the majority) from southern China. Large populations of Indian and Malay, and smaller communities of Achinese and Javanese from Indonesia, plus descendants of early Arab traders, add to the spicy multicultural mix that gives Penang its cosmopolitan ambience and cuisine.

BANGKOK

Bangkok, known also as Krung Thep or the City of Angels, is a fast-paced city of concrete and pollution. Yet beneath the sometimes charmless exterior lies an energetic city that is difficult to resist. The proud Thais have never been colonized by any European power and it was only in 1855, after two centuries of isolation, that King Rama IV opened up the Kingdom of Siam to the world. One year later, the British arrived—the first of a long line of Europeans. Trading houses and godowns (warehouses) soon appeared alongside the Chao Phraya River, just down from the Grand Palace. Many of these, as well as mosques and Chinese temples, can be seen along the riverbanks and in the small streets in the vicinity of the Oriental Hotel.

TRAIN PEOPLE

I can't help wondering what kind of people like to ride on this luxurious train. The answer is, all sorts. Romantics, nostalgics, and those who want to enjoy the glamour of the "exotic orient" in luxury: successful executives, industrialists, the occasional member of a royal family, fashion designers (Japanese designer Kenzo had taken the train shortly before me), retired folk who want to travel in style, the occasional pre-independence planter returning for a nostalgic visit, or a veteran who was here during World War II. One elderly English gentleman travelling with his wife is returning to the East for the first time in 43 years: he had been out here with the British army just after World War II. Travellers are predominantly English, German, Japanese, and American, with a sprinkling of other nationalities from over 60 countries.

THE BRIDGE ON THE RIVER KWAI

As we started from Bangkok, our first excursion is to the River Kwai and its notorious bridge, about 130km (80 miles) west of Bangkok. The 1950s Hollywood movie *The Bridge on the River Kwai* immortalized the British, Australian, and New Zealand Allied prisoners of war who worked to build the bridge and the Burma Railway. Under the command of Colonel Nicholson, played by Alec Guinness, the troops are forced to build a bridge over the river. Their Japanese captors demand that they use a British design, as the Japanese versions are unworkable. After much persuasion (torture, a few brutal killings, e.t.c.) the British commander agrees and it is built within the tight deadline demanded by Japanese army headquarters.

What the Japanese are unaware of is the sabotage the men are inflicting, even as the bridge is being built. Metal nuts are filed almost through, causing them to weaken without actually breaking, tightened nuts are unscrewed after passing inspection, fittings are surreptitiously dropped into the river, and white ants are gathered and buried beside unprotected foundation timbers. As the first train crosses the bridge, British commandos dynamite one span, causing the entire train to fall into the river.

The bridge is the culmination of the whole Burma or "Death" Railway project. The 415-km (260-mile) track through rugged and mountainous jungle was constructed as a convenient conduit for the Japanese to transport troops and prisoners of war, and to support them in their scheme to invade India. By May 1943, the Japanese had a working force of 61,000 Allied prisoners taken from the pool of British, Australian, Dutch, and American prison camps scattered throughout Southeast Asia. Around 250,000 Asians were also used as forced labourers, without the (doubtful) benefit of commanders who at least could

61

negotiate on their behalf. With orders from Japanese army headquarters to make "speedo," non-stop work shifts were instigated, lasting from 18 to 30 hours without a break. With little food or rest, and rampant malaria, dysentery, and cholera, there was no respite for the prisoners, who were kept working until they were unconscious or, in some cases, until they died.

An estimated total of 16,000 Allied soldiers and at least 80–100,000 Asian labourers died during the construction—a high price to pay for the railway, the building of which was completed within five months.

COLONEL BOGEY AND HIS MARCH

Our visit to the bridge is scheduled for mid-afternoon on the first day. The train makes a small detour from the main track to the town of **Kachanaburi**. It arouses great curiosity whenever it stops as both the local people and foreign tourists rush to photograph its gleaming silver lines. So, feeling like VIPs, we get down from the train and prepare for "The Bridge."

There is little evidence of the horrors that so appalled people around the world. Today Kachanaburi is a quiet place, and a popular holiday destination for Bangkokites. The wide river is crowded with floating hotels and restaurants that fill to overflowing during school holidays.

It's disappointing that we have no time to walk across the bridge or to visit the museum, but the full complement of passengers obediently follows the young guides down to the river, with the tinny strains of "Colonel Bogey's March" emanating from strategically placed loudspeakers.

After inspecting the bridge from a distance (the original curved spans that were shipped from Java, Indonesia, are still in use on the present, rebuilt construction), we board a large shaded barge, well furnished with cool drinks and a sound system that the guides use with great enthusiasm as they tell us a bit about the river and their town of Kachanaburi. Fortunately the trip is relatively brief, and on reaching the calm of Kachanaburi Allied War Cemetery No. 2, we are spared further explanations as

THAILAND

LEFT The reconstructed "Bridge on the River Kwai," at Kachanaburi, a silent memorial to those who died working on the infamous Burma railway in World War II

desultory early morning conversation, the sun rises—not an awe-inspiring dawn, but a good start to the day. One by one we disappear back to our cabins for breakfast and to arrange ourselves for the day as we rush on through the southern Thailand ricefields.

COLONIAL ARCHITECTURE AND ETHNIC ENCLAVES

That afternoon, after another elegant lunch, we reach the railhead at Butterworth, in the northern Malaysian state of Kedah. This is the departure point for our second scheduled stop: an excursion across the Penang Straits to the historic island of **Penang**. Here a jungle-covered mountain and a city that is a delightful mix of modern development, rambling colonial buildings, and colourful Indian, Malay, and Arab quarters combine to earn the island the sobriquet "Pearl of the Orient."

It is rare to find an urban centre nowadays that has been spared the depradations of modernization. Thanks to some enlightened planning 20 years ago, much of Penang's development has occurred outside the old city centre of Georgetown. So, while Penang is known for its numerous condominiums and one of Asia's largest "Silicon Valleys," the rich architectural heritage of old Georgetown has not been affected.

A trishaw takes us through street after street where crumbling pre-war Chinese shop-houses jostle with fine colonial buildings from the British era, (which ended in the 1960s with independence). Interspersed are several temples devoted to a pantheon of gods. The oldest mosque, the Acheen Street Mosque, dates back to 1808. Chinese temples and the charming St. George's Cathedral are found within the Heritage area. Many pleasant hours could be spent exploring the highways and

we are escorted round. The cemetery is one of two in the vicinity—a large, lawn-like place filled with concrete head-stones commemorating the Allied prisoners of war who died working on the railway. We read the wall plaques, look at the headstones, and return in pensive mood to the cool, welcoming confines of the train, and our journey continues.

Sitting in the air-conditioned bar with some energy-restoring gin and tonics to hand, we watch the lowering sun cast its lengthening shadows across the rice-fields as the train continues southwards. The world is bathed in the golden light that precedes a dramatic tropical sunset. Day slides into night.

After a 5:30 sunrise call, my companion and I reluctantly drag ourselves from our bunks and, clutching our camera gear, stumble down the swaying carriageway to the observation car at the far end of the train. It's always a good policy to check the sunrise, in case it's spectacular and a welcome photo opportunity. To my surprise, a few other enthusiasts are already there, standing sleepily in the cool morning air, coffee cups in hand. As we make

THAILAND

byways; our short excursion gives us just a little taste. Unfortunately, the E&O Hotel, designed by the Sarkies Brothers of Raffles Hotel fame, is undergoing long-term renovation.

After Penang, we head south, passing by **Taiping**, a 19th-century tin-mining centre. This historical town has an interesting background, retains some fine colonial architecture, and is set in a scenic part of the country. Surrounded with forested limestone mountains, it attracts Malaysia's highest rainfall; the landscape is reminiscent of China's Guilin.

By the time we reach the Malaysian capital of **Kuala Lumpur**, it's the dead of night and most passengers are asleep, thus missing the copper domes and Moorish spires of the city's main railway station. Built in 1911 according to the strict regulations laid down by British Railways, it has a roof strong enough to withstand the weight of a metre of snow. Most of the colonial buildings around Kuala Lumpur's station were built at the beginning of the 20th century—the majority are Moorish in style and well worth a visit on another occasion.

SMOOTH OPERATOR

The man responsible for the train's smooth operation is the train manager, Mr. Christopher Charles Byatt. His spare, hairless figure can be seen darting here and there, checking on the guests, food and wine, and troubleshooting any problems.

My first impression of this upright, shaven-headed man is rather negative, but Christopher turns out to be a charmer—an entertainer with a vast repository of stories. In perfectly accented British English, he regales me with colourful tales concerning previous guests, most unsuitable for publication. Christopher is a man well worth cultivating, a gentleman with Buddhist leanings and a wide experience that includes several years on the Venice–Simplon Orient Express.

SNAKING SOUTHWARDS

After Kuala Lumpur, the train passes into southern Malaysia, where over 21,000sq km (8,000 square miles) of oil palm estates and rubber plantations have been wrested from the rain forest. Malaysia, once the most prolific producer of rubber in the world, now lies in third place, behind Thailand and Indonesia, while its palm oil production has escalated to such an extent that it is one of the country's prime sources of income and has placed it high in world production stakes. In Malaysia palm oil can be found in almost everything the country produces, from cooking oil, soaps, candles, shaving creams, and lubricating greases to milk products, biscuits, and ice creams. Research is currently under way to assess its feasibility as a fuel for motor cars.

At Malaysia's **Johor Baru**, we reach the southernmost limit of the Asian continent, but the breakfast served in our cosy cabin keeps us occupied with far more mundane matters, and the geographical landmark passes us by almost unnoticed.

A painless ride across the Causeway brings us to Singapore and a quick stop at the new multimillion dollar Woodlands Customs and Immigration Checkpoint, where we disembark to complete all the necessary formalities—a rude awakening from the cocooned existence of the past two days. Fortunately, this is the only stop where guests are required to disembark from the train. After a ride through Singapore's older forested sections, the outlines of modern Singapore and Tanjong Pagar Station appear. We have arrived.

To paraphrase Robert Louis Stevenson, "To travel luxuriously is a better thing than to arrive." As train manager Christopher tells me, every trip is a different adventure, as the atmosphere changes with each group of guests. Many choose to repeat the trip at a later date. Given half a chance, I too would do it again, tomorrow.

THAILAND

GOING IT ALONE

be more likely to influence any add-on trips.

INTERNAL TRAVEL

It is possible to follow the same route as the E&O (without the luxury) on the normal rail services that run between Singapore and Bangkok. It will require three changes of trains.

The night train from Singapore to Kuala Lumpur (KL) connects with the morning train to Butterworth. There is also an afternoon train, which allows a few hours sightseeing in the Malaysian capital. Even the immediate vicinity of the station has some of KL's most attractive historic buildings, which are definitely worth a visit.

From Butterworth (allowing time for a day or two in Penang if required) the Bangkok International Express goes to Bangkok, stopping at the border town of Hat Yai for immigration formalities.

Sleepers are available from Singapore to Kuala Lumpur, and again from Butterworth to Bangkok. Through bookings can be made at either Singapore or Bangkok.

WHEN TO GO

Any time of the year is good to do the E&O Express journey as outside conditions don't affect the experience significantly. Weather conditions would

PLANNING

While most people prefer to make the whole journey in one, the E&O Express can be booked for a part journey—from Singapore to Kuala Lumpur or Butterworth, or from Bangkok to Butterworth. For some trips, an extension to the northern Thailand region of Chiang Mai can be booked at the same time.

Luggage required on the journey should be kept in a small soft bag that will stay in the cabin. Larger bags are kept in the baggage car at the front of the train, and these will not be accessible during the journey

HEALTH MATTERS

❑ Check on inoculations a month before leaving.
❑ Make sure you have full medical insurance.

WHAT TO TAKE

❑ Cabin luggage in a small suitcase or soft bag.
❑ Cash or credit cards for extra purchases and drinks on the train. (A bottle of your favourite beverage would minimize expenditure.)
❑ Walking shoes and a sun hat for excursions.
❑ Smart casual dress for daywear (jeans and T-shirts are not recommended), and smarter outfits for evenings.
❑ Some people find the swaying motion of the train a little disturbing on the first night — a sleeping medication may help.
❑ A good book for moments when you don't feel like socializing.
❑ Spare cash for tipping cabin and restaurant staff.
❑ Luxury toiletries are provided in your cabin, but you may wish to bring your usual cosmetics as well.

ON THE MENU

Apart from the superb meals of the set menu, the E&O offers an à la carte menu, which includes such delicacies as Scottish smoked salmon, Beluga caviar with blinis, and medallion of beef in ginger and lemon grass sauce, or panfried sea scallops. Meals can also be prepared without spices if you prefer.

THE POSTWAR ENCOUNTER

Train manager Christopher tells a chilling story of two elderly gentlemen guests, one British and one Japanese, who were both involved with the Burma Railway during the war years. They came to realize each other's existence and one day by coincidence—or fate—ended up alone in the bar car. After a few minutes of edgily facing each other, as recognition of the situation dawned upon them, they sat together over a drink, each sipping silently. As they finished, they stood and bowed before each went off his own way. An old score was settled.

THAILAND

Learning to Dive in Phuket

by Simon Richmond

Phuket, which offers the largest range of adventure activities of Thailand's islands is near the Andaman Sea's Similan Islands, one of the world's top dive sites. It was an ideal place for me to qualify as a diver and make my first trip into the aquatic world.

When it's raining cats and dogs in Phuket—Thailand's largest island and a magnet for over one million pleasure-seeking visitors each year—the best place to be is in the water. However, shivering slightly in the penthouse pool of a hillside hotel in the beach resort of Patong, and attempting for the third time to clear my flooded diving mask by blowing through my nose, I have cause to wonder whether being under water is such a good idea after all.

"You'll love diving," I was told by experienced diver friends. "Once down there, you'll never want to come up," they said. I wasn't too sure. I am a fan of aquariums and those graceful turtles and stealthy sharks, but I'd always been quite happy to observe them safely behind glass. I'd enjoyed seeing multi-coloured fish and corals while swimming, but that was in comfort, at the surface, using a snorkel.

However, if you want to explore the world fully, it is not a smart move to cut yourself off from the underwater mysteries and adventures of oceans and

 To undertake a diving qualification course you must be in good health and have sound swimming skills, such as being able to swim at least 183m (220 yards) and tread water for 10 minutes. It's also necessary to study a fair amount of diving theory in order to pass the test. Read the appropriate chapters in the manual before you start the course.

★★ Mastering some of the skills, such as flooding and clearing a diving mask of water, are challenging and can be unnerving at first. Any discomfort will fade once you've gained confidence. In terms of accommodation and eating, Phuket offers something for all tastes and budgets, from some of Thailand's most luxurious hotels to a lively traveller scene in Patong beach.

Whether you're learning to dive or just want to go snorkelling, the best pieces of kit to have are a mask, snorkel, and fins. All reputable dive operations and many places of accommodation will provide these free or at a small charge, but they can be in poor condition and might not fit as well as equipment that is tailored to your own needs. More experienced divers, or those who plan to take up the sport seriously, might consider buying their own Buoyancy Control Device (BCD) and breathing apparatus (regulators). The waters are warm, but a wet suit or Lycra body suit will aid buoyancy and protect against sunburn.

lakes—which cover well over half the globe. My trepidation had a lot to do with the fact that I wasn't a strong swimmer, but as Jeroen, co-owner of Fantasea Divers in Phuket, assured me, "You don't need to be. It's better to be a strong sinker!"

DIVER'S PARADISE

Phuket is one of the best places in Thailand to learn to dive. Other islands, such as Ko Tao and Ko Samui off the

ABOVE Small reef fish swim amongst the mixed corals of the Andaman Sea as a diver (INSET) is photographed under water against the sun
LEFT Scuba divers set off for deeper waters

east coast, are also popular, but they struggle to match the sheer number of dive centres in Phuket and particularly **Patong**, the main beach area, which long ago mutated from an idyllic hippy getaway into a fully fledged tourist town, complete with wall-to-wall gift shops, restaurants, and bars. Competition helps keep prices down and the surrounding diving attractions ensure that plenty of qualified dive masters from different countries are on hand to provide lessons in a range of languages you'd find hard to match in other parts of the world, let alone Thailand.

One reason for all the dive shops is Phuket's proximity to the Andaman Sea's nine Similan Islands, some 60km (37 miles) off the coast and designated a national marine park in the 1980s. Diving enthusiasts will tell you of the islands' famed attributes; how, save for two, they remain uninhabited and unspoiled by tourism; how the surrounding waters teem with a myriad plants and fish, including angel and parrot fish (*Pomacanthus paru, Scarus lepidus*), crown of thorns starfish (*Acanthaster planci*), turtles, and white-tip sharks; how visibility through the turquoise blue waters can be 30m (100 feet) or more. And, as much of the coral and fish life is within a couple of metres of the surface, a trip out to the Similans is worthwhile for non-divers, too.

The best time of year to visit the islands is from November to April, outside the monsoon season. But even if you arrive in Phuket during the wet months of summer, there are still plenty of diving opportunities around the Rajah Islands, to the south, or in Phang Nga Bay to the east. Snorkelling is an option in all these places, and if you don't have the time or money to invest in a three- or four-day diving certification course, all is not lost. One-day or "resort" dives will familiarize you with the basics of diving in a safe area of water. But to gain access to the deeper underwater paradises, to swim with the big fish, I had to learn the skills properly and this meant one thing: going back to school.

THEORY AND PRACTICE

I signed up for a four-day course, conducted under the auspices of PADI (Professional Association of Diving Instructors), the American-based organization that certifies some two-thirds of divers around the world. Given that it's vital you understand your instructor fully and that you'll be spending some time with them, it's worthwhile checking who will be teaching you and perhaps arranging to meet them beforehand. Also find out how many other students will be in your class; the smaller the

THE VEGETARIAN FESTIVAL

The island's capital, Phuket Town, is a fine antidote to beach culture, with its lively market, engrossing antique and craft shops, and remnants of dilapidated but evocative Sino-Portuguese architecture. If you can, visit around the end of October, at the start of the ninth month in the Chinese lunar calendar, to witness the exotic and sometimes repulsive rituals of Ngan Kin Jeh, the Vegetarian Festival.

The highlight of this festival (so called because of the strict vegetarian diet followed during the month-long period of ritual purification) is the parade of *nagas*, religious devotees who work themselves up into a dervish-like trance so they can skewer their flesh with metals rods, walk over hot coals, and undertake other such dangerous stunts without apparently suffering any of the usual consequences.

For those too squeamish to watch these displays of ritual masochism, the nine-day festival offers plenty of singing and dancing, colourful displays of altars in front of shops around town, and nightly fireworks shows. The best place to catch the festivities is at the Wat Jui Tui on Ranony Road.

group the more time you'll have with the instructor.

On my course were two other students: Issiah, a Singaporean flight attendant nursing his mobile phone like a comfort blanket, and Kira, a British teenager and the only one of us to have been on a one-day dive before. Duncan, our principal instructor and a former cook and holiday camp host from Britain, attempted to put us at ease by telling us that diving was not just a sport for "roughty, toughty, mega-fit types," and that it was a perfectly safe pastime as long as we observed basic procedures.

One of these procedures was filling out the medical questionnaire before the start of the course. Even something seemingly minor like a blocked nose from a lingering cold can have a serious impact on your ability to dive safely, so it's important that the questionnaire is answered honestly. If you're travelling with children, it's also worth noting that the minimum age for PADI certification is 12 years, and that 12- to 15-year-olds are classed as "junior divers" and must always be accompanied by an adult.

All dive courses include a sizeable chunk of academic training and, in this respect, PADI's are no different. Study is split into five modules, each accompanied by a video and seminar conducted by a dive master. The second element of the course consists of confined-water training—learning the basic diving skills in a controlled environment such as a swimming pool or shallow waters. The final segment takes you out into open water for four dives, to practise the newly learned skills. To pass the course, you must (a) get at least 75 per cent in a multiple-choice theory exam and (b) demonstrate competency in a range of basic diving skills.

TESTING THE WATERS

Duncan began by explaining what we would be doing over the next four days. The first morning would be spent in the classroom, studying modules one and two, before moving to a pool in the afternoon to become familiar with diving equipment and practise various skills. On Day Two, after zipping through the remaining three modules of the course, we would sit the exam. Days Three and Four would be taken up with four open-water dives.

This is not necessarily how all PADI courses are run. One of the system's advantages is its flexibility. Courses may also take either three or five days, depending on how quickly the instructor and the students want to go.

It soon became apparent to me why learning to dive wouldn't be just a simple matter of slinging on my scuba equipment and jumping in. Diving and breathing air underwater have significant effects on the body that must be taken into account if the activity is to remain safe and enjoyable.

For example, as you descend, uncomfortable pressure builds in your ears. The simplest technique for dealing with this "squeeze" is to block your nose and attempt to blow gently through it as you go down. More important, however, is making sure you always follow the golden rule of scuba diving: never hold your breath underwater and keep breathing continuously. If you do hold your breath, it's possible to injure and even rupture your lungs.

The piece of kit that allows you to breathe while diving is the scuba, or Self-Contained Underwater Breathing Apparatus. This consists of a tank (a high-pressure cylinder that stores compressed air), a valve to turn the flow of air on and off, a backpack to carry the tank, a regulator (the mouthpiece through which divers breathe a controlled amount of air), and a pressure gauge to monitor air supply.

THE FIRST DIP

Heavy as scuba gear is, its weight is often not enough to overcome the body's natural propensity to float. This is why divers wear belts threaded with several 1-kg (2-lb) lead weights to help them sink. But not everyone needs the same amount of lead.

"Better take some of those weights off," said Duncan, as I plummeted directly to the bottom of the pool. I was getting a first-hand lesson in negative buoyancy, something we'd studied in the theory section of the course earlier.

One of the main diving skills to learn is how to control your buoyancy underwater. This is done through a combination of deep, steady breathing and the use of a buoyancy control device, or BCD—an expandable bladder, often designed as a waistcoat jacket, that can automatically be inflated or

ABOVE Patong Beach, Phuket

deflated either to keep you afloat at the surface or to make you weightless underwater. The aim is to stay off the seabed and avoid crashing into dangerous rocks or delicate corals. The lightest touch can harm or kill organisms that have taken decades to grow.

Other skills to be practised relate to dealing calmly with problems such as getting water in your mask, the mask coming off completely, recovering your regulator if it comes out of your mouth, and running out of air.

Using some amateur psychology, Duncan asked us to start by doing what, in his opinion, was the hardest thing of all—to breathe underwater through our scuba equipment without a mask for one minute. What I had difficulty with, however, was getting the knack of the displacement method for shifting water out of my mask underwater. I flinched each time water went up my nose.

Then the course co-instructor, Thomas, gave me a tip: pinch your nostrils together while breathing out and tipping your head back. This did the trick and, as I refocused through the water-free mask, I was mightily pleased to see Thomas giving the OK signal that I had successfully mastered this skill.

UNDER EXAMINATION

We had several hours' homework the first evening, then Day Two involved completing modules three to five, which covered such topics as the aquatic environment, procedures to follow when you're diving from a boat, and how to use a compass for basic navigation. Most importantly, we learned about the effects of breathing air at depth and how, if not carefully monitored, diving can result in decompression sickness, otherwise known as "the bends."

Decompression sickness occurs when bubbles of excess nitrogen (which has been absorbed by the body while

breathing air at increased pressure) get trapped in the blood vessels and tissues on ascent. The way to avoid this dangerous medical condition is to master the use of recreational dive tables, which allow you to calculate the maximum safe time and depth limits for each dive, and the amount of time you should stay at the surface between dives.

Learning to use these tables trips some students up. It takes only a little practice, however, and I was glad I'd reviewed the manual in advance of taking the course and hadn't skimped on the homework Duncan had set.

By midday we were sitting the 50-question multiple-choice exam. Kira didn't make the pass grade, but as she'd be given a second chance the following evening, all was not lost. Duncan was encouraging: of the 300 students he'd taught, he'd had to fail only three: two were afraid of water and the other was medically unfit.

HEADING FOR OPEN WATER

Day 3 dawned and our small group was joined by three more students for the open-water dives. Cillian, a confident Irish lad, had done the first part of the

BELOW A crab rests (INSET), while a diver swims above orange sea fan coral

course at his resort hotel in another part of Phuket, while mother and daughter Fern and Tamalin had passed their exam and completed the confined-water training in South Africa before coming here.

This is another advantage of the modular PADI course; you can get the theory test out of the way in your own time and climate, then complete the enjoyable open-water stages at a dive school that also offers PADI courses in a warmer environment, such as Thailand. This was also the option chosen by Christopher Knowles for his PADI course in Borneo (see pages 198–207).

Fern had been encouraged to learn by her husband, a keen diver, but was yet to be convinced that under the sea was any place for humans to venture. Showing a sense of humour that I was beginning to warm to, Duncan made her my diving buddy and dubbed us "the nervous twins." Kira and Tamalin were the "young ones," and Issiah and Cillian the "sultans of cool."

It's important to go diving with a partner, or "buddy", for several reasons. They can help you put on and check equipment before the dive, remind you of the depth, time, and air supply limits, and give you emergency assistance should you need it. Apart from all that, it's much more fun diving with other people than on your own.

On the boat out to the reefs off the island of Rajah Yai, Duncan ran through the day's dive plan. We'd be practising various skills and then going for our first proper dive of around 40 minutes. He also reviewed the hand signals we'd be using to communicate with each other underwater. This is standard practice on any dive: work out a dive plan with your partner beforehand and then stick to it.

Into another world

The aquatic world is far from silent, but the main thing that novice divers notice is the eternal rush of bubbles from their scuba gear—and perhaps their hearts beating with the thrill of it all. All anxi-eties disappear once the real diving begins, which at best is as good a nature safari as you'll ever experience and far more relaxing than an equivalent ramble on land.

Even in the shallows around Rajah Yai, shoals of striped black and yellow sergeant-major fish swarmed around us. As we headed deeper, the corals became more dramatic and, with spiked sea urchins and crown of thorn starfish looming up from the bottom, I realized why it's so important to master buoyancy. It was very easy to go off into your own little world and become absorbed by a single fish or plant.

On the final day of the course, fine blue skies promised a good day's diving and my fellow learners were in an upbeat mood—especially Kira, who'd passed her re-test with 94 per cent. I still had to do my ten minutes of treading water (not having managed even five in the swimming pool), but was confident of success since salt water makes you buoyant and I'd been given a tip by Fern: keep your legs wide apart while paddling.

We head south again to Rajah Yai's Bungalow Bay, where some of our underwater skills tests are conducted in the presence of a curious yellow-fin fish. Once our training is over, we have time to relax and fully enjoy the marine life around us. I see a moray eel slithering through a maze of coral and hover as shoals of silvery fish pass by like a shimmering curtain. We spot lion fish and an octopus, but we keep our distance from the territorial female trigger fish and her sharp bite.

When Duncan gives the ascent signal I realize, with some amazement, that I actually don't want to leave this fascinating new world quite yet. Taking my time to rise through the calm blue waters, I'm already contemplating when to do my next dive. As I break the surface, I hear the best words of the last four days: "Welcome back on board, six more qualified divers."

GOING IT ALONE

INTERNAL TRAVEL

The main international gateway to Phuket is the airport, which is on its northwest coast (see also pages 40–49).

WHEN TO GO

November to April is the best time to visit the Similan Islands. During the monsoon season in summer, however, there is still good diving to be had in Phang Nga Bay (see pages 40–49) or the Rajah Islands.

DIVE CENTRES

The greatest concentration of diving operations is in and around Patong, but as many tour companies and dive centres include free pick-ups from hotels anywhere on the island, there's no pressing reason to stay there unless you want to.

The useful Phuket Island Access website (see Contacts) has links to local dive centres, plus photographs of marine life.

CHOOSING A DIVING COURSE

Before signing up for a course, check exactly what is included in the cost. For example, if you've already bought a diver's manual and dive tables, you won't need to pay extra for a course that gives you another copy.

Check the equipment you'll be using and staff credentials. Choose a centre that offer PADI or NAUI (National Association of Underwater Instructors) certificated courses. Find out if the dive centre is a member of Divesafe Asia, which runs Phuket's only decompression chamber.

One-day introductory dives start at around 3,000 baht ($80); the 3- or 4-day open-water courses are around 11,000 baht ($300). Most dive centres also offer the 2-day advanced open-water diver, 2-day rescue diver, 1-day medic first aid, and other speciality courses.

For qualified divers, day trips around Phuket include Ko Rajah Noi and Ko Racha Yai, some 30km (19 miles) south of the island, and Shark Point (Hin Mu Sang) and Ko Phi Phi to the east in Phang Nga bay.

DIVING EXPEDITIONS

The best way to dive around the Similan Islands is to join one of the 2- to 4-day expeditions on offer in Phuket, based on live-aboard boats. Generally everything, including food, drink, and diving equipment, is included in the price and, on the longer trips, a good range of dive sites will be visited. It's possible to do a day trip from Phuket to Ko Similan, but the journey takes 3 hours each way, leaving little time to enjoy the marine life. Longer trips can also be arranged, taking in the more northerly Ko Surin Islands, the submerged Burma Banks and the hundred islands and reefs of Myanmar's Mergui Archipelago—all areas where sharks and manta rays have been spotted.

WHAT TO TAKE

❑ Waterproof sunscreen.
❑ Swimwear and/or Lycra bodysuit or wetsuit, mask, snorkel and fins.

HEALTH MATTERS

❑ Take a basic medical kit.
❑ Check on inoculations a month before you go.
❑ Take out full medical insurance at home.

OTHER ADVENTURES ON PHUKET

Apart from diving, snorkelling, and sea kayaking (see pages 40–49), there are several land-based adventure activities available on Phuket. Tropical Trails organizes mountain-bike tours, jungle walks, and elephant hill treks in three different areas of the island. If you want to take off on your own, it's also possible to rent from them a 21-speed American Trek and/or Haro mountain bike, with helmet, lock, water bottle, and a Phuket trail map. Mountain biking is also offered by Siam Safari, which runs first-rate eco-tours including 30-minute elephant treks, walking trails, and inflatable canoe tours through the mangrove swamps. The Travel Company can arrange all the above activities and also offers several half-day and one-day adventure safaris around the island using small four-wheel-drive vehicles. These can be combined with elephant treks. Longer trips to the forests and waterfalls of Phang Nga and to the Khao Sok National Park, both north of Phuket, are also available.

See Contacts for details of all these organizations.

Steaming up to Mandalay

by Jill Gocher

The Road to Mandalay *is the name given to the luxury cruise ship that steams up and down the legendary Ayeyarwady River. After a visit to the Plain of Two Thousand Pagodas, I took it from Bagan to Mandalay. Trips ashore included visits to monasteries, a pottery, a goldleaf workshop—and the world's largest ringing bell.*

To explore Myanmar (formerly Burma) is to take a step back in time. It is difficult to believe in the very existence of the electronic age when the main forms of transport are still horse-and-carts, bullock carts, bicycles, ramshackle country buses, and rusty old cars. Industrial development is almost nonexistent and, apart from a few new luxury hotels in the capital, Yangon, and in Mandalay, things are low-key and traditional. The people, devout Buddhists, are gracious and charming.

Most visitors know nothing about Myanmar. Its closed doors have kept it out of world affairs so long that it has became an almost forgotten country. Vague recollections of George Orwell's *Burmese Days* (1935) and various descriptions of "A Golden Land" sit strangely with more recent reports from hawk-eyed journalists who come hunting the low-down on political dissents.

1 Anyone can do this river journey, although using local transport rather than the luxury craft requires a certain capacity for endurance.

★ The Road to Mandalay is five-star comfort all the way. Anyone with a back problem may want to opt out of the horse-and-cart ride on the Ava excursion. Accommodation of all levels is available in Yangon and Mandalay. Bagan has numerous guest houses and several pleasant 3-star hotels.

✗ You should bring a sun hat, walking shoes, mosquito repellent, and sun screen. A long-sleeved shirt is recommended for the sun sensitive.

THE PLAIN OF TWO THOUSAND PAGODAS

The Air Yangon flight from Yangon to Bagan arrives early in the morning and after a quick check-in with immigration and a payment of $10 per person for a visitor's pass, we leave the tiny airport to be greeted with an assortment of taxis, tour buses, and pony carts. I have arrived a day early so I can explore Bagan before joining the boat, and I decide on a taxi. After a little assiduous haggling for a good price, we head off to Old Bagan, about 5km (3 miles) south of Nyaung U village.

Situated on the eastern bank of the Ayeyarwady, Pagan, or **Bagan**, as it is now known, is just one of several classical civilizations that rose in the broad, fertile plains of central Myanmar. Mandalay and the ancient, almost mythical cities of Ava, Amarapura, Prome (Pyi), Sagaing, Mingun, and Shwebo, all lived and died alongside the Ayeyarwady River. This was probably the largest of these cities. The broad 42-sq km (16-square-mile) site on the Bagan Plain was, at the height of its power, scattered with more than 13,000 monuments.

Dispersed amongst the 2,000 or so pagodas, libraries, monasteries, stupas, and chedi (or *zedi*) that still stand are more than 100 monuments—a complex rivalled only by Cambodia's Angkor Wat and Indonesia's Borobudur.

Old Bagan is a delightful surprise. Negative reports on the forced relocation of the Old Bagan villagers,

plus stories of new roads and intrusive
tour coaches, had led me to expect
some kind of sterile theme park of
archaeological monuments. But this is
far from the case. While a new road does
cut through the site, all traces of a once-
booming tourist village have been completely obliterated, and the land is still
very much in use. Between the pagodas
and stupas are plots of corn, sesame,
peanuts, and garden vegetables, and

ABOVE Our boat at Mandalay
*BELOW The sun goes down on the Bagan
Plain and its ancient monuments*

M Y A N M A R

like as not you will see bullock carts creaking along the dirt tracks.

Added to the archaeological splendours is Bagan's timeless ambience and an indefinable charm that seeps into your consciousness. In recent years, the Burmese government in conjunction with UNESCO and the UNDP has begun a spate of renovations, and some of the more beautiful monuments are looking a little sharper around the edges as they are restored to something like their former outlines. Eventually, the government hopes to renovate all monuments within the site.

THE ROAD TO MANDALAY

I board *The Road to Mandalay* (*RTM*) about midday. After depositing my baggage, I take a look around the ship. The boat is of German origin, brought over by the Eastern & Oriental Company (E&O) several years ago to be refitted and upgraded to E&O standards at a cost of $5 million.

The staterooms are extremely spacious and plush, with separate shower and W.C. compartments. Wine chilling in the ice bucket, a range of opulent toiletries, a television with CNN and two video channels, and the intimate view of the river promise all that is required to make the trip enjoyable— enough to attract the rich and, sometimes, the famous.

Then it's time to head to the dining salon, to eye up the fellow guests and sample the lunch. For the first meal, an extravagant buffet of Indian specialities awaits us. Curries, dhal, salads, and Indian breads make a magnificent spread. Waiters are at hand, ready to respond to the merest flicker of an eye, and the ice water, tea, and wine are promptly delivered with a smile.

The 40 or so guests are a mixed bunch. A large group of rich Mexicans are about to embark on the second leg of their voyage, back to Mandalay. A Swiss physiotherapist and his mother and sister make up a small party. A group of Japanese journalists and an Austrian group seem to be enjoying themselves, and a distinguished-looking British couple appear to know everyone on the boat. *RTM* attracts an interesting and very well-heeled crowd.

The afternoon offers an organized tour of Bagan, but I choose to make my own arrangements and set off to visit a few pagodas with my trusty cart driver, Win Ko.

Win Ko (cart no. 134) is a delight. Born and bred in Bagan, he is a devout Buddhist and a humble man. He knows a lot about the monuments and just enough about business to allow him to earn a scanty living taking care of his passengers. He also knows how to look after his horse, which he feeds with

BURMESE TEA AND GREEN TEA SALAD

Food quality is obviously not a problem on *The Road to Mandalay*, but even luxury travellers may like to try some local food. It is generally quite safe to eat in smaller stalls as long as you follow the usual rules—if it looks good try it; if it looks dodgy, leave it alone. One of the most delicious meals I had was at an open stall on the banks of the Ayeyarwady at Mingun, where a cheerful local woman served fresh-fried river fish.

Things you might like to try include the delicious Burmese tea, sold in tea shops. This thick chocolatey-looking tea is brewed with milk and sugar, and is full of flavour. Regular teas pale (in both colour and taste) by comparison.

Green tea salad is a Burmese salad that has a piquant and interesting taste—and could become a favourite. It consists of green tea leaves and an assortment of sesame seeds, fried peas, peanuts, shrimps, garlic, ginger, and toasted coconut.

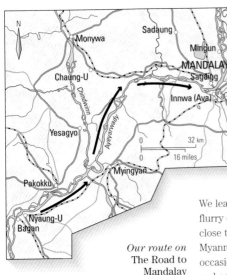

Our route on
**The Road to
Mandalay**

spices);
marinated lamb
brochettes with
vegetables and
Shan spices;
spinach and
tomato pasta
with sesame and
seared pimentos;
chocolate truffles; and
a selection of cheeses.

STEAMING

We leave Bagan about 10:30am amidst a flurry of activity, as our boat is anchored close to the landing point for the west Myanmar ferry. Ox carts, trucks, the occasional turbaned Shan states villager, and country buses gather in anticipation, together with foot passengers who sit and wait under a large tree. The food stalls do a roaring trade as plates of spicy fried noodles and cups of steaming Burmese tea are passed to enthusiastic customers. On the river banks an assortment of barges, sampans, and bamboo rafts, en route to markets downriver, adds to the colourful congestion.

The boat steams up the broad river towards Mandalay. The Ayeyarwady is a major transport conduit right through the centre of the country. Although it is not overly busy, all kinds of craft are

"grass and long beans"—and the animal's shiny glossy coat attests to his care. Every day Win Ko hires a cart (he can never scrape together the $60 or so required to buy one) and his place in the world is secure.

In the evening we take the cart to nearby **Minglazedi**, a favourite spot to catch the sunset. Half of Bagan's tourists are crowded on to the steep steps of the *zedi*. As the sun sinks behind the Ayeyarwady, cameras click almost simultaneously and the small crowd disperses.

That evening it's an elegant dinner on board and an early night, ready for a Bagan sunrise before the quick morning tour with the group. Breakfast is a delight: with fresh-baked breads and croissants, parma ham, French cheeses, omelettes, fresh fruit and juices, brewed expresso coffee and tea. Lunch has the flexibility of a buffet spread—a Burmese meal with Shan dishes, a Chinese, and a superb Indian feast. Dinner's highlights include Burmese vegetable samosas with light chilli sauce; grilled sirloin of beef with shitake mushrooms, shallots, and a confit of leek; rack of Kashmiri-style lamb on a purée of seasoned spinach and watercress; seafood chowder with roselle leaf and *chat marsala* (mild

---

BURMESE MAKEUP

The strange makeup worn by most Burmese, both male and female, is known as *thanaka*. The powder, derived from an aromatic tree bark, is applied in all kinds of artistic forms in circles and stripes large and small—and is believed to condition the skin and protect it from sunburn. For a Burmese, it would be unthinkable to go out without it. Thanaka comes in small cakes, sold at the market. It varies in quality: a good one is silky smooth, mixes easily with water, and applies smoothly to the skin.

MYANMAR

using the watery highway to transport goods, people, and priests. Navigable by steamer for 1,500km (940 miles) or over half its length, the river has long provided access to the interior. The British dubbed it "The Road to Mandalay," a name adopted by our ship.

The afternoon passes uneventfully as we steam northwards. The banks of the Ayeyarwady are dotted with pagodas and *zedis* every few hundred yards or so—a constant reminder of the devotion of the local people to their religion and the part it plays in their everyday life. That evening we drop anchor mid-stream, opposite a small pottery-making village that supplies half the country with marvellous earthernware pots. We go ashore, accompanied by giggling young villagers, and watch a young woman demonstrate her skills at the pottery wheel. In seconds a lump of clay has been masterfully transformed into a pot and then moments later, another. It's well after dark when we board the pilot boat back to the ship.

All transport on the Ayeyarwady stops at night. Because of unruly currents and the constant shifting of the sandy bottom, river traffic runs in daylight hours only and even then it is a hazardous affair, requiring constant monitoring of the waters ahead by small boats whose pilots use bamboo poles to gauge the depth and current flow.

Early next morning, long before breakfast, the engines have been revved and we are on our way once more, towards the fabled city of Mandalay. It is indescribably pleasant steaming along the broad river, even though there is not much to see. The high banks are wide

A MIGHTY RIVER

The Ayeyarwady starts its 2,170-km (1,350-mile) journey in the far north of Myanmar, high in the foothills of the Himalayas, source of many of Asia's legendary rivers—the Ganges, the Mekong, the Brahmaputra, and the Indus. The broad, slow-moving river flows south through the rugged and remote Kachin states, before it hits the fertile central plains, home to the many ancient kingdoms. Finally, it reaches the vast rice-producing delta in the south, where it splits wide into nine arms that empty into the Andaman Sea.

apart, with sweeping plains beyond, and the scene is enlivened by the occasional distant pagoda guarding the shores, an ox cart trundling along, or a group of children watching the passing boats.

Sitting on the boat allows time for small pleasures. Some guests choose

INSET Local river craft
RIGHT The U Bein bridge over
Taungthamon Lake at Amarapura, built
with timber from the ruins at Ava

to loll by the pool, others enjoy the air-conditioned comfort of the salons and find a quiet spot to read a book, or take a cool drink. *RTM* has no games or other embarrassments to mar the tranquillity. In fact, any organized activities other than the tours are conspicuous only by their absence. Privacy is respected, but the bar is the social centre.

We enjoy another delicious lunch, gazing out to the distant riverbanks. The buffet has a Burmese food theme and includes an excellent pork stew from the Shan states. The more enthusiastic guests start gravitating towards the upper deck as the British-built **Ava Bridge** appears—the only bridge to span the Ayeyarwady on its 2,170-km (1,350-mile) course. As it looms larger, a group of Japanese photographers get busy, snapping it from all angles.

More pagodas pass by, gleaming white in the strong afternoon sun, and then we are there. Across the river, the fabled Sagaing Hill beckons. With more than 600 monasteries and pagodas, it is Myanmar's spiritual capital.

We anchor outside the small **Shwe Kyet Yet** village. Some 20km (12 miles) downstream from Mandalay, it is to be our base for the next two days. Situated right by the river, the small village is worth exploring, and offers a cameo portrait of Burmese life. Early morning sees monks making their daily alms round, wandering through the misty streets in their maroon robes as the faithful kneel to give them rice.

ANCIENT AVA

A visit to the ancient and atmospheric ruined city of **Ava**, twice the royal capital of Myanmar, is scheduled for the afternoon. We arrive at the old city ramparts and take one of the picturesque horse carts that are waiting for us. Its huge wooden wheels bump unforgivingly over the rough roads that pass through flooded paddy fields.

Our maniacal, but good-natured young driver pops little leaf-wrapped packages of betel nut and lime into his mouth every few minutes. Between particularly difficult patches of road, he turns around, smiling with his red betel mouth, and cackles like a hyena. It is a hilarious journey that brings us to an old wooden monastery that mysteriously has managed to survive floods, famine, fire, and earthquakes for over 150 years.

After fighting through the small horde of souvenir sellers uttering the already familiar refrain "very old, madam, my father found it when he was digging the fields," we enter the dark, timber interior to hear the faint sound of a high-pitched chanting.

Around the corner we come across a group of very young monks. Illuminated by the slanting rays of the late afternoon sun, they kneel at low tables, reciting their scriptures. One by one they approach their teacher and after prostrating themselves three times, their heads touching the floor, each recites his verses to his teacher's satisfaction.

Sagaing Hill

Dotted over **Sagaing Hill** is a "little Bagan," where 600 monasteries and gold-topped pagodas gleam in the evening sunlight. Whereas Bagan is an ancient monument, Sagaing is very much alive, and Myanmar's spiritual capital. Its pagodas are living relics, in constant use, and the monasteries house over 3,000 monks. Monks come here from all over Myanmar to make retreats.

The goldleaf makers

In **old Mandalay town**, we make for the street of goldleaf makers. Housed in rustic shacks, with bamboo-tiled roofs, these men are practising a craft that hasn't changed in centuries. We squeeze into one tiny shack—and encounter a medieval, and faintly erotic scene: three men swathed in *lunghis* rolled up like loincloths, their brown skin glistening with sweat, stand beating piles of goldleaf with massive wooden mallets.

The gold is carefully prepared following a time-worn process. Three hundred leaves of pure gold, already beaten to consistency thinner than paper, are placed between sheets of purpose-made bamboo paper and packaged together with a covering of deerskin. Using a primitive (but accurate) coconut husk timer, the men beat each block for three hours, until the gold is as thin as a hair. After the beating, the exquisite gold leaf is sent to another house, where it is cut and packaged for sale. There is no need for weights and measures and intricate scales. It is such an ancient practice that everyone knows the exact price and weight. The price is 100 kyat a piece (less than 30 cents), which seems like a bargain.

A very big bell

Our final outing is to **Mingun Village**, 11km (7 miles) north of Mandalay, where we are to see the world's largest "ringing" bell. Seated on comfortable rattan chairs in a covered, flat-bottomed ferry we steam up the river for about an hour. As we approach, a stream of women, children, and clanking ox carts make their way to the ferry's docking point, ready to offer their services. Sweet young things come bearing fresh flowers. Our group splits up into small parties, disappearing in different directions with guides.

After a ramble around the village— and a stop to try some delicious fried river fish—we make it to the famed bronze bell. At 88 tonnes and 3.7m (12 feet) high, it is indeed very big— 14 times the size of the bell in St. Paul's Cathedral, London, and approximately half the size of the world's largest cast bell (which is cracked).

Commissioned by King Bodawpaya for his grandiose pagoda, the bell was cast in 1790. On completion its creator was executed, preventing him from ever making another. The Mingun (Mantara Gyi) Pagoda, started between 1790 and 1797, was to be the biggest in Myanmar, standing 150m (490 feet) high, but the king died before it was completed and the project was abandoned. Guarding the pagoda from the river entrance are the backs of the world's largest griffins. In the 1838 earthquake their front ends disappeared into the Ayeyarwady. Rising at least 9m (30 feet) from the river bank, their backs present an imposing sight.

GOING IT ALONE

INTERNAL TRAVEL

Getting up to Mandalay is best done by air. There are daily morning and afternoon Air Yangon flights between Yangon and Bagan or Mandalay. Two express trains run daily, in each direction, between Yangon and Mandalay (morning and night). There are also buses and hire cars.

Booking a flight with Air Mandalay or Yangon Airways in Yangon works out much cheaper than booking through a travel agent abroad.

WHEN TO GO

The best time to travel on the river is at the end of the rainy season, between October and January. The landscape is still lush and green from the rains and the river is high. October can still be quite warm but by November it begins to cool off. On the plains, a light jacket or sweater is enough, but in the mountain areas you will need a warm jacket. As the dry season progresses, the landscape browns and the sunsets get redder.

Where to Cruise

The stretch of the Ayeyarwady River from Mandalay to Bagan is the most popular with tourists, but it is not the only one: Myanmar has over 8,000km (5,000 miles) of navigable rivers and the Ayeyarwady alone has 1,500km (940 miles). With all kinds of boats plying their trade along the Ayeyarwady, cruising possibilities are numerous. Boats and ferries run for much of its length from way up north. One of the most scenic stretches is reputedly that

between Mandalay and Bhamo. Other ferries ply downriver to Twante and Pathein, in the delta.

A very interesting option, for those with time and an adventurous spirit, would be to go from Mandalay all the way down to Yangon.

ARRANGING A CRUISE

Arrangements depend on the kind of cruise desired. *The Road to Mandalay* operates only between October and April, after which the river gets too low. Ferries operate all year. Check with the ferry office in Yangon.

MONEY SAVERS

Change your dollars into *kyat* (pronounced "chat") in Yangon's downtown Scott's Market for the best rates.

Make your airline bookings on arrival in Myanmar. The two recommended airlines, Mandalay Airways and Yangon Airways, offer tickets at least $10–20 cheaper than travel agents outside the country. Both airlines use new French, propeller-driven planes. With the current dearth of foreign tourists, there is no difficulty in obtaining a seat on a plane even on the day before departure. The same goes for the new interna-

tional hotels where, with the current room glut, rates are negotiable, even in the best hotels.

TO GO OR NOT TO GO

With so much negative publicity on Myanmar, it is difficult to know whether or not to visit. My advice is go. Try to ensure that your money gets to those who deserve it. Take a private guide rather than a big tour company. In Bagan find a private horse-and-cart driver rather than a tour bus. Be positive. Try to make your visit to this beautiful country count. Every little bit that we pay private shops and individuals will help to make the people's lives a little less hard.

WHAT TO TAKE

- ❑ Light cotton clothes.
- ❑ Mosquito repellent.
- ❑ Sun screen.
- ❑ A good hat.
- ❑ Walking shoes.
- ❑ In winter, a sweater or light jacket for the plains.
- ❑ Smart casual clothes for wearing aboard *The Road to Mandalay.*

HEALTH MATTERS

- ❑ Take a basic medical kit.
- ❑ Check on inoculations a month before you go.
- ❑ Take out full medical insurance.

TRAVELLERS' TIPS

Don't talk politics with local Burmese in public; it can be dangerous for them. If you do want to try and get the low-down, try talking to your guide, but not in the presence of other Burmese. When our guide was asked a sensitive question by one of our group he had to try joking his way out of it and made a point of saying "there are spies everywhere." Best to let sleeping dogs lie unless you are sure no one is around.

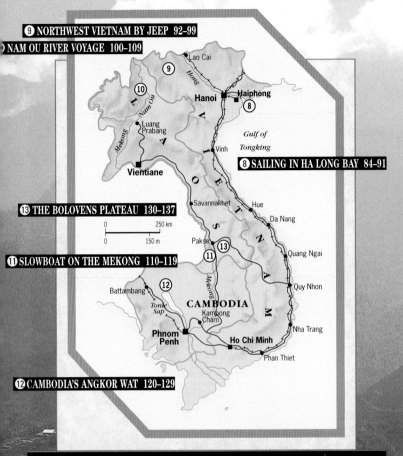

⑨ **NORTHWEST VIETNAM BY JEEP 92–99**

⑩ **NAM OU RIVER VOYAGE 100–109**

⑧ **SAILING IN HA LONG BAY 84–91**

⑬ **THE BOLOVENS PLATEAU 130–137**

⑪ **SLOWBOAT ON THE MEKONG 110–119**

⑫ **CAMBODIA'S ANGKOR WAT 120–129**

Lao Cai

⑨

Hanoi ■ Haiphong

⑧

Gulf of Tongking

Luang Prabang

Vinh

Vientiane

Savannakhet

Hue

Da Nang

0   250 km

0   150 m

Pakse

⑪ ⑬

Quang Ngai

Quy Nhon

Battambang

⑫

CAMBODIA

Kampong Cham

Tonle Sap

Nha Trang

Phnom Penh

Ho Chi Minh

Phan Thiet

VIETNAM•
CAMBODIA•LAOS

Laos is one of the undiscovered gems of Southeast Asia—wilder than Vietnam, less developed than Thailand, with a serenity bred out of its deepset Buddhist religion. The joy of travel in this lovely, landlocked country is the thrill of visiting one of Asia's least known destinations. Neighbouring Cambodia is home to Angkor, that world-renowned, captivating city of ruined temples, and, for those in search of history and adventure, one of life's unrivalled travel experiences. Bordering both Cambodia and Laos, Vietnam is, in so many ways, a land of contrasts, one that lives up to its classic images of misty paddy fields and dramatic limestone towers, boat people, coolie hats, and water buffalo.

A sweeping view of Sa Pa in the Tonkinese Alps, Vietnam

VIETNAM

Smooth Sailing in Ha Long Bay

by Jill Gocher

The calm emerald waters and other-wordly scenery of Ha Long Bay make it perfect for sea canoeing. I combined my exploration of the 1,000 or so islands, deserted beaches, and bizarre sea caves and grottoes with a relaxing soujourn on a beach and a hike through the Cat Ba National Park on Cat Ba island.

I'd often wondered about sea canoeing and now, in one of the world's most perfect locations, it was time to give it a try. After days of fruitless hunting around Hanoi for the right trip, I noticed a promising-looking advertisement in a tourist magazine. A new company was offering pioneer weekend canoeing trips to Ha Long Bay prior to launching a bigger programme. Mr Kien, manager of Buffalo Tours, was full of enthusiasm for his new venture, which would offer canoeing enthusiasts new canoes and U.S.A.-made equipment.

A typhoon off the coast of the Philippines meant my two would-be companions had to cancel their trip, so I was the sole guest for the weekend. I decided to go along anyway, but, pleasant as it was travelling solo, I would recommend a larger group for this kind of adventure—two or three people would fine.

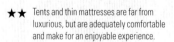

 This route requires good health and a moderate level of fitness—enough to enjoy sleeping in a tent on a fairly hard surface and paddling leisurely for five hours a day or more, depending on the route taken.

★★ Tents and thin mattresses are far from luxurious, but are adequately comfortable and make for an enjoyable experience.

 Bring waterproof, high-factor sun cream, sunglasses, a hat, shorts, long-sleeved T- shirt, a swimming costume, and mosquito repellent. A sleeping sheet will also be useful.

TO THE SEA

The journey to Ha Long Bay makes a less than auspicious beginning to this adventure. Kien picks me up at 7:30am and then it is a 160-km (100-mile), four- to five-hour ride over bumpy roads to Baie Chai, the harbour for Ha Long Bay trips. We drive for about three hours, passing ricefields and small villages, and finally arrive at **Dong Trieu**, a ceramic-making village. We head to the "Hong Noo Fast Foods" shop for a break and a very welcome cup of coffee.

After Dong Trieu, the road deteriorates dramatically. In Vietnam, roadworks are sporadic, so a new, smooth section is followed by a bumpy and dusty patch where our speed drops to around 10kph (6mph). It is with a great sense of relief that eventually, an hour and a half later, we arrive.

In the new harbour, a kilometre before Baie Chai, Ha Long's main town, dozens of converted fishing boats jostle together, awaiting passengers. They are all fitted out for the comfort of tourists with tables and long bench seats, in an open saloon. With names like *Ha Long Princess* or variations on that theme, these boats are the mainstay of Ha Long Bay tourism, for every visitor to Baie Chai will take at least one cruise across the bay—and Ha Long Bay is one of Vietnam's top tourist destinations.

There is scarcely time to meet my guide, Nam, and buy a bottle of water, before I am whisked into the waiting

HA LONG BATTLES

This peaceful bay was twice the scene of battles against the Chinese, who with a mind to possession invaded the Bay in AD 938 and again in 1288. The Vietnamese, innovative in their use of natural defences, managed to outwit their more powerful enemy. After embedding bamboo stakes, sharpened and tipped with iron, in the sands across a nearby river mouth, General Ngo Quyen used men in small, shallow-draft boats to lure the Chinese closer. As the Chinese reached the trap, the tide fell and their boats were impaled on the bamboo stakes. The Chinese leader, Admiral Hung-ts'ao Too, was drowned, along with more than half the crew. Three hundred years later, the same thing happened again in an almost identical manner. This time, it was Vietnamese General Tran Hung Dao who set the trap and again the result was so decisive that the Chinese thought no more of invading Vietnam by sea—in the Ha Long Bay area at least.

boat, and we set off to the sea and the beckoning islands.

Without warning, lunch appears, prepared in the makeshift galley by the fishermen crew. The Vietnamese, being used to difficult conditions, can whip up a feast with the barest minimum of utensils. Give them a wok and a charcoal cooker, fresh vegetables, and the ubiquitous fermented fish sauce "*Nuoc Mam*," and they are in command of a dozen delicious dishes. Our lunch is an assortment of fried fish, crabs, prawns, meat, and vegetables cooked in that curious eastern "Western style" found in so many travellers' cafés. But it is plentiful and tastes good enough.

INTO THE MAZE OF KARSTS

We eat while we are motoring across the bay towards the distant limestone towers. An assortment of craft pass by— fishing boats, sampans, the odd tourist boat, a barge loaded to the gunwales with coal from the nearby mining town of Hon Gai. The picturesque junks so often seen in photographs have largely disappeared from Ha Long Bay, and the only one I saw was a tourist boat. We near the first limestone formations, cut from the mainland, according to legend, by the tail of a huge dragon as it thrashed its way into the sea. In the late afternoon, as the sun sinks low, the bay takes on a new magic. Shafts of light slant between the limestone karsts that loom ahead, and the sea sparkles with a million dancing lights.

Tonight we are camping on **Ba Cat Island**, a deserted island in the middle of Ha Long Bay. It is not to be confused with the better-known Cat Ba island, which is home to the Cat Ba National Park and, with it, a fast developing tourist industry.

We enter the maze created by the karsts, strange remnants of an ancient seabed pushed out of the water in some ancient geological upheaval. The water is a deep emerald green, a likely looking home for dragons—or for the Tarasque, a 30-m (98-foot) black, snake-like creature that's said to inhabit the bay.

As we near our destination, the boat slows down. The crew are obviously searching for something. Then, a smaller, far less luxurious fishing boat than ours appears from behind a limestone tower. This, apparently, is to be

FISHERMEN'S CORACLES

A Vietnam speciality, the fishermen's lacquered and woven wood coracles are an old tradition. Round-bottomed with a circular or lozenge shaped, and no rudder, they are rather like a big tub, but the fishermen manage them effortlessly as they glide along using a long paddle—a technique not mastered overnight.

the backup boat that will transport us to Ba Cat Island and then carry our gear to Cat Ba Island the next day while we paddle the canoes.

The rather surly crew turn out to be part of an army patrol unit rather than bona fide fishermen. Apparently, Ha Long Bay has long been the lair of smugglers and other undesirables who use the caves for hiding all kinds of

weaponry, booty, and ammunition, and the tour company (or the government) considers it good policy to safeguard any foreign visitors. I feel suitably reassured.

After transshipping in midstream, we head through more limestone karsts. Rising straight from the sea, they tower above us. Finally, under a pinkening sky, we anchor close to the island and then, balancing camera gear, tents, bags, and

LEFT Fishing boats present a busy scene near Cat Ba Island, while tourist boats (ABOVE and INSET) take a more leisurely cruise

bodies in the low canoes, we paddle ashore. It's a fairly tricky manoeuvre, but it's managed without mishap.

SETTING UP CAMP

The tiny island of Ba Cat is mostly towering rock and scrubby vegetation, with a beach just big enough to house a dozen tents if necessary. With only two tents tonight, there is plenty of space. As I photograph the setting sun, Nam and his assistant, Nguyen, put the tents up—roomy, two-person models, with fly covers and plenty of zips and screens to deter unwanted night visitors. I don't know exactly what sort of wildlife one might encounter on Ba Cat Island, but I'd rather it was outside than in. Later we return to the boat for a dinner of rice and fried pork with vegetables and fresh flower crabs bought from some local fishermen with cigarettes and a few dong.

Silence and an almost perfect peace descends with the night. We paddle the short distance to the island and say our good nights. The mattresses that night are thin, but they provide adequate cushioning against the coral stones and insulation from the cold sand. The island's three inhabitants soon settle into a peaceful sleep.

Sound carries easily across the still waters of Ha Long Bay. A few fishermen trawling for squid call out, sounding as if they are just metres away. Their calls enter my dream and a group of tribal elders sit around a campfire at my tent door. They disappear when I open my eyes to investigate the sounds of other fishermen.

Around seven I awake, as the first rays of sun hit the beach, to a celestial vision of calm green waters, gleaming in the morning light. Slanting rays break through gaps in the rocky towers. Near by, a fishing boat is preparing to move, and reluctantly we too get ready to set off. While the boys pack up, I photo-graph this scene of serene beauty, trying to capture the moment on film.

A DAY'S CANOEING

After a breakfast of fried noodles and coffee, we make our plan for the day. We will canoe for about five hours from Ba Cat to Cat Ba Island. Our plywood kayaks are Vietnamese-made. Like a whale or any sea creature, they are heavy and cumbersome out of the water but surprisingly light and seaworthy once immersed. Their long waterline makes them glide through the water, with minimal effort. Even a novice could master the basics in a matter of minutes. I take the smaller, one-man canoe while Nam and Nguyen take the bigger, two-seater craft, where paddling is shared.

We slide into the canoes from the boat and set off, gliding through the calm waters in the cool of the morning. As the sun gains height, so does the temperature and by 10am, it is quite sweaty work, relieved with frequent sluicings of sea water and the occasional swim. We go close to rocky overhangs, past sea caves and more huge limestone towers rising straight from the water.

Life looks different from a water-level vantage point. Everything is more immediate, and you feel more in touch with your surroundings. As you pass small fishing boats, you can enjoy exchanges with Vietnamese fisherfolk, who, friendly at the best of times,

TRAVELLERS' TIPS

- ❏ Don't pitch your tent too close to the sea. High tides at night can have you waking to wet feet.
- ❏ Take water with you when canoeing or buy some before boarding the boat to Ha Long Bay. Deserted islands don't sell it and it's a necessity when paddling in the hot sun.
- ❏ Bring a sleeping sheet, preferably a silk one (for comfort and portability). You can buy them in Hang Gai Street in Hanoi for a few dollars.

respond with enthusiasm. With wife, baby, a child or two, and sometimes a grandmother, they all squeeze into a space the size of a small bathroom.

As we enter **Cat Ba Bay**, there is a very light swell, enough to provide the smallest of thrills. Once we are past the entrance point, the waters are flat and still once again. The shadow cast by a large limestone tower provides a few moments of welcome relief from the sun's burning rays. We don't dip our hands or faces in the water any more once we're in the bay. Hundreds of boats are moored there and while they look colourful and mildly exotic, the water quickly becomes a sewer—a repository for food scraps, refuse, plastic bags, and other unmentionables. Even the drips off the paddle become suspect.

Our arrival in Cat Ba Bay by canoe provides the fishermen with some lively entertainment. Frequently they call out, motioning to come alongside and pay a visit. I go over to a couple of the boats and exchange a few basic pleasantries and lots of smiles. Then it's time to move on—unless I am going to climb aboard and share a cup of Vietnamese tea.

Remote Cat Ba Island is surprisingly urbanized. Some new mini hotels with good views over the bay are crammed together in a strip, offering bed and board for a few dollars. Karaoke bars lurk around corners and even on boats in the bay, but it makes a pleasant base for a day or two.

CAT BA NATIONAL PARK

Later in the day I visited the **Cat Ba National Park**. It's a 16-km (10-mile) or half-an-hour motorbike ride through the centre of the island. Hiring a bike in Cat Ba is extremely easy, whether it's from one of the drivers who cruise the street looking for business, or from one of the open-fronted cafés, where signboards list their services.

Buses run (infrequently) to the park, and groups are taken by bus, but the best way to see the country is on a motorbike, whether riding pillion or driving yourself. After climbing out of hot little Cat Ba town, the road opens out to give spectacular views across the town and Ha Long Bay. Then vegetation takes over as the road passes through picturesque valleys of brilliant green *padi*. Tiny villages and small Chinese farmhouses dot the landscape.

Beyond the park entrance at Trang Trung, the road leads to more limestone

HA LONG BAY'S LEGENDARY CAVES

The picturesque and often misty Ha Long Bay has inspired generations of Vietnamese poets. Even the name "Ha Long," which means "where the dragon descends into the sea," is poetic.

The limestone caves too, have fired visitor's imaginations, resulting in romantic names and fanciful folk tales. The Vietnamese love the idea of dying for love or suffering for honour and many stories repeat variations of this theme. The Maiden Grotto or Virgin's Cave owes its name to the story of a rich old man who rented his boat to a poor couple. The couple had a beautiful daughter named Nang He and when they were unable to pay their debt, the boat owner forced them to give up their daughter to marry him. As she refused to share his bed, he had his servants beat her; when she still refused to acquiesce, he had her imprisoned in a grotto where she eventually starved to death. Later, fishermen found her body and buried her there. Strangely, a rock emerged, resembling the shape of the beautiful Nang He.

The Dau Go Cave or Grotte des Merveilles (Cave of Wonders) is Ha Long's most famous. Named by some intrepid French tourists who visited in the late 19th century, the cave is filled with stalactites and stalagmites resembling animal, bird and human forms.

VIETNAM

karsts and another stretch of Cat Ba's convoluted coastline, 17km (11 miles) away. With a few days on the island, you could explore numerous walks and inviting paths outside the town.

The typically Vietnamese entrance to the park, built of concrete blocks, is not particularly inviting. But beyond this and the small zoo housing monkeys and deer, development peters out and concrete walkways give way to more inviting dirt paths and the start of the lowland forest. This is not the primeval, equatorial rain forest of the lower latitudes. Here is a lighter, sparser jungle, home to a variety of wildlife. Most visible are the colourful butterflies that flutter about the water holes. The 21 species of birds include

hawks and hornbills, and a transient population of migrating birds that stop over in the mangrove forests and beaches. Rabbits, gibbon, squirrels, fruit bats, loris, and macaques all live in the jungle.

The return drive, just before sunset, is simply beautiful. The temperature has dropped and is delightfully cool, and an evening mist is settling in. Smoke from the woodfires wreaths the valleys and ricefields as the sky turns from pink to a darker hue of purple.

The next morning, regretfully, we leave on the 6:00am ferry for **Hai Phong**, catching a magnificent sunrise on the way. The early start allows enough time for a brief exploration of the old port city. With its shaded streets of old colonial buildings, Hai Phong is an interesting place, worth a few hours. Tour groups are rushed round to see a pagoda and a tapestry factory, but the town's relaxed atmosphere invites a slower pace and I just wander around the old streets and take an early lunch before catching the 2:00pm train to Hanoi. The train's seats are wooden and hard, but the swaying motion is hypnotic, and a welcome change from the bumpy car ride.

LEFT Local people collect lumps of coral for sale to tourists
BELOW Sunset canoeing through the karsts

GOING IT ALONE

INTERNAL TRAVEL

From Hanoi, trains, buses, and cars all go to Ha Long Bay. The train to Hai Phong takes 2 hours, and from there it is possible to connect with one of the two daily ferries that run to Cat Ba Island. From Cat Ba Island, it is quite easy to arrange 1- or 2-day cruises around Ha Long Bay. It is cheaper from here than from Baie Chai. For convenience and a reasonable price (under $30 for 2 days) many visitors prefer to take a fully organized tour from one of Hanoi's traveller's cafés (see Contacts).

WHEN TO GO

The best time for canoeing is in the hotter months of August and September, but expect some rain. October, or possibly November, is probably the best month, when the weather is almost guaranteed to be sunny and warm, nights are cool, and rain is not expected. The winter months tend to be foggy, and warm and sunny one week, cold and cloudy the next.

SEA-CANOEING TRIPS

Only one company, Buffalo Tours (see Contacts), organizes the sea-canoeing trips. They can be overnight, a week, or even longer. The company has 40 new U.S.-made sea kayaks. Three to seven people make a manageable number, although the company can handle larger groups.

OTHER ADVENTURES IN HA LONG BAY

The waterfront cafés facing the bay in Cat Ba offer a limited range of activities, including guided hikes through Cat Ba National Park and motorbike trips across the island. Bikes, mostly sturdy old Russian geared ones, rather than the easy to drive, automatic Honda Dreams, can be hired with or without a driver for around $5 a day (less if you bargain).

With a few hours and a simple map, it's easy to cross the island, exploring the park and small villages beyond the park entrance.

The best park excursion is a 4- to 5-hour walk covering about 7km (4 miles) of steep trails across seven peaks to a secluded beach. Have lunch here before taking the waiting boat back to Cat Ba town. Leave as early as possible, before the heat of the day sets in.

As you walk along the waterfront, fishermen will call out, eager to take you out in their sampan for an hour, a day, or even a week for a tour of the harbour or a longer exploration of Ha Long Bay. It is cheaper here than at Baie Chai.

If you want to relax, beach sitting, is popular at one of the two beaches about 1km (½ mile) from Cat Ba town—an easy walk through a small pass to the east of town.

HEALTH MATTERS

❑ Food is generally safe. Freshly prepared and fried foods are better than food that has been lying around. If you have doubts about a place, don't eat there.
❑ Bottled water is recommended and is readily available all over Vietnam. Prices vary enormously.
❑ Ice is reputed to be made from treated water, but those with tender digestive systems should probably avoid it.
❑ Bring mosquito repellent. Although there are few mosquitoes around, it pays to be careful. Dengue fever and malaria can be very real problems.

MASTERING VIETNAMESE

Most Westerners find it almost impossible even to get a grip on Vietnamese, let alone master it. Just managing some of the numbers, "coffee with milk," "chicken noodle soup," "Hanoi Railway Station" and "thank you" demands masterful effort. The niceties of everyday conversation are way beyond anyone except a full-time scholar. Part of the difficulty lies in the use of tones. One simple word, like "ga," can mean chicken, railway station, and a host of other things, depending on which part of throat the word is uttered from.

Northwest Vietnam by Jeep

by Jill Gocher

This is a spectacular journey around Vietnam's northwest frontier—over 1,000km (600 miles) on the country's toughest roads, through rugged mountains, high, misty passes, vast ricefields, and untrammelled jungle. The route is enlivened by colourful markets, tribal villages and, in stark contrast, historic prisons and battlefields.

Vietnam's remote, northwestern provinces are still little visited, promising real adventure to those who love to explore. The unsurfaced roads are slow and rough—hot and dusty in the dry months, cold and muddy in the wet. From Hanoi the road heads northwest, touching the Chinese border at Lao Cai before moving further north to the one-time French colonial retreat of Sa Pa and the end of "civilization" as we know it. After that it is unadulterated Vietnam, where raw new towns of Vietnamese settlers contrast strongly with the earthy minority villages tucked away in mountainous areas. Dien Bien Phu's historic battlegrounds, on which the French were decisively thrashed by the Viet Minh in 1954, and Son La's French prison, which once housed Vietnamese freedom fighters, are sombre reminders of recent history.

ON A CLEAR DAY...

I began by taking the overnight train from Hanoi to Lao Cai, which sits on the Chinese border at the top of the Red River Valley. This way, I saved myself 380km (240 miles) of unneccessary road travel. From Lao Cai to **Sa Pa** is a pleasantly panoramic bus ride through the Tonkinese Alps.

When I arrive in the mountain trading town the early morning air is clear and the visibility superb. Mount Fang Xi Pang (or Mount Fansipan), at 3,143m (10,310 feet), looms above the ramshackle buildings of the town—

so close it seems you could almost touch it, although in reality it is a good two or three days' walk away. This is a rare sight in Sa Pa and one to be treasured: my last visit to Sa Pa saw five days with 5-m (15-foot) visibility—and that was on a good day.

Sa Pa is one of Vietnam's tourist spots that has retained its fresh appeal. Scattered across nearby hilltops a few French villas remain from colonial days—most were destroyed in the Chinese invasion of the 1970s. Sa Pa is also a traditional trading centre: the minority people come for a big day out to attend the weekly market, to catch up on local gossip and—the younger ones at least—to search for a suitor.

With their distinctive indigo-dyed, homespun outfits and silver jewellery, the Black Hmong are the most visible of Sa Pa's minority inhabitants. The less outgoing Red Zao women are easily recognizable in their extraordinary embroidered indigo pantaloons, long embroidered jackets and, most

 You need only the ability to endure a little discomfort while travelling in a jeep. Doing the trip in an air-conditioned Land Cruiser would be less physically punishing, but also less rewarding.

★★ Accommodation ranges from basic through comfortable to luxurious (in Sa Pa).

A warm jacket will be needed in the winter months. Take good walking shoes or boots if you are planning to go trekking in the mountains.

MINORITY PEOPLE OF NORTHWEST VIETNAM

Vietnam is inhabited by 57 different ethnic groups—more than most other countries in Southeast Asia. A high proportion of these tribal minority people live in the hills surrounding Sa Pa and to the northwest. Mostly of Sino-Tibetan origin, they migrated from southern China millennia ago, taking to the valleys and high plains of northern Burma (now Myanmar), Thailand, Laos, and Vietnam.

distinctive of all, bright red headgear, wrapped and folded in layers, reminiscent of the Duchess in *Alice in Wonderland*. Until recently, Red Zao girls would congregate at Sa Pa's Saturday night "love market" to be serenaded with traditional chants. However, to escape prying eyes and taunting from the Vietnamese, they have now moved far away from this public venue to a secret location.

Although many of the tribal people are quite shy, tourism draws many of the older Hmong and Zao women into town each day in the hope of selling their merchandise. Authentic silver jewellery is a thing of the past, and all that is available now is derivative. However, there are always some good pieces of weaving and plenty of new "tourist clothes" to be found.

The market area dominates the town centre. A big new concrete market has replaced the earlier, more atmospheric wooden structure. Cavernous and dark, with rudimentary stalls manned by women selling huge bowls of steaming noodle soup (*pho*), fresh-fried doughnuts, and thick milky *café su'ua*, the old market was a popular haunt with both tribal minorities and Western tourists. Perhaps the new market will settle down to a more comfortable dinginess after a few years of use.

BEST-LAID PLANS

My original plan was to stay in Sa Pa for a day or two, making a few minor forays into the surrounding valleys, then taking a jeep westwards to Phong Thô and Lai Chau before heading on to Diên Biên Phu. But Nam, my guide, casually mentions that tomorrow (Thursday) is market day in Phong Tho, so we change the plan and decide to leave after lunch. The best market in the area, almost completely undiscovered by tourists, is not to be missed.

Nam soon returns with an army jeep and a driver. These old Russian jeeps may not be beautiful, but they are sturdy, trustworthy, and strong—as good as any horse.

The road to Phong Thô is long, hot, and bumpy—and the Russian jeep, designed for the severe winters of the Tundra, is not fitted with an abundance of windows. The tiny triangular window in the corner doesn't catch much breeze when you are bumping along at 5kph (3mph). It does however, keep out some of the dust.

Phong Thô is only 80km (50 miles) away, but it takes a long three hours through magnificent scenery to reach it. Illuminated by the late afternoon sun and a creeping evening mist, the mountain peaks are touched with a golden light. The road climbs into the Hoang Lien Ranges, known as the Tonkinese Alps by the French. **Mount Fan Xi Pang** is the highest peak. These old roads follow the contours of the mountains, clinging to the edge, so they are long and winding, with few steep passes. After circumnavigating most of Mount Fan Xi Pang, we come to an open plain where strange limestone hillocks rise from the farmland.

The new town of Phong Thô is a major disappointment. In the middle of a beautiful valley, circled by these strange, almost surreal limestone mountains, it consists of badly constructed, garish concrete blocks. *Pho* (noodle) shops and karaoke bars are signs of the times.

VIETNAM

We eat across the road from the town's concrete hotel, at Mr. Tuan's *pho* shop, dining on delicious springrolls, fried pork wrapped in vegetables, shrimp fritters, barbecued pork, mountains of vegetables, soup, and a bottle or two of *tzao*, the heady local moonshine, to wash down the beer. It wasn't at all bad.

CONCRETE AND LOUDSPEAKERS

Days start early in Vietnam. At 5:00am (or was it 5:30?) the loudspeakers shatter the quiet of the night, broadcasting raucous communist propaganda for the benefit of the minority folk, according to Nam, although most minority folk live far

ABOVE AND LEFT Flimsy-looking suspension bridges are a feature of the spectacular and evocative landscape of the Northern Highlands
RIGHT INSET Our jeep, windows intact

from town. Whatever the cause and whoever it was for, it is loud and unwelcome, and it's not yet even light. Across the road, trucks that had stopped for the night start revving up their engines loudly, while other drivers perform their noisy ablutions.

The market, it turns out, is several kilometres back, right out of Phong Thô town and far from any tourist hotel. So, after a steaming bowl of the mandatory *pho*, it's back to our jeep and on the road again till we reach the village.

The market is easy to spot. People in various styles of exotic dress crowd the main road. At the roadsides, diminutive ponies belonging to Hmong men stand saddled, perhaps waiting to make a quick getaway. In the midst of a walled compound, the main market buzzes with activity as stalls engage in brisk trade.

Nam informs me that Sunday is the big market day, but Thursday is busy

around the head, all very modish. I also notice a few Red Hmong girls. These girls used to add horsehair to their own substantial tresses to create enormous bouffant styles, wrapped around the head and then topped with silver ornaments. Now they use a kind of wool, to similar, attractive effect. It is really bizarre to see these sensationally dressed people acting quite naturally, without a hint of self-conciousness faced with a stream of visitors.

The rest of the morning is taken up with a long and very hot drive to **Lai Chau**, the provincial capital until it was moved to Dien Bien Phu. By the time our jeep arrives, having passed some very attractive villages en route, it is full of sweaty, grumpy folk—but salvation is near. Sitting in Lai Chau's one restaurant/hotel is a large Canadian, Steve, who is working on a mineral exploration project. Steve gives me the best piece of advice of my whole trip: if you want to survive in a Russian jeep, get the driver to remove the window. It is held in by just three bolts, and they can very easily be taken out. In seconds, that much-cursed window is slung into the back and Anh, the driver, follows suit with his window. The afternoon's drive is a breeze.

and colourful enough to satisfy me. Along one wall sit several blue-handed women selling mounds of a sticky paste. It is indigo, a natural dyestuff extracted from the indigo tree and used by many ethnic groups for dyeing their handloom cloth to the requisite blue-black. Blue jeans, too, were probably originally dyed with this natural substance. This particular paste comes from China, transported across local trade routes on horseback, far from the prying eyes of the authorities.

Already, within 80km (50 miles) of Sa Pa, we have left the Red Zao people behind, and we are now into the territory of the Black Zao, whose women wear layers of black garments, put together in a very chic manner. Their long hair is wrapped in thin plaits

To Dien Bien Phu

Climbing into forested hilly country, we enter Red Hmong territory. Simple villages, similar to those of northern

VIETNAM

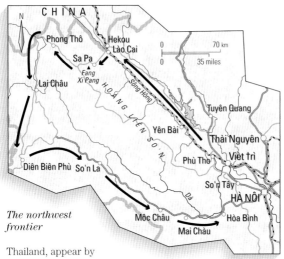

The northwest frontier

of war, the museum proves quite interesting. Inside the spacious hall, an air-conditioner, turned on for our benefit, wheezes ineffectually in the corner. The entrance fee brings us the chance to gaze at wall-sized black-and-white war photographs, glass cases stuffed with war memorabilia, and a video that comes in English, French, or Vietnamese. It shows old war footage and a reasonable description of the battle, facilitated by the large-scale model of the Dien Bien Phu Plain. In spite of my professed lack of interest, the museum is worth a visit.

Not yet finished, we sweat up to the top of Eliane 1, the most intact of several French strongholds. Surrounded by a rusty barbed-wire fence and a gate that opens to the occasional visitor, it contains a memorial erected to Vietnamese heroes of exceptional bravery, plus a rusting tank or two. The tunnels used by the Viet Minh have fallen into disrepair and cannot now be visited.

The view of the town from the hill gives some idea of the layout that Colonel de Castries had planned for his great victory. Most of the battlefields have given way to "urbanization," but enough remain to give us an idea of how the unfortunate battle was conducted.

Later we visit de Castries' Bunker on the "country" side of town. Surrounded by soybean fields, this heavily fortified bunker was once the centre of command. Unlike the Cu Chi Tunnels in south Vietnam, de Castries' Bunker is unfurnished and comes without any kind

Thailand, appear by the side of the road. Built on the crests of small wooded hills, they look dusty and hot and apparently far from a water source. The bamboo houses are thatched and basic, but in the golden afternoon light look beautiful. A few Hmong girls walk down the road, their full, pleated and dyed hemp skirts swinging jauntily as they walk.

We arrive in **Dien Bien Phu** after dark and search for a hotel—difficult as many of the better ones are full. At my insistence, we finally arrive at the Airport Hotel, a perfectly acceptable place with just one modest neon sign proclaiming its name.

Dumped into the middle of a wide plain, Dien Bien Phu is dusty and flat, a wide open cowboy town of karaoke bars and dance halls and new prosperity. It sprawls untidily along one side of the very same airstrip that the French used to land their troops in 1954. On the other side of the airstrip are plain fields. A small road demarks town and country. On one side is the town, on the other, soybean fields.

Nam specialized in war studies during his recent university days and is itching to air his knowledge. So we head off to the museum, a dusty few blocks walk away. Housed in yet another revolutionary style, square cement blockhouse surrounded with the detritus of explanation. There are many other sights, including a French War cemetery and a Vietnam War cemetery with tombs honouring the war heroes.

BLACK T'AI COUNTRY

Just outside town, the road turns west towards the Lao border, an area worth exploring, but we head south, towards Son La and into Black T'ai territory, the most scenic part of the whole trip.

The T'ai like to build their sturdy stilt houses by running water. Their idyllic farmlands occupy fertile valleys. Small villages of bamboo-roofed houses cluster together, looking across acres of emerald *padi* to the wooded hills beyond. It is harvest time, and scenes of peaceful agricultural activity are played out all along the road.

The T'ai women are known for their skills at the handloom, weaving home-grown cotton and silk into decorative pieces like the black headscarves they all wear. Each village has its own patterns. The faint clacking of a backstrap loom confirms that weaving is still part of the village agenda, even if a creeping modernity means women spend less time at the loom than in the past.

TO SO'N LA

Late afternoon brings us to **So'n La**, a mountain town whose major draw is the old French prison. Built early in the 20th century, it housed Vietnamese freedom fighters and later, in an abrupt turn of

events, French political prisoners. Much of the prison was destroyed by American bombs during the Vietnam War, but enough has survived to make it worth a visit. It's a chilling experience to push open the heavy iron doors of the solitary confinement cells in the cellar. These were easily flooded and when inmates became too unruly, a quick turn of the taps would soon silence the unfortunate creatures. No one ever escaped from this prison.

A few kilometres outside the town are hot springs where several bath houses have been set up. For a very small fee you can take a refreshing break from the rigours of the journey.

MARVELLOUS MAI CHAU

There's more magnificent scenery on the road to **Mai Chau**, a small town situated in one of Vietnam's most beautiful valleys. Hemmed in by towering limestone peaks, it's a little Shangri-La. In the valley are White Thai villages, while higher up the mountain are Hmong and Muong communities. The often misty mountain tops and valleys lend a surreal beauty to the scene. Trekking is particularly good in the region.

Tourists can easily stay in a White Thai village here. Every Monday, Wednesday, and Saturday, the villages fill with Western tour groups who have come for a night. Other nights are relatively quiet. The houses are large, clean, and perfectly comfortable.

THE BATTLE OF DIÊN BIÊN PHU

The French commander, Colonel de Castries, believed the broad plain of Diên Biên Phu, hemmed in by mountains, would make an impregnable base from which to attack Ho Chi Minh's Viet Minh. However, he underestimated their tenacity and bravery, inadvertently setting a trap for his own army. On November 20, 1953, while six battalions of French troops parachuted into Diên Biên Phu, General Giap moved into position with 55,000 Viet Minh. Some 200,000 porters wrestled heavy artillery up steep mountainsides to key positions overlooking the valley and the French. By March 1954 the shelling started and the French strongholds fell one by one. The French surrendered, and on 24th July, 1954, Vietnam was divided along the 17th parallel—communist to the north and capitalist to the south. It was not a peace destined to last.

ABOVE Highland panorama
INSET A tank at Dien Bien Phu
BELOW Hmong women in indigo clothes

Sitting on the floor surrounded by mats and cushions and eating off low trays, we enjoy a splendid meal of fried chicken, rice, and vegetables and then troop off to a house where we join a Vietnamese group watching the village speciality—a cultural performance. Fortified by a few glasses of *tzao* rice whisky and some mekong fire water from Thailand, we settle down to watch some T'ai dancers.

The audience is seated on the floor around the walls, watching the girls give a graceful display of traditional dance. When the Vietnamese get ready to display their karaoke style, we decide it's time to head off to another house, where a Belgian group are putting on a show. This was even better, particularly the special dance at end—a celebratory drinking song. After much singing and armwaving, we get to the point: a large ceramic pot in the middle of the floor, fitted with a dozen hollow bamboo straws. This type of ceremonial alcohol pot is popular with several tribal groups across Southeast Asia. Everyone dances around the pot, to the tune of windpipes and accordion, and takes turns in sipping the sweet rice wine and then dancing some more. Once the wine and dancing is finished, we wander happily home through the darkened, sleeping village. In spite of the extra income earned from the tourists, the villagers are mostly farming folk who rise at dawn to tend their fields.

During our absence, mosquito nets and curtains have transformed our house into a dormitory with cosy individual sleeping spaces. Sounds of night preparations soon peter out as the whole room settles into a quiet slumber.

Next morning, after breakfasting on more bowls of steaming *pho*, we wander around the nearby fields, and then it's time to return to Hanoi.

As we bump along in this dusty, overheated sauna on wheels, sometimes I wonder, is this what I really want to be doing? Why is this a trip I have been intrigued with for years? There is no answer. At other times, especially after the windows have been removed, it is just wonderful.

GOING IT ALONE

INTERNAL TRAVEL

Hire a car in Hanoi from one of the tourist cafés or check the noticeboards in the tourist cafés of Hanoi's Old Quarter for others advertising to make up a group.

Alternatively, take a night train (wooden bench sleepers only) from Hanoi to Lao Cai, then a bus to Sa Pa (this cuts 380km/240 miles off the car journey).

WHEN TO GO

The best time to do the trip is in the cooler, often misty months, November–January, when temperatures range between 8°C (46°F) and 20°C (68°F). October is close to perfect, if a little warm, and being right at the end of the rainy season, the countryside is green and lush.

The rainy season is not regular, but there is usually rain between June and September. February and March can also be wet.

ARRANGING A CAR AND GUIDE

Jeeps and guides who know the country are available in Sa Pa (although the English is not perfect). Ask in the Auberge or at any of the small tour companies along the market road. As soon as people know you are looking, they will seek you out.

Talk with your guide before you set off to ensure you both know what you want. If you take a driver who doesn't speak much English, check with the company that he knows what is required of his passengers. If you are interested in visiting minority people or spending time on photography, make sure the guide/driver is willing to stop when you want. A trip can be spoiled if your guide makes you feel rushed.

PLANNING

Remember that all cars come with a driver. There are no self-drive jeeps, but

it is possible to rent a motorbike. An alternative mode of transport to the Russian jeep is an air-conditioned Land Cruiser—this would offer a more comfortable, but less intense experience.

HEALTH MATTERS

Inoculations against hepatitis are recommended, as are malaria pills. Bring a small first-aid kit of plasters, Lomotil, antibiotic cream and pills, and painkillers. If you have a dust allergy bring anti-histamine tablets (or take a Land Cruiser rather than a jeep).

TRAVELLERS' TIPS

❑ If you are not particularly interested in military history, miss Dien Bien Phu and save time for more pleasant places.

❑ If you take a Russian jeep, get the driver to remove the windows by loosening the three big bolts below them.

❑ Allow at least 2 or 3 days in Sa Pa. Even a week is not too long. The altitude makes for cool temperatures—perfect for trekking in the surrounding countryside.

❑ Try to obtain permission before photographing people. A smile, a nod, and indication that you wish to photograph are all that is needed. If someone declines, respect their wishes.

❑ Never hand out Western medicine unless you are qualified to do so.

❑ Take sweets or pens and books for the village children. They are still a rare treat. Some have never tasted a sweet other than sugar cane.

WHAT TO TAKE

❑ Bottled water.

❑ Walking shoes.

❑ Insect repellent.

❑ Sleeping sheet (buy a silk one on Hanoi's Hang Gai Street).

❑ A torch.

❑ Tissues and toilet paper.

❑ Sunscreen and hat.

❑ Basic first-aid kit.

❑ Small denomination notes for purchases.

❑ A roll-up dry bag to keep dust and moisture out of cameras and other electronic items.

❑ A warm and/or waterproof jacket (it can be cold in Sa Pa). In the winter months, it is cold all over the northwest, so bring a hat and sweater.

Nam Ou River Voyage

by Ben Davies

From the remote northern region of Laos, the Nam Ou River flows through a wilderness of jungles and rugged cliffs to the magical city of Luang Prabang. I took one of Laos' great adventures, travelling northwards by river and returning by road.

High up in the northern reaches of Laos, the Nam Ou River narrows, twisting around giant boulders and towering limestone cliffs clothed in dense tropical vegetation. Seated in narrow rows, we clutch on to the side of the boat as it lunges through rapids sending sheets of water over our rucksacks (now tightly sealed in polythene). Only the giant roar of the engine and the whooping noises of my travel companions (an Australian photographer and his charming Thai wife) register in my mind as we continue upriver towards Ban Hat Sa and the border with China.

Travelling up the Nam Ou is a thrilling experience. It's not simply the wild and beautiful landscape through which you pass, or the sudden glimpses of ethnic minority villages you spot through lush jungle foliage. Rather it's the thrill of journeying into the very heart of one of Southeast Asia's least-known countries. Until recently, Western tourists were barred from this mountainous region, flanked by China to the north and west and Vietnam to the east. Even now roads are in appalling condition. But for those with the time and the adventurous spirit, a journey to northern Laos offers a unique opportunity to travel to one of Asia's last great frontiers and, with a little bit of luck, all the way back again.

ANCIENT ROYAL CITY

My journey up the Nam Ou had begun a day earlier in the magical city of **Luang Prabang**, situated on the confluence of the Mekong and the Khan rivers. This ancient royal city (home of the last Lao monarch, King Savang Vatthana) is about as close as you can get to a mountain Shangri-La, with its splendid temples and its sleepy garden walkways bathed in rich perfumes of flame trees and lush forest shrubbery.

"Were it not for the scorching sun, it would be paradise," wrote the great explorer Henri Mouhot on arriving in Luang Prabang shortly before his death in 1861. Even a century later, it's hard to fault that sweeping statement.

To see the place at its most beautiful, get up before dawn and wander out on to the streets to watch the monks as they file down the narrow alleyways past lines of the Buddhist faithful who donate food and occasionally lotus flowers to make merit. After breakfasting on toast and coffee, walk—or

Expect the unexpected with long boat rides, enormously uncomfortable bus rides—and an unrivalled sense of adventure. For greater ease, arrange a guide through Sodetour (see Contacts).

★ If you want comfort, you can take your pick from a variety of excellent hotels in Luang Prabang (this is a city that can easily be viewed as a holiday destination in itself). Along the Nam Ou River, accommodation is extremely basic with dormitory-style beds, shared bathrooms, and almost zero tourist infrastructure.

Take binoculars to view the birdlife in the jungles and along the river. You will need walking boots, sun hat, and sun protection for the boat journey.

better still take a bicycle (almost every hotel or guest house rents them)—to the 16th century **Wat Xieng Thong** (Golden City Temple), set in a tranquil compound off Xiengthong Road. This is the oldest of Luang Prabang's temples, famed for its elaborate carvings and mosaics as well as its graceful, sloping rooftops and elegant *sim* (ordination chapel). Even more exquisite is **Wat Mai**, a short distance to the west, next to the Royal Palace. A former home of the great Buddhist leader Phra Sangkharath, this remarkable building is decorated with bas-reliefs of pure gold, depicting one of the last reincarnations of the Buddha.

Overawed by so much finery, I take the steep path that leads up 329 steps to **Mount Phousi**. Literally translated, the name means "marvellous mountain." From this lofty summit, next to the shimmering golden spire of Wat Chom Si, you will be rewarded with the ultimate spectacle of the town far below, surrounded by forests and hills.

After all the exertions, there's only one way to round off the day. Take a pew at one of the riverside restaurants overlooking the Nam Khan or the

THE MEKONG CONNECTION

From Houei Xai, on the Lao border with Thailand, there are regular slowboats and speedboats along the Mekong to Luang Prabang. The trip takes around 5 hours on the fast boat and 10 hours on the slowboat, although you can make a pleasant overnight stop in the town of Pak Beng, which lies mid-way. Alternatively, Mekong Land organizes luxury 2-day/1-night river cruises, overnighting in a Lao-style lodge on the river bank near Pak Beng (see Contacts).

Mekong, order a *Beer Lhao* (the highly drinkable local brew), a plate of *larb moo* (spicy pork) or *khai pehn* (dried seaweed), and watch the sun set over the mother of all rivers.

CAVES AND WATERFALLS

Most hotels and tour operators in Luang Prabang offer day trips to the finest sites in the vicinity. There's one in particular I could not miss. An hour's drive to the south of town by rented jeep brings us to the **Kwuang Sy Waterfalls**, which rank among the most gorgeous in the whole of Laos (at their best between September and February). The falls are not high, but the spectacle of water cascading down the multi-tiered hillside into an oasis fringed by palms and lush tropical foliage is the perfect complement to Luang Prabang's temples. Even the potholed road journey to the falls is more than made up for by glimpses of hunters, clad in their traditional *phasins* (black embroidered wrap-arounds) carrying beautifully carved but archaic-looking muskets in search of a few winged species for their dinner.

Another pleasant trip can be made to the **Pak Ou Caves**, a 20-minute speedboat ride up the Mekong, home to more than 4,000 Buddha statues made of wood and gold and dating back as much as 300 years.

MOUHOT'S LAST LOVE

It was the great French explorer and naturalist Henri Mouhot who provided some of the finest early descriptions of Laem Prabang in the mid-19th century. Mouhot, who is credited with rediscovering the ancient Khmer ruins of Angkor Wat, arrived in Laos in 1860 after more than four years' travelling through some of the most remote regions of Siam and Indochina. His love affair with Luang Prabang was to prove his last, and in 1861 he died of malaria. He is buried in a simple white grave a short distance from his beloved city on the banks of the Khan River.

Back in Luang Prabang, we set about chartering a fast boat to take us up the Nam Ou, recruiting a driver and a skilled navigator to plot a course around the rocks and rapids now all the more dangerous for the lack of rains (expect to pay around $75 for the five-hour trip to Muang Khua).

The following morning at 6am we catch a motorized tricycle known as a "jumbo" to the river bank at Ban Don, stopping at the market (Talaht Sou) on the way to buy bottled water, baguette bread, and "Vache qui rit" cheese, which is found throughout Asia.

We don our crash helmets and life vests (you should not leave without them) and Souvanna, our boatman, guns the 40h.p. Toyota outboard engine— with a loud blast and a shudder we are off, speeding up the Mekong River before branching to the right up the Nam Ou, beneath a towering overhang of awesome limestone cliffs.

ABOVE AND BELOW Towering limestone cliffs are the backdrop for our river trip
RIGHT Looking down on the little village of Muang Noi from the bridge over the Nam Ou

THE BIRDS AND THE BEES

Laos boasts a dazzling array of flora and fauna with over 400 species of birds, 69 species of bats, six species of flying squirrels as well as tigers, leopards and sun bears. The kingdom's original name, Lane Xang, which was acquired in the 14th century means "Land of Million Elephants." Unless you are extremely fortunate, you are unlikely to see wild elephants. But you should keep your eyes open for beautiful and rare birds such as the sunbird (*Nectarinia arachnothera*). Laos also boasts more than 1,000 species of wild orchids including the spectacular blue *Vanda caerulea*. Other flowering plants include hibiscus, frangipani and acacia.

JOURNEY UP THE NAM OU

As we bounce along the surface of the river vibrating like plates of jelly, two facts become abundantly clear. Laos is a breathtakingly beautiful country. And the Nam Ou is one of the last great opportunities to explore the remote north before the advent of mass tourism.

The views from our speedboat are stupendous: palm-fringed mountains, *heua ha pa* (paddled wooden boats) with the passengers clutching colourful parasols to keep off the sun, and small villages flanked by young teak plantations.

The first major settlement that we come to (after two hours) is the most impressive. Muang Noi lies at the foot of gigantic limestone cliffs that reach up into the clouds. Its main road sports a line of one-storey shacks, along with a couple of newly opened guest houses and pool halls. From the nearby concrete bridge there are magical views over the river to the mountains beyond.

From Muang Noi, we continue north through remote countryside, skirting sudden eddies or clusters of rocks sticking out from the water. It is late afternoon when we reach the town of **Muang Khua** and the light is softening. On the river bank, a crowd of locals are soaping themselves down in the water, their sarongs neatly tied around their bodies to preserve their modesty. My friends join them, diving into the fast-flowing water that cuts through this astoundingly beautiful landscape of rolling hills and rain forest.

In Muang Khua as in many other northern towns, luxurious accommodation does not rank high on the list of priorities. The main hotel (situated 75m/80 yards up on the left) doesn't even bother with a name. Its rooms are spartan and a trifle damp, but full of character. The best way to cope is to do what the locals do: imbibe large amounts of *lao lao* (potent rice whiskey) or *Beer Lao* and go to sleep very early.

Besides its no-name hotel and its delightful suspension bridge that crosses over the Nam Phak River on the far side of town, Muang Khua has another historical claim to fame: the French had a presence here until 1954, when their forces were ousted in the aftermath of the infamous battle at Diên Biên Phu (see pages 96–97).

THE UPPER REACHES

The next day, in the company of a local policeman (whose fare costs him just a third of ours), we take the last and most scenic leg of our river journey into the remote upper reaches of the Nam Ou. According to our new boat driver (a swanky local by the name of Soung), this isolated region is home to elephants, tigers, and rare clouded leopards (*Leo nebulosa*), although we see no evidence of them. The people who live along the banks of this stretch of river are known as the Lao Loum, or lowland Lao. These genuinely friendly people, who migrated from the southern provinces of China in the 6th and 7th centuries, live in remarkable solitude. You may come across one solitary thatched hut perched halfway up a hill, inhabited by a farmer and his wife. In the next valley there is another almost identical hut, and a kilometre further on, a third. Even dropping down for a glass of fermented rice whisky with the neighbours must take an evening of walking.

From Muang Khua it takes two hours in a fast boat to complete the difficult but dramatic stretch of the river to **Ban Hat Sa** (it is often impassable during the dry months from February to July). The Nam Ou continues further north from here towards Ban Suayngam and the Chinese border, but a succession of rapids hinders further progress.

There is, however, alternative transport. Every day a public jeep leaves Ban Hat Sa at around midday—or whenever it is so full that it appears incapable of going anywhere. This ancient vehicle then crawls along some 20km (12 miles) of painfully rutted dirt track at a maximum of 20kph (12mph). Occasionally it stops while the driver or mechanic replaces some vital part of the engine. Finally after two hours, we arrive in the provincial capital of Phongsali.

ETHNIC TRIBES

In **Phongsali** there's a delightful little market in the old part of town, which sells a variety of unidentifiable roots, fruits, and vegetables and is frequented by both the local people and the ethnic minorities. The market, like the town itself, reflects the rich and colourful tapestry of this far-flung province situated high up in the mountains near the Vietnamese and Chinese border. Prior to the Sino–French treaty of 1895, Phongsali was an independent principality attached to southern China. Today it remains the most isolated province in the far north, home to minority tribes, to opium fields (under no circumstances should you approach them), and to increasing numbers of Chinese attracted by trading opportunities over the border.

After checking in at the Phongsali Hotel, a large and ugly establishment that commands pole position in this town of 20,000, we dine on *khao phoun* (noodle soup) and *kayo cuon* (spring rolls) before exploring this peculiarly picturesque town with its old wooden houses and narrow cobbled alleyways.

Beyond Phongsali an unbroken ridge of mountains extends north as far as the Chinese border and south towards the town of Oudomxay, more than 220km (135 miles) away. These highlands are inhabited by as many as 25 ethnic minorities, among them the Phou Noi (recognized by their white leggings), the Akha (or Ekaw) with their black headdresses adorned with silver coins, and the warrior-like Hmong, who were recruited in the mid-1960s and early 1970s by the C.I.A. to fight the Lao communists or Pathet Lao. According to local mythology, these people, characterized by their heavy silver necklaces and enormous turbans, arrived in Laos on a flying carpet. Anthropologists, however, place their original home in southern China, where they were enthusiastic cultivators of opium poppies.

We spend just a day in Phongsali, exploring the town, climbing the nearby Mount Fou Fa ("Mountain in the Sky"), and following paths into the countryside, where the hilltribe people sometimes walk barefoot for days carrying sacks of egg plants, corn, and opium, which they barter for household goods. (For the time being, the Lao government forbids overnight stays in their villages.)

JOURNEY OVERLAND

The following morning dawns cool and overcast. We arrive at the bus stop opposite the Phongsali Hotel at 7am (the official departure time). There is no bus, but there are plenty of passengers clutching sacks of rice, pigs tied up with string like Christmas turkeys, and clumps of bamboo.

Eventually the bus (it is a converted truck) heaves into sight in a thick pall of

LAOS

black exhaust. Everyone piles on to the seats (which are wooden planks) and we are off. Travelling by road may be the most uncomfortable way to cross northern Laos, but it has its rewards—such as the sheer beauty of the countryside and the intriguing vignettes of everyday life that you experience, not to mention the euphoria of real, unorganized adventure. Soon the views grow ever more magnificent, until even the pain of the crowded bus and the smell of leaking exhaust are almost forgotten.

LEFT A public jeep leaves Ban Hat Sa daily for Phongsali—a slow and uncomfortable journey BELOW Loading up at Luang Prabang on the Mekong. Luang Prabang is an enchanting and ancient city known for its temples, including (INSET) Wat Xieng Thong

L A O S

At **Ban Yo** (74km/46 miles), a small village situated at the foot of the hills, a few shell-shocked passengers climb off, to be replaced by more sinewy farmers and tribespeople for whom potholes and ruts are all they have ever known in life.

The fact that there are any roads at all is something of an achievement, given the sheer poverty of the Laotian people. Average annual income is estimated at just $200 per person. What is more, population density in the far northern region is put at just nine people per square kilometre, one of the lowest levels in Southeast Asia.

From Ban Yo, a dirt track threads through the rugged countryside past **Akha villages** that cling precariously to clearings on the mountainside. In places, entire sections of the road have been swept away by landslides. In others, the bus lurches to one side to avoid giant boulders that obstruct our progress.

It takes nine hours to reach **Udom Xai**, a characterless trading town where we spend the night (there are several hotels and guest houses). The next morning, we catch one of the regular buses for the five-hour journey to Luang Prabang and the gently lapping waters of the Mekong and Khan rivers.

TEMPLES AND RELICS

On my last day, I take a 40-minute flight to **Vientiane** (pronounced Wieng Chan), the modern-day capital of Laos. This city, situated on the banks of the Mekong, has suffered numerous invasions. It was razed by the Thais in 1828 (when its king was left suspended in a basket above the river), attacked by the Vietnamese, Burmese, and Khmers and, most recently, occupied by the French. What remains is a delightful if incongruous mixture of rambling old colonial villas, grand tree-lined boulevards, temples, pagodas and, these days, ugly shop-houses and even traffic jams.

The best place to stay is the Auberge du Temple, a charming converted villa on the outskirts of town. After checking

---

PLA BUK

Ranked as one of the largest river fish on the planet, the famous Pla Buk, often known as the *Pangasianodon gigas*, can weigh up to 300kg (660 lbs) apiece. This giant river-bed dwelling fish, which grows larger than a full grown man, was once believed to inhabit underwater caves of gold. Like many of Laos's most populous species it has become severely depleted in recent years as a result of over-fishing, but there are hopes that new breeding programmes could provide a new lease of life for the monster of the Mekong.

---

in, I catch a tricycle to the city's most revered monument. **That Luang** ("great sacred stupa") is reputed to hold a part of the Buddha's breastbone. It was first plundered by the Chinese and Burmese before being reduced to a heap of rubble by the Siamese. It was restored in the 1800s and today its 30-m (100-foot) high spire dominates the skyline: it is shaped like a lotus bud surmounted by a stylized banana flower and a parasol.

Vientiane boasts two other noteworthy religious monuments. To the west, between the morning market and the river, is **Wat Sisakhet**, the city's oldest (and most impressive) temple complex, containing more than 2,000 Buddha statues in magnificent niches. Off Thanon Setthathirat, the **Wat Ongtu** (temple of the heavy Buddha) contains a 16th-century bronze sculpture weighing in at a mighty 3 tonnes.

On my final evening, I take a stroll down Thanon Fa Ngum, the street named after the country's longest ruling king, marvelling at the grand teak and casuarina trees that line this bustling promenade, stopping by the colourful hawker stalls to order *nan wan* (sweet jelly in coconut milk), and watching the sun set over the Mekong. Tomorrow I'm flying back to Bangkok. But for now, I'm still in one of the most remote and captivating countries in Southeast Asia.

GOING IT ALONE

INTERNAL TRAVEL

Luang Prabang can be reached by a 40-minute Lao Aviation domestic flight from the Lao capital Vientiane or by a six-hour speedboat ride from Chiang Kong, on the border with Thailand.

Boats up the Nam Ou River to Ban Hat Sa can be organized on arrival at Luang Prabang. However, if no public boat is leaving, you may be forced to pay for the entire boat (around $100).

Buses are overcrowded and unreliable, but unless you arrange your own transport, they are the only way to get around. They generally leave early in the morning and arrive at their destination some time before dark.

PLANNING

The best time to take a boat up the Nam Ou River is during the cool months between October and the beginning of February when the river is sufficiently high after the monsoon rains.

In the hot season from February to July temperatures often exceed 35°C (95°F) and the river is often impassable.

From June to the end of September it is the rainy season, when tropical downpours alternate with fine days and roads are difficult to pass without a four-wheel-drive vehicle.

FINDING A BOAT

From Luang Prabang, speedboats travel up and down the Nam Ou River to Muang Noi (2 hours), Muang Khua (4 hours), and Ban Hat Sa (6 hours). Slowboats take double the time, but cost less and can be a pleasant alternative. Make sure you agree a price before leaving (foreigners are almost inevitably charged more than locals). And if there are no public boats, be prepared to rent the entire boat (generally around $20 an hour for the fast boat). Be warned that from the beginning of February through to July, the river may be too low to navigate, especially the final section from Muang Khua to Ban Hat Sa.

There are a couple of operators who organize tours or tailormade trips up the Nam Ou River (see Contacts).

ACCOMMODATION

Luang Prabang and Vientiane offer a wide range of accommodation, from beautiful colonial-style hotels to cheap guest houses. In the smaller towns along the Nam Ou River, accommodation is extremely basic and hotel rooms often comprise little more than single beds with a communal shower outside the room.

WHAT TO TAKE

❏ Water and food for the boat journey.
❏ Sun hat and sunscreen.
❏ Plastic bag in which to keep things dry.
❏ Toiletries and tissue paper.
❏ A torch and matches.
❏ Local currency to pay for boats, buses, hotels, and food.
❏ Warm clothes during the cool months.

HEALTH MATTERS

❏ Northern Laos is a malarial zone. For the most suitable anti-malaria tablets, consult your doctor prior to departure.
❏ Bring repellent and mosquito coils, and at night wear long-sleeved shirts and long trousers.
❏ Bring a small first-aid kit that includes antiseptic cream, plasters, and dysentery tablets.
❏ Drink only bottled water.
❏ Wash or peel all fruit and avoid ice.
❏ Inoculations against hepatitis are recommended, but you should seek advice from your doctor.
❏ Take out comprehensive medical insurance.

REGISTRATION WARNING

Wherever you stay in Northern Laos, remember to register your arrival and departure with the immigration officials in the local police station. This may be situated near the river pier or, in the case of passengers arriving by plane in Luang Prabang, at the airport. Failure to obtain an arrival stamp and a departure stamp can result in a fine or major bureaucratic hassles.

Slowboat on the Mekong

by Ben Davies

In the southern reaches of Laos, beyond the towns of Savannakhet and Pakxe, the most beautiful stretch of the Mekong River flows past the pre-Angkor ruins of Champassak to Khong Island and the dramatic Khone rapids. I spent three days cruising this splendid stretch of water aboard the luxurious Vat Phou.

Southeast Asia's greatest river is born high up in the Tibetan Himalayas in one of the most remote corners on Earth. From this inauspicious beginning, the Mekong, known as the Mother of All Rivers, flows through the rugged mountains of south-western China, passing through Burma and Thailand before entering Laos near the town of Houei Xai. For some

1,900km (1,200 miles), it then cuts through this lush and beautiful country, finally crossing over into Cambodia and Vietnam for the last leg of its journey to the South China Sea.

Decades of war and political turmoil have until recently kept adventurers away from the Mekong, destroying the dreams of early explorers to travel the full length of the river. These days, with the opening up of Laos, Cambodia, and Vietnam, it is once again possible to travel by boat along certain stretches of the Mekong.

The most popular section is from Chiang Khong on the Thai–Lao border to the beautiful ancient city of **Luang Prabang** (see pages 100–101), a journey of about five hours by speed boat (or two days on a slowboat). But for travellers in search of something a little more luxurious, the southern stretch of the Mekong from Pakxe (Pakse) to the rapids of Don Khong Island, is an even more rewarding alternative.

Navigable all year round, this 140-km (87-mile) stretch of water offers dramatically varied countryside as well as the chance of a visit to the ancient Hindu and Khmer temple of Wat Phu (or Phou). Most of all, it offers the opportunity of a magnificent cruise on one of the world's finest rivers.

The best time to take a voyage on the Mekong is during the winter months, from October to the end of February, when the weather is temperate and the river is at its most beautiful. This is a time when the waters are still high from the monsoonal rains. It is also a time

 As with any tropical country, you will need a basic level of fitness for walking in the heat. From March to May temperatures can often exceed 35°C (95°F).

 If you want to travel in comfort along this stretch of the Mekong, the best option is to take a 3-day cruise aboard the *Vat Phou*. The 34-m (110-foot) vessel has 12 rosewood cabins (with twin beds), a dining room, and a magnificent viewing deck. You should make advanced reservations through Mekong Land (see Contacts).

 Take a comfortable pair of walking boots for exploring the Khmer temples and rapids. In the monsoon season, make sure you have waterproofs and mosquito repellent.

when some of Laos' most famous religious festivals are held, including Bun Pha Wet, which celebrates King

BELOW The Vat Thou, *with its elegant sun deck (INSET), offers an opulent view of the southern reaches of the Mekong. It's a journey best made between October and February, when this stretch of the river looks its most spectacular*

Vessanthara's reincarnation as a Buddha, and Magha Puja, which marks the end of the Buddha's time in the monastery.

"Mother of All Rivers"

It is mid-morning when the luxurious *Vat Phou* leaves its moorings in the old French town of Pakxe, manoeuvring out into the middle of the Nam Se River before steaming into the Mekong proper. From on deck, our motley group of passengers—an eccentric Italian journalist and his wife, two French dentists and their families, a Spanish teacher, and I—can just make out the mountains of Champassak province to the south and, further off, the hazy outline of Thailand tapering off into the distance.

Sipping our *Vat Phou* fruit cocktails, we sail downstream, passing clusters of wooden houses and glittering Buddhist temples that seem to sprout out of the lush undergrowth. With each curve of the river, the scenery becomes wilder and more rugged, the limestone cliffs towering on either side of the Mekong until soon Pakxe is little more than a dot in the distance.

To be honest, I had never intended to explore southern Laos by luxury boat and certainly not to join an organized adventure tour group. Like many travellers, I have always associated river adventure with dug-out canoes, manifestly unsafe vintage cruisers, and mosquito-infested river banks. And yet I found I rather liked the experience. Travelling on an organized cruise saves time and hassles. And because there's a guide (speaking English and French),

you learn more than you would otherwise about the people and the environment in which they live. More than anything, a luxury cruise enables you to enjoy the Mekong in comfort, without worrying about where you are going next and what you will do.

Life on board the *Vat Phou* soon settles into a steady rhythm. After breakfasting on French bread, scrambled eggs, and mouthwatering tropical fruits (including exotic rambutans and bright orange-coloured papaya), we move to the sun deck, lazing on beautiful bamboo settees and rattan mats, watching the magnificent river scenery as it passes slowly by. Lunch is served at 12:30 by crew members dressed in finely woven Lao sarongs. That still leaves plenty of time for trips ashore, for afternoon naps, or the opportunity to admire some of the most spectacular landscape in the whole of Laos.

Temples and monsoons

The rain is already falling as we draw alongside land, a short distance from the ancient town of **Champassak**. Formerly one of the centres of power for the 6th-century Chenla empire, this quiet little town is now better known as the jump-off point for the Khmer temple of **Wat Phu**, a 15-minute bus ride to the southwest.

Although Wat Phu cannot compare with its better-known peer Angkor Wat in Cambodia, its imposing setting at the foot of the Phou Pasak Mountain lends a special power to the crumbled walls and piles of weathered masonry. It was

SOURCE OF THE MEKONG

The first recorded attempt to find the source of the Mekong took place in June 1866, when two gunboats under the command of Doudart de Lagree set sail from Saigon with the aim of navigating the full length of the river. The voyage, however, was to end in tragedy when they were forced to abandon ship. Later expeditions also foundered on the Keng Luang Rapids and further downstream near Khemmarat. Indeed, it was only in April 1995 that a Franco-British expedition announced that they had discovered the source of the Mekong, 5,000m (16,500 feet) up at the head of the Rup-Sa Pass in Tibet.

A TASTE OF LAOS

If you have never eaten Lao food before, try these local specialities:

❑ *Laap*, made of finely chopped and seasoned meat with onions, lemon, and chillies.

❑ *Khao niao*, a type of sticky rice that accompanies almost every meal and is typically served out of small rattan baskets.

❑ *Neung paa*, a steamed fish.

❑ *Tam maak hung*, a spicy salad sometimes known as sotam and made from shredded green papaya and chilli.

❑ *Khao phun* or flour noodles

❑ *Tom khaa kai*, a spicy soup made with chicken and coconut milk.

❑ For the local brew, try *Beer Lao* or *lao lao*, a potent form of rice whiskey.

discovered by the French explorer Francis Garnier in 1866, but its previous history remains shrouded in mystery. Archaeologists believe that the original Hindu complex was built as early as the 6th century, at least 200 years before work commenced on Angkor. In the 11th century the temple was turned into a Buddhist shrine by the Khmers, with construction beginning during the reign of King Jayavarman VI (1080–1107).

Approaching the grand processional causeway from the east, we follow our guide past a pair of ruined sandstone pavilions containing carvings of Shiva, the Hindu deity with powers of reproduction. But it is higher up, beyond a pavilion dedicated to Nandi the Bull (another common Hindu feature), that we come to the main temple sanctuary, situated near a shallow cave through which flows a sacred stream. Here we see the most delightful carvings, ranging from dancing heavenly nymphs (*apsaras*) to Indra riding on a three-headed elephant.

Visitors fired up by visions of Indiana Jones's "Lost Ark" will enjoy Wat Phu's own little secret. Legend has it that a priceless Emerald Buddha is hidden somewhere inside the complex, although so far nothing has been discovered.

By the time we descend from the uppermost level, the temple is wholly obscured by the monsoonal downpour. Back on board, we pass through the rugged foothills of the Annamite Mountain Range, on either side of the river. In the late afternoon, the *Vat Phou* moors alongside the village of **Ban Boun** and we are taken for a guided tour of this simple community set amidst lush ricefields on the banks of the Mekong.

FOUR THOUSAND ISLANDS

At first light, the engines of the *Vat Phou* splutter into life. Continuing our leisurely voyage downriver, we enter a stretch of water so vast that it almost resembles an ocean. Only the distant villages and the lines of waving children on the far bank tell us that we are inching forwards towards the Cambodian border and the Khone falls.

Soon, the Mekong takes on a different guise, dividing into a maze of channels that cut through this magnificent countryside like the tentacles of an octopus. The Lao call this part of the river See Pan Done (Four Thousand Islands) after the countless islands that emerge from this giant waterway. It is said that during the rainy season the Mekong reaches a breadth of 14km (9 miles), creating treacherous whirlpools and sudden eddies that make further progress increasingly hazardous.

After mooring alongside the northern tip of **Don Khong**, which is the largest of the islands in the Mekong, we are driven to **Wat Chom Thong**, a Khmer-influenced temple built some time in the early 19th century and now inhabited by Buddhist monks clothed in beautiful saffron robes. This crumbling

wat, surrounded by coconut palms
and sturdy-looking mango trees, is
renowned for its finely carved wooden
window shutters.

Temples are not the only thing for
which this picturesque island of 55,000
inhabitants is renowned. In December
the fun-loving people hold a five-day
boat-racing festival on the Mekong (Bun
Suang Heua), nurturing their energies
with ferocious amounts of rice wine. To
experience this singular event, or simply
to tour the sacred caves and temples on
the island, it's best to hire a bicycle from
the Auberge Sala Done Khong, an old
teak hotel in Muang Khong.

From Wat Chom Thong, we cross
over to the mainland on a rustic catamaran made from antique oil drums lashed
together with wooden planks. It's a
scenic 30-km (19-mile) drive further,
through glistening ricefields to the
widest rapids in the whole of Southeast

*ABOVE One of the many falls that make up
the raging Khong Phapheng rapids. It is
near here that you may see the freshwater
Mekong dolphins*
*RIGHT A more peaceful riverbank scene,
at Pakxe*

WATERFALLS AND PLATEAUX

If floating down the Mekong gives you an appetite for exploring the surrounding region, try combining the river cruise with a visit to the beautiful Bolovens Plateau and the waterfall at Tadlo, a two-hour drive to the northeast of Pakxe (see pages 130–7). The really adventurous can travel by bus (or take a tour) to one of the country's last frontiers beyond Attapeu, near the mountainous border with Vietnam.

Asia. In the distance the Khong Hai Mountains delineate the border between Cambodia and Laos.

VOICE OF THE MEKONG

We hear the mighty **Khong Phapheng Falls** long before we reach the river bank, their tumultuous roar growing ever louder at our approach. Measuring 10km (6 miles) in width and made up of literally hundreds of raging cascades and precipitous channels, they have not surprisingly been named "the voice of the Mekong" by the local people.

In the shadow of these gargantuan falls we take an incongruous lunch of fresh fish, sun-dried beef, and salad, served on china dishes carried from the boat by crew members. Afterwards, we wander down the path that leads to the edge of the water.

It was Garnier (see page 113) who first reported the existence of the rapids in 1866, when they forced him, en route to China, to abandon his vessel and continue his travels over land. Later

explorers also had their dreams of navigating the full length of the Mekong shattered by these raging torrents.

In the late 19th century, the French built a 5-km (3-mile) stretch of narrow-gauge railway to transport cargo around the Khong Phapheng and Li Phi falls (the old locomotive can still be seen near the railway bridge at Ban Khone). Such was the zeal of the French, that they even dismantled their boats piece by piece and then reassembled them on the far side of the rapids.

Locals will tell you that beyond the falls you may occasionally catch sight of freshwater dolphins. The dolphins, with their bluish-grey colouring, are best seen during the winter months, between December and May, when they gather in the late afternoons. But these days, their very existence has been threatened by dynamite fishing, a popular pastime over the border in Cambodia.

VOYAGE UPRIVER

In the early afternoon, we set off once again, this time upriver, passing villages half-concealed behind thick clumps of bamboo and papaya trees. Occasionally small fishing boats dart out from the shoreline. Besides that, there is little sign of life. One of the most striking things about the Lao people is their totally lackadaisical outlook on life. While the Chinese are renowned for their business acumen and the Vietnamese for their hard work, the Lao have long been held up as an example of delightful indolence.

This can be blamed partly on the people's insatiable appetite for *lao lao*,

DOLPHINS OF THE MEKONG

They are called *Orcaella brevirostris* or *paa khaa*, have bulging bluish-grey foreheads, and reputedly live in small numbers in the rivers in Laos, Myanmar, and Cambodia. The best time to see the dolphins of the Mekong is in the late afternoon, when you may occasionally glimpse them leaping through the murky waters. And dolphins are not the only Mekong speciality: in the northern stretches of the river, you may also come across the rare *pla buk*, known as the monster of the Mekong (see page 108).

a potent form of local rice whiskey that is found almost everywhere, despite the fact that it is officially discouraged. So keen are the Lao on this fearsome drink, that they even place it in small glasses as offerings for their house spirits.

But there's another reason for the people's *joie de vivre*, for here on the Mekong, hard work is rendered almost wholly unnecessary by the abundant gifts of nature.

We halt in the late afternoon at the village of **Baan Paou**, where the simple self-sufficiency of the people is almost palpable. Like so many other villagers on the Mekong, the inhabitants of Baan Paou are wholly reliant on the river for their food, their water, their irrigation, and even their transport. In the evening, entire families can be seen washing in the river or casting fishing nets on its clouded surface. Further downriver, clothes are soaped and neatly laid out on the banks to dry.

That night, a major storm breaks out directly overhead. Torrential rain streams down the windows of our luxury vessel. Outside, on the river bank, a few naked children play in the rain, their laughter trailing away into the distance, barely heard above the crashes of thunder.

JUNGLE TEMPLE

The following morning the sky is overcast, the sun hidden behind thick monsoon clouds. But the air is cool and pleasant, and a fresh breeze blows along the river. Shortly before 10am, the *Vat Phou* moors alongside **Ban Noi**, another fine little village perched on the fertile banks of the river. From here, we follow our guide along a narrow trail that leads for 1km (½ mile) through tall trees to the ancient ruins of **Oum Muang** (alternatively known as Oup Muang or Muang Tomo) deep within the jungle.

Built some time between the 6th and 9th centuries, around the same period as Wat Phu Champassak on the opposite bank of the river, Oum Muang luxuriates

in its sheer isolation. Here there are no crowds or guides, just a feeling of total abandonment. The remains of two stone sanctuaries are all that now stand. Elsewhere, spread over an area the size of a football field, lie beautiful moss-covered slabs of laterite, faded sandstone carvings, and the remains of a seven-headed naga snake that still guards the temple complex. Probably the temple was abandoned by the warlike Khmers at the end of the 13th century and has since been left to the forces of nature.

From Oum Muang, we walk back through this picturesque village of wooden houses before continuing our journey upriver.

Later on in the afternoon, we go ashore to climb to **Wat Phou Ngoy**, a hillside Buddhist retreat that offers superb panoramic views of the Mekong. Then we are off once again, sipping cocktails and savouring our last night on the Mekong. The next morning, at precisely 7am, the *Vat Phou* steams into **Pakxe**, marking the end of our short stay in paradise.

PASSENGER BOAT TRAVEL ON THE MEKONG

For adventure travellers who do not have the budget to cruise down the river on the *Vat Phou*, all is not lost. You can enjoy a magnificent, if less opulent boat trip aboard one of the motorized passenger vessels that leave from Pakxe.

The boats take two hours to Champassak (it's best to stay overnight there) and a further eight hours to Don Khong. The price is the same whether you travel inside the overcrowded boat or on the flimsy roof (most people prefer the latter as you can enjoy the magnificent views). To avoid getting serious sun stroke, make sure you bring a hat or an umbrella for shade. Baguette bread, bottles of water, and other snacks are worth their weight in gold on this long, crowded, but immensely rewarding journey.

GOING IT ALONE

INTERNAL TRAVEL

You can get to Pakxe either by air (there are twice-daily flights from Vientiane) or by road via the Thai border crossing at Chongmek. If you are travelling from Bangkok, the easiest and most pleasant way to get to Pakxe is to fly to Ubon Ratchathani in northeast Thailand, from where you can hire a taxi at the airport (600 baht/$16) to take you as far as Chongmek. Once you have crossed the border into Laos, a selection of ancient buses and cars ferry passengers to Meun Khao, from where it's a 10-minute hop over the river to Pakxe.

Most tour operators will be able to arrange transport to Ubon as well as onward connections.

WHEN TO GO

The best time to go cruising on the Mekong is in the cool season, between October and the end of February, when the skies are blue and temperatures range from 15°C to 30°C (59–86°F). From March to May, temperatures often exceed 35°C (95°F) and the low level of the water can make river transport difficult.

From June to the end of September is the rainy season, when tropical downpours alternate with fine days.

PLANNING

Prior to your arrival in Laos, you will need a tourist visa. These can be obtained through your tour operator or travel agents in Bangkok (allow 2 days).

ARRANGING A BOAT

The *Vat Phou* operates 3-day/3-night scheduled cruises from Pakxe for around $450 per person stopping at Wat Phou Temple, Oum Muang Sanctuary, Khong Island, and the Phapheng Falls. Prices include spacious twin-bed cabins, food, and tours. Reservations should be made in advance through Mekong Land in Bangkok (see Contacts). They can also arrange transfers to Vientiane, Ubon Ratchathani, or the beautiful former Laos capital, Luang Prabang.

Those who want to go it alone can use one of the regular public boats that leave from the jetty in Pakxe for Champassak, taking 2 hours (foreigners almost inevitably pay more than the locals). There are

also crowded ferries that go the whole way to Don Khong, taking around 10 hours. Travel agencies in Pakxe may be able to arrange boat charters to Don Khong for up to 20 people.

ACCOMMODATION

Accommodation in Pakxe ranges from the upmarket but ugly Champassak Palace Hotel to a range of cheap hotels and guest houses around the market place. Elsewhere in Champassak province and on Khong Island, there's a handful of standard hotels as well as several cheaper guest houses.

HEALTH MATTERS

❒ Southern Laos is a malarial zone. Consult your doctor prior to departure and take precautions.
❒ Bring insect repellent and mosquito coils; at night wear long-sleeved shirts and trousers.
❒ Carry a small first-aid kit that includes antiseptic, plasters, and-dysentery tablets.
❒ Drink boiled or bottled water only.
❒ Wash or peel all fruit and avoid ice.
❒ Make sure you have comprehensive medical insurance.

LEFT Following our guide through the jungle to the ruined temple of Oum Muang
ABOVE The ruins of Wat Phu, a fantastic lost city near Champassak

Cambodia's Angkor Wat

by Ben Davies

The greatest archaeological site in the whole of Southeast Asia lies in the northern reaches of Cambodia, beyond the lapping shores of the Tonle Sab Lake. Angkor Wat is a supremely rewarding destination in itself, best viewed as part of a five-day journey that will take you by boat to the delightful capital of Phnom Penh.

Dawn over Angkor Wat must rank as one of the finest spectacles on Earth. As the first rays of light stream over the horizon, the five majestic towers, soaring to 65m (215 feet) high, are silhouetted against the Cambodian sky.

Greater even than Pagan in Myanmar (Burma) or the Khmer temple of Pimai in neighbouring Thailand, Angkor has no equal in Southeast Asia. Its exquisite artistry and the sheer number of temples (there are more than 400) lend it an overwhelming power and splendour that even decades of war and political turmoil have been unable to dull.

Approaching the temple from the west, we follow our young Khmer guide across a giant stone causeway, before entering the main Angkor complex. Built in the 12th century by King Suryavarman II, Angkor Wat took 30 years to construct, with as many as 100,000 slave workers toiling night and day. Known literally as "the city," it is dedicated to the Hindu deity Vishnu, whose followers regard him as the supreme saviour.

The level of artistry is no less extraordinary inside the galleries that lead off the main complex. Intricately sculpted bas reliefs, extending for 800m (875 yards) range from the delightful *apsaras*, or heavenly dancers, with their finely chiselled bangles and bare breasts (they were supposedly modelled on the king's harem) to the monkey kings from the Hindu epic *Ramayana*.

But the most famous carving of all is the **"Churning of the Oceans of Milk,"** a momentous work of art showing 88 *asuras* (devils) and 92 *devas* (gods) engaged in a tug of war using a giant serpent that is wrapped around the mountainside. The two groups are trying to achieve immortality, watched by heavenly female spirits who sing and dance in encouragement.

By the time we leave Angkor Wat two hours later, the sun is already high in the sky and the first groups of tourists are beginning to arrive; they have missed seeing the dawn break. Well-rewarded for our early start, we retire to the small collection of tea houses situated almost directly opposite the entrance of the temple, and breakfast on baguettes, fried eggs, and coffee, before taking the road north to Angkor Thom.

1 If you arrive in Angkor during the hot season, from March to May, you may have to put up with walking in the searing heat. That aside, you will need only a very general level of fitness.

Accommodation in Siem Reap, the sleepy little town that lies 7km (4 miles) south of Angkor, ranges from luxury five-star hotels to simple guest houses. Good European and Asian food can be found in hotels and restaurants. Alternatively, you can take a pleasant breakfast or lunch in the small tea houses directly opposite the entrance to Angkor Wat.

Bring at least double the amount of camera film that you think you may need. Walking shoes, sun hats and sun cream, are a prerequisite, along with waterproofs if you plan to travel in the monsoon season.

Exploring Angkor

My journey to Angkor had begun a day earlier when I joined a couple of friends in Bangkok for the 1½-hour Bangkok Airways flight to Siem Reap in northern Cambodia. Arriving at the small airport, we caught a taxi for the 7-km (4-mile) ride to the heart of town and booked in at the Apsara Guest House, a pleasant two-storey hotel with an open terrace and plain but simple twin rooms.

Although most visitors to Angkor book a tour well in advance, it's just as easy and considerably cheaper to make arrangements on arrival. The best way to explore the temples is by hiring a motor-bike driver (most double up as guides); this can be organized by your hotel. Cars with drivers are also available. This provides far greater flexibility than any group tour can offer. It also means that you can spend as little or as much time as you want in any particular temple.

For the majority of people, three days in Angkor is generally sufficient to see the sites, including Angkor Wat, Angkor Thom, Ta Phrom, and Bantei Srei (often referred to as the "grand tour"). If you are short of time, it's just about possible to squeeze the major temples into the one-day "petit tour."

To get the best out of Angkor, there are two imperatives. Get up at dawn to explore the temples, then make sure that you return to your hotel in the heat of the midday sun for lunch, a swim, and a nap. In the mid-afternoon, you can continue from where you left off. This will allow you to see the ancient monuments in their best light. It will also ensure that you do not end up speeding from one temple to the next like an Exocet missile, a condition that affects many of Angkor's most enthusiastic proponents.

Walled City

From Angkor Wat, we follow a tree-lined road that runs north for 3km (2 miles) to **Angkor Thom**, a complex that is in some respects just as impressive. At its height of power, this walled city was home to as many as one million people, spread over 9sq km (3 square miles) and equalling in scale and beauty anything standing at the time in Europe.

Entering the ancient city through one of five grand causeways, we pass sculpted balustrades of *nagas*, the legendary aquatic serpents celebrated throughout Southeast Asia, as well as gods, demons, and three-headed stone elephants.

The centrepiece of Angkor Thom, both physically and symbolically, is the **Bayon Temple**. Built at the end of the 12th century by King Jayavarman VII, it features an upper and lower courtyard with more than 1,000m (1,100 yards) of carved reliefs, and one of the Khmers' most extraordinary achievements: elaborate stone towers carved with giant smiling faces that appear to stare down at you from every angle.

According to our guide, these 200 serenely smiling faces may represent the "Bodhisattva," an individual who after many births, deaths, and rebirths reaches a state of enlightenment, but selflessly stays on to help others find salvation. The best time to view the Bayon is in the early morning or late

KHMER ARCHITECTURE

The temples of Angkor are more than simply works of art. They are also symbols of the Khmer cosmos. The central *prasat*, or tower, typically represents Mount Meru, the mythical home of the gods at the centre of the universe. The colonnaded galleries and enclosures signify the mountains, while the moat symbolizes the ocean. Not all the temples have an identical structure. By the 12th century, the architectural style had become increasingly elaborate as the god-kings of Angkor attempted to outdo each other in the size and complexity of their creations.

afternoon, when the light is soft and the place is eerily deserted. By the time we leave the Bayon, the sky is filled with dark clouds and the first raindrops are falling. We take shelter under a colossal gateway, high enough to allow an elephant to pass under it, complete with parasols. Back aboard our motorbikes with our guides, we then drive back to Seam Reap, 7km (4 miles) to the south.

GODS AND KINGS

One of the most remarkable things about Angkor is the sheer number of kings who ruled over it. In total, 23 monarchs held sway over a kingdom that at its peak extended from Burma to southern Laos, and as far afield as northeast Thailand.

The first-known god-king was Jayavarman II (reigned 802–850), who founded the Khmer empire and instituted the tradition of temple building. But it was Jayavarman VII

(reigned 1181–1201) who is remembered as presiding over Angkor's finest period. During his reign, he built not only Angkor Thom and the Bayon, but Preah Khan and Ta Prohm.

Although Jayavarman's successors were to rule for another two centuries, Angkor went into decline. In 1431 it was attacked by the Siamese and finally abandoned by the Khmers.

The history of Angkor is all the more poignant given Cambodia's tumultuous past. How could a nation of such greatness find itself marred by virtual civil war for more than 200 years? Some scholars argue, however, that the same autocratic streak that created Angkor was also responsible for creating the Khmer Rouge, the radical Maoist army that killed more than one million innocents in a bid to return the country

LEFT Mystical moments at Angkor as dawn breaks over Srah Srana and (BELOW) as a storm gathers
FAR LEFT Young boatmen take to the waters of the Tonlé Sap

to the Year Zero.

After lunching in town, we take the 20-minute bike ride east of Angkor Thom to **Ta Prohm**, one of the most enchanting temples in the whole of Angkor. It was the French naturalist Henri Mouhot who first stumbled across this ancient ruin, sticking out of the jungle canopy, in 1860. Ta Prohm has since been left largely to the forces of nature. Trees 30m (100 feet) high grow out of the ancient passageways, their roots sprouting forth like immense tentacles that even the gods of Angkor have been unable to stop.

Overawed by the immensity of the scene, we sit in silence until the shadows lengthen and the dappled light fades. Then we join our guides and drive for 10 minutes back to the East Entrance of Angkor Wat, and from here we watch the sun set over this great palace of the gods.

TEMPLES AND LEPERS

The next morning, we rise early to ensure that we get to the ruins before first light. Clambering after our guides through the darkness, clutching one feeble torch between us, we finally emerge at the top of **Phnom Bakheng** (60m/200 feet high) to witness the sun rise over this simple mountain temple that offers quite unrivalled views of the surrounding countryside.

It's a short distance north from Wat Bakheng to the 11th-century **Baphuon Temple**, built by King Udayadityavarman II and dedicated to Shiva. This pyramidal structure, shaped like Mount Meru, the home of the Khmer gods, is now undergoing renovation, but it has been described as one of the greatest of Angkor's temples.

Another exquisite work of art lies a two-minute walk further to the north. The **Elephant Terrace** and, a short distance beyond it, the **Terrace of the Leper King** contain fine 7-m (23-foot) high carvings of members of royalty, as well as finely sculpted elephants, *garudas* (half man-half bird), and the five-headed horse Balaha, which was an incarnation of the Bodhisattva. The Terrace of the Leper King is believed to have been the work of Jayavarman VII, a monarch who may have suffered from leprosy.

In the early afternoon, we head off once again, this time following a dirt track that winds 5km (3 miles) past the airport to the giant **Western Baray Reservoir**. On this vast and tranquil expanse of water built by Udayadityavarman II, it's possible (but only after the rains) to take boat trips to the Western Mebon in the centre of the lake. The reservoir is also famed for its birdlife, including its egrets, herons, and wild duck—best seen between January and May.

JOURNEY TO BANTEI SREI

On our final day in Angkor we get up early once again, watching the sun rise over the ritual cleansing pond of Srah Srang before continuing north on a 25-km (15-mile) journey to **Bantei Srei**. This spectacular sidetrip is worth taking for the scenery alone: a narrow dirt track threads its way through a succession of villages and paddies, now freshly planted with young rice plants. Many hotels and travel agents organize minibuses here, sometimes with an

---

OVERLAND ROUTE

If you want a real adventure, take the overland route from Poipet on the Cambodian border with Thailand to Sisophon and Siem Reap. It will take at least six hours and is unbelievably uncomfortable (you travel by pick-up), but it offers awesome views of the countryside. Make sure that you have a Cambodian visa before you leave, as you cannot arrange one on arrival at the border. Also check with the Cambodian embassy on the security situation: if there are any doubts about safety, take the plane.

armed escort. But travelling by motorbike is more fun and, so long as your guides check on the security situation before leaving, just as safe.

Bantei Srei was one of the first temples in Angkor to undergo large-scale restoration work, under the direction of the French École Française d'Extrême Orient, in the 1930s. Enormous trees surround the small courtyard, and here our guide points out some of the finest examples of Khmer sculpture: exquisite reliefs of Shiva and his spouse Uma, as well as pink sandstone carvings of gods, guardians, and mythical beasts. Built in the late 10th century by the Brahman tutor of King Rajendravarman, this Hindu temple, with its collection of mini-shrines, marks one of the high points of the early Angkor period.

In the heat of the midday sun, even would-be adventurers need a rest, and so we return to Siem Reap for a lunch of chicken curry, washed down with copious quantities of Angkor Beer, the exceedingly pleasant local brew.

In the afternoon, our guides collect us for the last time to bring us to **Preah Khan**, a 12th-century temple that lies a short distance north of Angkor Thom. Less well known than the famous Ta Prohm, this temple, whose name literally means Fortunate City of Victory, is in some ways just as impressive. Its long vaulted galleries and processional walkways once played host to 97,000 men, including 444 chefs and 2,298 servants who were charged with its upkeep. Nowadays, its darkened corridors have been invaded by tree roots and creeping, luxuriant shrubs, beyond which lie richly

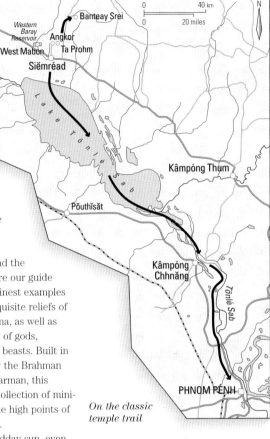

On the classic temple trail

decorated lintels and panels. Many of them are currently being restored under a programme of the World Monuments Fund.

RIVER JOURNEY

After three days on the "grand" Angkor circuit, we are ready to take the next leg of our journey south, across the beautiful **Tonlé Sap Lake** to Phnom Penh.

After purchasing our ticket in the hotel (it costs $25 one-way including transfer), we board a passenger boat in the village of Jong Khneas. We sail past a sparkling patchwork of fishing villages on stilts and several floating markets selling such mouthwatering local delicacies as ducks' eggs (eaten just before they are hatched), dried salted

fish, and bananas of all shapes and sizes.

Twenty minutes later, we are transferred to a sturdy 76-seater Malaysian metal-hulled speed boat for our voyage into the largest freshwater lake in Southeast Asia. The sheer size of the Tonlé Sap is awesome. During the rainy months from mid-May to early October, it swells from 3,000 to 7,500sq km (1,160–2,900 square miles), flooding the surrounding region and driving the villagers to higher land. But during the dry season, the waters of the Tonlé Sap drain back south into the Mekong.

The concentration of fish is no less extraordinary. The Tonlé Sap (literally "great lake") yields as much as 10 tonnes of fish per square kilometre, making this one of the richest inland fisheries on earth. Even the fish exhibit remarkable characteristics.

ABOVE The Silver Pagoda at Phnom Penh
BELOW Saffron-robed buddhist monks at Angkor
RIGHT Nature has taken over at Ta Prohm, where trees grow out of the temples

CAMBODIA

The famous walking catfish, known as the *hok yue* or elephant fish, can spend several hours out of the water, enabling it to flip-flop its way to deeper pools.

From Kompong Chnang, a lively little fishing port situated some two-thirds of the way down to Phnom Penh, we emerge from the great lake into the Tonlé Sap River. Soon river boats are darting across the surface of the water from the small fishing villages along the river's edge, shaded in mangroves and rich tropical foliage.

Down below, in the large air-conditioned cabin, "entertainment" consists of a few violent Khmer videos and a small and singularly tasteless cake handed out to each passenger. Besides that, there's nothing much to do except watch the magnificent scenery or sleep. Finally, after five hours, the boat draws alongside the municipal ferry landing at **Phnom Penh**.

CRUMBLING ARCHITECTURE

Legend has it that the Cambodian capital was founded on the spot where a rich old woman by the name of Penh discovered four images of Buddha. To commemorate this fortuitous event, she built a temple on a nearby hill in 1372. The temple here (Wat Phnom Penh) has since become a revered monument, while the small settlement has been transformed over the years into a bustling riverine capital.

If you have time to visit only one site within the city, make sure it's the **Royal Palace** on Samdech Sotharos Boulevard. This building, which was constructed in 1866, contains one of the richest shrines in the world. The floor of the **Silver Pagoda** is covered with 5,329 silver tiles, each tile weighing 1.1kg (2½ lb).

Most day tours will also include a trip to the splendid **National Museum of Arts** (also called Museé des Beaux Arts) on 13 Street, and the Russian market on 182 Street, with its antique tea chests, raw silks, lacquerware, and fine Khmer scarves.

But behind its lively exterior, Phnom Penh hides a deep melancholy. When the victorious Khmer Rouge swept into the capital on April 17, 1975, the entire population was force-marched out into the countryside as part of Pol Pot's bid to establish a radical Maoist-style agrarian society. Hundreds of thousands of the inhabitants died of starvation or exhaustion. Others were bludgeoned to death in mass extermination camps.

Evidence of those chilling atrocities can be found at the **Tuol Sleng Museum**, known as the Museum of Genocide, on 103 Street (not for the fainthearted), as well as in the infamous **Killing Fields of Choeung Ek**, 9km (5 miles) to the south of town.

On our last afternoon in Phnom Penh, we hire a tricycle to explore the city, travelling along the wide tree-lined boulevards past magnificent colonial villas built by the French almost a century ago. Down on the busy water-front, a collection of bars and fine restaurants overlook the Tonlé Sap River, providing a perfect end to our five-day journey in this beautiful, but tortured country.

FOOD AND DRINK

In Cambodia you can enjoy everything from the most delightful French cuisine to the numerous local specialities, including *trey chorm hoy*, or steamed fish, and *samla machou bangkang*, a spicy prawn soup. For other popular Khmer dishes, order *khao phoun*, a type of rice noodles, or *an sam chruk*, a roll of sticky rice filled with soyabean cake and chopped pork. Always make sure that the food is freshly cooked and that you peel any fruit to avoid stomach problems. Bottled water is widely available, as is the popular, locally produced Angkor Beer.

GOING IT ALONE

INTERNAL TRAVEL

From Bangkok there are daily flights to Siem Reap (1½ hours) on Bangkok Airways. There are also frequent connections with Phnom Penh on Thai Airways International (50 minutes). Air-conditioned speed boats take 5–6 hours from Siem Reap to Phnom Penh, although they may not operate at the height of the dry season. There is also an overland route from Aranyaprathet on the Thai border to Poipet, Sisophon and Siem Reap, but you should check on security conditions prior to your departure.

WHEN TO GO

The best time to visit Cambodia and the temples of Angkor is during the winter months, from the end of October until the end of February, when the skies are blue and temperatures average a pleasant 27°C (81°F).

From March to May temperatures average 32°C (90°F) and can soar as high as 38°C (100°F). Between May and October it is the rainy season, although sudden downpours usually alternate with sunny spells.

At the height of the dry season, from March until May, the Tonlé Sab may be too low to travel by boat.

PLANNING

Before leaving for Cambodia, check with the embassy for safety updates and the latest visa requirements.

TOURING THE RUINS

The best and most flexible way of exploring Angkor is to rent a motorbike with a guide/driver from outside your hotel or guest house. Drivers charge a fixed daily rate and will generally know the whereabouts and history of the surrounding temples.

Alternatively, cars and drivers are available from the major hotels. It's even possible to hire bicycles from guest houses (it is 7km/4 miles from Siem Reap to Angkor).

A wide range of tour operators in Phnom Penh and in Europe/U.S.A. organize trips to Angkor ranging from one day to one week. These trips often combine stop-overs elsewhere in the region, including Saigon and Hanoi in Vietnam, Luang Prabang in Laos, and Bangkok in Thailand.

Entry fees to Angkor range from $20 for a 1-day pass to $60 for a week pass. The fee covers all the sites in the entire Angkor complex except for Bantei Srei.

ACCOMMODATION

If there's one place on Earth where it's worth splashing out on a luxurious hotel, it's Angkor. But good hotels don't come cheap. The magnificent old colonial Grand Hotel d'Angkor, refurbished by the Raffles group, costs upwards of $130 a night. But for those on lower budgets there is a wealth of choices ranging down to a couple of dollars a night.

WHAT TO TAKE

See page 120.

HEALTH MATTERS

❑ Make sure that you consult your doctor at least one month prior to departure for the latest update on recommended inoculations as well as protection against malaria, which is wide-spread outside the major cities of Cambodia.

❑ To reduce your chances of sickness, drink bottled water, peel or wash any fruit, and avoid eating uncooked vegetables.

❑ Bring a small first-aid kit with antiseptic, plasters, and dysentery tablets.

❑ Most importantly of all, before you leave home, take out comprehensive medical insurance.

PERSONAL SAFETY

Despite two democratic elections and one of the most expensive peace-keeping operations in the history of the United Nations, Cambodia's law and order situation remains fluid. Travellers who fly direct to Siem Reap and Angkor, however, need not fear. There is security around the major sites, but you should inquire about local conditions before visiting the outlying temples. And never walk off the beaten track, as large areas of land have been mined. Finally, if you plan to travel overland from Thailand or to take the boat to Phnom Penh, check with your embassy first for the latest situation.

LAOS

Exploring the Bolovens Plateau

by Ben Davies

In a remote corner of southern Laos, vast tracts of rain forest crowd in on enchanting waterfalls, jungle rivers, and the villages of ethnic tribes. I ventured into this isolated region for a six-day tour travelling by vintage car, bus, boat, and elephant.

The car that ferried us into southern Laos from the Thai border town of Chongmek was not like other vehicles. It had masking tape holding its doors together, a cracked windscreen and an engine that made the sound of a jumbo jet at take-off. The brakes were of a similar vintage to the rusty exterior (it was an ancient Morris Minor). Every time the driver wanted to slow down, he would pump-prime the brakes with a great flourish of his diminutive legs, allowing us to drift to a gradual standstill.

This unsatisfactory state of affairs lasted for some 20 minutes as we drove at a snail's pace through some of the grandest countryside imaginable. Then the inevitable happened. Crossing a single-lane bridge, we encountered an oncoming vehicle. Once again our driver went into pumping position. But this time to no avail. Slowly, inevitably, we advanced until with a neat little crunch we hit the approaching vehicle, coming to a sudden halt over a dried-up river bed in the middle of nowhere.

Travelling in southern Laos is full of such surprises. First of all there's the almost complete lack of tourist infra-structure (at present there's only a handful of operators that put together trips as far as Attapu, using private transport). Then there's the primitive nature of the hotels, where you must often share bathrooms and even squat over toilets. Finally there's the Lao people's remarkable lack of urgency, which means that things seldom work out quite the way you expect them to.

But if you want to travel to one of the most remote and beautiful countries in Asia, Laos is the place to choose. Here you will find not only magnificent scenery, jungle rivers, ethnic tribes, and fine waterfalls, but also some of the friendliest people and one of the richest cultures imaginable. Most of all, you will find the real spirit of adventure that is fast disappearing even in the furthest

In the monsoon season, between June and the end of September, expect to get out and push cars or even buses over appalling stretches of road. At other times of year, abundant mosquitoes and lengthy boat and bus rides are also an inevitable part of this magnificent adventure.

★ You won't find too much in the way of crea-ture comforts on this route, except at the pleasant resort in Tad Lo (where bungalows overlook the waterfall) or in the incongruous-looking Champassak Palace Hotel in Pakse. Elsewhere, expect basic rooms with mosquito nets and shared bathrooms. Because any tourist infrastructure is almost wholly absent, it is best to organize a guide and transport in advance (see Contacts).

Comfortable walking boots are recom-mended, along with swimming gear, sun protection, and hat (for the boat trip).

RIGHT We trundle off into the jungle sitting behind the elephant's mahout, or driver, on the bamboo seat that's strapped around the elephant's girth

flung corners of Southeast Asia.

BANKS AND BUSES

The town of Pakxe lies at the confluence of the Mekong River and the Don River, within easy reach of the famous Khmer ruins of Wat Phu and Dong Kong Island (see pages 100–9). It is a town of clashing styles with a colourful central market, surrounded by ugly new shop-houses and faded colonial villas. Established by the French as an administrative post in 1905, it has few attractions itself other than as a transit point for road and river traffic.

In the local bank, we change our money into the memorable local currency known as the Lao Kip. Its biggest distinction is the sheer volume of paper: a $50 note comes back as a stack of notes the size of a paving stone.

From Pakxe, we catch a three-wheeled motorized contraption known as a jumbo to the bus terminal, which lies 2km (1¼ miles) to the southeast of town. Now if you imagine buses to be modern, roadworthy vehicles with reclining seats and air-conditioning, think again. Typically, a minimum of 70 passengers squeeze into rows of wooden seats (literally planks) designed for a maximum of 30 people. Two dozen more passengers then sit on top of the bus, merrily clutching on to an assortment of baskets, vegetables, and spare tyres.

Every time one of these remarkable vehicles approaches a police station, it will screech to a halt at the side of the road, so that the passengers who are sitting illegally on top of the bus can clamber inside. Then as soon as the vehicle has lurched past the checkpoint, it stops again to allow the passengers to climb back on to the roof like monkeys in the jungle.

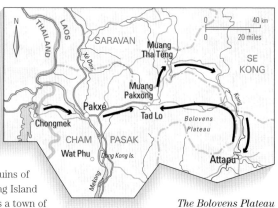

The Bolovens Plateau

From Pakxe, it's a stunning two-and-a-half-hour drive northeast to the village of Tad Lo, which lies at the foot of the Bolovens Plateau, on the border of Saravan and Champassak provinces.

At the small turn-off, we stagger off the bus in a blissful state of relief and follow the dirt track that winds its way through the village past grunting pigs and clucking chickens to the **Tad Lo** Resort and waterfalls, signposted 1.5km (1 mile) away.

ELEPHANTS AND WATERFALLS

Set among shady trees overlooking the burbling Tad Hang waterfall, the collection of simple (if over-priced) bungalows belonging to the Tad Lo Resort provide an ideal base from which to explore the surrounding region by foot—or elephant.

We rise at first light the following day, wandering down to the water's edge for a swim in the Xe Xet (pronounced Houai Set) River. After a breakfast of French bread and omelette at the resort restaurant, it's off for another Tad Lo speciality: elephant riding.

At the pre-appointed time (7am), our two mahouts (elephant drivers) arrive at the resort on their large four-legged protégés—one a 40-year-old elephant with an unquenchable appetite for sugar cane and palm fronds, and the other her half-tonne younger sister. To climb on board these jungle giants is easy.

From the second floor of the resort, you simply place one foot on to the elephant's head, and then with the help of the mahout lower yourself down on the two-person bamboo seats that are tied fast around their enormous girths. Then we are off, swaying along a dirt path that leads south, before fording the river to the picturesque villages and lush jungle vegetation beyond.

Elephants in Laos are something of a national symbol. Indeed, in the latter part of the 14th century, under the Lao prince Fa Ngoum, the country was known as Lane Xang, "Land of a Million Elephants." These days, these awesome and majestic creatures are somewhat less in evidence (only 3,000 Asiatic elephants—smaller than the African variety—are believed to live in the wild). But our two lumbering sisters provide a pleasant reminder of glorious times past.

By the time the sun is directly over-head, the novelty of elephant riding is beginning to wane, and so we return to the beautiful restaurant at Tad Lo Resort for a lunch of coq au vin (not recom-mended), fried rice and fruit, followed by a lazy afternoon swim in the shady pool above the **Tad Hang waterfall**.

RATS AND BATS

Whether it's food or drink, Laos has a few of its own unique specialities that rank alongside some of the world's most unusual gastronomic forms of sustenance. For drink, try *Beer Lao* or *lao lao*, a potent local rice whiskey. For something even stronger, ask for *choum*, a ferociously powerful spirit made from fermented bananas and stored in jars out of which it is imbibed using straws. Then there are a few Lao delicacies you are unlikely to find at home, such as barbecued rat, roasted bat, or pig's intestine soup. For more con-servative eaters, there are noodles, fresh fish, and other mundane dishes.

ETHNIC TRIBES

If elephants are one Tad Lo speciality, ethnic tribes are the other. So the following morning in the company of Souk, our irrepressible Lao guide who speaks Thai (but not English), we go in search of these diminutive people. In total, Laos is home to some 45 ethnic minorities, of which 12 are found in the vicinity of Tad Lo. These range from the Alak (an Austro-Indonesian ethno-linguistic group) to the Nge, the Xouei, and the Ta-oy.

Don't expect to find colourful costumes, however. While these semi-nomadic people, known collectively as the Lao Theung, have kept many of their traditions and superstitions intact (the Alak test the prospects of a marriage by killing a chicken, for example), they generally wear sarongs and a T-shirt. They live in small thatched huts often distinguished by their rounded roofs.

One of the most fascinating of the ethnic groups is the Katou, a Mon-Khmer tribe who moved to the plateau during the 1960s and 1970s to escape the American bombings of the Ho Chi Minh Trail to the east. According to Souk, these shy people, who are famous for their brightly coloured *paisin* or sarongs, sacrifice up to six buffalo every year (in February or March) in a costly ritual aimed at appeasing the spirits.

If you don't have a guide (it's best to arrange one in advance through Sodetour in Pakxe, see Contacts), don't despair. You can take a pleasant two-hour walk along the narrow trail that leads upriver past the upper Tad Lo falls to the villages of Baan Tad Soon and Baan Kien Tang Le. From the main road (near the bus stop), you can also re-cross the bridge and visit some of the surrounding villages on the river bank, stopping for a swim as you go. However, the Lao government has banned tourists from overnighting in the local villages, so you have little choice but to return to Tad Lo at the end of the day.

In the evening, as the sun goes down behind the hills, we sit out on the resort terrace listening to the croaking of tree frogs, the chattering of cicadas, and the distant sound of water cascading down the falls below.

RIVER JOURNEY

Christened the "coffee route" by the French settlers who came here in the 1920s and 1930s, the road from Tad Lo to Tha Teng and Sekong takes you through some of the most fertile countryside on Earth. The region's elevation (1,200m/4,000 feet above sea level), along with its mild climate, have made it ideal not only for arabica and robusta coffee, but for teak, cardamom and even durian, the infamous oval fruit prized for its aphrodisiac qualities.

Despite the recent monsoon, which has turned parts of the route into mud slides (we get out to push on two occasions), it takes little more than an hour to reach Tha Teng (35km/22 miles) and then it's a further two hours to the town of Sekong in the remote eastern region of the country.

Overnighting in Sekong, an ugly brick town best known for its luminous green-painted cockroaches that are hung on bits of string in the market, we set off with our guide the following morning for the biggest thrill of the entire journey— a ride down the **Kong River**.

To rent a boat, or more accurately a motorized canoe, to Attapu costs around $10–15 per person (minimum $40 per boat) and the journey takes about six or seven hours. But it is worth every minute, cutting through remote jungles and cliffs inhabited only by minority tribes (it was long rumoured that U.S. soldiers listed as missing in action during the Vietnam war were held here).

At times we cross over sudden rapids, at times there is so little water that we must almost push the canoe through the narrow gorges that rise from the banks of the river.

By late afternoon, it is raining and the countryside is all but obscured beneath a thick veil. Ahead the river curves around the hills for the last time. To stretch our cramped legs, we draw alongside dry land and climb out on to the mud banks of the Kong River, framed by the distant mountains of the Bolovens Plateau.

THE FINAL FRONTIER

It's dusk when we arrive in the town of **Attapu**, perched on the confluence of the Kong and Sekhaman rivers. Known to the Lao as "Garden Town" after its magnificent setting of flowered lanes and lush tropical plants, this picturesque

ABOVE A dozen of Laos's 45 semi-nomadic ethnic minorities live in villages accessible from Tad Lo
LEFT A typically well-laden bus stops near Attapu

town, which until two years ago was out of bounds to tourists, is one of the great unknown destinations of Laos.

Attapu has neither smart hotels nor nightclubs (we stay in the spartan Tavivan guest house). After 10pm, when the generators are switched off, it does not even have electricity. But what the town lacks in modern infrastructure, it makes up for in charm, with its quaint old wooden houses, its rustic inhabitants who wash in the river alongside the water buffalo, and its lively morning market selling rattan baskets, monstrous-sized fish, and a multitude of bananas in all shapes and sizes.

If you learn just one phrase in Lao, make sure that it's "*sabai dee*". This literally means good day and is the polite form of greeting. If you say it with sufficient enthusiasm, it may also win you friends.

To the east of Attapu, near the Vietnam border, lies the infamous Ho Chi Minh Trail. Extending through the hills and jungles of Cambodia and Laos, it provided the main supply route for Vietnamese communist forces fighting the U.S.-backed South Vietnamese. By the time the war ended in 1975, more than one million tonnes of bombs had been dropped on this area, the biggest tonnage dropped per square kilometre in history. Even now, more than 20 years later, unexploded bombs litter the border area and you are strongly advised not to travel too far afield without a guide.

We spend little more than a day exploring the beautiful lush countryside and the waterfalls around Attapu, pressured by lack of time and the persistent monsoon rains. These now threaten the nearby roads with landslides, raising the prospect that we could be stuck here for at least another couple of days, cut off from the outside world.

OVER THE MOUNTAINS

From Attapu, there's only one way to get back to Pakxe: by a spectacular but

tortuous route (180km/112 miles) that twists and turns through the mountainside with magnificent views first of ricefields, then of jungle-clad mountains and finally of lush coffee plantations. Twice we get out of our vintage bus: once to allow the bus driver to cross a flooded river bed and another time so that he can change a tyre that has been reduced to ribbons by the sharp boulders.

But this seven-hour bus trip is not just a test of human endurance. It provides an insight into one of the greatest natural problems now confronting Laos. Along some stretches of the route, vast tracts of monsoon forest (mainly Asian rosewood, teak, and other hardwoods) have been hacked out of the jungle. Ostensibly the clearing is to make way for new settlements and for coffee and fruit plantations. But there is another more sinister reason. Officially, Laos's forest resources are being depleted at less than 0.9 per cent a year, one of the lowest levels of any country in the region. Unofficially the figure could be as high as 4 per cent, as a result of large-scale and often illegal logging.

For a glimpse of one of the highest waterfalls in the whole of Laos, we jump off the bus at Ban Pak Kud (next to the KM38 sign, a 20-minute drive west of Pakxong). From here **Tad Phan** is signposted on the left hand side (1km/½ mile) at the end of a track that leads past coffee plantations. Tad Phan tumbles an astonishing 130m (430 feet) down the mountainside and is a place of considerable beauty. But beware: the mud paths down to the falls are steep and slippery, and should not be attempted under any circumstances in the rainy season.

From Pakxong, we catch a pick-up truck known as a *songthaew* (literally two rows) for the final leg of our journey down Highway 23 to Pakxe, the end of our adventure through one of Asia's last great frontiers.

G O I N G   I T   A L O N E

INTERNAL TRAVEL

Get to Pakxe either by air (there are twice-daily flights from Vientiane) or by road via the Thai border crossing at Chongmek.

If you are travelling from Bangkok, the easiest and most pleasant way to get to Pakxe is to fly to Ubon Ratchathani in northeast Thailand, from where you can hire a taxi at the airport to take you as far as Chongmek. Once you have crossed the border into Laos, ancient buses and vintage cars ferry passengers to Meun Khao, from where it's a 10-minute hop over the river to Pakxe.

From Pakxe, buses run to Tad Lo, Sekong, and Attapu. Many of the roads, however, are in appalling condition, especially during the rainy season.

WHEN TO GO

The best time to visit southern Laos is between October and the beginning of February, when the skies are clear and temperatures range from 15 to 30°C (59–86°F).

From the end of February to May, temperatures often exceed 35°C (95°F) and the Kong River can be impassable by boat.

From June to the end of September is the rainy season, when tropical downpours alternate with fine days. At this time of year, some stretches of road around Attapu and Sekong are extremely difficult to negotiate without a four-wheel-drive vehicle. The landscape, however, is at its most beautiful and tourist numbers are minimal.

PLANNING

Prior to your arrival in Laos you will need a a tourist visa. These can be obtained through travel agents in Bangkok (this generally takes two days) or at the Lao embassy.

ACCOMMODATION

Accommodation in Pakxe ranges from the upmarket but ugly Champassak Palace Hotel to several basic hotels and guest houses. In Tad Lo, there's the pleasant Tad Lo Resort, although you should make an advance reservation through Sodetour. Elsewhere in Sekong and Attapu, accommodation is extremely basic.

FINDING A GUIDE

Sodetour organize tours or tailormade trips to Tad Lo, Sekong, and Attapu using four-wheel-drive vehicles, which can negotiate the roads all year round.

You may also be able to negotiate a guide to travel with you by bus, although in high season you are strongly advised to make arrangements in advance.

You can rent a car and driver from the Champassak Palace Hotel for around $50–70 a day. Sodetour also rents out cars and drivers.

While it is quite possible to travel to Sekong and Attapu on your own, the lack of tourist infrastructure can make the journey at best time-consuming and at worst unpleasant.

WHAT TO TAKE

❑ Warm clothes. (November–February).
❑ Waterproof bags.
❑ Map and compass.
❑ Walking boots.
❑ Sleeping sheet.
❑ Water bottle.
❑ Toiletries and tissues.
❑ A torch and matches.

HEALTH MATTERS

❑ Take anti-malaria tablets.
❑ Use mosquito repellent and coils.
❑ Wear trousers and long-sleeved shirts at night.
❑ Bring a basic health kit.
❑ Arrange full medical insurance prior to departure.

TRAVELLERS' TIPS

❑ To get the best out of your trip, arrange a guide in advance.
❑ Time is a flexible commodity in Laos. Things rarely happen quite when they are supposed to.
❑ As a rule of thumb, boats and buses leave at dawn and arrive before dusk.
❑ Change only small amounts of foreign money into Lao Kip at one time, as many hotels prefer payment in U.S. dollars.
❑ On arrival in Pakxe and Attapu, you are advised to register with the local immigration officials at the police station.
❑ Don't expect people to speak English. If you are determined to go it alone, take a dictionary.
❑ During the rainy season from June to September, allow plenty of extra time if you are going by public transport, as roads in the south can be extremely difficult.

⑮ ISLAND-HOPPING AROUND LANGKAWI 148–157

0   200 km

0   100 m

⑮ Alor Setar

Kota Baharu

George Town ■

Kuala Terengganu

⑭

Ipoh

MALAYSIA

• Kuantan

Kuala Lumpur ■

Melaka

Johor Baharu

■
SINGAPORE

⑭ MALAYSIA'S JUNGLE RAILWAY 140–147

MALAYSIA

H ome of the world's oldest rain forests and the tallest, most glittering skyscrapers, Malaysia is a study in startling contrasts. As well as being one of Southeast Asia's most ethnically diverse countries, it is also one of its most stable: the friendliness of the people and their relative prosperity make travel here a joy. Although Islam is the dominant religion, animist Malay, Chinese, and Indian cultures also play an important part in life, adding spice with their foods and colour with their temples and festivals. Malaysia abounds with opportunities for trekking, wildlife spotting, diving, snorkelling, and other water sports. Its steaming jungles are bursting with exotic, often unique animal and plant life; treks can be organized in the 11 national parks, and there are scores of other state-managed forest parks and reserves that attract fewer tourists, so increasing the chances of spotting wildlife. The idyllic islands of Langkawi, off the peninsula's northwest coast, offer, away from the luxurious resorts, treks through mangrove swamp and rain forest, visits to limestone caves, and exciting diving.

Tea estate, Cameron Highlands, central Malaysia

MALAYSIA

Malaysia's Jungle Railway

by Simon Richmond

The east coast town of Kota Baharu, where traditional Malay pastimes and arts are fostered, is also the access point for the chugging jungle railway to Taman Negara, the country's top national park and trekking destination.

Travelling in Malaysia often seems like visiting two different countries. Fly into high-tech Kuala Lumpur International Airport and sit in a traffic jam on your way to view the capital's sparkling steel and glass Petronas Towers (currently the tallest building in the world) and you'll believe that the country is a fully paid-up member of the modern world. Cross to the northeast coast town of Kota Baharu, where trishaws ply the quiet streets and the night market stops briefly for evening prayers, and you realize your original assessment needs some readjustment.

> **4** It really depends on what you do within the national park: there are several easy trails lasting no more than half a day, while the longer treks can be very challenging, especially the ascent of Gunung Tahan, Malaysia's highest peak. The canopy walkway is not for those who suffer from vertigo.

> ★★ The third-class train journey is no-frills, but far from unbearable; take plenty of your own food and drink and you'll be fine. In Taman Negara, the comfort level depends on what you decide to do: the resort's best chalets are the ultimate in comfort, but don't expect much sleep if you opt for a night at one of the extremely basic wildlife observation huts (hides). The hides and fishing lodges have mattresses, which don't fare well in the jungle's humid conditions despite being stored in metal wardrobes. Take your own sheets (these can be hired from the resort's housekeeping department) and a mosquito net. If it has been raining, be prepared for a bloody encounter or two with leeches while trekking.

> ✗ For trekking in Taman Negra: walking boots and inconspicuous clothing (so as not to scare off wildlife). For river tubing: a T-shirt to protect against sunburn.

Kota Baharu, capital of Kelantan state, has long been a law unto itself. Physically isolated by the mammoth swath of jungle and mountains running through the centre of the peninsula, the town is one of the most Islamic places in Malaysia, fiercely proud of its local traditions and such arts as shadow-puppet plays and the making of giant kites.

Most people stop in town en route to the idyllic Perhentian Islands, some 60km (38 miles) to the south, off the coast of the neighbouring state of Terengganu. While waiting for the next bus out, they discover Kota Baharu's quirky museums, fantastic central market, with its cornucopia of colourful photo opportunities, and the night market, which serves some of the most delicious food in the country.

But I was in Kota Baharu for another reason: to take a journey on what is known as the jungle railway from Tumpat, on the coast, through the centre of the peninsula to Gemas, southeast of Kuala Lumpur. I was in no hurry and the slow daytime train is the ideal way to get a glimpse of life at the edge of the jungle as I made my way to Malaysia's premier national park and adventure destination, Taman Negara.

CROSSING THE RIVER

I had a day to pass in Kota Baharu before catching the early morning jungle train, so I opted for a trip across the wide and muddy Kelantan River in the genial company of Roselan Hanafiah, the town's highly recommended tourist guide. Roselan, organizer of Kota

Baharu's free cultural performances (see box below), also runs half-day trips that combine visits to the homes of a master puppetmaker and a kitemaker with a pleasant boat trip along the river.

"This is off the tourist map," Roselan keeps saying with, surely, a tone of irony given that I'm in the company of two Italian tourists on a trip that he's probably run hundreds of times before. But there's some truth in what he says, for it's surprising how few visitors to Kota Baharu explore the surrounding villages. Even if they did, they'd more than likely see dusty and generally unattractive places. But with Roselan as your guide, doors open and you find yourself in the fascinating company of Pak Su, a puppetmaker and top *Wayang Kulit* (shadow play) performer.

Pak Su is sitting cross-legged by the window of the home he shares with his family of 13. He's working on one of his puppets, made from translucent buffalo hide. He sticks to traditional patterns for each of the characters in the shadow plays, hammering them out of the hide with umbrella spokes and motorbike tools. He paints colours on with dyes and felt-tip pens, and fixes strings into place with a quick dab of his ever-smouldering cigarette.

After tea, cake, and the inevitable puppet-buying opportunity, we set off by car for another boat ride from a jetty beside the islands clustered in the Kelantan River delta. The boat chugs downstream to a village where the tour finishes up with inspections of a batik factory and the workshop of Ismail Bin Jusoh, an aged kitemaker. He makes a brief appearance to demonstrate how the filigree pattern is applied to his lightweight creations. If you want to see more of this kind of work, head for Kampung Kijang, a ten-minute bus ride from the centre of Kota Baharu, and search out Shapie Ben Yussof. You can't miss his workshop on the main road, flanked as it is by two giant black kites.

THE LONG TRAIN JOURNEY

Cockerels are squawking as I make my way to **Wakaf Bharu**, even though the sky is still inky black, dotted with a dazzling array of stars. At the station the platform is beginning to fill up with passengers, mainly hardy-looking female market sellers with bundles and baskets of produce on their way to towns in the interior. In a small room further down the platform old ladies are rolling out their prayer mats, donning white robes, and kneeling towards Mecca.

The train pulls in on time at 6:20am. Some of the torn leather seats in its shabby third-class carriages are already taken by passengers who boarded at the start of the line in Tumpat. A couple of Dutch backpackers cause a stir as they negotiate a spot to store their souvenir giant kite. Windows are opened so that fat hands of bananas, sacks of stinky durian fruit, and other bulky parcels can be bundled on in the five-minute pause the train makes.

It will take over ten hours to reach my destination—Jerantut, one of the gateways to the Taman Negara National Park—and I soon understand why: the

CULTURAL KOTA BAHARU

Kota Bharu is one of the best places for traditional Malay arts and pastimes. Between March and October free performances are held Monday, Wednesday, and Saturday at Kelantan Cultural Centre, on Jalan Mahmood, five minutes' walk from the State Museum. Typical shows include demonstrations of *Rebana Uni*, the playing of giant decorative drums; *Gasing Uri*, the spinning of large wood and metal tops, and *Gasing Pangkah*, a battle between two spinning tops; *Bulu Ayam*, volleyball played using feet only with a chicken-feather shuttlecock; and *Silat*, a combination of dance and martial arts. Spectators can try all these activities. Evening shows take place on Wednesday (shadow puppet plays) and Saturday (traditional music and dance).

MALAYSIA

train stops every ten minutes or so at some dusty station or isolated halt to load and unload passengers and their belongings. But this is the whole point: the jungle railway passenger service has run 500km (300 miles) through the interior of Malaysia since 1931; it's the equivalent of the local bus in an area where there are still few roads.

If you're feeling peckish on the journey, the choices are either the lacklustre offerings of the buffet car (Styrofoam cartons of unappetizing chicken and rice or fish curry and rice) or to buy from the women who walk along the carriages selling small plastic bags of boiled speckled eggs, clusters of rambutans, nuts, and sweets. I opt for a boiled egg and a plastic bag filled with tea from the buffet and eat while I watch the sun rise, at last, through the jungle palms in a kaleidoscope of colours.

RIGHT Taman Negara National Park offer numerous exciting possibilities for exploring its rain forest, which, at 130 million years old, is the oldest in the world BELOW On the jungle train, women sit surrounded by bags of produce to sell at market FAR RIGHT Central market, Kota Baharu

GOING SOUTH

By late morning the dawn chill has been replaced by soporific heat, eased only slightly by the breeze from the open windows and whirling fans. Many of the market women disembark at the first major town, **Kuala Kerai**, on whose station platform I notice a fish tank and neat flower beds. Still the train remains busy, with more women in patterned

frontier town of **Gua Musang**, 50km (30 miles) south, deep in the interior of Malaysia. Here imposing limestone outcrops, riddled with caves, thrust out of the jungle, abutting the railway.

Shortly after leaving Gua Musang, the railway crosses from the province of Kelantan to Pahang and continues towards the former state capital **Kuala Lipis**, important at the end of the 19th century for gold and tin mining. Modern methods have brought gold-mining companies back to the area recently, but the town still has the air of a colonial relic. On Fridays, when hundreds of tribespeople and locals gather for Kuala Lipis's bustling night market, it's easy to feel you're caught in a time warp.

Kuala Lipis is also the access point for the **Kenong Rimba State Park** (128sq km/49 square miles, with trekking trails, caves, and a couple of waterfalls. Facilities here are much more basic than in Taman Negara (expect to camp out a couple of nights), but fewer visitors means a greater likelihood of spotting wildlife. Although it's possible to explore the park solo, you'll get more out of the experience if you hire a guide or take an organized trek from Kuala Lipis.

For those in search of the full jungle experience, however, Taman Negara—Malaysia's first and largest national park (4,343sq km/1,677 square miles)—is hard to beat. The train arrives at the small town of **Jerantut** shortly after 4pm, missing the last sampans up the Tembeling River to the park headquarters by a couple of hours. But the

headscarves, surrounded by sacks and baskets, small children sucking sweets, and old men smoking and gossiping.

Wispy clouds hang low around the distant jagged mountains as the train pulls into the village of **Dabong**; south of here is the Jelawang Country Park, a favourite spot for camping and trekking trips from Kota Baharu. The countryside is most spectacular, however, at the

143

overnight stop allows me to attend the free briefing at Sri Emas Hotel on activities in the park and to weigh up the many options for the next few days. I also go shopping, as the prices for provisions for any hiking trip are cheaper here in Jerantut than at the few stores there are in the park.

INTO TAMAN NEGARA

Even on the shortest trip you'll have time for some of the milder jungle experiences of **Taman Negara**: hiking up Bukit Teresek—the 342-m (1,122-feet) peak near the park headquarters; crossing the canopy walkway—the 450-m (1,480-feet) rope bridge through the tree tops; taking a boat trip or floating on an inner tube down the Tembeling River. With a few days to spare, take one of the longer trails and either camp or stay in one of the fishing lodges or observation huts (known as hides) overnight; the further you get from the park headquarters at Kuala Tahan, the better your chances of spotting wildlife.

First, however, I needed to get to the park itself. Of the two routes (by river or by road), the agricultural tour in a minibus organized by Sri Emas Hotel is faster and more interesting. It stops off along the way at cocoa, rubber, and palm oil plantations, and the guide gives a short explanation about the crop. You also have a chance to try hacking down the huge globes of orange palm oil fruit with a lethal scythe attached to the end of a long and very heavy pole.

By noon the bus has arrived at **Kuala Tahan**, the village across from the park headquarters and the Taman Negara Resort. Many visitors now opt to stay in Kuala Tahan because accommodation and food prices are cheaper than at the resort, where the only budget accommodation is in the hostel or at the campsite. It's worth noting that close on 40,000 tourists a year visit Taman Negara, so if you're planning on staying during any of the holiday periods it's important to make accommodation bookings well in advance and to be prepared for crowds on the shorter trails.

EXPLORING THE JUNGLE

I cross the Tembeling River to the park on the 30-second shuttle service. As I check in at the resort, a praying mantis lands on my leg and a livid green snake slinks idly across the wooden steps—a welcome to the jungle that could hardly have been better stage-managed.

Taman Negara contains one of the oldest tropical rain forests in the world. It began life as the Guning Tahan Game Reserve, set up in the 1920s to preserve wildlife across the states of Pahang, Kelantan, and Terengganu. In 1939 it became known as the King George V National Park, and it got its current name (meaning national park) when Malaysia gained independence in 1957.

The peninsula's highest mountain, Gunung Tahan, (2,187m/7,175 feet) lies within the park. To climb the mountain, following an undulating 55-km (34-mile) trail from the park headquarters, takes a week, and encompasses the full range of jungle terrain from steamy lowland dipterocarp jungle and rivers to the higher altitude elfin forests—an eerie, damp world of stunted trees coated with moss, ferns, lichens, and orchids. This is the only trek in the park for which you must be accompanied by a guide, which will cost around RM500 ($135) for seven days; make enquiries at the Park and Wildlife Offices next to the resort about any trips that you might be able to join.

Most visitors stick with easier hikes, all along clear, well-marked trails. The most popular is the one that leads towards the canopy walkway 1.5km (1 mile) east of the resort, past Bukit Teresek. If you're afraid of heights, or of swaying rope-and-plank bridges, the walkway is not for you. Alternatively, the 450-m (492-yard) circuit, made up of nine bridges between eight treetop platforms, is a ramble through the canopy level of the jungle, where most animal and bird activity takes place. There are also good views along the Tembeling River and down 30m (100 feet) through the trees to the jungle floor.

UP THE TAHAN RIVER

Buy a permit and you can go fishing within the park. Popular spots are Kuala Kenian and Kuala Perkai, some 28km (17 miles) northeast of Kuala Tahan, and Lata Berkoh, 8km (5 miles) north-west. **Lata Berkoh**—a picturesque series of cascades on the Tahan River— is also a favourite destination for motor-ized sampans from Kuala Tahan. I opt to make the four-hour hike there in the afternoon, staying overnight at the fish-ing lodge and catching a boat back the next morning, so as to avoid the crowds who picnic and swim there each day.

Shortly after leaving the park headquarters, I spot a monitor lizard waddling across the trail, the largest fauna I encounter during my hike, which otherwise takes me past thousands of small insects, including termites, giant ants, and purple and blue butterflies. Fallen tree trunks block the path occasionally, almost as if the jungle has deliberately put obstacles along the way to liven up the trek. There are a couple of shallow river crossings and a short uphill stretch, but nothing too demanding.

I meet hardly any other people, save for a group of Orang asli—the original people of peninsular Malaysia—who've set up a tiny camp of bamboo huts in a clearing. Children scamper shyly in and out of the huts and in one corner a man is kneeling by a fire, tending a row of blow darts, which are still used by the Orang asli for hunting. A written notice pinned to a nearby tree offers blow pipes for sale, priced according to length. It also informs you it will cost RM5 ($1.50) to take a photograph.

Chirping cicadas crank up the late afternoon noise level as I ford the Tahan to reach the fishing lodge, which has two bedrooms, each with a pair of bunk beds, a covered veranda, running water,

The jungle railway

and toilets. My companions for the night are Roded from Israel, Lieke from Holland, Gavin from Australia, and Nicole from England. Roded and Lieke have spent the day hiking from Kuala Trenggan, 12km (7½ miles) to the east, where the resort runs some upmarket jungle lodges. Gavin and Nicole will be headed in the same direc-tion in a couple of days to stay at the hide, Kumbang, where you're almost guaranteed at some point during the night to see a tapir feeding.

Nightfall finds us all gathered on the fishing lodge veranda enjoying a candlelit supper of barbecued fish caught fresh from the Tahan River. Lightning flashes momentarily illuminate the jungle, rain drops rattle the tin roof and somewhere in the dark an iguana cackles hysterically.

JUNGLE NIGHTS

In the morning, the iguana is still laughing. As the first daytrippers invade our jungle idyll, I take the boat ride along the tannin-stained waters of the Tahan River back to Kuala Tahan. This is Taman Negara at its most beautiful. Neram trees arch across the water, their roots tenaciously clinging to the river banks. Lianas droop in Hollywood-jungle style and floating logs do impressions of sleeping crocodiles as the longboat glides around bends and through the gentle rapids.

The overnight rain has raised the river levels, promising an exciting white-water ride down the Tembeling by inner tube—an activity offered by most of the floating restaurants at Kuala Tahan. First you're ferried by longboat some 4km (2½ miles) upriver past several mild rapids, then you're left to drift back to Kuala Tahan over a couple of hours, lolling in a giant black rubber doughnut. For the most part this is a leisurely activity, the rapids being too far apart and too gentle to provide more than a mild thrill.

Much more exciting is the night trek with Wan, a guide from the Parks and Wildlife Department. At the start of the hour long exploration of jungle close to the resort, Wan gets us to turn off our torches to experience total darkness and begin listening for animal sounds. Treading lightly along the path, we pause as Wan's torchbeam picks out a scorpion's lair in a cleft of a tree and an exotic orange stick insect on a leaf.

Half-way through the trek, we stop, switch off our torches again and wait, our eyes adjusting slowly to the blue/green glow of phosphorescent fungus on the ground. There is a rustling in the bushes. The sound comes nearer and waves of excitement tinged with fear grip the group. A moment later the noise is directly behind us and our torches flick on to reveal a spiny porcupine, squealing a warning to its jungle brethren while we in turn squeal with delight.

LEFT Jungle walkway, Taman Negara

G O I N G   I T   A L O N E

INTERNAL TRAVEL

There are regular flights to Kota Baharu's airport, 9km (6 miles) northeast of the town centre, from KL, Penang, and Alor Setar. A taxi into Kota Baharu costs RM16 ($4). Long-distance buses arrive at either the Langaar or Hamzah bus stations, both a couple of kilometres (about a mile) south of the centre. The local bus station is next to the night market, and is where buses from the neighbouring state of Terengganu stop. For train details, see below.

WHEN TO GO

In the dry season—November to May—trees and plants are in bloom and migrant birds arrive from Siberia and China. May to August, in the wet season, is best for seeing jungle animals.

ARRANGING A RIVER TRIP AND HOMESTAY

Roselan Hanafiah is the man to track down at the Tourist Information Centre if you want to arrange a river trip or a homestay programme around Kota Baharu. The river trips are daily except Friday and generally take a maximum of three people. The homestay programmes, lasting 3 days/2 nights can be with either a puppet-maker or kitemaker and include lessons in each craft.

THE JUNGLE TRAIN TRIP

A taxi from Kota Baharu to Wakaf Baharu, the closest train station, 7km (4 miles) west of the town, costs RM15 ($4). Trains depart daily for destinations south: morning trains are third-class only; evening trains are faster and have second-class sleeping berths, worth paying extra for only if you're heading on down to Singapore, since the service arrives at Jerantut at 2am. In the opposite direction, there are two overnight services for Kota Baharu from Jerantut. Jerantut is also connected to KL by a direct overnight train service. Times are subject to change, so it's best to check schedules with local tourist offices and KTM (Keretapi Tanah Melayu, the train operator).

TAMAN NEGARA BY BOAT AND BUS

Sri Emas Hotel and Jerantut Guesthouse, both in Jerantut, organize two ways of getting to Kuala Tahan and Taman Negara's park headquarters. Increasingly popular is their 2-hour mini-bus tour. The more traditional alternative is to drive to the jetty at Kuala Tembeling and take a motorized sampan up river for three hours. A good idea is to take the bus into the park and the boat back, since the river journey downstream is faster than up. If you're really in a hurry, you can take the Taman Negara Resort 1-hour speedboat service. From the Istana Hotel in KL, a direct bus service (4 hours) to the jetty at Kuala Tembeling runs daily, connecting with boats to Kuala Tahan.

HEALTH MATTERS

Take anti-malaria tablets and use mosquito repellent. Bring a first-aid kit, and arrange full medical insurance before you leave home. It's wise to wear a T-shirt to protect against sunburn if you go river tubing.

ESSENTIAL FOR TAMAN NEGARA PARK

❑ Register on arrival at the park HQ or the Tembeling jetty.
❑ Buy an entry permit and camera permit at the HQ.
❑ Book an overnight stay in the fishing lodges at Lata Berkoh of Kuala Perkai, or in a hide in the park.
❑ Hire camping equipment from the HQ campsite.
❑ Bring good walking boots (those for hire are often in a sorry state).

TIPS FOR JUNGLE TREKKERS

❑ Loud noises scare away wildlife. This also means it's best to walk in small groups. And stop to listen: you might not see many animals or birds, but you'll certainly hear plenty.
❑ Take your time. It's hot and humid, so rushing about will only make you uncomfortable.
❑ Read a guidebook before you start so you know what to look for. Bring a torch, hat, and water.
❑ The most active times for wildlife are dawn and dusk. Take time to rest during the midday heat, like the animals.
❑ Bright clothing scares off wildlife.
❑ Look for the small. The chances of spotting big game, such as elephants and tigers, are very slim. But there are myriad smaller animals and plants, from exotic ferns and butterflies to termite colonies and fungi. Bring binoculars.

MALAYSIA

Island-Hopping around Langkawi

by Simon Richmond

Beside the luxury resorts and the fanciful legends of the 99 islands of Langkawi, off Malaysia's northwest coast, lies a world of unspoiled nature and beguiling rural charm. Ancient rain forests, mangrove swamps, and caves are some of the attractions off the beaten tourist path.

One of the many legends that is told in the islands of **Langkawi** is that they were once cursed. Mahsuri, a beautiful, kind young woman was falsely accused of adultery by her jealous mother-in-law. As the execution-er's knife was plunged into her heart, white blood spurted, out proving her innocence, and as Mahsuri breathed her last, she damned Langkawi for seven generations.

People on the islands will swear this story is a fact, even though the date of the supposed events varies from less than 200 to 750 years ago. The History Association of Kedah in conjunction with the Kedah State Museum believe they've tracked down Mahsuri's direct descen-dants on the island of Phuket, Thailand. Whatever the truth, the curse has long

since been lifted because Langkawi is now one of Malaysia's most upmarket holiday destinations, a prosperous island with uncrowded beaches, virgin jungle, and generally low-key development.

The catalyst for this change was the arrival on the island about 40 years ago of a young doctor from the state's capital Alor Setar. As I sailed across the Straits of Malacca to reach **Kuah**, Langkawi's main town, I was intrigued to find exactly what it was that had so captured the heart of this Dr. Mahathir Mohammed, Malaysia's future prime minister, and encouraged him to push for the island's designation as a duty-free port in 1987 and its subsequent transformation into a pit-stop for the international jet set.

Of the islands that comprise Langkawi, clustered some 30km (20 miles) off the far northwest coast of Malaysia, only two are permanently inhabited: the largest, Pulau Langkawi, and Pulau Tuba, 5km (3 miles) south, and home to a small fishing community. For most visitors the point of coming here is to remain cocooned in the luxury resorts, lounging on the beaches and relaxing. But those seeking mild adven-ture will not be disappointed either. Newly laid roads make for a pleasant motorbike or car tour of Langkawi's scattered sights. Half a day can be passed hopping between the islands, swimming in a freshwater pool, spotting

1 The most thrilling thing you can do, apart from risking a dive with a dodgy operator, is to go paragliding. It lasts only five minutes and is huge fun—even if you get a dunking in the sea on take off-and landing.

★★ Langkawi has some of the best hotels in Malaysia and its roads are in excellent condition and empty of traffic. Renting a vehicle is practically the only way to get around the island. This is not a destination for those without money; if you're on a bud-get, other island resorts in Malaysia or nearby Thailand offer better value for money.

Besides your camera and binoculars, no special equipment is needed.

wildlife, and even going paragliding for a bird's eye view of the scenery. The best activities, however, are nature walks in the jungle and a cruise into the fascinating mangrove forests.

The best time to visit Langkawi is in the dry season between November and May, when the island is home to migrant birds from Siberia and China and the trees and plants burst with flowers. Even during the wet season, in the remaining months of the year, there is plenty for the nature lover to see and do. The fruiting season, from May through to August, is the best time to see animals feeding in the jungles. Fireflies make an appearance between June and July, and in early August you might be lucky enough to catch sight of Langkawi's strangest natural phenomena: small fish hobbling on their gills across the paddy fields, after hibernating for a year in the dry earth.

A MOTORBIKE TOUR

Don't be fooled by its size. Langkawi might be only about 500sq km (190 square miles) and take no more than hour and a half to cross by car, but by motorbike you'll be pushed to see all the major sights in one day and you'll find that on a round trip you can cover anything up to 70km (45 miles). If you're not in any hurry, hire a bike for a couple of days and take your time looking around.

I make an early start and set off north from my hotel at Pantai Cenang along the coast, around the landfill created for the new airport runway, towards the waterfall **Telaga Tujuh**, or "Seven Wells." A rollercoaster-like road, twisting over and around many a small hill, and past Pantai Kok—one of the island's most attractive beaches— takes me to the base of the hill, from where the waterfall is a stiff 200-m (650-foot) climb.

The picturesque waterfall, which ends in a cliff-edge drop with a view of the ocean, takes its name from the

seven moss-covered pools created by the pounding water in the rock. If the waterfall is in full flood, it's possible to slide from pool to pool, but this is not recommended unless you want a bruised back. So much for the prevailing legend that this is a favourite spot for fairies to bathe and that they have bequeathed the waters healing powers.

I return to the main road and ride 20km (12 miles) or so east across the north of the island, past numerous paddy fields in which water buffalo wallow, to the sprawling **Kompleks Budaya Kraf**, the Craft Cultural Complex. Designed to show off the full range of Malaysia's arts and crafts, this consists almost exclusively of tourist gift shops, but is partially redeemed by the demonstrations smiling local women give of basketmaking and clothweaving. I spend an amusing half-hour playing the traditional marble game *congkak* with a couple of the younger girls, who giggle at my fumbling attempts to grasp the rules.

An even quirkier attraction lies some 10km (6 miles) further along the road, past the roundabout with what appears to be a giant pile of buffalo dung on it, and towards Kuah. This is the **Galleria Perdana**, which houses over 2,500 state gifts and awards presented to Prime Minister Dr. Mahathir and his wife. There's everything from china and cars to jewellery and Japanese dolls, but two of the more extraordinary gifts are a portrait of the good doctor, from Beijing, made of horsehair (the guard tells me

---

THE PADANG MATSIRAT

Another of Langkawi's legends concerns the Padang Matsirat or Field of Burnt Rice. Not long after the princess Mahsuri's death, the entire crop of rice was set fire to, either by the villagers themselves in the face of invading Siamese, or by the pillaging and looting Siamese. Either way, today locals claim that blackened rice can still be seen in the sand, especially after heavy rains.

MALAYSIA

BELOW and LEFT Pulau Langkawi is the largest of around 100 islands that make up Langkawi. The island is best explored by hiring a motorbike or four-wheel-drive from the main town, Kuah, or at beach resorts. Island-hopping boat trips are also popular

RIGHT Langkawi has a choice of good hotels. At Bon Ton it is possible to stay in a refurbished kampung (village house). One of Langkawi's best restaurants is part of the same complex

MALAYSIA

proudly that it took 100 people working non-stop for three months) and a full-length Astrakhan wool coat and cap from the president of Turkmenistan—just the thing for tropical Malaysia.

THE EAGLE HAS LANDED

Kuah itself is worth only a short look, its main attraction being that it has the island's largest concentration of shops. The jetty is dominated by the huge sculpture of a brown eagle—the symbol of Langkawi—its wings spread ready for take-off towards the inviting islands to the south. Near by, the gardens of Lagenda Langkawi Dalan Taman are dotted with more giant, colourful sculptures relating to the island's legends. Lack of shade makes it an unpleasantly hot spot to hang out, however.

Before I return to my hotel, I have one last place to visit: **Makam Mahsuri**, the tomb of the ill-fated beauty. Despite being something of a tourist honeypot, the tomb is surprisingly hard to locate, and I have to keep a sharp look-out for the direction signs. Once they get there, most visitors rush past the simple white marble mausoleum to the traditional *kampung* (village) house on stilts, which has been carefully restored, and the well from which Mahsuri once drew water. I munch on a *kuih peneram*, a sweet snack I bought at a stall in the grounds, and listen to local musicians beat on drums, wondering what Mahsuri would think of Langkawi now.

ISLAND-HOPPING

The second-largest island of the group is **Pulau Dayang Bunting**, Island of the Pregnant Maiden. Its freshwater lake, Taski Dayang Bunting, is a charming place to while away a couple of hours and is a fixture on all the "island hopping" tours around Langkawi. It's the first stop on my trip from the Pelangi Beach Hotel with a group of 12 other guests and, before we dock at the landing for the short walk to the lake, the boatman pauses to point out one

MAGIC WATERS

Mahsuri is not the only legendary lady of the islands. The celestial princess Putri Dayang Sari lends her name to Pulau Dayang Bunting, Island of the Pregnant Maiden. One story has it that Sari was seduced by an earthly prince and their union produced a child, who died seven days later. The distraught princess threw her dead baby into the freshwater lake on the island, blessed the waters, and returned to the heavens. Today, women wanting a child still come to bathe in the lake's magical waters.

possible reason for the island's name: the silhouette of a pregnant woman formed by the rolling crest of the hills (see box, above, for another story).

The Italian couple in our group, Paulo and Isabella, think that the small lake, backed by steep, wooded hills, looks like a Scottish loch. But there is a difference—the emerald waters are beautifully warm for swimming. For those who don't fancy a swim, there are pedalos and canoes for hire, and a floating wooden sundeck from which to admire the view. All too soon it's time to return to our boat, past the curious macaque monkeys who clamber down from the trees to watch us, and we hop over to the next island.

Pulau Singa Besar, the Island of the Big Lion, has been designated a wildlife sanctuary and, if you're lucky, you'll catch sight of lizards, mousedeer, more monkeys, and hornbills as you follow the specially laid paths around the island. More likely, you'll encounter the animals that have been introduced to the island, such as horses, deer, and peacocks, all of which appear somewhat lost and lonely in the alien environment of Pulau Singa Besar's camping ground.

There isn't enough time to explore the whole walkway through the mangrove trees before my boat leaves Pulau Singa Besar for the final destination of the day. It's a short trip to the tiny island of **Pulau Beras Besah** (Wet Rice Island), a good spot for swimming, with a fine sandy beach. Here I decide to have a go at paragliding. A fellow guest warns me that I might be sick, but I don't. I just feel elated as the wind catches under the parachute and I'm hoisted off the beach, dragged along like a kite flown from the speedboat below me. The bird's eye view of the islands is incomparable. But I can't stay airborne for ever, and all too soon it's time to land back on the beach and let the next customer take a turn.

SNORKELLING AND DIVING AT PULAU PAYAR

An hour's boat ride south of Langkawi, between the smaller islands of Pulau Kaca, Lembu, and Segantang, **Pulau Payar** is one of the best places in the area for snorkelling and diving, with the chance to see colourful tropical fish as well as black-tipped reef sharks and giant turtles. With its vast range of corals (said to be the best in Malaysia), the area has been designated a marine park, but this hasn't stopped the largest of the tour operators, Langkawi Coral, building an enormous floating pontoon directly above the reef to service its popular snorkelling and diving tours.

It's a great shame that the environmental standards of the tour companies are not higher, for Payar is a

potentially rewarding place to visit. Care should be exercised, especially, when choosing a dive company (see Safety First box, page 157). The company that I used fell well short of the basic safety requirements any diver should be looking for. We were not given a chance to check our rental equipment before setting off, and as a result some of it malfunctioned dangerously during the actual dive. Nor was any member of the group asked about previous diving experience.

INTO THE JUNGLE

What's really put Langkawi on the international holiday map in recent years has been the opening of several luxurious resorts in remote parts of the island. The most famous, perhaps, is The Datai, one of only two hotels to share exclusive use of the gorgeous beach **Pantai Datai**. In the far northwest corner of the Langkawi, it has a view directly across to the southernmost islands of Thailand. Constructed of local stone and timbers, The Datai blends almost seamlessly with its magnificent jungle surroundings. It's these that I set off to explore in the grey light of dawn, with the hotel's naturalist guide Irshad Mobarak, an ex-banker turned conservationist.

From the road leading up to The Datai, Mobarak points through the trees to the jagged edge of Gunung Mat Cincang, a limestone massif shrouded in primeval rainforest. "You're looking at the oldest rock formation in Malaysia, over 550 million years old," he announces, before launching into detailed and lively explanations of the flora and fauna around us. We start on the road because this will give us the best chance of spotting wildlife—the jungle is so dense, there is little light to allow animals to be seen.

Pausing in front of what appears to me to be three trees entwined together, Mobarak explains that we're witnessing a slow assassination. The strangler fig is

---

LIGHT READING

Some 5km (3 miles) west from Kuah, towards the centre of the island, the Book Village is a half-hearted attempt to make Langkawi a mecca for secondhand book lovers. The cottages within the pleasantly landscaped grounds have few books to choose from; the most interesting shop is one that has a selection of old magazines from around the world that would make ideal beach or poolside reading.

actually a liana vine, and grows by dropping its roots from the upper branches of the host tree and planting them in the ground. Over the course of 30 years or more, the life is squeezed out of the host as the fig applies what Mobarak calls, slipping back into the language of a banker, "a hostile takeover."

A troop of dusky leaf monkeys swings through the treetops as we stop again to learn about the medicinal properties of various jungle plants that can be used to make natural astringents, antiseptics, and contraceptives. At our feet, two species of termites have created busy motorway systems, along which thousands of worker termites stream back and forth from their distant nests

in a beguiling display of natural co-ordination.

You don't need to be a Datai guest to take part in these fascinating walks, nor do you need to wake at crack of dawn. Mobarak also guides groups around the hotel at dusk, a time when it's possible to see civet cats, giant red flying squirrels, and the colugo (*Cynocephalus volans*), a rare member of the flying lemur family, as well as several species of birds and bats.

Bird-watchers will want to accompany him on a sunset trip to **Gunung Raya**, at 883m (2,897 feet) Langkawi's tallest peak and easily accessible by a winding 11-km (7-mile) road which, for the most part, runs along the canopy level of the forest, where much plant and animal life is found and which is home to the great hornbill (*Buceros bicornis*). At 115cm (45 inches) from the tip of its yellow bill to the end of its black and white tail, this is the largest bird in the islands.

LEFT Kuah, Langkawi's main town, is strung out along the seafront, with views to the southern islands
BELOW LEFT To learn about epiphytes— and more—take a walk in the jungle from Datai with the hotel's natural historian
BELOW Planting rice

INTO THE MANGROVES

At the northeastern cape of Langkawi is **Tanjung Rhu**, Casuarina Bay, where casuarina trees fringe a beach that at low tide you can walk across to the islands of Pulau Pasir, Pulau Gasing, and Pulau Dangli. Boats cluster at a small jetty in the mouth of the lagoon and can be hired to reach **Gua Cherita**, the Cave of Tales, accessible only by sea. Take a torch so you can locate the faded traces of ancient writing on the walls. One story has it that these are verses from the Koran, another that they are the last scribblings of survivors from an Indian vessel, shipwrecked here in the 13th century.

The most interesting trip from Tanjung Rhu combines exploring caves watching birds along the rugged coastline with sailing into the mangrove forests along the Kilim and Kisap rivers further south. I join three young female vets, two from England and one from Malaysia, and a party of four German tourists for the half-day tour. Our guide is Osman, a part-time snake charmer who today, I'm pleased to note, has only brought along a bright green iguana in his backback for company.

The first stop is one of the floating fish farms sheltering in the lagoon. Submerged nets are strung between a chequerboard of wooden planks floating on blue plastic barrels and each square of netting contains a different fish or type of seafood. We peer into one and see an enormous grouper surface for a snack of dead sprat, its sharp teeth glinting momentarily in the sun before it sinks back into the water. Not everything here ends up on a plate; the farm also breeds colourful tropical fish for the island's aquarium.

THE CHARCOAL FACTORY

As we head out to sea and follow the dramatic limestone cliffs fashioned by centuries of exposure to the elements, we spot many types of bird, but binoculars give a closer view. Brown eagles and white-bellied eagles hover overhead as we pull into the mouth of Gua Dedap to inspect the cavern entrance. Here the boat is too wide to make it through to the lagoon beyond, but we have no problem getting to the next cave, along the remarkably beautiful Kilim River.

Gua Kelawar can be reached only at high tide, when the narrow channels through the mangroves become navigable. The acrid smell of droppings is potent evidence that the cave is home to thousands of fruit bats, but Osman shines his torch into their tiny eyes anyway, to let us see them as they hang from the roof. A wooden walkway runs in a circular route through the chamber, in one entrance and out another, and at one point we find ourselves wading through water up to our shins.

Before we get back on the boat, Osman tells us about the two main types of mangrove that grow here. The Raisufara can be chopped down and turned into charcoal, but the Barbutah should be avoided at all costs. Breaking off a leaf he shows us the milky sap. "If this gets in your eyes you'll go blind," he warns, "and if you put three drops in someone's tea, they'll get stomach cramps, vomit blood, and die in three days." The only antidote comes from the roots of the same tree.

Returning to the coast, we encounter a longboat filled with mangrove logs and follow it to the charcoal factory in the Kisap River further south. The scene we encounter there is nothing short of Dickensian, giving a glimpse of life under Mahsuri's curse. Naked children wave from piles of logs on the bank, in front of a house and a factory made of wood and palm leaves and covered almost entirely in soot. The Thai man and his family who make the charcoal here are, we're told, happy because even this is a better living than they would make in Thailand. It proves a thought-provoking climax to both the half-day coastal nature trip and my week enjoying the luxury and beauty of the rest of Langkawi.

GOING IT ALONE

INTERNAL TRAVEL

Langkawi's airport, on the west side of the island, is served by daily flights from KL, Penang, and Ipoh, as well as by international services from Singapore, Taipei, and Kansai International in Japan.

There's a choice of ferries to the island. From Kuala Perlis on the Thai border there are nine fast boats daily, taking 45 minutes one way. Slower ferries operate from Kuala Kedah further south, 8km (5 miles) from the city of Alor Setar. From Penang there's one ferry a day at 8:30am, which takes 2½ hours. If you're coming from Thailand, there's also a fast ferry three times daily from Satun.

WHEN TO GO

In the dry season—November to May—trees and plants are in bloom and migrant birds arrive from Siberia and China. May to August, in the wet season, is best for seeing jungle animals.

RENTING A MOTORBIKE

Motorbike rental shops abound in the beach resort Pantai Cenang, and you should be able to hire the cheapest models for around 30 baht ($8) for 24 hours. Make sure you check the bike over fully and give it a test ride before handing over your cash.

Also ask for a helmet; few people wear them on the island, but it is the law and you could be fined if you're caught without one.

You'll have to fill up the tank with fuel, so make sure you know where the nearest petrol stations are.

RENTING A CAR

Car hire is also available at the ferry jetty in Kuah and at several hotels around the island; check first that the people you're hiring from are fully licensed to rent out vehicles. At both the Pelangi Beach and its sister establishment the Burau Bay, a Vitara Jeep-style vehicle can be hired for RM150 ($40) for 24 hours.

BOATS TO THE ISLANDS

Island-hopping boats, which visit Tasik Dayang Bunting, Pulau Singa Besar, and Pulau Beras Basah, depart twice daily from Kuah's ferry jetty. For a small extra cost, most of the hotels at Pantai Cenang organize their own boats to the same islands; taking one of these will save you the hassle of getting back and forth from Kuah.

A more expensive and more stylish are Dynamite Cruises' day trips, run by New Zealander Lin Ronald on an 18-m (60-foot) sailing ship *Dynamo Hum*. The trip departs from the Porto Malai marina at the south-western tip of Langkawi and includes a buffet lunch with drinks. Depending on the weather and season, Dynamite Cruises also offer a trip around the mangrove forests and rocky inlets on Langkawi's northeast coast.

ORGANIZED NATURE WALKS

Irshad Mobarak's company Wildlife Langkawi organizes the nature walks around The Datai as well the coastal nature safari from Tanjung Rhu into the mangrove forests, a dusk trip to Gunung Raya to spot hornbills, and longer jungle treks around Gunung Mat Cincang. Another naturalist offering jungle treks and mangrove tours is Jurgen Zimmerer, a German ex-pat.

WHAT TO TAKE

- ❑ Waterproof bags if you visit in the wet season.
- ❑ Water bottle.
- ❑ Toiletries and tissues.
- ❑ Sun cream and hat.
- ❑ Binoculars for spotting wildlife.

HEALTH MATTERS

- ❑ Take anti-malaria tablets.
- ❑ Use mosquito repellent and coils.
- ❑ Wear trousers and long-sleeved shirts at night.
- ❑ Bring a basic health kit.
- ❑ Arrange full medical insurance prior to departure.
- ❑ Check on vaccinations with your doctor at least a month before leaving.

SAFETY FIRST

At the very least before taking any diving or snorkelling trip:
- ❑ Ask to check out the equipment you'll be using before you get on the boat.
- ❑ Check the credentials and experience of the diving instructor and whether the company is affiliated with a member of a reputable body such as PADI.
- ❑ Find out about the boat you'll be using; if the seas turn rough, the small open-sided boats used by many companies are not a good place to be if you're at all prone to seasickness.

SUMATRA • JAVA

⑯ RACING DOG RIVER RAPIDS 160–169

Banda
Aceh

Medan
⑯

Sibolga

S u m a t e r a (Sumatra)

Dumai

Pekanbaru

K e p u l a u a n

Padang

Jambi

▲
3805m

Bangka

Palembang

Bengkulu

Tanjungkarang
Telukbetung

0		400 km
0	200 m	

Jakarta

J a v a   S e a

Bandung

Semarang

*J a w a
(Java)*

Surabaya

Yogyakarta ⑰

Malang

Bali

⑰ THE GREAT BOROBUDUR 170–177

O f the great con-
catenation of islands that
form the state of Indonesia, Java and Sumatra
are perhaps the names best known to the outside world. A paradise of
magnificent natural landscapes and home to a variety of ethnic
groups, Sumatra is for its size sparsely inhabited, with a population of
only about 40 million. Yet it is a vital part of Indonesia's economy,
accounting for 60 per cent of the country's oil and petrol production.
Physically, it is mountainous and highly volcanic, the explosion that
created Lake Tobo probably being the greatest in the Earth's history.
Java, to the southeast, is the cultural centre of Indonesia. Although
much smaller than Sumatra, it hosts 60 per cent of the population,
and has been the birthplace of the greater part of Indonesia's many
magnificent kingdoms and the source of its greatest art. It is not
merely a political centre. There are 120 volcanoes in Java, of which
about 30 are active. As a result, Java has some of the most fertile
earth in the world, which sustains its massive population and which,
according to Sir Stamford Raffles, was to a great extent responsible
for the great Javanese civilization.

*The water-filled crater of Mount Sinabung, northern
Sumatra*

SUMATRA

Racing Dog River Rapids

by Simon Richmond

Scaling active volcanoes, slogging through treacherous jungle, and braving the rapids of merciless rivers are part of the northern Sumatra adventure experience. Chilling out afterwards with the orangutans at Bukit Lawang on the edge of Gunung Leuser National Park is essential.

The knock on my guest house door comes at dawn. We were supposed to be climbing the volcano at 4am, so as to catch the sunrise over the hill station of Brastagi, but two hours later we're only just starting. I've been less than a day in north Sumatra and I realize I've slipped into what the locals call jam karet—rubber time.

The unpredictable nature of travel in the many islands of Indonesia is part of its attraction. You're never quite sure what's coming next—or when it's coming—but you can be sure the experience will be memorable.

Sumatra's most adventurous activities—such as white-water rafting on the upper reaches of the Wampu River or the Asahan River closer to Lake Toba—are not for the fainthearted or inexperienced. There are softer rafting options for travellers who'd prefer not to risk life and limb. A fair degree of fitness is necessary for the jungle trekking and volcano climbing.

Don't expect to be able to keep to a strict timetable in Sumatra, and be prepared for standards at the top end of the accommodation range to to be lower than those in other parts of Southeast Asia. On the plus side, it's possible to travel in considerable style on a limited budget. Another factor to take account of is the possibility of civil unrest.

A good pair of walking boots is essential for jungle hikes, as well as all-weather gear. Waterproof bags are important if you want to keep your gear dry while rafting. A light, long-sleeved shirt and trousers will keep jungle insects at bay, and you'll need warmer clothing for both Bukit Lawang and Brastagi at night.

The plan for my week in north Sumatra had been unveiled shortly after I'd arrived in **Medan**, capital city of the fourth largest island in the world, by Halim, who was himself a bit of a surprise. He turned out to be an energetic German—previously called Georg (he changed his name when he adopted Islam)—who was hooked on dare-devil adventures in wild rivers and untamed jungles.

Together with his young assistant, Igun, we'd drive immediately to **Brastagi** and camp overnight beside Lake Kawar, where I'd get some canoeing practice. The next morning we'd climb Mount Sinabung, the higher of the two volcanoes near the former Dutch colonial-era hill station, then we'd hire an off-road vehicle and driver to take us to a remote hillside village. From here we'd trek through the jungle to the upper reaches of the Wampu River and camp beside a powerful waterfall. The final day would be a six-hour canoe trip, braving the rapids of the Wampu River and ending up a short drive from Bukit Lawang, famous for its Orangutan Rehabilitation Centre.

I'm assured that the upper Wampu is graded III on the white-water scale (see box page 164) and that its lower reaches are part of the standard rafting day trip from Bukit Lawang, fine for novice paddlers such as me. However, when I ask why the Wampu is also known locally as Laubiang (the Dog River), Halim says "because only a dog will survive if it falls in."

UP THE VOLCANO

A few salubrious Dutch-era villas remain around Brastagi, but today it's little more than a down-at-heel, one-road town that's a convenient pit stop en route from Bukit Lawang to Lake Toba to the south. Lying 1,300m (4,265 feet) above sea level on the Karo Plateau, 68km (42 miles) from Medan, it's also a cool (and rainy) retreat, so you'll need to bring warm, waterproof clothing.

The plan to camp and climb Mount Sinabung is scratched because of the heavy rain; the track up the 2,451-m (8,041-foot) volcano will be too slippery. Instead, we take rooms in a guest house at the foot of Gundaling hill, north of the town centre but closer to **Mount Sibayak**, so we'll have a head start when climbing the still-steaming 2,095-m (6,873-foot) volcano the next day.

Guides abound in Brastagi, but you won't need one for the easy three-hour climb up Sibayak, a well-trodden route that begins north of the town's colourful fruit and vegetable market. At a shack at the end of the pot-holed road, we pay the small charge for climbing Sibayak, sip fortifying cups of thick coffee, then follow a track that sidles around the volcano, seeming to go more downhill than up.

Two kilometres (1¼ miles) from the summit, a recently constructed hairpin-bend road leads to concrete steps and a path laid across the moonscape-like ridge, punctuated by murky green pools of sulphurous water and hissing geysers. The final 100m (330 feet) to the jagged summit, crowned by an unmanned weather-monitoring station, is too crumbly to climb safely without mountaineering gear, but we have a spectacular view of Mount Sinabung and the mountains encircling Lake Toba. Do bring something warm to wear, since the wind can chill to the bone.

We take a different, more taxing route down, towards the hot spring village of Semangat Gunung. Few of the 2,000-odd steps on the steep slope are intact, most having been washed away,

leaving a dangerously pitted path to negotiate. I take it slowly, but my legs are at full wobble by the time we emerge from the jungle at the tangle of rusting pipes that pump water to a thermal power station. A sign lists the people who have gone missing or got into difficulties climbing Sibayak, underlining the necessity to stick to the official route.

AN AFTERNOON IN PERBESI

The next stage of the journey takes us through the fertile countryside around Brastagi, the heartland of the Karo Batak people. It's dotted with their picturesque *adat* houses, easily identified by their distinctive thatched roofs, decorated with colourful gables and buffalo horns. The more isolated Karo villages, such as **Barusjahe** and **Dokan**, are the better ones to head to, being less touristy than places like **Lingga**, where you'll be asked to pay if you take photographs of the locals.

There are no pretty houses at our destination, the dusty pit stop of Perbesi on the main road south of Brastagi, but all we want to do is hire a four-wheel drive vehicle that can handle the deeply rutted mud track leading to the highland hamlet of Rih Tengah. A deal is struck at 1:30pm, we load our bags on board the Toyota Land Cruiser, and then we spend the next four hours cooling our heels while the driver and village mechanics ensure it's up to the demanding journey ahead. I pass the long afternoon hanging out with the locals, whose lips are stained livid red from chewing *sirih* (betelnut). Entertainment is provided by a squealing pig, trussed up in a sack, being hauled on to the roof of a bus that's already packed to the gills.

The dearth of public transport means that when the Land Cruiser is finally ready we find ourselves giving a ride to eight other people. They come in useful when, at one point, the Land Cruiser has to be pushed out of a particularly muddy spot. Night falls, cloaking the rolling highlands in total darkness. The mud

track becomes even more hellish, but the skilled, chain-smoking driver pushes on. Two and a half hours later, with much relief, we arrive in **Rih Tengah**, to be greeted by a gaggle of curious villagers. Mats are rolled out in one of the tin-roofed houses for us to sleep on and the evening ends with drinks by candlelight, the village generator having broken down.

LEFT The crater of a steaming Mount Sibayak
ABOVE and BELOW The decorative homes of Lake Toba's Batak people are distinguished by their sharply gabled saddleback roofs

CROSS-COUNTRY HIKE

It's raining the next day as we start a four-hour trek from the village to our campsite on the **Wampu River**. There's some discussion about getting an ox-drawn cart to transport the bags for part of the route, but in the end Halim hires three of the villagers as porters, one of whom carries his beloved "second wife"—a sky blue kayak made of cross-link polyethylene, a superstrong plastic used for modern white-water craft. They're soon well ahead of us on the route that leads past Rih Tengah's vegetable and rice fields, towards the

southeast corner of Gunung Leuser National Park.

The track plunges into a shady pine forest and then emerges on a plateau, where sharp-edged grass reaches to our armpits. All around are spell-bindingly beautiful hills, peeking out from between misty clouds, and in the distance I can hear rushing water, a sign that we're nearing the Wampu. For the 1.5-km (1-mile) downhill stretch to the river, I'm led hand-in-hand by one of the surefooted porters along a frighteningly steep track through a dense forest of spiky trees. As if this isn't nerve-racking enough, there's a final 800-m (900-yard)

WHITE–WATER DETAILS

The main rivers for white-water rafting, canoeing, or kayaking in north Sumatra are the Alas, flowing through Gunung Leuser National Park, the Wampu near Bukit Lawang, and the Asahan, south of Lake Toba. On the international scale of rating rapids (from I for leisurely to VI for highly dangerous), the most challenging river is the Asahan, which scores between IV and V; a journey along this should not be undertaken by the inexperienced.

The lower reaches of the Wampu and the Alas are fine for novices. Note that the American white-water specialists Sobek no longer run trips along the Alas, and Pacto (one of the main tour companies in Medan) is advising against it because of damage done to the jungle during the 1997 forest fires.

Rafting is a potentially dangerous activity so before signing up:

❑ Make sure you'll be provided with helmets and life jackets in good condition.

❑ Inspect the raft or canoe for wear and tear.

❑ Check there are spare paddles, in case any are lost during the journey.

course of slippery rocks to brave alongside the bubbling river before we reach the campsite close to the 30-m (98-foot) high Wampu waterfall.

We must cross the river to reach the campsite, so the black rubber inflatable canoe is unpacked and pumped up. Halim and Igun ferry me and our bags across and we just have enough time to bid farewell to the porters and put up one of our two tents before the rains start again, beating down in a torrent for most of the afternoon. By 5pm the storm has abated sufficiently for the camp to be better established, but the river has risen a couple of metres and has turned into frothy chocolate milkshake. We may have to spend an extra day in the jungle waiting for conditions to improve.

THE RIVER WILD

The next day the water level has dropped back and the Wampu is again sparkling in the sunlight. Halim feels we can run the rapids in relative safety, so we decamp and prepare for the river trip. With Halim leading the way in his kayak, I'm seated at the front of my canoe and Igun is steering from the rear. I get a quick lesson in paddling techniques, before our bags are loaded into the centre of the canoe and we set off towards the first set of rapids.

The closer you are to a river's source, the more frequent are the rapids. The higher water level has increased the current, cutting down the recovery time between the rapids and making this journey more fraught—or thrilling, depending on your point of view. My point of view, kneeling at the prow, legs wedged tightly into the sides, is nothing short of terrifying, as the rocks rear up at speed and foaming water crashes around me.

Be prepared to be thrown out of a canoe or raft on such a white-water expedition. Halim had briefed me the previous night on what to do if this happened: keep hold of your paddle and try to put your legs out in front of you, so you can bounce away from rocks. It might seem like you're swimming for ever, but eventually there'll be a calmer stretch of water where you'll be able to grab hold of a branch or rock on the river bank and wait for the expedition leader to pick you up.

We've been paddling down the Wampu only 15 minutes when crunch time comes. In furious rapids, we collide head on with an enormous black boulder, bounce off to one side and slide into a whirling watery abyss. The next thing I know is that I'm in the river, clinging on to a bent paddle and desperately shouting for help as I become human flotsam. Halim is soon beside me and I grab on to the kayak, only to see bags being swept away downstream. The only luggage saved is mine.

A SECOND DUNKING

The next major set of rapids is approached with more caution. A recent landslide has littered the river with dangerously sharp rocks and debris and the current is too fast for us to go through by canoe, so we spend an hour portering the craft along the river bank to safer waters. Then a navigation slip flips the canoe again and I'm back swimming, like a barking dog, through a good kilometre of the Wampu.

Dark clouds are gathering above and thunder rumbles ominously as we paddle on, aiming to make our landing point at Bohorok before nightfall. In counterpoint to the threatening weather and malevolent river conditions, the lush screen of virgin jungle, broken by waterfalls and cascades is truly beautiful.

The periods of calm between the rapids grow longer, the rains remain at bay, and by 2pm we've arrived at the point where the rafting day trips that operate from Bukit Lawang begin. The jungle thins out and locals start appearing on the river banks or in boats, fishing, washing or just playing in the now tamed waters. There are still some tricky rapids to be negotiated, but

A PROTECTED AREA

Now that much of Sumatra's lowland forest has been chopped down, Gunung Leuser National Park has become vital refuge for the island's rarest animals, including orangutans, rhinos, elephants, and tigers, not to mention thousands of other species of flora and fauna, some unique. Covering 800,000ha (2,000,000 acres) across north Sumatra and Aceh provinces, and including Gunung Leuser— at 3,455m (11,335 feet) the island's second highest mountain—it was one of five national parks established by Indonesia in 1980, but has been a protected area since the 1930s.

compared to what has gone before they feel like child's play and, weirdly, I find myself missing the mind-blowing thrill of what had gone before.

We pull up to the pebbly banks at 5pm, after eight shattering hours on the river. Halim and Igun have lost nearly all their gear, but we're delighted to have survived all that the Wampu could throw at us. Eddy, a chuckling local, brings his van to transport us the last couple of kilometres to the holiday cottages at Bukit Lawang and the first comfortable night's sleep I've had in three days.

GUNUNG LEUSER NATIONAL PARK AND ITS ORANGUTANS

What brings most visitors to **Bukit Lawang** isn't white-water rafting, but the opportunity to go trekking in **Gunung Leuser National Park**, the natural habitat of some 2,000–3,000 orangutan. Treks into the park and surrounding jungle are mainly organized from Bukit Lawang, which is on the park's eastern side, and **Kutacane**, in the central Alas Valley. The park headquarters are at **Tanah Merah**, 5km (3 miles) north of Kutacane, and you must stop off here or at the office in Bukit Lawang to arrange a permit.

If you want to be sure of seeing the remarkably human-like, but endangered apes—they live only in Sumatra and Borneo—the best place to head is the **Orangutan Rehabilitation Centre**, at the far western end of Bukit Lawang and the primary reason the village has boomed into a major pit stop on the Sumatran travel circuit in the last two decades. With extinction threatening the

species, the centre was set up by the World Wide Fund for Nature to retrain the apes for life back in the forest after years of caged or domesticated existence (there is a ready black market in

ABOVE White-water rafting and tubing— two ways to experience the currents of northern Sumatra's rivers
BELOW Feeding time at Bukit Lawang's Orangutan Rehabilitation Centre

Sumatra for these cuddly beasts as pets). With around 200 orangutan successfully rehabilitated since the centre began in 1973, their numbers have been boosted.

I attend the afternoon feeding session for the orangutans who have been released into the park. It's a stiff 15-minute hike up to the viewing platform in the jungle above the Bohorok River and for the first half hour no apes appear, the deliberately mono-tonous diet of bananas and milk having, perhaps, done its trick of encouraging them to search elsewhere in the forest for food.

Eventually a female ape, with a baby clinging to her hairy breast, comes swinging up to the platform for an after-noon snack. With no other takers, she gets to scoff the lot and delights the visitors by posing, supermodel-like, for the cameras.

Returning to the centre of Bukit Lawang, I pass several people floating in rubber tubes along the crystal clear waters of the Bohorok, a popular activity offered by many of the local guest houses. It looks fun and refreshing but, having just survived the roaring Dog River, I can wait awhile before I take another dip in Sumatra's wild rivers.

LAKE TOBA

There's no better place to kick back in north Sumatra than **Samosir**, a peninsula that rests like an island within the mystically beautiful **Lake Toba** (Danau Toba), 160km (100 miles) south of Medan. Formed some 75,000 years ago in a cataclysmic volcanic eruption, Lake Toba is the homeland of the Batak people, whose distinctive culture—encompassing beautifully decorated houses with sharply pointed projecting gables, elaborate tombs, and traditional singing and dancing—thrives in the villages of Samosir.

The best place to stay in Samosir is **Tuk Tuk**, a stubby outcrop on the west side of the island, and the ideal way to get around is to hire a moped (around 30,000Rp ($4)

CLIMBING GUNUNG LEUSER

The starting point for the ascent of Mount Leuser is the village of Blangkerjeren, just outside the northwest corner of the park. Set aside at least ten days for the climb, which progresses from virgin rain forest through steep, rocky montane forest to open alpine meadows.

per day including fuel). Don't bother with a full 90-km (55-mile) or so tour around Samosir's perimeter; the best stretch of road and views is from Tomok, near Tuk Tuk, round to Pangururan on the west coast, from where you can drive up to a panoramic viewpoint on Mount Belirang or take a diversion to a hot spring. Along the way, make sure you stop off in Simanindo, to catch one of the twice-daily (once on Sunday) morning dance shows, at the Batak Museum.

Another popular way to explore Samosir is to do the 45-km (28-mile) hike across the steep highlands. This can be done in a long day if you start early from **Pangururan**. Alternatively, you can start from Tomok, on the east side, and spend a night in the central village of **Ronggurni Huta**. This means you'll be tackling the steepest part of the climb first, but will get to the highest point before the afternoon clouds have settled on the lake, obscuring the view.

The most direct track is the steep, winding path that starts at **Ambarita** and takes you past the splendid **Simangande** waterfall, which cascades down the sheer cliffs, on the way to the village of **Dolok** in the mountains—a climb of around four hours. It's another 12km (7½ miles) from here to the small **Sidihoni Lake**, from where it's all downhill to Pangururan.

Think twice before taking a moped along this track as the road is in extremely poor condition. A very basic map is avail-able from the Gokhan Bookshop in Tuk Tuk, but it's as well to keep checking with locals along the route to make sure that you're on the right track.

GOING IT ALONE

INTERNAL TRAVEL

Medan, Sumatra's largest city, is the international gateway to northern prt of the island. Polonia International Airport is practically in the centre of the city, while ferries arrive at Belawan, 26km (16 miles) to the north. There's no reason for hanging around Medan longer than you have to and, if you arrive early enough, you should be able to make it to Bukit Lawang, Brastagi, or Lake Toba within a day.

The chaotic long-distance bus terminals are both on the outskirts of Medan; Amplas Terminal, 5km (3 miles) south of the centre, is for destinations south, including Lake Toba, while Pinang Baris Terminal, 9km (4½ miles) northwest of the centre, serves north-ern destinations, including Bukit Lawang, Brastagi, and Aceh.

Bus fares are cheap, but taxis are also relatively inexpensive, so worth considering for long-distance journeys; Poltaks is on Jl Brig. Jen. Katamso and you can either wait here for a shared taxi to fill up or charter the whole cab.

There are private minibus services, too, which link north Sumatra's main tourist destinations.

WHEN TO GO

The driest time of the year to travel in northern Sumatra is from May to September, with the onset of the rainy season from September to October. However, it's always hot and humid and, if you're trekking in the jungles you can count on rain at any time of the year.

WHAT TO TAKE

- ❏ Waterproof jacket.
- ❏ Walking boots.
- ❏ Warm clothes for nights.
- ❏ Insect repellent.
- ❏ Light, long-sleeved shirt and trousers to keep insects at bay.
- ❏ Waterproof bags to keep things dry while rafting.

RIVER TRIPS

In Bukit Lawang, the best rafting day trips are offered by Bohorok Adventures, at the Seven Cs tour office near Bukit Lawang Cottages (around $30). Wild River Adventures, near the bridge across to Anggrek Leuser Inn, and the Back to Nature Guesthouse, upriver towards the Orangutan Rehabilitation Centre, organize cheaper trips, but their gear isn't quite as good.

For longer trekking and raft-ing trips along the Wampu and other rivers in Sumatra contact P.T. O'Learys Indonesia Adventure Holidays (see Contacts).

GUNUNG LEUSER NATIONAL PARK

For details, pick up a copy of an excellent booklet by Mike Griffiths available from the visitors centre in Bukit Lawang and the headquarters in Tanah Merah.

The Orangutan Rehabilitation Centre is open to visitors daily 8–9am and 3–4pm. You must first get a permit from the PHPA office (daily 7am–3pm), in the centre of Bukit Lawang, for which you'll need to show your passport and pay 4,500Rp (60¢).

Hiring a guide for a hike or trek through the jungle costs from $10 per person. 2- and 3-day treks, including meals, camping gear, and permits cost from $35 and $50 per person. Inner tubes for floating down the Bohorok River can be hired from many outlets for 1,500–2,000Rp (20–25¢) a day.

The bus between Bukit Lawang and Brastagi goes via Medan; an alternative is to hike. The traditional route, taking 3 days, goes through areas largely cleared of jungle, and costs around $70 for a guide, camping gear and meals. Ask at the tourist office about the 4-day trek on a new track through the jungle for about $100.

HEALTH MATTERS

Malaria has been reported from Pulau Weh and from poor, remote areas of the mainland. The risk is much greater on Nias, off the west coast, and on most of the outlying islands, so you'll need to take precautions if travelling to these areas.

MORE TRIPS

Guest houses in **Brastagi** can arrange guides for hikes up both Mount Sibayak and Mount Sinabung. They also offer tours to the Karo villages in the surrounding area and into the jungle, including trips to Gunung Leuser National Park and rafting on the Alas River. The Sibayak chain of guest houses are a good first stop.

In **Bukit Lawang** it's also worth checking out trips to the settlement of Tangkahan, where you can stay at the Bamboo River Guesthouse.

From **Kutacane**, the place to head for is the rain forest research centre at Ketambe.

The Great Borobudur

by Christopher Knowles

Cradled by palm-covered hills and smoking volcanoes, a short distance outside the bustling sultanate of Yogyakarta, the immense Buddhist pyramid called Borobudur is an astounding testament to the genius of early Javan civilization.

Getting to Yogyakarta from Manila is a long business. And if at Manila airport you are assured that your luggage can go all the way through, don't believe it. The route takes you via Singapore and Jakarta where, unfortunately, you must clear immigration and customs, procedures that are likely to take some time. Long enough, certainly, to miss a connecting flight should it depart within an hour of landing, as in my case. Although the Indonesian people in general are congeniality itself, the immigration staff at Jakarta airport are, to put it mildly, unsympathetic to the plight of the harassed traveller. On the other hand, Garuda Airlines were perfectly willing to alter my ticket and put me on the next flight, some three hours later.

BELOW Some of Borobudur's 72 trellised stupas, each hiding a statue of Buddha

YOGYA BY NIGHT

Darkness had fallen over **Yogyakarta** by the time that flight touched down, but the heat was as stifling as if it were noon. As I emerged into the arrivals area a bunch of sweetly scented flowers was thrust into my arms and Roswitha introduced herself. Married to an Indonesian and resident in Yogya, as it is known, (and pronounced "Jogya"), for 12 years, she hailed from Munster, in Germany. Clearly half-besotted and half-infuriated with life in Indonesia, she exactly reflected the colourful, contradictory nature of the country.

My hotel, the Jogyakarta Village Inn, was an exceptionally attractive place to stay. Centrally located, it is built around a tropical garden of flowers and bushes, which screen a swimming pool. The bedroom, painted in the earthy shades of green and ochre that characterize

 A visit to Borobudur is difficult only for those who find great heat intolerable. The site is exposed to the sun and, to fully appreciate it, you must climb of several flights of steps. But with a sun hat and water, this should not be problem if you take the climb slowly.

★★ Yogya has all types of accommodation, but it is as well to try and find a hotel in the centre of the town in order to enjoy fully the atmosphere of the city. The Yogyakarta Village Inn has an excellent location and plenty of charm, and is reasonably priced.

For the trek up Mount Merapi you will be better off with walking boots, but trainers or stout shoes will do as long as there has been no rain. A torch will probably be offered by the guide, but a good one of your own is recommended. It may well be cool when you set out but when the sun comes up, the heat quickly follows. A waterproof is always a good idea. Take snacks, a water bottle, and your camera. A parasol, umbrella, or sun hat is essential for the visit to Borobudur.

Indonesian batik art, had a canopied iron bed and traditional furniture. Little ceramic pots containing various ointments are put out for guests' use. The dining room is an open-sided hall of richly decorated wood with the texture of fruit cake and looks out to the pool and garden.

But there was not much time to enjoy all of this. Roswitha took me off to dinner and then for a short tour of Yogyakarta at night. We wandered the night vegetable market, noting the presence of two very masculine transvestites, and then went on to the park in front of the Sultan's palace, or *kraton*, where a strange custom prevails. In the centre of the park there is a pair of large trees; at the roadside a vendor rents out blindfolds to passersby. Don your blindfold and try to walk from the edge of the park to a point between the trees: if successful, make a wish and it will come true. Needless to say, what seems easy turns out to be practically impossible. The chances are that what may assuredly seem to be a straight line will become a 90° turn. I certainly found it to be so, although the stifled giggles of Roswitha, who thought that she was following me stealthily, hardly helped.

PRESERVED FOR PROSPERITY

The pyramid complex at Borobudur is absolutley massive, and it is astonishing that the monument has survived so completely and in such condition. Fortunately for us, it was buried under volcanic ash until 1815 and, although it has since suffered as a result of lightning, colonial rapacity, and bombs planted by political extremists, a complete restoration project was undertaken between 1973 and 1984. This, according to Mathias, involved the complete dismemberment of the monument followed by a laborious, stone by stone, reconstruction.

MARKETS AND MARKETEERS

Yogyakarta, lying in Central Java, about 40km (25 miles) inland from the Indian Ocean, is an attractive, restless town of shops, markets, palaces, and classical Dutch architecture. Generally considered to be the cultural heart of Java, with its own identity, even, to some extent, its own distinctive life, Yogya is immensely proud of its traditions and, above all, of its royal family.

All this I learned next day from Mathias, who was to take me to Borobudur that afternoon. In the morning, however, there was a chance to delve into the workings of the city. At a district market I was introduced to the various fruits, cereals, and nuts of the area, and to the different types of soya. The marketeers, each of whom sat with an air of seeming contentment and unending patience, were keen to sell their wares to a foreigner, just for the fun of it—but, to be honest, there was not much I could do with a kilo of tapioca. It was interesting, however, to note how neighbouring sellers tended to deal in the same wares with no apparent jealousy, a neighbourly homogeneity that was replicated in the pottery area, on the edge of Yogya, which is almost a village in its own right, composed entirely of pottery workshops. Although each piece is beautifully coloured and exquisitely crafted, mostly by hand, much of the pottery could be used for practical purposes, as well as decorative ones, while it is has the additional merit of being very, very cheap.

Although **Borobudur** is located only some 40km (25 miles) northwest of Yogya, it took a good hour to get there because of the fickle nature of the traffic. And there were other obstacles to our progress: every time we came to a halt at a junction, or at traffic lights, young musicians appeared at the windows to serenade us—not, it is sad to report, because of love of music and zest for life, but because of Indonesia's economic plight. Within Indonesia, Java, which has a huge population, has been hit especially hard. It was ironic that in a country that at first seems so filled with good things, where markets are overflowing with food, many people are unable to buy enough to eat.

The reason to visit Borobudur is to see the massive decorated ziggurat that ranks with Angkor Wat in Cambodia as one of the great relics of Buddhism in Southeast Asia. Built atop a small rise facing Mount Merapi and partially surrounded by hills and vast tracts of coconut palms, it stands in an extensive park, where once would have stood a settlement dedicated to the shrine.

Exposed as the site is, the sun beats down on it unrelentingly. The pyramid itself is a 20-minute walk from the entrance, brushing aside the many offers of drinks, coconuts, parasols, and assorted souvenirs, all of which are thrust in your face en route. If you can avoid making eye contact with the pedlars, they will eventually peel away; but should you inadvertently acknowledge their presence, then it is a devil of a job to shake them off. In the heat the constant badgering can be wearing.

In Buddha's footsteps

Given that Borobudur is one of the major attractions of Java, there are times, apparently, when the site becomes crowded, its great size notwithstanding. The early morning is therefore the best time for seeing it, before the onset both of visitors and of the great heat. On the day of my visit, however,

From Yogyakarta to Borobudur

there was almost nobody at Borobudur, which may have explained the constant, desperate attentions of the sellers. The pyramid itself is immense. Built of grey stone bricks between A.D. 750 and 850, it is far broader than it is high, and its sombre imposition on the countryside brings to mind a blackened Victorian Gothic cathedral. Whilst the overall shape is pyramidal, it is not a straight-line pyramid like those in Egypt. There are six square terraces rising to four circular platforms upon which is a series of bell-shaped stupas. The walls of the various terraces are decorated with finely chiselled relief sculptures that tell the story of the life of Buddha and illustrate the Buddhist cosmic vision.

THE ART OF BATIK

Batik is found elsewhere in the region, but is a speciality above all of Java, and in particular of Yogya. The meaning of the word batik is obscure, although it may derive from the Malay word tik, to drip, and perhaps succeeded tattooing as a mark of status. Essentially batik is a form of resist dyeing woven cloth, the resistance provided by beeswax. Traditionally, the liquid wax is poured on to the cloth from a pot with a long spout, a process nowadays largely replaced with stamping. There may follow a number of rewaxings and dyeings, during which the batik sometimes cracks. Although Westerners regard cracking to be a characteristic of batik, Indonesians tend to regard it as a flaw.

To understand the story as told on the monument, you should follow the so-called Pilgrims' Way by walking clockwise from the eastern gate, which is probably the first one you will come to. The whole route has a total length of about 5km (3 miles). If this is too much to ask on a hot day, all you need to do is look at any one piece of sculpture and simply wonder at the skill and artistry of the craftsmen and architects and perhaps gain some insight into Buddhist philosophy or Javanese life 1,200 years ago.

Mathias had very sensibly allowed me to go to the top alone, from where there are extensive views of the encircling countryside and, importantly, a cooling breeze—if you find yourself in the right position to catch it. Meanwhile, at the bottom, Mathias waited for me in the shade of a tree. As the sun began to set, we made our way beneath willowy palms and amid flowers in all their gilded tropical brilliance back to the park, where we sat and drank coconut milk directly from the shell, before returning to the hotel.

PROBLEMS WITH POLYGAMY

Later that night (at 1:30 the next morning, to be precise), I was to meet Mathias again, prior to the trek up the slopes of **Mount Merapi**. In the meantime, after dinner, Roswitha turned up to show me more of the town. There was a choice—either the traditional shadow puppets, or traditional Javanese dance.

We went to the dance, which took place in a small open theatre in a back street. Sadly, we were the only members of the audience. The dances, sedate in the extreme, are hypnotic. The gorgeously costumed, exquisite dancers exhibit daunting powers of physical control in performing convoluted, highly symbolic stories at the slowest pace imaginable. The orchestra, largely made up of traditional gongs and drums, performed in that desultory, though precise, fashion that is the hallmark of musicians throughout much of Asia. They talked , smoked, and dozed all the way through the performance as if they were altogether detached from it; yet they never missed a cue or a beat, and remained in exact unison at all times.

ABOVE The scale of Borobudur is startling: over 2 million blocks of andesite were used
BELOW LEFT Dancers prepare for a performance at a kraton, *or palace*

After the performance, Roswitha suggested that we drop in at another *kraton*, this one belonging to the sultan's brother. It was his birthday the next day (he has a birthday every 35 days) and there was to be more dance and music in his honour. As before, the performance was to take place in an open-sided hall. The large orchestra was in place, but since there appeared to be a break in the proceedings Roswitha led me around the back of the hall to have a look at another royal room. We poked our heads around a doorway to find the sultan's brother himself, in full regalia, in conversation with some cronies over a cigarette and a cup of tea. Roswitha asked in her fluent Javanese if we might have a look around. Permission was granted, and we inspected the ornate, dimly lit hall, which seemed to be a cross between a chapel and a ceremonial chamber. There was a single large shrine, surrounded with ornate script and symbols, and several portraits. After the show, as we made to leave, the Sultan's brother engaged us in conversation, and then asked us to sit down to take some tepid, sweet tea with him and his friends.

We sat there for a good hour in the stifling heat of the the tropical night, listening to their conversation—which, Roswitha disclosed to me with a smirk, was largely "boys' talk." Certainly, there was a lot of laughter over the difficulties this man was having with his four wives, of varying ages. It was, to me, curious how they were prepared to talk about these things before a Western woman in a way that, I felt sure, they would be unwilling to repeat before an Indonesian.

Entertaining though it all was, there was the little matter of having to get up at 1:30am for the trip to Merapi, so we made our excuses and left.

AN EARLY START

Mathias duly arrived at the appointed hour and we set off. The journey, in the same general direction as Borobudur, was much quicker than it had been the day before. Shortly after 2am, having followed a winding road up the lower slopes of Merapi, we came to the village of **Kaliurang**, at 900m (2,950 feet), and the Vogel Hotel, from where the trek was to begin. The place was in complete darkness, and there was no sign of life. After a while Mathias was able to rouse somebody, the lights went on and a few other walkers (who sensibly had stayed in the hotel and therefore didn't have to get up so early) began to drift in.

By about 3am everyone was ready, at which point our guide delivered a briefing on the volcano and its inherent dangers. It seemed that since **Merapi**, one of the six most active volcanoes in the world, had been fairly active at that time, we were not allowed to go beyond the edge of the so-called "Danger Area;" and that before we left a telephone call would be made to a volcano observatory to obtain up-to-date activity readings. We were assured, furthermore, that the guide would be carrying a mobile telephone in case the observatory should need to contact him; and that in the event of an imminent eruption, we would probably have about an hour to get back down again. All of which, though no doubt true, was delivered with melodramatic gravity. It transpired that one of the reasons we were to undertake the trek at that ungodly hour—apart from catching the sunrise— was that volcanic activity tended to take place in the early morning, shortly after dawn. Finally, after being issued with torches, we set off, leaving Mathias to return to the minibus for a sleep.

ROUTE MARCH TO THE CONE

To begin with, the route took us along roads, and then along stony paths that fairly quickly entered woodland, or forest. Of course, even with torches, we were unable to see very much. But the sounds of the forest, the clickings and whirrings of insects, the occasional hooting of a bird, were all around us. Soon the path was no more than a mud trail, along which we were marching at a considerable rate. Why we had to proceed with such urgency was not clear, although it did somehow inject a hint of drama into proceedings. Still, after an hour we rested for a few minutes, and took the opportunity to unwrap a bar of chocolate and take a few sips from a water bottle. There followed another 45 minutes' forced march, until eventually we came to a halt at a grassy platform not so very far from the tree line at the base of Merapi's cone, which we could but indistinctly make out as the first glimmers of light appeared. At this point our guide retired to the shade of the nearest tree for a little sleep.

We had hoped that in the gloom we would witness the orange and red glow of lava dribbling down the side of the cone. Sometimes it is possible to see it, apparently, but not that morning. The sun rose around us and the lights of the city below became paler and paler. Now we could clearly see Merapi's classic volcanic cone, which rises to 2,911m (9,550 feet), and the constant drift of steam from its crater. In front of us, a long winding slash in the undergrowth, like a grey river coursing down from the summit, turned out to be the route of the last serious lava flow. After a while we clambered down on to it, climbing over the boulders that the hot lava had dragged down with it, and brushing against the coal that was created there and then as trees were incinerated in the extreme heat. Part of our descent took us along this lava river before we rejoined the path through the trees.

By now the sun was fully risen, warming the forest to the usual high levels of humidity. Our guide suddenly ducked into the undergrowth to re-emerge clutching a massive spider that covered most of his face as he held it up for our disgusted delectation. It was not venomous, of course, but the sheer size of it could frighten you to death.

Before long we stopped again, for breakfast, at a little forest kitchen and café made of leaves and sticks. There was tea or coffee, as many banana fritters as you could eat; and a most beautiful view of Merapi, which against a blue sky and framed by palm and pine, made the perfect volcanic picture. The rest of the descent was a pleasant saunter among jackfruit trees, whose globular green fruit was being harvested by pickers on ladders, down to Kaliuran, where Mathias emerged from the minibus, rested and serene.

GOING IT ALONE

INTERNAL TRAVEL

By air The jumping-off point for a visit either to Borobudur or Mount Merapi is the fascinating city of Yogyakarta, which lies in the eastern part of the island of Java, in Indonesia. Yogya is most conveniently reached by air from Jakarta, from where there are several flights each day on the Indonesian national airline, Garuda. Flying time is about 1 hour. There are also regular daily flights to and from Denpasar, capital of Bali, which last about 45 minutes.

By bus A comprehensive bus service links all the major towns of Java and Bali. Ticket prices reflect whether the buses have air-conditioning or not. The journey from Jakarta to Jogya, a distance of about 700km (440 miles), is 12 hours; from Surabaya the journey time is 8 hours; from Denpasar in Bali 16 hours. Yogya bus station is some 4km (2½ miles) southeast of the city centre. Note that privately run luxury buses also operate these routes at greater expense (find agent offices at the bus station and in the city centre).

By train Yogya's railway station is in the centre of the city and is linked to both Jakarta and Surabaya.

There are several classes of carriage:'Ekonomi' class with wooden seats and no reservation; 'Bisnis', with comfortable seats and fans;'Eksekutif' with air-conditioning. There are also sleepers on the most luxurious services.

Journey time to Yogya from Jakarta is between 9 and 12 hours, from Surabaya between 5 and 7 hours. Prices at the lower end of the scale are very cheap, while the cost of the most comfortable services approaches that of flying.

WHEN TO GO

Temperatures, which 25/26°C (47/49°F), do not really vary throughout the year. However, the dry season coincides with the so-called east monsoon between June and August, so this is probably the best time for visiting.

GUIDED TOURS FROM YOGYA

Once in Yogya, it is very easy to make arrangements for guided visits around the city, and to Borobudur and to Mount Merapi. Getting around the city by oneself is not difficult, but if you are short of time, and given the heat and the distances involved, a guide with transportation is definitely recommended. Paramita Tours (see Contacts) offers a friendly, reliable service and can arrange visits and accommodation.

GETTING FROM YOGYA TO BORUBUDUR

To get to Borobudur by yourself from Yogya you can either go by taxi or (much cheaper) take a bus from the bus station or from a stop on Jalan Magelang, in the city centre (1½ hours). There is a bus to Kaliurang for the climb up Merapi.

WHAT TO TAKE

- ❏ Sun hat and cream.
- ❏ Comfortable shoes with good grip or walking boots.
- ❏ Rucksack.
- ❏ Torch.
- ❏ Waterproof jacket.
- ❏ Camera film.
- ❏ Insect repellent.
- ❏ Bottled water.

HEALTH MATTERS

- ❏ Take anti-malaria tablets.
- ❏ Use mosquito repellent and coils.
- ❏ Wear long trousers and long-sleeved shirts at night.
- ❏ Bring a basic health kit.
- ❏ Drink bottled water.
- ❏ Arrange full medical insurance before departure.
- ❏ Check on vaccinations at least a month before leaving home.

THE SULTAN OF YOGYA

Yogya was founded only in the 18th century by Prince Mangkubumi after a dispute with his brother the Susuhunan of Surakarta. The prince assumed the title of sultan and the dynastic name Hamengkubuwono, which means the universe in the lap of the king.

For a while Yogya became the most powerful Javanese state and later a symbol of independence as a result of its stance against the Dutch colonialists. As a result, Yogya became a Special District answerable directly to Jakarta, and although the Sultanate no longer exists, the current Sultan, who continues to live in the *kraton*, has become the local governor, a reflection of genuine popular support.

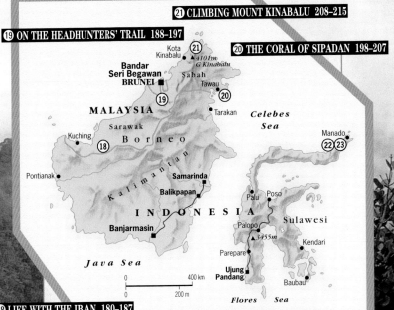

21 CLIMBING MOUNT KINABALU 208–215

19 ON THE HEADHUNTERS' TRAIL 188–197

20 THE CORAL OF SIPADAN 198–207

18 LIFE WITH THE IBAN 180–187

22 THE TARSIERS OF TANGKOKO 216–223

23 MANADO'S CORAL PARADISE 224–233

Kota
Kinabalu
▲ 4101m
G. Kinabalu
**Bandar
Seri Begawan
BRUNEI** ■
Sabah
Tawau
MALAYSIA
Tarakan
*Celebes
Sea*
Manado
Kuching
Sarawak
B o r n e o
Pontianak
K a l i m a n t a n
Samarinda
Balikpapan
Palu
Poso
I N D O N E S I A
Palopo
Sulawesi
Banjarmasin
▲ 3455m
Kendari
Parepare
Java Sea
0   400 km
0   200 m
**Ujung
Pandang**
Baubau
Flores   Sea

BORNEO•SULAWESI

T he islands of Borneo and Sulawesi, both straddling the Equator, are among the largest in Southeast Asia. Borneo, composed of the independent sultanate of Brunei, the states of Sabah and Sarawak (parts of Malaysia), and of Kalimantan (belonging to Indonesia), has always caught the imagination of Westerners, and with good reason. It is a land renowned as the home of the orangutan and the world's largest flower, of one of the highest mountains in Southeast Asia, of some of the best diving in the world, and of people who still live in longhouses. Sulawesi (formerly known as Celebes), lying across the Macassar Strait to the east, is altogether different. Highly volcanic, it is divided into four provinces, known simply as North, South, Central and Southeast Sulawesi. Nowhere on the long, asymmetrically shaped island is more than 40km (25 miles) from the sea, yet, as the island is composed largely of mountain, rift valley, and torrential rivers, getting from one part of the island to the other—even by sea—was, until the advent of the aeroplane hazardous. So Sulawesi, too, is a place of fabulous variety.

*Razor-sharp Pinnacles are a feature of Gunung Mulu
National Park, northeast Sarawak*

BORNEO

Life with the Iban

by Simon Richmond

In the far reaches of the beautiful Batang Ai river system, the Iban, Sarawak's largest indigenous tribe, still live in wooden longhouses and practise ancient forms of farming and hunting. I ventured on an extended tour from Kuching, the best way to gain a fascinating insight into their life.

Also known as Sea Dyaks, though they live hundreds of kilometres from the ocean, the Iban make up around a third of Sarawak's population. In this Malaysian state on the northwest flank of Borneo, the medley of races splinters into even finer subdivisions with the indigenous people— known collectively as Dyaks—comprising the Iban, Bidayuh (or Land Dyaks), Melanau, Kayan, Kenyah, Kelabit, and Penan. These last two are sometimes grouped together under the name Orang Ulu, "people of the interior." And it is to meet such people—and to visit their homes, known as longhouses—that many travellers come to Sarawak.

As a visitor to **Batang Ali**, I look at the jungle and see a thick mass of exotic trees, plants, grasses and creepers. However, the Iban, my guide Christopher (himself an Iban tribesman) tells me, see a supermarket, hospital, and warehouse. Moving swiftly from one plant to another, Christopher points out food, medicine, emergency water supplies, fishing rods and nets, weaving material, even protection against evil spirits.

Later, we stand at the crest of the hill in **Kuching**, watching over the Hilton Batang Ai Longhouse Resort and the beguilingly beautiful man-made lake on which it sits. Here a giant Chinese urn marks the 90-year-old tomb of an Iban warrior. Every year, relatives pay their respects at this spot, leaving offerings of money and bottles of *tuak*, the local grog. The lake may have flooded traditional Iban lands, but ancient rituals continue.

PREPARING FOR THE TRIP

My journey to Batang Ai had begun four days earlier in the appealing capital city Kuching, former seat of power of the Brooke family, the White Rajahs of Sarawak for just over a century from 1841. Although Kuching is now a thoroughly modern Malaysian city, it has managed to retain its colonial charm—best appreciated on a walking tour of the compact centre, where a fort and imposing neo-classical style buildings nestle side by side with Chinese shophouses, mosques and a colourful, lively riverside market.

The best place in Kuching to prepare for any trip to a longhouse is the excellent (and free) **Sarawak Museum**,

 In the dry season, you must expect to have to get out of the longboats and push them over the rockier rapids. The jungle trekking is easy, but requires a general level of fitness.

★★ If you want comfort, the only option is to stay at the Hilton Batang Ai Longhouse Resort and take day trips to the genuine longhouses. Otherwise, expect to rough it to some degree. To be fair, the Hilton's longhouses, despite successfully combining the comforts of a top-class hotel with the adventure of the jungle, are not what most people have in mind. The resort, however, does provide a fantastic opportunity to relax at the beginning or end of a journey deeper into the Batang Ai National Park and surrounding river areas to find the real thing.

Take binoculars to view the birdlife in the jungles and around the rivers. You'll also need good walking boots if you're going jungle trekking.

Iban territory

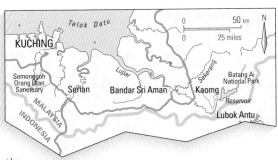

housed, incongruously, in a mansion bult in the style typical of Normandy, France, and set in manicured gardens. There is also a more modern building across the main road, Jalan Tun Abang Haji Openg. Exhibits include stuffed and preserved wildlife, including the skeleton of a giant snake and a dental plate recovered from the stomach of a crocodile. In the ethnographic section find recreated longhouse interiors of different tribes, displays of wood carvings and evocative black and white photographs that give an impression of how life was once lived by Sarawak's tribes.

To experience what life is like for the jungle-dwelling Iban today, I join a tour organized by Borneo Adventure to their adopted longhouse **Nanga Sumpa**, one of the most remote in the Batang Ai area. The initial road journey by air-conditioned minibus towards the hydro-electricity dam that created the Batang Ai reservoir, some 250km (155 miles) east of Kuching, will take four hours, to be followed by a 1½-hour longboat ride to the longhouse on the Delok River.

Mathew, my guide for this trip, is a personable 30-year-old Bidayuh. I'm also joining Marci, an energetic, middle-aged Texan businesswoman now living in Australia. While Mathew shops for food supplies at the bustling market town of Serian, I have fun sampling exotic local produce. These include *jering*, a sour-tasting fruit inside a tough khaki shell shaped like that of a terrapin, the floury-textured, ruddy orange-coloured *buah tamong*, and the vinegary *asam paya*—hard brown berries on a stick. Serian's Chinese-run general stores are also well stocked with suitable gifts for the constant stream of longhouse visitors.

ACROSS THE RESERVOIR

Having paused for lunch at a Chinese restaurant in the tiny village of **Lachau**, we finally arrive at the reservoir jetty by 3:30pm. The boatman taps his watch anxiously as we load our gear into the longboat for the smooth journey across the crystal-clear man-made lake. A disastrous flash flood the week before has put the locals on safety alert, so it's important to reach the longhouse before any afternoon rains set in.

Captaining the boat is Jonathan, the Iban elder in charge of tourism at Nanga Sumpa, while Manang, the community's shaman, navigates the river channels, past drifting logs and branches torn by the flood. Swallows swoop low over the astoundingly beautiful waters, the surface of which mirrors the surrounding jungle and skies.

When the dam was completed in 1985 it flooded an area of around 90sq km (35 square miles), submerging

---

ARTS AND CRAFTS

To be sure of buying authentic examples of Sarawak craft, such as wood carvings, woven baskets, mats, and the distinctively patterned *pua kumbu* cloth, wait until you visit a longhouse, where such goods are often sold, and generally much cheaper than in Kuching, although the range is much wider there; explore the shops of Main Bazaar, but be aware that many of the cheaper items will be from Kalimantan, the Indonesian side of Borneo.

sections of the Lemanak, Engkari, and Ulu Ai river valleys. Batang Ai National Park, created in 1990 and covering just over 24,000ha (60,000 acres), begins at the confluence of the Engkari and Ai rivers. We glide past the park offices and the small boarding school for children from the surrounding longhouses.

ABOVE Cooking sticky rice and chicken in bamboo, a local delicacy
BELOW Traditionally, longhouse visitors are entertained with dancing and music
RIGHT Many Iban longhouses are nowadays roofed with corrugated iron

On the steep river banks patches of jungle are being cleared to plant rice and other crops. The mountains rising above the dipterocarp rain forest mark the border with Kalimantan, Indonesian Borneo, and the country from which the Iban migrated several centuries earlier in search of new land to cultivate. It was during this expansion period, from the 16th to the 19th centuries, that the Iban fought with the Melanau and Bidayuh tribes along Sarawak's coast and the practice of head-hunting gained notoriety.

B O R N E O

LONGHOUSE STYLE

You'll search in vain for severed heads in longhouses today. Likewise, if you're harbouring thoughts of longhouses as rustic time capsules, and their residents as semi-naked peasants, think again. Nanga Sumpa, like many other longhouses, is populated by shrewd folk dressed in baseball caps and T-shirts. One home has a television, where the community gathers to watch sporting events such as the World Cup; and posters of pop singers, soccer heroes, and movie stars adorn some walls. But I soon learned that, despite these modern trappings, in many other respects this is a traditional Iban dwelling.

Made of wood and raised on stilts, **Nanga Sumpa** stands beside the river, which serves as the water supply, sanitation system, and transport network. Squealing piglets and scruffy cocks (used for cock fighting, a favourite pastime) rummage in the garbage and muddy puddles beneath the carved log ladder leading up to the longhouse. The main building is a row of 28 individual apartments under a shared roof, home to around 200 people.

Each family has their own *bilik* (living space), which might be divided between living/sleeping room and kitchen. Inside each *bilik* the most treasured possessions will be the giant antique Chinese urns, used for storing food. Other possessions, such as the specially woven mats for sitting on, are stored in the *sadau* (loft) above. The *ruai* is the covered corridor running the length of the longhouse and used communally as a living space, while outside is a parallel *tanju* (open platform).

Along the *ruai*, residents are whittling away at a wood carvings, weaving *pua kumbu* (the traditionally patterned blankets), idly gossiping or just snoozing in the shade. Lounging pet dogs and energetic children complete the picture. The posse of kids who had greeted our arrival hang around as we check into the guesthouse on the opposite side of the river from the longhouse.

At other longhouses the correct form is to be introduced to the *tuai rumah*, the headman, and offered a sleeping spot on the *ruai*. But I'm glad of the arrangement at Nanga Sumpa, which maintains a degree of privacy for both Iban and visitor. The guesthouse is decorated with pretty local crafts, and has comfortable mattresses protected by mosquito nets, and decent showers.

FISHING IBAN-STYLE

The next day, in the company of local tribesmen Johnny and Muntai, we head further upriver to stay overnight in one of Borneo Adventure's basic wooden jungle cabins in an idyllic part of the jungle. These furthest reaches of the **Batang Ai National Park** are home to hornbills, gibbons, wild boar, and the increasingly rare orangutan, which we hope to spot on a trek into the hills.

The river narrows and twists over rapids en route to the cabins. We pause while the guides chop down bamboo, whose trimmed stems are used as improvised cooking pots. Muntai also demonstrates the *jala*, the weighted net used in traditional Iban fishing. With a third of the net draped over one shoulder and the remaining two-thirds bunched in each hand, he casts the net in a single fluid motion so that it fans out in a graceful circle before sinking and trapping the fish underneath it.

In the hands of an expert such as Muntai, who can also pick the right spot on the river, the *jala* will yield a healthy supper. During the languid afternoon, Mathew and I practise casting on the pebbly river bank in front of the wooden cabin, but without success. We feel only slightly better when Johnny and Muntai return empty-handed from their night-time hunting expedition in the jungle.

In the morning we cross the river and follow the trail up the mountain ridge in search of orangutan. Mathew cautions us to tread quietly so as not to disturb the wildlife, but during the two-hour trek the only sign of the apes is their empty nests in the upper branches of the trees. Still, the sweeping views from the ridge across the mountains towards Kalimantan are worth the walk, and the boat journey back is serenely beautiful.

Longhouses like Nanga Sumpa might make some of their living from tourism, but it's farming that provides the steady income. During the day most able-bodied Iban are out tending crops or preparing the jungle for future plantings. A contingent passes by as we cool off at a waterfall and swimming hole on the way back to Nanga Sumpa.

EVENING ENTERTAINMENT

After a riverside picnic we return to the longhouse for our final evening. Marci and I join some more guests and cross the bridge to the longhouse for the formal presentation of gifts to the *tuai rumah* and some informal evening entertainment. A few Iban have put on their best sarongs, but otherwise there are no traditional costumes. The long-house children are gathered against one wall. Some shyly come forward to perform their slinky little dances, while others jive around confidently.

It's the done thing to join in, so Marci and I demonstrate our own halting moves to the rhythmic beat pounded out on the *engkeramung*, a gamelan-like instrument of gongs and chimes. When the dancing is over, the longhouse women rush forward to display their handicrafts: patterned *pua kumbu*, wood carvings, baskets, beads, and distinctive black clay pottery—an ancient tribal craft revived in this community. There's no obligation to buy, but the clay pots are so exquisite it's hard to resist.

The following morning the heavens open and the river begins to swell. Fearful of another flood, we waste no time on protracted goodbyes. In the boat, half-closing my eyes against the driving rain, I'm glad that I'll have a day to relax and dry out back at the Hilton resort. But Marci throws herself into the spirit of the journey; she keeps reminding me, "It's an adventure!" And so it is.

LONGHOUSE ETIQUETTE

❑ Only enter a longhouse following your guide or having first been invited in: apart from being disrespectful, there may be a temporary *pemali* (taboo) on new visitors because of a recent childbirth or death.

❑ Remove your shoes, particularly before entering the individual living quarters of the longhouse or sitting on the woven mats rolled out along the communal area.

❑ Be modest: old ladies may walk around bare-breasted, but don't take this as a cue for topless sunbathing. Wear shorts or a sarong when swimming or washing in the river.

❑ Present gifts directly to the headman, who will distribute them accordingly.

❑ Accept the food and drink you're offered, if only to try a little, and don't worry that you're eating too much since it's polite to entertain guests lavishly.

GOING IT ALONE

INTERNAL TRAVEL

There are regular flights to Kuching airport, 11km (9 miles) south of the city, from Kuala Lumpur, Singapore, and Kota Kinabalu, as well as a few other regional Malaysian cities. A taxi into the city costs RM16.50 ($4); buy a coupon from the kiosk by the taxi stand outside the airport.

WHEN TO GO

Any time of the year, but it's best to check with the tourist offices and travel agents on any strange weather patterns that might threaten to put certain sections of the jungle out of bounds; it's no fun being caught out by a flash flood.

PLANNING

The recommended way to organize a trip to an Iban longhouse is through a reputable travel agent in Kuching (see Contacts); many of the communities are linked to particular companies. It's important to choose your agent carefully since some longhouses—particularly along the Skrang and Lemanak rivers—have developed bad reputations for being tourist traps.

Things to look out for when booking a tour include:

❏ How far away the longhouse is—the shorter the journey, the more likely it is that the community will have become jaded with constant foreign visitors.
❏ Whether the company provides lifejackets for the boat rides.
❏ What meals are included.
❏ Where you'll be sleeping—the better outfits have their own accommodation away from the main longhouse to minimize visitors' impact on daily life.

If you opt to stay at the Hilton Batang Ai Longhouse Resort, you can arrange day trips to a range of longhouses in the area. The resort also offers fishing, jungle trekking, and mountain biking tours.

If you're determined to do a longhouse trip solo, be prepared to pay for expensive boat charters and for a lot of waiting around and chatting to locals en route to the Batang Ai area. Head for Sri Aman, 150km (95 miles) southeast of Kuching, the starting point for trips up the Skrang River. Further away from Kuching, it's also possible to arrange visits to longhouses along the Batang Rajang River.

HEALTH MATTERS

❏ Take anti-malaria tablets.
❏ Use mosquito repellent and coils.
❏ At night wear trousers and long-sleeved shirts.
❏ Bring a basic health kit.
❏ Drink bottled water.
❏ Arrange medical insurance before departure.
❏ Check on vaccinations at least a month before leaving home.

WHAT TO TAKE

❏ Walking boots for jungle trekking.
❏ Waterproof jacket.
❏ Gifts to present at the longhouses.
❏ Insect repellent.

LEFT and INSET Sarawak's rivers are still the Iban's lifeline: their houses line the country's river banks

EATING AND DRINKING

Fish, chicken, rice, and local vegetables, such as jungle ferns, form the basis of Iban cuisine. On well-organized trips you'll get the chance to try sticky rice and chicken steamed in bamboo. Larger longhouses may have a small shop selling basic provisions—this will be the only opportunity you'll have to buy snacks and drinks to supplement what you bring with you. *Tuak* (rice wine), the traditional Iban tipple, tastes a bit like dry sherry and is very palatable; you'll be offered some in the longhouse while watching the dances. At some places these dances are performed in traditional costumes, while at others it's something you pay extra for. If you're uncomfortable with the contrived nature of such displays, consider timing your visit to coincide with the *gawai* (harvest) festivals in May and June, when the merrymaking is authentic.

BORNEO

On the Headhunters' Trail

by Simon Richmond

*Giant caves, home to millions of bats, are the introduction to the Gunung
Mulu National Park in northeast Sarawak. You can hike and boat along the
park's historic jungle trail, and there is also the chance to scale the
lethally sharp Pinnacles.*

I was prepared to be disappointed.
With so many of the world's great
caves now easily accessible to visitors, it's increasingly difficult to get
worked up about yet another illuminated
interior of weirdly shaped stalactites and
stalagmites. Deer Cave in **Gunung Mulu
National Park**, Sarawak, however, is
something else.

For starters it's thought to be the
world's largest cave passage—just over
2km (1¼ miles) long, 174m (580 feet)
wide, and 122m (400 feet) high—big
enough to accommodate a fleet of jumbo
jets. To take in the full grandeur of the
cavern entrance you must sit down and
tilt your head as far back as it will go.

4 The Headhunters' Trail is easy to follow but it
does get waterlogged and there's a river to
ford. The mountain climbs should not be
approached lightly, and the Pinnacles trail is
especially taxing because of the slippy,
jagged rocks.

★ Apart from the Royal Mulu Resort at the park
entrance, expect no frills at the camps,
beyond what you bring in your own backpack.

 A good pair of walking shoes, sun hat, large
water bottle, rain and swimming gear, a torch,
insect repellent, and sarong (to use as a sheet
and/or a towel) are all essential items. An air
mattress and earplugs are recommended if
you're aiming to sleep in the jungle, while a
long-sleeved shirt and trousers will also serve
as protection at night from the insects.
Essential equipment for adventure caving
includes a torch and, preferably, a helmet.
More specialist equipment is not available
within the park so you'll have to bring it
yourself. For climbs up Gunung Mulu you'll
also need a sleeping bag.

The local Penan and Berawan people
called it Gua Payau or Gua Rusa, both
meaning **Deer Cave**, because this is
where the animals used to shelter. These
days the constant stream of visitors
keeps away the deer, but not the cave's
other inhabitants: over a million bats. In
good weather, the best viewing time is
dusk, when the bats emerge, in a
malevolent cloud of flapping black
wings, from the dark recesses of the
cave to hunt for food.

As I arrive at the cave it's beginning
to rain, so there will be no mass exodus.
However, evidence of the bats is all
around. The first thing to register is the
overwhelming smell of ammonia, rising
from bat guano that coats the cave floor
in a seething brown sludge. Three to
six tons of the stuff are deposited each
day, creating a moist environment for
millions of tiny creatures—which makes
me glad that I'm wearing a hat and a
tough pair of boots.

A little way into the passage, our
guide, Veno, tells us to look up, back
towards the southern entrance. At this
point the rocks briefly conspire to create
the silhouetted profile of Abraham
Lincoln (although British visitors might
think the face, with its prominent chin,
is more reminiscent of television sports
personality Jimmy Hill). At the end of
the concreted trail into the cave
another visual wonder awaits—a lush
enclave of vegetation, called the
"Garden of Eden," fostered by the
sunlight that floods in through a hole
in the cavern roof.

Gunung Mulu National Park

Deer Cave is certainly the most impressive of the "show caves" in Sarawak's largest national park, covering 544sq km (210 square miles) of primary rain forest and rugged mountains. Some 25 underground chambers have so far been explored in what is considered to be the largest limestone cave system in the world. Even though modern explorers have been attracted to the area since the 1850s, less than half of the estimated 1,000km (625 miles) or more of cave passages within the park have been fully surveyed.

A Royal Geographical Society expedition in 1976 made the case for protecting the area as a national park, but it wasn't until 1985 that Gunung Mulu was ready for tourism. Now, around 15,000 visitors a year trek the 3km (2 miles) from the park headquarters to Deer Cave and three others: the nearby Lang's Cave, a much smaller chamber with well-lit stalactites and stalagmites; Clearwater Cave, Asia's longest at 107km (67 miles), and the connected Wind Cave, so called because of the cool draughts that naturally air-condition parts of the cavern. It's possible to arrange bespoke tours through some of the other chambers and passages (see box, page 193).

The park has much more to offer than caves, however. The pristine rain forest, irrigated by crystal clear rivers and streams, makes Gunung Mulu ideal jungle trekking territory. There are also two challenging climbs: Gunung Mulu, at 2,376m (7,725 feet) the park's tallest peak—which my companion, Adam, successfully tackled—and the Pinnacles, towering spikes of limestone shooting out of the jungle near the summit of Gunung Api (1,732m/5,682 feet)—which I planned to attempt.

Jostling in the scrum around the check-in desk at Miri airport, I have cause to wonder if I'll make it to the park at all. I thrust my ticket forward and am rewarded with one of 18 boarding cards for the tiny twin-propeller plane. Once up in the air, the view of the twisting rivers, thickening jungle, and lofty mountains is tantalizing. I also notice, however, the vast patches of charred, dead trees, victims of the disastrous forest fires in 1997.

My plan for the four days in Gunung Mulu is to explore the show caves, climb to the Pinnacles, and trek along the so-called Headhunters' Trail to the northern exit from the park. With two nights of basic jungle accommodation ahead, followed by a night in a longhouse, I decide a soft start is required and opt for a night in the park's most luxurious accommodation, the Royal Mulu Resort. This also suits Adam, who has just completed the exhausting three-day ascent of Gunung Mulu.

Climbing Gunung Mulu

Conquered in 1932 by Edward Shackleton—who followed the trail established by a Berawan rhinoceros hunter, Tama Nilong, along its southwest ridge—**Gunung Mulu** remains a challenging climb. The terrain switches from steamy jungle at the base to primary rain forest on the lower slopes and, rising into the clouds, the eerie and dark moss forest. Two or three nights are spent in basic accommodation on the mountain.

There are four camps along the 24-km (15-mile) trail up Gunung Mulu. If you hit the trail straight from the plane in the afternoon, you will be able to cover the relatively easy 6km (3¾ miles) to Camp 1 the first evening, and then you can do the relentless climb through primary forest to Camp 4, just below the summit, on Day 2. From here the approach to the summit can be made in the early morning, before the clouds gather at the peak and obscure the view.

The last stretch includes some vertical slopes where ropes have been installed to allow you to pull yourself

ABOVE Kenyah women are the most distinctive of Sarawak's ethnic peoples, with pendulous ear-lobes stretched by the weight of brass ornaments

up—leave everything but essentials at Camp 4, to collect on the way down. Here, the forest gives way to stunted trees, with numerous clumps of carnivorous pitcher plants, some bigger than a fist. At the summit, a small tin hut gives basic shelter in bad weather. On a good day, the last few kilometres provide dramatic views over the jungle, Gunung Api to the north and the snaking brown line of Sungei Tutoh far below. Stay at Camp 3 on the return trip, where you could be woken by the calls of gibbons, and you should be back at HQ in the afternoon. An alternative, if you get an early start from the park headquarters, is to hike to Camp 3 on Day 1, to the summit and back to Camp 4 on Day 2, and back to park HQ on Day 3.

Gunung Mulu is less visited than the other trails in the park and you may well have the mountain to yourself. With few

ABOVE The view of the spiky limestone Pinnacles that is the reward for those who make it to the top
LEFT Longboats take visitors along the rivers to some of the park's immense and spectacular caves

people on the trail, there's a good chance you'll hear and maybe see such local wildlife as macaques, pit vipers, wild pigs, and the Borneo pheasant.

200 STEPS TO A YOUNG LADY

Day 2 of our stay at Royal Mulu Resort begins with a leisurely cruise along the Melinau River to the other show caves. The longboat ride takes just 15 minutes, but if you fancy making more of an

HEADHUNTING: THE TRUTH

The Gunung Mulu park authorities have fostered the swashbuckling myth that the so-called Headhunters' Trail was once the route followed by Kayan warriors on head-hunting forays into enemy territory. Locals such as our guide, Petrus, say that the only heads taken were of Japanese soldiers during World War II, who were using what is basically the main road through the jungle as their supply route and fell foul of the enemy.

effort, the alternative is an easy 1½-hour hike through the jungle to caves.

Steps into and walkways through the caverns have been built by the park authorities, so there's no problem penetrating either Wind or Clearwater Cave. The gusts of cool air in **Wind Cave** provide a brief respite from the rising heat outdoors. Beyond the natural atrium, the walkway leads into the King's Chamber, dripping with knobbly rock formations. From here, a 4.5-km (2¾-mile) pot-holing route leads to **Clearwater Cave**. You need to be fit and have some caving experience to undertake this challenging underground trek, which will involve some swimming and takes around six hours.

The easier option is either to follow the exterior walkway for five minutes to Clearwater Cave, or to hop back in the boat for an even faster transfer. Two hundred steps lead up to this cave's entrance, festooned with one-leaf plants. The first small chamber passed is the **Young Lady Cave**, so-called because an over-imaginative explorer fancied one of the stalagmites had the look of a maiden with flowing hair. Look carefully and you'll notice white crabs, scorpions, and spiders keeping the lady company.

Although Clearwater Cave stretches for 107km (67 miles), the walkway goes only a short way, to an observation point over the subterranean river. A couple of

Australians set off for a 1.5-km (1-mile) adventure caving jaunt following the river back out to the jungle, and pop up later while the rest of the morning's visitors are cooling off in the luscious—and surprisingly chilly—watering hole at the foot of the steps.

HIKING TO CAMP 5

At midday Adam and I leave the day trippers at the caves and proceed by longboat to **Long Berar**, the confluence of the Berar and Melinau rivers. If the water levels are low, it's often necessary to push the boat over the rapids. The previous day's rain has ensured that this isn't the case, so we can relax and then enjoy a picnic lunch of curried chicken and rice before starting on the first 8-km (5-mile) section of the **Headhunters' Trail** to Camp 5, our base for the next couple of days.

Our guide is Petrus, a stout and friendly Berawan, who was on the Royal Geographical Society's cave exploration team from 1980 to 1984. He soon sets us straight on the trail's name (see box, above), but regardless of the truth, it's easy to imagine being ambushed in jungle so thick that the afternoon light struggles to break through the canopy of dipterocarp trees to the trail below. It's something of a relief to emerge on the sun-splashed, rocky banks of the river halfway and rest. When porters arrive I realize we are indeed being followed by a tour party of nine, spotted at the caves earlier. If we're to get a decent spot at Camp 5, it's time to get a move on.

The trail is wide and easy to follow, with only the occasional muddy or waterlogged patch to negotiate. By 4pm, we arrive at the camp, a sturdy and spacious wooden building with a veranda, kitchen, and bathroom facili-ties, beside the inviting Melinau River and overshadowed by the breathtaking limestone massif of Gunung Benarat. The black gash halfway up the sheer rock face of the 1,580-m (5,183-foot) tall mountain is Tiger Cave, which has yet to be surveyed as no one has found a way of reaching it—or, come to that, the summit of Benarat.

REACHING THE PINNACLES

The 2.4-km (1½-mile) trail up to the **Pinnacles** —a forest of limestone spikes sticking up above the treetops near the top of Gunung Api—is, however, well trodden, and awaits me the following day at 6am when I'm woken by Petrus. It helps if you're fit, but the key factor in climbing the mountain successfully is to take plenty of water; a litre is the very minimum, while two or more is even better. Given good conditions, the climb there and back should take between five to eight hours, so you need not carry anything more than a light snack and a poncho or rain jacket in case the weather turns. If it's been raining heavily the night before or in the morning, the guides will cancel the climb because the danger of slipping on the sharp rocks is too great.

MORE CAVING

Some of the tour companies and guides at the park headquarters offer adventure caving trips in at least 15 caves, where you might have to wade or swim through subterranean rivers, squeeze through narrow rock passages, climb, and even abseil. The caves are graded from 1 (easy, suitable for novices) to 5 (the most difficult, with many hazards, suitable only for experienced cavers). At three of the show caves (Deer, Clearwater, and Wind) it's possible to continue off the beaten track and take more challenging routes, some of which are suitable for inexperienced cavers. You'll need some caving experience and must be physically fit if you're thinking of exploring the Sarawak Chamber, the world's largest cave chamber.

I begin climbing at 7:30am along with 16 other people, who eagerly tear off through the jungle to the first set of ropes up a short cliff face. After this initial clamber, the route is pure slog through dense forest for a good couple of hours. The climbers soon separate into three distinct groups: the front runners, the middle section, and the stragglers, puffing away at the rear. Once a pace has been established the climb becomes easier and is actually most enjoyable in the final section, where I have to haul myself up ropes and across ladders strapped to the savage rocks. The obligatory park guide is nowhere to be seen, but getting lost isn't a problem since the trail is well marked.

After such a build-up the Pinnacles themselves come as something of an anticlimax. These 50-m (165-foot) tall spikes of limestone, eroded from Gunung Api over millions of years, are an impressive sight, but the viewing spot—a narrow ridge, which is itself a pinnacle—is far from a comfortable place to linger, especially when all the daily climbers have arrived. The crowds don't seem to deter the grey squirrels who scamper around the rocks in search of crumbs from the packed lunches.

The descent has to be negotiated even more carefully; one false move and you could end up impaled on a pinnacle. Just to make the going really stressful, it starts to rain about a third of the way down. After a total of six hours (three hours up and three hours down) I'm one of the first to limp back into camp, only to be informed by Petrus that the record for an ascent is 45 minutes.

THROUGH THE JUNGLE

While I'd been climbing, Adam—still stiff from his Gunung Mulu trip—had opted for a leisurely day exploring the sights at ground level around Camp 5. The main place to head is the **Melinau gorge**, a narrow crevice with 100-m (300-foot) rock walls, cut through by the river, around 3km (2 miles) from Camp 5. On

the way, there's a fine swimming spot at a bend in the river, where the current has carved out a natural pool deep enough to dive into.

Mist is rising from the jungle at 7:30am as we start the final day's 11-km (7-mile) hike along the Headhunters'

RIGHT The climb to the Pinnacles involves slogging through dense forest and hauling yourself up ropes and ladders ABOVE and BELOW Gunung Mulu's Fairy Caves and Wind Cave are part of the biggest cave system in the world

Trail. The torrential rain of the previous evening, which had beaten a deafening tattoo on Camp 5's corrugated iron roof, has ceased, but has left parts of the trail badly waterlogged. After a couple of hours of delicately negotiating these patches, we give up and resign ourselves to wet feet.

The puddles are just a minor inconvenience compared with the fast-flowing **Terikan River**, which blocks our way along the trail at the 6-km (3¾-mile) mark. Petrus strips off and

BORNEO

porters our bags across. I follow, keeping a tight grasp of the rope that has been strung from bank to bank, struggling to maintain my balance in the strong current, water lapping around my chest. While we dry off on the opposite bank, Petrus points out Lubang China, the Chinese Cave, where it's said that two Chinamen died, trapped by the rising river after a storm.

Continuing along the trail we hear the calls of hornbills high up in the trees and spot the tracks of a civet cat. A rustle in the distance signals the movement of a troop of macaques, but this is the closest we come to actually seeing wildlife in the dense forest. Just before noon, we arrive at Kuala Terikan, where boatmen are waiting to transfer us out of the park. The beers they've bought in an icebox slip down nicely with our sandwiches. After pausing at the Kuala Mentawai Rangers Post to inform the park authorities of our safe passage along the trail, we continue downriver to **Rumah Penghulu Sigah**, the longhouse that will host us for our final night.

To the longhouse

Of the two longhouses that accept guests along the Medalam River (the other being the Rumah Bala Lasong, rebuilt in concrete), Rumah Penghulu Sigah is the more attractive, still being largely constructed of wood. The longhouse, home to over 300 people, is enormous, with 44 homes joined together, sharing the communal interior corridor (*ruai*) and outdoor veranda (*tanju*). In front are neat flower gardens, chicken coops, a clinic, boat-building hut, and Roman Catholic chapel, while behind are a sizeable school, fish pond, and vegetable patches.

It's the custom to be introduced to the headman on arrival, but he's away on business so our welcoming party consists of the longhouse children who scamper excitedly asking "What's your name?" over and over again. Adam is intrigued to see whether the longhouse

still has any enemy heads hanging around, but the only trophies on show appear to be those won by the local soccer team.

Eventually the headman returns and apologizes profusely for his absence. We're invited into his home for dinner and provided with space on the veranda for sleeping. The evening progresses with a spirited choir practice in the chapel and a sampling of *tuak*, the dry sherry-like rice spirit, in the company of the headman, who tells us that all the severed heads were buried a long time ago, when the people became Christians.

Crowing cockerels and the boom of the communal radio ensures we're all up early the next morning for the last leg of the trip downriver towards Limbang, the end of the trail. We board the longboat and leave behind this rural idyll, glancing back at a scene of water buffalo paddling in the muddy shallows of the Limbang River, against a backdrop of palms and paddy fields—just the kind of thing the English landscape artist John Constable would have painted had he been born in Sarawak.

HORNBILLS

The fauna and flora of the Mulu area of Sarawak is exceptionally rich and varied. Within the boundaries of Gunung Mulu National Park, 1,500 species of flowering plant and 109 species of palm have been recorded, along with 74 amphibian, 50 reptile, 47 fish, 281 butterfly, and 458 ant species. The 262 species of birds that have been spotted include eight varieties of hornbill. Unique to tropical Africa and Asia, hornbills make a magnificent sight as they flap noisily across the forest. Their big horny bills are topped with large, variously coloured 'casques', or growths. The largest species is the rhinoceros hornbill (*Buceros rhinoceros*) distinguished by its long orange-red casque, banded black and white tail, and *kronk krank* call in flight.

GOING IT ALONE

INTERNAL TRAVEL

From Miri The main gateway to the park is the town of Miri, from where the easiest route to Mulu is the 35-minute flight. If you take the early morning flight from Kuching, it's possible to connect at Miri and be at the park the same day. There are, however, only two flights daily and since the Twin Otter planes carry a maximum of 18 passengers it's essential to book ahead.

From Mulu airport take either a minibus or longboat to the park headquarters, where you must register and pay small fees for park permits. If you're on an organized tour all transfers and paperwork will be taken care of for you.

From Marudi There are also flights to Mulu from Marudi, on the Batang Baram River, which is where you'll also have to head if you're planning on reaching the park by boat. Before starting on this day-long overland route, it's best to check at the tourist information offices in either Kuching or Miri on the latest public transport timetables, charter costs for boats, and river conditions.

From Limbang Another alternative is to approach the park from Limbang, close to the border with Brunei. Limbang airport is about 2km (1¼ miles) south of the centre. From here take a bus or boat to the logging village of Nanga Medamit, from where you'll need to charter a boat for the 3–4-hour journey to the ranger's post of Kuala Mentawai, at the northern edge of the park.

Permits can be arranged here and there's also accommodation, including self-catering facilities. Bring all food and supplies as there are no shops or cafés.

To get to the start of the Headhunters' Trail at Kuala Terikan, you must continue along the river by longboat for at least another hour.

WHEN TO GO

There's no particular time of year when you should avoid travelling in Sarawak since the tropical climate is constantly humid. In and out of the monsoon season, expect short bursts of rain, usually in the afternoon or at night.

PLANNING

The traditional route is to follow the Headhunters' Trail from the park headquarters to Kuala Terikan, which will take at least 3 days if you opt to climb the Pinnacles. It's essential to book your accommodation in the park as far in advance as possible since the number of beds is limited. This is especially so at Camp 5, the starting point for the Pinnacles climb, where it only takes a few large tour groups to arrive together and the place is filled up.

COSTS

The only problem you might encounter travelling independently to and around Gunung Mulu National Park, is the mounting cost of fees for guides (usually compulsory) and boat charters. This is why many visitors planning to visit the show caves and the Pinnacles take an organized tour (see Contacts).

The best strategy for minimizing guide fees and boat charters is to team up with other groups of people.

Guides for Deer Cave, Lang's Cave, Clearwater Cave, and Wind Cave start at RM20 ($5). For the 2-night/3-day trip to the Pinnacles the minimum cost is around RM110 ($30), and slightly more for the trek up Gunung Mulu. For the entire head-hunter' Trail expect to pay at least RM200 ($50) in guide fees before adding on the even more expensive boat charters.

GUNUNG MULU PRACTICALITIES

❏ You are required to take an official park guide when climbing Gunung Mulu, despite the route being well marked by red and white paint.

❏ In damp weather, leeches are unavoidable.

❏ Camp 2 is just a pitch for a tent next to a stream; the others are tin-roofed huts on stilts in varying states of disrepair, but with adequate shelter and rudimentary cooking and toilet facilities.

❏ Above Camp 2, water is available only from the camps' rain tanks, and should be boiled or purified.

WHAT TO TAKE

❏ Walking boots.
❏ Rain and swim wear.
❏ Sun hat and cream.
❏ Insect repellent.
❏ Torch for caving.
❏ Bottled water on climbs.

HEALTH MATTERS

❏ Take anti-malaria tablets.
❏ Use mosquito repellent and coils.
❏ At night wear trousers and long-sleeved shirts.
❏ Bring a basic health kit.
❏ Drink bottled water.
❏ Arrange medical insurance before leaving.
❏ Check up on vaccinations with your doctor.

The Coral Wall of Sipadan

by Christopher Knowles

*It took time to adapt to the submarine world of the diver, but once I had overcome
the mental turmoil that besets the beginner, the silent, iridescent beauty of the coral
reefs off the little island of Sipadan became addictive.*

Malaysia was in something of an uproar when I arrived. The Commonwealth Games were in full swing, but the unremittingly cheerful celebration of the event could not conceal the fact that a popular reforming minister had just been arrested. The angry demonstrations of his appalled followers, which happened to coincide with my arrival (and also that of Queen Elizabeth II), threatened to provoke the government into taking the sort of draconian steps that could have made my visit uncomfortable.

It is worth mentioning this only because such goings-on can sometimes introduce a note of uncertainty to an already exotic destination. As it turned out, the trouble was confined mostly to the capital, Kuala Lumpur, with life continuing as normal everywhere else in what is, after all, a large country.

KL (as the capital is usually called) has

You don't need to be super-fit to gain your open-water diving qualification but you do need to be able to swim for 183m (200 yards), tread water for ten minutes, and have no significant medical problems.

★★ At Kota Kinabalu there is accommodation of all types. On Sipadan the accommodation in huts on stilts is simple but comfortable, with all basic amenities. It is, however, in very short supply and you are advised to book well in advance. You will probably have to share a room but you can enquire about single supplements.

Diving equipment can be hired at both Kota Kinabalu and Sipadan; or you may take your own. Note that there are no shops to speak of on Sipadan, so make sure that you bring everything you need for your stay.

BELOW Divers prepare for a beach dive on the perfect coral island of Sipadan, one of the best places in the world for scuba-diving RIGHT A diver off Sipadan gets close to a large soft coral (Sarcophyton) *in amongst some staghorn coral* (Acropora)

BORNEO

a brand new airport, built to coincide with the Games in 1998, which, for anyone having to spend any time there, is an air-conditioned heaven. It is, of course, a heaven that to the uninitiated breeds illusion; for as soon as you step out of the door, you are smothered by hot, clammy air and the sweetly fetid odour of the tropics that goes with it.

TO KK

Kota Kinabalu (or "KK"), the former Jesselton, a surprising 2½ hours' flying time from KL—Malaysia is a big country—is located on the western seaboard of Malaysia's share of the island of Borneo, known as Sabah. It is a medium-sized resort town strung out along a narrow strip of coastline between a jungle-clad ridge of jagged hills, and the shallow South China Sea. Facing the town is the island of Pulau Gaya; while from behind the hills Mount Kinabalu emerges massive and solitary, as if it has been transplanted here from the Himalayas. The town has an unfinished feel about it and sort of peters out into shanties and over-ambitious building projects. There are, however,

LIFE ON THE BEACH

Although the island is small, back on the beach there is plenty to enjoy if you are patient. The butterflies are large and brilliantly coloured. Huge monitor lizards, up to 1.25m (4 feet) long, plod around the accommodation huts looking for scraps. There are big coconut crabs, which clamber up palms in search of coconuts (their pincers, which have evolved to break open the coconuts, are best avoided). Every day those who are interested can take a guided walk through the jungle; and every two days there is the possibility of watching the release of the baby turtles that have been hatched by Borneo Divers (to prevent them being taken by monitors and birds presumably).

numerous shops, the style of which is a cross between Chinese department stores and Arab souks and a number of markets. Above all, it is filled with that particular mix of cultures that forms the Malaysian people; and no more charming, kindly people could you wish to meet. Go into a bakery, express interest in the taste of local cakes and you may find yourself leaving with a bag of them, you no poorer and the shopkeeper certainly no richer.

LEARNING TO DIVE

There are a number of reasons to visit Sabah, orangutan-spotting and simple beachcombing among them. I was there, however, to tackle two rather more energetic activities for which the region is famous—scuba diving at Sipadan, a coral island to the east of Sabah; and trekking up Mount Kinabalu. But that was all in the future. To dive at Sipadan you have to be a fully fledged open-water diver, which was to mean a few days of hard work at KK in order to gain my PADI (Professional Association of Diving Instructors) qualification. PADI is one of three principal diving associations in the world and the one favoured by Borneo Divers, who were providing my instructors. For more details on the PADI course, read Simon Richmond's account, Learning to Dive in Phuket, pages 66–73.

My course would take place on the island of Mamutik, a short speedboat journey from KK. Behind the boat the bulk of Mount Kinabalu, which I would look at with a mixture of trepidation and disbelief, rose forbiddingly. After 15 minutes or so we were on Mamutik, with its shoals of glittering fish at the jetty, its huge butterflies, and its chattering birds.

You can stay on the island merely to enjoy sea breezes and island tranquillity; or you can follow a path around the island and go bird-watching; or you can just snorkel above the reef. But most visitors come here to learn to dive in the warm, shallow water.

THE RULES OF THE GAME

Because Sipadan is so small, you will find that certain rules must be observed to ensure smooth running at the Borneo Divers resort. At the entrance to every public area (including the accommodation huts) there is a bowl filled with water. You must dip your feet into this before entering, to remove sand from them. You are asked to remove all dirty dishes and glasses after meals and place them on a table outside the restaurant. Tea, coffee, cold drinks and bananas or crackers are freely available at all times, which is a small but significant advantage—diving creates quite an appetite. Under water, you are asked to touch no living creature, whether it be coral or turtle.

GETTING STARTED

As it turned out, I was the only student. On the first day, under the tuition of Joseph, I sat (very jetlagged—it would be better to tackle this fresh in mind and body) through a series of videos divided into five modules, to get the basic idea of what scuba is all about. The videos are rather ambivalent, on the one hand telling you how wonderful is the world of scuba and undersea diving and on the other terrifying the living daylights out of you with talk of the dangers of decompression and nitrogen narcosis.

On Day 2, with Alex as my tutor now, I was allowed in the water, complete with air tank, BCD (buoyancy control device), mask, and assorted regulators. The initial dives take place in "confined" water, that is to say in a swimming pool or, as in this case, in a shallow roped-off section of seawater.

The first moments after you sink beneath the waves are frankly terrifying, the fear coexisting uneasily with euphoria as the realization dawns that you are under water, yet able to breathe. The cardinal sin, as far as

diving is concerned, is to hold your breath but that is exactly what you want to do. Why that should be is hard to say—the unaccustomed noise of your breathing perhaps, or because you want to breathe through your nose, yet cannot. You have also to learn to curb a natural desire to flail wildly about (which serves only to expend more energy and therefore more oxygen) and achieve "neutral buoyancy." All of this begins to happen naturally as you spend more time submerged.

A vital part of the course consists of learning how to cope with the emergencies that are supposed never to happen. Your mask, for example, is ripped off by a passing whale shark (a gargantuan but otherwise harmless creature), so you have to control your nasal passages, as you continue to breathe through your regulator. Or you run out of air and have to share a respirator with your "buddy" (in diving you never go anywhere without your buddy). With the help of teachers like Joseph and Alex the difficulties, which at first appear insurmountable, are somehow overcome. The consequence is a feeling of control, after which it is possible to begin to relax and enjoy the experience of swimming beneath the surface, to a depth of up to 30m (100 feet) once you are qualified.

IN OPEN WATER

Eventually come the "open-water" dives, which involve travelling a little way out to sea by boat, donning all the equipment, giving one another a brief check to ensure everything is in order, and then falling into the water in one of two ways—stepping out from the side or, as in the movies, by tipping over backwards. Now it is possible to follow the divemaster with something like calm detachment, watching as he dabs at giant clams, as he discovers intricately patterned shells more usually seen for sale in souvenir shops (except that here their lodgers are still at home) or as he pokes his hand into a cleft where a small

ABOVE A diver photographs some staghorn coral. Divers must always be very careful not to damage the coral
RIGHT The sun goes down on a beach near Kota Kinabalu and, after dark, a Sipadan ranger shows tourists a nesting turtle

nurse shark is lurking. Perhaps he spots a blue-spotted stingray, which kicks away in a cloud of muddy sand at his approach. Strange sounds come at you: motor boats passing overhead or the muffled boom of an explosion as a grenade is chucked in the water—an effective, if illegal, form of fishing locally.

On the penultimate day of the course, as we emerged from the deep, we were witnesses to the fickle nature of the tropical climate. A twister hurtled furiously across the bay to the mainland, seemingly engulfing one of KK's flimsy suburbs, thereby eliciting in the following day's paper the headline: "It's NOT a tornado!," presumably an exhortation to a volatile population to keep calm.

There are a few more tasks to perform on the final day. Your mask must be cleared of seeping water while you are submerged, then removed and replaced at depth. You must find your way back to a given point by using a compass. Then you must swim for 183m

(200 yards) without stopping and tread water for several minutes. Finally there is a written multiple-choice examination (which may be taken in your home country, ahead of the practical part of the course). And that is that—I am now a fully qualified recreational open-water diver, ready to take on the wall of coral at Sipadan.

A CORAL IDYLL

One of the best places in Asia for scuba-diving—probably one of the best in the world—is the islet of **Sipadan**, an atoll off the eastern coast of northern Borneo. Reaching it is a fairly tortuous affair. As usual in Malaysia, getting anywhere requires an early start, in this case at 4am—a painful experience, given that I

BORNEO

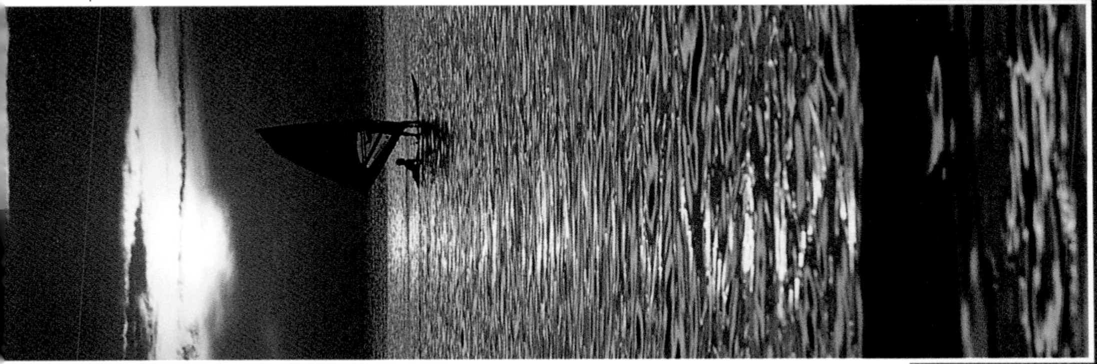

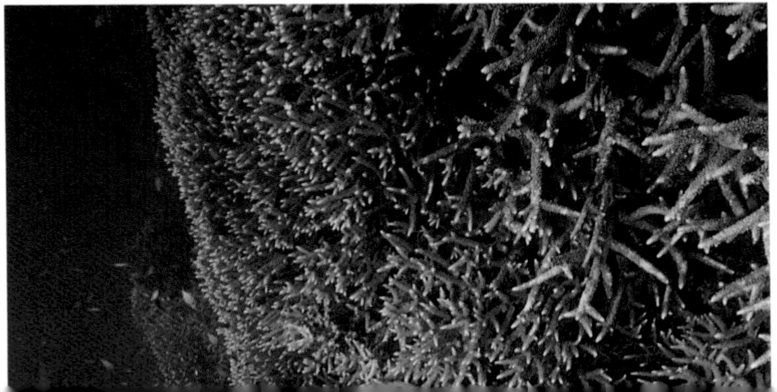

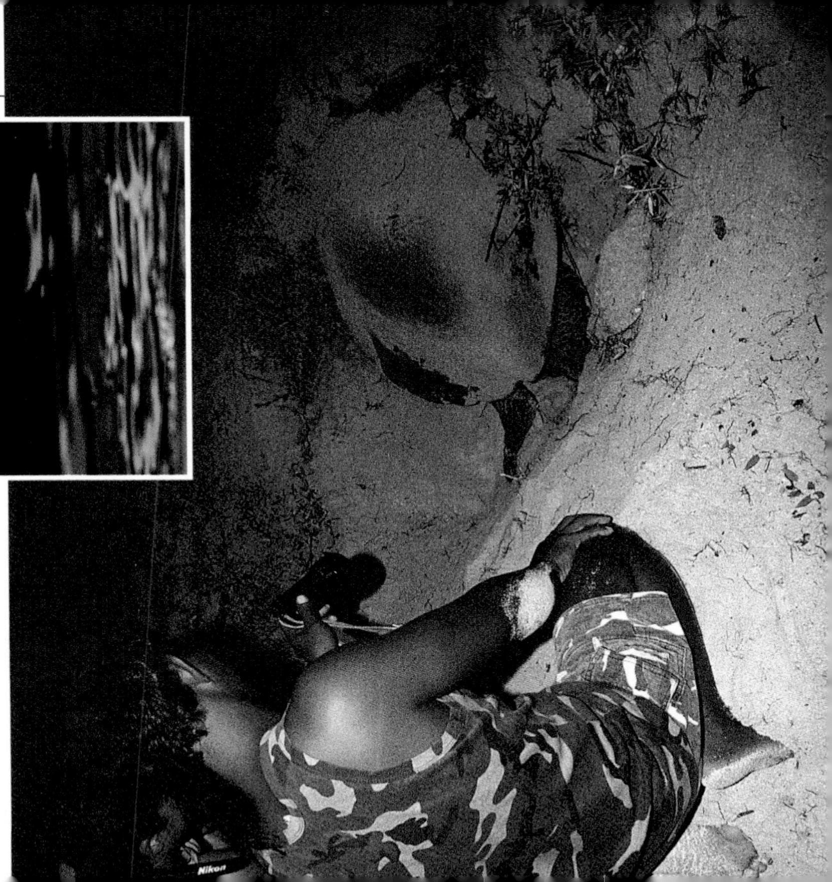

had only returned from Mount Kinabalu at 8 the previous evening. From KK it is an hour's flight to the town of Tawau. From there it is a two-hour bus journey to the port of Semporna. Finally, it is an hour by fast launch out to sea, passing on the way, if you are lucky, schools of leaping dolphins. The helmsman likes to make the best use of the 400-horse-power of the engines, so he begins by banking steeply out of Semporna harbour at high speed to give us a thrill.

Pretty soon we are out at sea. We pass one village built entirely on stilts and then scud across the waves towards Sipadan. When finally it appears, a solitary lozenge on the horizon, it is everyone's idea of a perfect coral island. It is very small (you can walk around it in 20 minutes) and is fringed by a white beach enclosing a dense little thatch of jungle. Beyond the beach is a ring of coral, extending some 45m (50 yards). And then, where the aquamarine meets the sapphire, a sheer drop of 2,000m (3,200 feet) down to a wall of coral-encrusted limestone, a haven of kaleidoscopic marine life.

Once we arrive at the resort a Borneo Divers representative gives us our briefing and we are introduced to Rajid, who is to be our divemaster. This is followed by a short tour of the immediate area, so that we know where everything is (including the dreaded decompression chamber, in the event that any of us develops the "bends") and learn the few basic rules of the establishment.

BEACH DIVES

Our rooms are clean, with lights, plugs, electric fan, and a simple bathroom. I am to share with Ray, an Englishman who has been living and working in Sabah for the past several months, and who is also a novice diver (though a much more confident one than I am). By now we had become a considerable party, members having joined at various places along the route from KK. In KK itself early that morning I had met Prakash,

and a very fortunate meeting that turned out to be; for I had managed to forget to pack my swimming costume. My short trousers would have done instead, if the hotel in KK had not somehow contrived to misplace them at the last minute. Prakash is able to lend me his spare costume, and his spare pair of shorts—a lucky break, since on Sipadan what shops there are deal in postcards, T-shirts and not much else.

In the afternoon our first excursion into the deep is a so-called beach dive (as opposed to diving from a boat), which in this case takes the form of a sort of sub-aqua orientation. Those of us who need to rent equipment get kitted out at the equipment hut, from where we plod directly to the beach and into the water. After wading and paddling 45m (50 yards) out to a point near the end of the jetty (which also doubles as a bar, known as the Drop-Off Café), we deflate the BCD and are enveloped in the warm water. We open our eyes, and as the bubbles disperse, there we are, hovering over the edge of a coral cliff, poised above a profoundly blue abyss.

The visibility is breathtaking—myriad little fish dart and flit around us. We descend further. A white-tip reef shark approaches but veers away, evincing only the minimum of curiosity. In front of me, a turtle paddles towards Ray, who is looking in the other direction. He turns to face front and then squirts away to the right as the turtle comes beak to face with his mask. I want to laugh, but in the circumstances, laughter is not recommended. We descend to 18m (60 feet) before returning to the surface.

Later that afternoon a few of us go for another beach dive, which turns out to be a salutary experience. Beneath the unruffled surface there can be a mighty current to deal with. My legs, tired from climbing Mount Kinabalu the day before, cannot fin adequately and I am rising uncontrollably to the surface. Ray, being a conscientious "buddy," follows me up to the top to make sure that all is well.

At the end of the day

Evening comes on. The sun sets in spectacular fashion, streaking the sky crimson and magenta. People gather on the pier to watch. Darkness descends, the water laps against the jetty piers. Beams of light flash beneath the waves as a few hardy souls take night dives and report back with sightings of 2-m (6-foot) bump head parrotfish. But dinner awaits and very good it is too: soup, *sashimi* of freshly caught tuna, rice and fish dishes, chips, and fresh fruit.

Sipadan is a convivial place. What strikes a novice diver most is the good-time element. A surprising number of people smoke, and there is a fair amount of drink taken, although excessive intake of alcohol is not to be recommended. In fact, there is a generally lively air in the evenings, and such a variety of people. Michael is a lawyer from Australia. Prakash is involved in the construction of large houses for wealthy Australians and seems to get to know everyone on the island in the first couple of hours.

Then there is Axel, an employee of the German post office who is taking a nine-month extended break—his is a job he can go back to anytime he likes.

DIVE VIDEOS

At the end of each day much time is spent poring over the books that illustrate the submarine flora and fauna of the region, in an attempt to ascertain just what we have been looking at. Help sometimes comes in the form of the videos shown each night after dinner. They are made by Stephen Fish (this is his real name), an American who who makes his living on Sipadan by accepting commissions to accompany visitors on their dives. The videos don't come cheap, but then a personalized film featuring you and a shark is something more than the average holiday snap.

Andrea and Cristina, from Rome, are dedicated sea photographers; Claudia, from Switzerland, is back-packing for a year; Rene and Rahel, also from Switzerland, are just taking a holiday. Susan, an industrial hygienist from America is an avid rower; and her friend, an air stewardess. Some people I just observe, but don't meet. There is an old man, with a handkerchief on his head against the sun, who is helped each morning into a plastic canoe by a young man at the pier, from where they both paddle off for a tour of the island.

Wall diving

The next day there are three dives available. Generally speaking, the first is always the deepest and we go down to 30m (100 feet), which is close to the maximum depth recommended for "recreational" diving. There are Moray eels poking their vicious-looking snouts out of their hiding holes; a vast glittering shower of jacks school down the side of the coral. A pair of huge tuna patrol by; territorially minded trigger fish dart from crevices—someone told me that they had their fins bitten by one particularly aggressive individual. One of our party saw a barracuda. There were more sharks and turtles and an array of clown fish, parrot fish, and many others that we would try to identify under the fans in the restaurant after our return.

Then I began to get low on air, Rajid handed me a bag of putrefying rubbish that he had collected from the ocean floor and suggested that I surface. In the process my mask went missing. In diving circles this is considered hilarious and I was not allowed to forget it for the duration of my stay. "See anything interesting this morning?" "Only a manta ray wearing a scuba mask."

Back out at the Drop-Off Café, the sea is lit up again. Not this time with underwater torches, but with the phosphorescent algae or plankton that sometimes illuminate the waves like sub-aqua star dust. On some evenings the divemasters gather together on the pier and sing, to an accompaniment of guitars and a sort of drum improvised from bottles and tins. With the blinking phosphorous around them, and the echo of chirruping insects and geckos, it is a scene of almost supernatural beauty.

The rhythm of the days and nights on Sipadan is unchanging, their character formed by what has, or has not, been seen beneath the waves. Of course there is always something to see, from the vividly streaked nudibranches (types of sea snails) to scorpion fish, pipe fish lingering transparently just under the surface, and, even in these limpid waters, distant, unidentifiable shapes. The boats take you out to different parts of the reef, each one noted for something particular—Barracuda Point, Coral Garden, Turtle Cave. It is not even necessary to dive. Just by snorkelling out to sea for 45m (50 yards), you can hover face-down over the abyss to gaze into another, silent world. And, if you are really lucky, you may find yourself in the shadow of a whale shark, or a killer whale.

Borneo Divers are highly respected operators

B O R N E O

GOING IT ALONE

INTERNAL TRAVEL

Kota Kinabalu is served by direct flights from the Malaysian capital of Kuala Lumpur, and is linked by air to all the major towns and cities of Malaysia.

The town is also served by long-distance buses, so (with changes) it would be possible to get there from Sarawak and Kalimantan. There is also a thrice-daily boat service to Pulau Labuan, the island resort popular with wreck divers to the south of KK.

WHEN TO GO

The temperature does not vary much throughout the year and the monsoon rains have become unpredictable. However, the driest months tend to be January to April. Visibility is best for diving between mid-February and mid-December.

PLANNING

For Sipadan, it might be as well to book the whole journey, if you can afford it (i.e., flight to Tawau, transfers to Semporna and Sipadan) through Borneo Divers or one of the other operators on the island, such as Sipadan Dive Centre (see Contacts). Tawau is served by air from KK, KL, Lahad Datu, and Sandakan in Malaysia, and from Tarakan in Indonesia. It is served by boats from Tarakan (via Nunukan), and from Sulawesi.

KK to Tawau is possible by bus (about 11 hours). From Tawau it is 110km (70 miles) to Semporna—there are regular minibus services between the two.

DIVING COURSES

Although the coral reefs are not especially interesting for experienced divers, KK is a good place to learn to dive, for the water is warm and shallow. Borneo Divers offer 4-day courses on Mamutik Island, which is a short boat journey from the jetty close to Jin Datuk Saleh Sulong. Scheduled boat services operate all day, although they are not entirely reliable. However, if a service does fail to materialize, there are always plenty of freelance boatmen ready to step into the breach, with whom you can negotiate a price. The 4-day course (starting at 900RM/$240 per person) includes:

❑ full tuition
❑ video presentations
❑ exam fees
❑ requisite number of dives (with boat)
❑ equipment hire
❑ lunches

Borneo Divers tends to be more expensive than other companies, but is probably the most widely respected dive operator in Asia.

DIVING ON SIPADAN

Sipadan, being small and exclusive, is an expensive place for diving. The daily cost of $200 includes:

❑ transfers to and from Semporna
❑ accommodation
❑ all meals
❑ three boat dives per day
❑ unlimited beach dives

Equipment hire is extra.

In order to make sure you see everything, a stay of at least two days is recommended. Although the main reason for going to Sipadan is to dive, it is worth noting that the snorkelling is also spectacular (but expensive).

Stephen Fish will come with you on your dive and immortalize your journey to the submarine world with his underwater video camera. It is not cheap at $120, but if other members of your group are interested the cost can be shared.

ESSENTIALS

MasterCard is more widely accepted in Malaysia than other credit cards.

WHAT TO TAKE

❑ Swimming costume.
❑ Relevant diving qualification certificate.
❑ Flip-flops or equivalent.
❑ As few clothes as possible and washing powder.
❑ Torch.

HEALTH MATTERS

❑ Take anti-malaria tablets.
❑ Use mosquito repellent and coils.
❑ At night wear trousers and long-sleeved shirts.
❑ Bring a basic health kit.
❑ Drink bottled water.
❑ Arrange medical insurance before leaving.
❑ Check up on vaccinations with your doctor at home.
❑ Bring any prescribed medication with you.

SAFETY FIRST

The Buddy System is designed to ensure that potential problems are either preempted or dealt with swiftly once you are under water. Each diver teams up with another. They check each other's equipment before going under and keep an eye on each other while submerged. Hand signals enable divers to communicate with each other in emergencies.

BORNEO

Climbing Mount Kinabalu

by Christopher Knowles

Sabah's Mount Kinabalu presents an awesome, not to say alarming, sight to the uninitiated climber. Few experiences however, equal the sense of accomplishment when you find yourself at 4,200m (14,000 feet), with a sea of cloud at your feet.

It was only the day before that I had gained my open-water diving qualification. Celebration would have to wait, however, because the very next day there was the small matter of the ascent of Mount Kinabalu.

At 6am John, a Malaysian of Indian extraction, came to pick me up from my base in **Kota Kinabalu** (KK), the Hotel Holiday. Immediately, I was deposited at a restaurant for breakfast while he went off on an errand. It is as well to realize that sometimes in Malaysia early starts seem to be arranged on a "just in case" basis, which is all to the good, as "just in case" frequently becomes "I knew that would happen." After some time he returned

4 If I give the impression that this adventure was hard, then that is as it should be. Although no actual climbing is involved, it is essential to realize that this is quite an arduous hike. On the other hand, people of all ages tackle it and succeed—it is largely a question of will.

★★ Accommodation is variable. In Kota Kinabalu there are hotels of all descriptions from basic to luxury. The overnight stop on the mountain is in, at best, a simply equipped hostel but the number of places is limited, so book ahead as far as possible. Meals are available and there is a small shop. There is also accommodation at the base of the mountain at Park HQ.

⚒ The following may be useful: a waterproof rucksack, an umbrella, a torch, a water bottle, chocolate or dried fruit to eat during the ascent and descent, a fleece (a light but very warm jacket), gloves, waterproof walking boots and jacket, walking stick. If necessary, gloves can be bought at a village on the way to the park.

with Marc and Maarten, lawyers from the Netherlands, who were to be my companions and counsellors during the difficult hours ahead.

The journey to the mountain takes between two and three hours, depending on the traffic. From the suburbs of KK there is a fast dual-carriageway, which becomes a winding mountain road as it approaches the lower slopes of Kinabalu. Any road journey in Malaysia is a hair-raising experience and the drive from KK to Gunung Kinabalu (as the vast park enclosing the mountain is called) is no exception. It is all, no doubt, a question of local technique, but overtaking manoeuvres in Malaysia are alarming to the uninitiated Westerner. The roads, moreover, though well made in general, may suddenly, for no discernible reason, degenerate into a brief series of trenches and troughs before returning to normal.

TO BASE CAMP

The route, through a tropical landscape of plantations, logging haciendas with hillsides denuded of timber, and lush palm bushes, brought us to a sort of base camp, or Park HQ, that is to say to the entrance to the **Gunung Kinabalu Park**. If the weather is clear—which it often is in the early morning—it is worth photographing the spectacular views of the mountain on the way as the opportunity may not arise again. Even if it does, you may not, after the climb, feel much like taking advantage of it.

The three of us waited for John in the comparative cool (we were at

1,585m/5,280 feet) as he disappeared into the Park HQ office to register us with the authorities. We looked with amused disbelief at a notice recording the fastest times for an ascent and descent of the mountain, something like 2 hours, 40 minutes. It did my patriotic blood good to see that the record was held by a Briton, but I don't think that it did very much to assuage our feelings of apprehension. Nonetheless, a fairly light-hearted atmosphere prevailed among the cheerful pilgrims at the bottom.

AN OPTIMISTIC CANTER

After registration (for which passports are required) there is a further 4km (2½ miles) to the starting point of the "climb" itself. John drove us to the Power Station, which marks the beginning of the trail and, with, a cheerful wave, sent us on our way.

In tow was Raimin, our mountain guide. Raimin was tireless. He had almost no knowledge of English and was able to answer our questions only with either "yes" or "no"—giving us little confidence that the question had been properly understood. But he stuck to us like glue, never missed a trick and would, I am sure, have willingly carried our rucksacks had we asked.

We set off at an optimistic canter, all the more so as the first couple of hundred metres consisted of descending steps. They, however, constituted the last bit of downhill that we were to see for quite some time.

Very soon the steps started. Still feeling fresh, we continued for a while to climb with the same enthusiasm, all of us trusting that the steps were merely a prelude to a firm, comfortable trail that would curl gently in a slowly ascending loop around the girth of the mountain. We could not have been more wrong. The steps went on and on. And on. At first we exchanged words, but pretty soon the inclination to talk gave way to a determination just to keep going.

At this stage we were climbing

SPECTACULAR FLORA

Most interesting of all the plants around the mountain are perhaps the nine species of carnivorous pitcher plants. The largest is the Rajah Brooke, which has been observed to hold several pints of water and be capable of killing a creature as large as a rat. In general, however, pitcher plants stick to insects, which cannot sustain grip on the slippery inside of the flower and which then slide down to their doom. Ask your guide to look for examples. The world's largest flower is also found in the area of the park (though not on the route to the top). *Rafflesia* (named after the famous colonialist and botanist Stamford Raffles) can reach a width of a metre (over 3 feet) or so. Size notwithstanding, it is difficult to spot as it flowers for only a few days, usually between May and July.

---

through dense bamboo forest. When we paused, apart from our panting, there was not a sound to be heard. Giant ferns rocked gently at the slightest breath of air.

We knew that the way was marked at every half-kilometre but it was an unpleasant surprise to come across the first marker only after what seemed an eternity. However, a small shelter, the first of many soon appeared, and we gladly made use of it. I produced some dried mango (dried fruits are supposed to be good for energy and for reducing the effect of altitude), while Marc and Maarten took out a bar of chocolate. We sat munching in gratified silence, taking thoughtful sips from our water bottles. We looked at each other and laughed. It was going to be a long day.

HARD SLOG

The steps, mostly of stone set into the orange soil, or flights of thin wooden bars, became more uneven as we went

up, requiring us to find an idiosyncratic rhythm to deal with them. As the time passed, we did just that, locking ourselves into a sort of trance that enabled us to keep going. Maarten, the wiriest of the three of us, turned out to be

ABOVE It is compulsory to register with the park authorities and to hire a guide to climb with you
LEFT Head above the clouds: it's a tough climb, but most complete it in two days
BELOW Kota Kinabalu, starting point of the expedition

something of a mountain goat, soon leaving Marc and me to plod on at our own donkey-like pace. Every 50 paces or so we would stop to recover our breath, the intervals of course becoming shorter the higher we rose and the thinner the air. Then we would turn a corner and there would be Maarten awaiting us in a shelter. Time for more chocolate. Raimin, unflappable and exhibiting not the slightest sign of physical exertion, sat down on a rock near by and

BORNEO

THE MOUNTAIN'S CLIMATIC ZONES

The Gunung Kinabalu Park, in which over half the world's families of flowering plants are said to be represented, has a plethora of interesting flora and fauna, partly on account of its range of climatic zones. Within 3km (1¾ miles) the vegetation ranges from lowland tropical rain forest (up to 1,300m/4,300 feet) to alpine and cloud forest (from 2,000m/6,600 feet upwards). The climb takes you mostly through this last zone, where orchids, pitcher plants, and rhododendrons flourish. Beyond 2,600m (8,670 feet), among the rocky outcrops, you will see the gnarled and stunted tea trees, and finally only mosses and Alpine buttercups, which manage to cling to the soil-less summit area.

contentedly smoked a cigarette. A ground squirrel, evidently used to snacks, lurked timidly in the vicinity. Small olive green birds hopped from branch to branch. Marc said "I am beginning to appreciate some of Holland's qualities" (i.e., it's flat).

By now we were starting to meet people coming down. They gave us pitying glances but assured us, with the lofty air of those who have accomplished what they set out to do, that it was all worthwhile and that if we thought this was hard, then we hadn't seen anything yet. We also met up with old friends—I had met Hank and Heidi during my diving course at KK, and Maarten even bumped into somebody who was related to a friend of his in Holland. We had also, from time to time, to make way for people running up the mountain—we would know they were coming because of the speed of their footfall, at complete variance with the heavy plodding steps of our group. We could only stand and wonder at them, as they sped up the slope before us, in preparation for the annual Climathon, which takes place

every October. Were they mad, or were they alien life forms? Walking at a more sedate pace but no less remarkable, were the local people carrying supplies up to the mountain huts. Small and wiry, and often female, they made this journey regularly.

From lush green bamboo forest we passed up into rhododendron forest of wide leaves with their glossy, plastic sheen and pink flowers growing out of twisted and desiccated branches. At km 3 (mile 2) we stopped for lunch, which had been provided at Park HQ. Only 3km (2 miles) to go.

The comparative evenness of the steps gave way to a boulder-strewn path like a Roman road after an earthquake. The bushes became squatter and sparser and the intervals between pauses shorter. Yet our pauses were not long, just enough to catch our breath, giving us sufficient strength to reach the next objective that we had set ourselves.

A BREATHER

And then, after 6km (3¾ miles), and at 3,550m (11,830 feet) altitude, there it was: the **Laban Rata Resthouse**, our home for the night, a large hut perched on the edge of the mountain. It had taken us 4 hours, 59 minutes—less, we could claim, than five hours. For me, who had booked some time in advance, the prospect of a hot shower was about as appealing as a shower had ever been. For Marc and Maarten, who had booked only the day before, there was another five minutes to go up the slope to a simple dormitory, from where they would have to descend for their meals.

In fact, other than being on the spot for meals, my supposedly more luxurious hut held few advantages. There were six of us in my room and all the taps produced icy water. But there was hot food and drink and that peculiarly pleasurable feeling of relief that comes when something has been difficult—the one that almost convinces you that it was fun.

Marc and Maarten went to sleep for a while, while I enjoyed a pot of Milo (the ubiquitous Swiss/Southeast Asian chocolate drink). Outside there was nothing to be seen except the swirling cloud below. We were all begging for it to dissipate so that we could look down from our 3,300-m (11,000-foot) eerie on to our achievement. When finally it broke there was a rush to the balcony to record the moment.

At 6pm we ate dinner and pretty soon afterwards retired to bed. We still had 3km (2 miles) to go to the summit and we were to start at 3am—not an altogether pleasing prospect. And exhausted though I was, I was totally unable to sleep. Perhaps it was the altitude, perhaps it was a streaming mind, I don't know. But others had the same problem. You occupy a twilight world between sleep and wakefulness, conscious that you are not asleep, yet your mind wanders off at will. There was a lot of rain, too; but by 2am it had ceased and soon, after a cup of hot tea, we were ready for the off—sort of. The aim was to make the summit by 5:40 when the sun was supposed to rise.

THE FINAL PUSH

The ground was wet and, other than our candle-like lights from torches, it was pitch black. Dozens of us proceeded upwards, forcing weary legs into gear to cope once more with the steps. Lack of sleep and the altitude made it difficult, and this time even Marc outdistanced me. Gradually the procession thinned out, and the vegetation did too, eventually giving up altogether, unable to gain a foothold on the dense, gritty, grey rock that we were now treading. As the steps gave out, however, ropes took their place; and there were one or two points where the darkness was a definite bonus, because there was undoubtedly a considerable drop to the right which I was happy not to see. Of course, it would have to be dealt with on the way back; but that was some time ahead.

In the meantime all that mattered was somehow to keep going.

By 5:40 **Low's Peak**, the highest point of Mount Kinabalu, was an isolated promontory, shaped something like a crooked thumb, at the far end of an expanse of sloping grey granite. The first faint glimmers of the sunrise were by now apparent and I was taking a breather every ten or fifteen paces. It was also very cold. Torches were being extinguished and we could see the silhouettes of the early arrivals on the peak making the final push up to the top. At this stage I felt like calling it a day and watching the sunrise from where I was, but with the help of Raimin, who had faithfully stayed by me the whole time, I pressed on. At 6 o'clock I had made it to the summit at Low's Peak (4,102m/13,458 feet), just in time to catch the full splendour of the rising sun as it sent a pink wash through the sea of cloud that lapped at the slopes below us and through which pierced other, distant peaks. Numb fingers, prised from soaking gloves, fumbled to pull a camera from a pocket in order to record the sheer exhilaration of being here, at the top of this bleak place above the clouds.

NEVER AGAIN?

It was too cold to stay very long and everyone turned around to begin the clambering descent. Now that we had made the ascent, nothing held any fears for us (not even the ropes) and we could afford to be cheerful. The sun began to thaw us out and to disperse the clouds. Way below us the morning steam rose from the fresh green of the forest.

After an hour we were back at the huts, in time for breakfast and another cold shower. With rucksacks refilled, we set off, confident that the descent would be a breeze. Not so: different muscles, yes, but the same pain. It took us just under four hours. It meant that we had walked something like 12km (7½ miles) over extremely difficult terrain since

getting up that morning and 18km (11 miles) since yesterday. Only the wonder of having completed the ascent allowed us to think better of the descent. Near the end the heavens opened and we covered the final kilometre in 15 minutes, jellied legs notwithstanding.

As we took shelter from the downpour at the gatehouse at the bottom, a trickle of weary people joined us. As each person staggered in, there was a shake of the head and a muttered "Never again!" Well, perhaps not,—but then you have to have done it once to be able to say that.

GOING IT ALONE

INTERNAL TRAVEL

The main point of arrival and departure for Mount Kinabalu is the coastal town of Kota Kinabalu (KK), which sits in the shadow of the mountain on the western seabord of Sabah, Malaysia's northern share of the island of Borneo.

Kota Kinabalu is served directly by regular flights from the Malaysian capital of Kuala Lumpur, and is linked by air to all the major towns and cities of Malaysia. There are also direct flights from KK to international destinations such as Hong Kong, Singapore, Manila, Brunei, Seoul, Jakarta, Taipei, and Tokyo. It is also possible to fly here from Kalimantan (Indonesian Borneo).

The town is also served by long-distance buses so it would be possible to get here from other parts of Borneo such as Sarawak.

There is also a thrice-daily boat service from Pulau Labuan, the tax haven island to the south of KK popular with wreck divers. Journey time is 2½ hours.

KK's railway station, 5km (3 miles) to the south, serves Beaufort and Tenom.

To reach Park HQ, which lies about 60km (37 miles) east of KK, either organize a trip that includes transfers from and to the town (there are plenty of operators in town, including Borneo Divers—see Contacts), or take a minibus or bus for Ranau,

LEFT Clouds swirl around the stark rock faces of Mount Kinabalu
INSET On top of the world as the sun rises

asking to be dropped at the park. The journey will take 2–3 hours. Larger buses (there are at least two services per day) tend to be slower but may well be air-conditioned and are of course more spacious. There is no main bus station in KK but buses for the park tend to leave from Jln Tunku Abdul Rahman.

WHEN TO GO

It is generally accepted that the best time for a visit to the mountain is during the dry season; March or April offer the best opportunity for clear views. The worst time is probably November and December, which fall in the middle of the wet season. It is possible to offer only very broad generalizations since in truth the climate here is very fickle.

PLANNING

Since the number of people allowed on the mountain at any one time is limited, it is essential to book your accommodation well in advance (although last-minute bookings are by no means out of the question).

In the period of the annual Climathon, in early October,

accommodation may be particularly hard to find.

ESSENTIALS

Note that it is compulsory to climb with a local guide, and remember to take your passport for registration at the entrance to the park.

Note also that MasterCard is more widely accepted in Malaysia than other credit cards.

WHAT TO TAKE

- ❑ Waterproof walking bootsand jacket.
- ❑ A fleeece top or jacket.
- ❑ Passport.
- ❑ Insect repellent.
- ❑ Swimwear if visiting Poring Hot Springs.
- ❑ Spare batteries and film for your camera.
- ❑ Water bottle.

HEALTH MATTERS

- ❑ Take anti-malaria tablets.
- ❑ Use mosquito repellent and coils.
- ❑ Wear trousers and long-sleeved shirts at night.
- ❑ Bring a basic health kit.
- ❑ Drink bottled water.
- ❑ Arrange comprehensive medical insurance before departure.
- ❑ Check on vaccinations at least a month before leaving home.

HOT BATHS

Over 40km (25 miles) from Park HQ, though within Gunung Kinabalu Park, Poring Hot Springs offers a welcome way of soothing aching muscles after the climb of Mount Kinabalu. Set in a pretty garden beyond a suspension bridge over a river, the hot sulphur baths are in the form of deep, tiled pools with taps. Once you find one that works, you can immerse yourself up to the neck for as long as you like. There is also a restaurant, accommodation, and the chance of a jungle canopy walk along a ropeway 35m (115 feet) above ground. Arrange a taxi or minibus from Park HQ, or in advance at KK.

The Tarsiers of Tangkoko

by Christopher Knowles

My trek into the remarkable Tangkoko National Park, located in volcanic northern Sulawesi behind a beach of black sand, was to seek out the enchanting, nocturnal tarsier, one of the world's smallest primates, the playful black macaque, and a host of other endemic species.

In **Manado**, less than 50km (100 miles) north of the Equator, I picked up the jeep that was to take me to the Tangkoko National Park, where I was to go trekking in search of tarsiers and black macaques. Along with the jeep came a driver, James, and, I was relieved to find, air-conditioning—which for a foreigner from a temperate climate, is sometimes better than food or drink.

Although the direct journey to Tangkoko should have taken no more than three hours, we ended up making a (very worthwhile) detour to see some of the gorgeous scenery of the Minahasa Highlands.

After 40 minutes or so, you come to the town of **Tomohon**, built in the shadow of a number of active volcanoes in the hills above Manado. It is worth spending the night here and then in the early morning walking up to one of two nearby volcanoes, the higher of which rises to 1,585m (5,200 feet). From the Happy Flower Homestay it is possible to walk directly up to the crater of **Mount Lokon**, which is not at the peak of the mountain as you would expect, but as a result of Lokon's most recent outburst, in a declivity just adjacent.

The path up through the slopes of Mount Lokon was unexpectedly reminiscent of an English farm track, despite the presence of tall and willowy coconut palms. Perhaps it was because of the slightly cooler air, and the smell of the fertile volcanic earth, which here produces very untropical vegetables, such as carrots and cabbages.

The heat, of course, soon regained its tropical strength as the morning wore on, but, at this altitude, there was none of the suffocating humidity that there is on the coast at Manado. The path curved pleasingly around the girth of the mountain before passing through an area of forest where butterflies danced before me to the accompaniment of rustlings of lizards scurrying into the undergrowth. Soon the forest path emerged into the open air, and then plunged back into a patch of dense elephant grass. I forced my way upwards as the path steepened,

3 This is not a difficult trip for anyone reasonably fit. The walking through the jungle is mostly flat and the paths are clear. The heat, however, is oppressive and the insects are potentially a major irritant. Getting there by public transport would be taxing.

★ For the trek in the forest, you must wear clothes that will cover you as much as possible. In the heat this is not comfortable, but not only are there mosquitoes in the forest, there is also a mite or louse that apparently lurks in rotting wood and vegetation and which, if it gets on to your skin, leaves an irritation that may itch for months on end. There is accommodation to suit all tastes and pockets in Manado itself, but at Tangkoko you must stay in one of the simple homestays, among which the Ranger Homestay is apparently the best equipped. Jenli, the head ranger, is in the process of building his own homestay. Bring your own towels and soap.

⚒ Take plenty of insect repellent, a torch, camera, binoculars, spare batteries and film, walking boots and socks, and rainwear. If you want to go swimming, don't forget your costume.

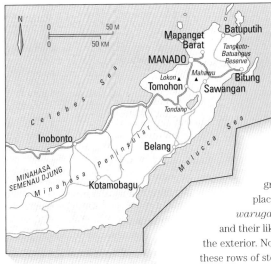

In search of wildlife at the tip of Sulawesi

the Dutch colonists, when Christianity swept all before it, the native people of Sulawesi, who were animists, favoured entombment above the ground. The dead were placed in a sitting position in *waruga*, hollow stone tombs, and their likenesses were carved on the exterior. Now, in a jungle setting, these rows of stone huts, surrounded by the more recent Christian graves of Dutch colonists and their converts, make an arresting sight. In fact, this congregation of tombs is an artificial one, since the tombs were originally scattered all over Minahasa and were only assembled here after a cholera outbreak early in the 20th century, to create a sort of open-air museum. Yet it felt nothing like a museum. To somebody walking up the road to the cemetery, it would appear that James and I, the only people there, had come to pay our respects to our relatives or our ancestors.

Religion, in its Christian form, is evidently very important to the Sulawesi people. The villages are dominated by grandiose churches, whose brilliant white facades and stepped eaves are reminiscent of Dutch colonial architecture. Many of these settlements, which are usually fairly small, have not one but several churches, each catering to the adherents of a different denomination.

There was a marked contrast between the serenity of the churches and the raucous methods of salesmanship adopted by local shopkeepers. It is sale by attrition. Huge speakers are posted outside the shops and music broadcast as loudly as possible in order to drive the customers in. If it works, it must surely only be because it is quieter

suddenly reaching the peak, and a path at the very lip of the steaming caldera. The air was filled with the stink of sulphur and, at intervals, the hissing of escaping steam. Inside the crater there was a small green lake, and rocks splashed with brilliant sulphurous yellow. The path continued around the circumference of the crater, and it would have been possible to have made a complete circuit, were it not for the possibility, in a changeable breeze, of our being engulfed in a cloud of poisonous gas.

But it was not necessary to go that far to appreciate the fascination of the crater (and the not unreasonable fear that it might erupt at any moment) or to admire the views northwards towards Manado and the outlying islands, including Bunaken; and southwards to the several other Minahasa volcanoes that stood sentinel over the plain below.

A RELIGIOUS OUTLOOK

From Tomohon it was still a three-hour journey to the village of Batuputih and the Tangkoko National Reserve, located on the coast to the west of Manado. On the way we made a stop at the village of **Sawangan**, the site of a very curious collection of tombs. Until the coming of

SULAWESI

in the shop than outside on the street. The smaller villages on the other hand, which depend entirely on farming, are tranquil in the extreme. They are fragrant, too, because northern Sulawesi is a centre for clove production. The cloves are placed on rattan mats to dry in the sun at the roadside, and their spicy aroma filled the air and circulated around the car as we drove through. All of the villages were filled with horse-pulled versions of the Philippine jeepney—little brightly coloured and chromed surreys, hauled by rugged little ponies and usually containing pairs of women enjoying a few moments of modest splendour.

THE ROAD TO TANGKOKO

Eventually the quality of the road surface started to deteriorate seriously. James did not seem too concerned about it but I could imagine that in the event of heavy rain the road would be impassable. As it was, we very nearly become

RIGHT Carved waruga *tombs at Sawangan's cemetery. Built to hold bodies in a sitting, foetal position, they are unique to the region*
BELOW Manado's night market

enmired in a stretch of grey sand, and were able to escape only because we were on a slope and therefore able to coast back to the bottom, before starting again. And yet a local bus, crowded as usual with passengers, luggage, and livestock, hove into view behind us and sat on our tail until James pulled in to let it pass; after which it bucked away from us in a cloud of smoke and dust.

By now the road had become no more than a wide track weaving through an area of thick palm forest. From time to time we passed farmworkers at the roadside making palm oil but otherwise—apart from an abandoned mechanical digger, a sorry splash of orange paint and smashed glass—there was nothing around us but a wide expanse of green. Then the sea appeared beyond the palm tops. "Ten

minutes," James grinned. And indeed, soon after, at about four in the afternoon, we pulled into the little village of **Batuputih**, right at the edge of the **Tangkoko National Park**.

Our accommodation, the Ranger Homestay, was directly opposite the park entrance and had been chosen because it was the only homestay with mosquito nets. While this was clearly a great advantage, the rooms were otherwise very simple, with a basin of water and a ladle to act as a shower, and a small electric fan that stirred, just a little, the humid air.

James went to locate our guide. Jenli was the head ranger, a local man who had developed an interest in the welfare of the forest and who, after a time just watching the work being done to preserve its flora and fauna, turned

MOUNT MAHAWA

A rewarding trip from Tomohon—and an easier one than the trek to Mount Lokon—is to take a local bus to another volcano, adjacent to Lokon—Mount Mahawu. Enquire locally about the current level of activity of the volcano, then find a bus going to Rurukan (if you have no transport of your own), tell the driver "Gunung Mahawu," and you will be dropped off at the appropriate path.

professional. After 12 years as a ranger, he knew the forest paths intimately. Life, though, is never quite that simple and even this living was complicated by unscrupulous competition. He had to compete with the amateur guides from the village, who, attaching themselves to visitors, would tell blatant lies to obtain the work. We, for example, had been told on our arrival that Jenli had disappeared from the village dead drunk. In the past, clients who had made reservations with him had arrived to be informed that he was dead and buried.

INTO THE JUNGLE

We drove over what seemed an impossibly narrow wooden bridge and, having registered at the park office, entered the park itself. After a drive of a couple of kilometres along a forest trail, we halted and got out. Armed with torches, long trousers enclosed in socks and boots, long-sleeved shirts, and mosquito repellent thoroughly applied to those parts of the body unavoidably exposed to the light, we followed a path into the undergrowth.

Just beyond the trees to our left, the sound of rolling surf washed over us eerily from the invisible sea. The air was heavy and humid as the light began to fade, and the sounds of the tropical night—multifarious whirrings and whistlings and hootings—started up, sounding out through the forest twilight. Lianas, the long stringy roots made

famous by Tarzan, hung at our sides and whippy arcs of rattan bowed across the paths; yet, although we sometimes had to duck to miss huge ferns or palm leaves, or jump over a fallen tree trunk, the path was generally easy to follow. Giant ficus trees towered above us, their granite-coloured trunks supported by roots that surround the base in folds like crinoline skirts.

After an hour we stopped. Jenli approached a tree and looked inside a hole in its trunk. He came back nodding his head in satisfaction—he had found a nest of tarsiers. It was not yet completely dark and he suggested that we wait there for these nocturnal creatures to emerge for their nightly hunting excursions.

Within a few minutes it was pitch black. Jenli watched the surrounding bushes intently. Abruptly he arched forward to shine his torch into the round, dazzled eyes of a little creature the size of a large mouse. Its long thin tail hung down as it stared, absorbed, into the beam of light. Its eyes, like those of the more famous lemur, were disproportionately large, giving it an air of wide-eyed innocence.

It was an animal of great appeal and charm, but we soon had to switch off the torches to let the poor creature continue with its hunting. Then, just as we turned away, there was a crashing in the undergrowth, followed by a cry of "Oh, we really have to stop meeting like this!" and there, in the dark and in the middle of the jungle, stood Mark and Clare, the South African couple I had met a few days before when I was diving on Bunaken island.

We had accomplished what we wanted to that night and so returned home. Mark and Clare, who did not have the benefit of a vehicle to transport them along the trail in the pitch black, accepted the offer of a lift. They got down at the gate, inviting us to watch them leave by another bridge, the classic rope and board confection that, in movies, sways dangerously across a gaping chasm, or in this case, a muddy river about 5m (15 feet) below it. The bridge did sway, and there were several slats missing. Jenli whispered to us that several people had fallen through the gaps only the week before. In the thick darkness, the torches were not much help; but they made it safely across and we shouted our goodbyes to each other, in anticipation of yet another providential meeting.

A BRIEF AUTOBIOGRAPHY

The next morning—early, needless to say—we would be returning in search of more. Over dinner of fish and fruit back at the homestay, meanwhile, I was treated to the story of James's early life. He had trained for some time at a seminary to become a Roman Catholic priest before realizing that, as he put it, his vocation was incorrectly motivated. He was, he had discovered after four years, more motivated by the pursuit of women, to which end he had at one point even considered becoming a sailor, based on the old "girl in every port" formula. In the end, perhaps through parental pressure, he had found himself studying tourism in Jakarta before coming back to find work in Manado. But now he was about to get married to a Muslim girl (much to the disgust of his family), which would mean a move to her home town and a yet another vocation, this time as a rice merchant.

After dinner I wandered on to the road outside the homestead gates. A small cluster of children were playing marbles in the dust, watched by chattering neighbours. Above us all, the midnight-blue sky, a spangled starscape, seemed to be brushed by tall, shadowy coconut palms.

At five the next morning we were up and ready to re-enter the forest for a three-hour trek. Still in darkness, the forest was a hive of activity—we could hear the chattering of the tarsiers, but they were not our objective now. We were in search of larger prey. At the base of a ficus tree Jenli stopped to point out a hole high in its trunk, the home, he said, of a pair of nesting hornbills. To see them we would have to await the return of the parents from their hunting expedition. So we stood around waiting for dawn, listening to the cawing of parrots and sniffing the damp, steamy air. As the sunlight reached down to us, there was a heavy, rhythmic flapping above our heads as the first of the adult hornbills settled on the upper branches of a neighbouring tree.

He, or she, sat there preening its feathers, in patient expectation of its mate. The mate was a long time coming, so patience is definitely a virtue in hornbill-watching circles. And when the mate arrived there was much caressing, preening and pecking with surprisingly gentle dexterity, given the size of their great, multicoloured beaks, before the two of them flew in quick succession into the nest to tend to their offspring.

THE BLACK MACAQUES

Now we were to shift our attention from the high branches to the lower ones, for we were off in search of the black macaques, an ape unique to Sulawesi, which inhabits the forest here in consid-erable numbers. A passing local woman pointed out something to Jenli and we hurried along another path behind him towards the sound of animated activity. When we arrived at its source we found ourselves surrounded by at least 30 gambolling jokers of all sizes, a troop of black macaques. There was the lead male, sitting on his haunches and keep-ing a weather eye on his charges; a couple copulating energetically; and several young monkeys chasing each other from branch to branch—all of this within a few paces of where we stood. Of course they knew we were there, but they completely ignored us. None approached us for food or to warn us off. Apparently we held no fear for them

bu at the same time—and just as gratifying—sentimental tourists had evidently not spoiled them. Gradually the troop moved deeper into the forest (each troop controls its own area) and for a while we followed, enchanted, until it was time to break away and start the return trip through the woods.

We went by way of a another giant ficus tree. Inside, it was entirely hollow, but its roots crept in an intricate tangle up the interior of the trunk, like a gigantic brandy snap. Further on, James invited me to shine my torch up into the trunk of another tree, and there was a host of small, round orange beads suspended in mid-air, the eyes of a colony of bats.

TANGKOKO OR BATUPITIH?

Confusion can arise between the names of Tangkoko and Batuputih. Tangkoko is the name given to the area of the park taken from the mountain of the same name. In fact much of the reserve covers the lower slopes of the mountain. Batuputih refers only to the village at the end of the road from Bitung, and may be the name used by buses that ply the route between the two.

Eventually the sound of the surf returned and before long we were on a beach of black volcanic sand. The jungle, with its dense fruit-bearing trees, came almost to the water's edge. We turned on to the beach and strolled along it until we came to a clearing where the car was parked.

No doubt return journeys into the jungle would bring new delights. There are very long pythons in there—up to 12m (40 feet), so it is said—and the babirusa, which is a sort of wild boar. It is possible to spend the night in the jungle too; but for me the treks had been fruitful enough.

To my relief, the journey back to Manado was quite painless. I had antici-pated problems returning up some of the pitted slopes, but James steered us through skilfully. We gave a lift to an English couple and a New Zealander, Mike, with an artificial leg. In love with travel, he had been in an appalling accident on holiday in Crete, but he was the very personification of good cheer, and held no grudges. His optimism and determinataion made any discomforts I had endured in order to see such magi-cal places as Tangkoko, seem as nothing.

ABOVE Bananas to go: in Manado
RIGHT In an area of active volcanoes, a
beach of black volcanic sand edges the jungle

GOING IT ALONE

INTERNAL TRAVEL

The most obvious point of arrival for Tangkoko is the port of Manado, about 3 hours' drive away on the opposite western coast. In Manado it is not difficult to arrange a car and driver to take you to Tomohon and on to Tangkoko.

By air The easiest way of getting to Manado is by air. From Jakarta there are daily services on Garuda, the Indonesian national airline (journey time 90 minutes). There are also daily flights to and from other major cities in Indonesia.

There are a few international flights operating in and out of Manado. Silk Air, the regional carrier of Singapore Airlines, operates at least twice a week to Singapore. Bouraq operates once a week from Manado to Davao, on the southern Philippine island of Mindanao. Garuda has been thinking of operating flights to and from Japan, but no decision has yet been made.

By bus It is possible to reach Tangkoko by bus from Manado. Start from the Paal II Terminal and take a bus for Bitung. Change at Girian.

By boat You can also get close to Tangkoko by boat. Manado's main port, Bitung, is well located, only about 2 hours by road. Pelni, the Indonesian state shipping line, runs fortnightly loop services to various ports in Sulawesi, as well as to Jakarta and Surabaya. There is also a weekly service (normally Tuesday, taking 35 hours) from Bitung to Davao in the Philippines, and various services to Balikpapan in Kalimantan (Indonesian Borneo). If you arrive by boat, continue to Tangkoko by bus. An intermittent boat service runs between Bitung and Batuputih, but no clear information is available.

WHEN TO GO

The temperature is more or less unvarying, but the driest months are August and September, and the wettest December through February. The monsoons are unpredictable, and it would be worth checking locally, as the road to Tangkoko is likely to be impassable after heavy rain.

PLANNING

All visitors entering the park must employ a local guide and must register at the entrance. Try to take on one of the official rangers—not only are they the best informed but they are doing their utmost to fight the trade in illegal animal smuggling. The Smiling Hostel in Manado can help with this. There are plenty of locals willing to act as guides but they are not official rangers.

WHAT TO TAKE

- ❏ Swimming costume.
- ❏ Walking boots and socks.
- ❏ Light clothes that cover all flesh (or at least the legs).
- ❏ Insect repellent.
- ❏ Rainwear.
- ❏ Torch and spare battery.
- ❏ Binoculars.
- ❏ Water bottle.

HEALTH MATTERS

- ❏ Take anti-malaria tablets.
- ❏ Use mosquito repellent and coils.
- ❏ Wear long trousers and long-sleeved shirts at night.
- ❏ Bring a basic health kit.
- ❏ Drink bottled water.
- ❏ Arrange full medical insurance before departure.
- ❏ At least a month before leaving home, check with your doctor what vaccinations are needed.

SULAWESI

Manado's Coral Paradise

by Christopher Knowles

A fabulous reef and coral wall rings the volcanic island of Bunaken, which lies offshore from the port of Manado. Here I found a paradise for both the snorkeller and the scuba diver.

Manado, a port on the Celebes Sea, close to the Equator, lies at the very northern, volcanic tip of Sulawesi, which is the eccentrically shaped Indonesian island located to the west of Borneo and to the south of the Philippines. The capital of the province of Minahasa, **Manado** is a substantial and thriving town of some 200,000 people, and is an almost essential point of embarkation for visitors to the region.

Much of the town exudes an air of languid prosperity. The port itself, littered with worn-out ships, has the faintly run-down aspect that it has probably borne for the last one hundred years. It looks out to several offshore islands, of which **Manado Tua**, with its perfectly shaped volcano covered in vegetation as dense as moss, is the most prominent. In the waters that lap that volcanic island, the coelacanth, the prehistoric fish first discovered off the coast of South Africa in 1937, was found for the first time in Asian waters in 1997. Adjacent to Manado Tua is a long, flattish island, with a hump of forest along its spine. This is **Bunaken**, home to one of Asia's finest diving reefs, a coral-encrusted wall that falls 180m (600 feet) into the ocean depths.

Bunaken, along with Manado Tua and three other islands close by, is surrounded by a 75,000-ha (188,000-acre) marine park, a beautiful deep-sea garden as yet unspoilt by visitors. However, tourism is a potential threat to the coral. Boats belonging to some of the cheaper dive operators tend to damage the coral with their anchors, one of two good reasons not to use them (the other being that their equipment may not be the best).

FROM MANADO TO BUNAKEN

If you are not staying in one of the luxury hotels in Manado, the main point of information is the Smiling Hostel, a cheaply priced backpackers' guest house close to the port area. The hostel can arrange diving, as well as boats out to Bunaken. The journey to the island from Manado takes about 40 minutes by motorized outrigger. As it does its best to plough through the squally waves, you look back to Manado's ancient Chinese temple, which dominates the

If you don't already have a diving qualification, you can take a PADI course on Bunaken. The diving is excellent and although the current at the reef wall needs attention, the level of concern and care shown by Froggie Divers is outstanding. Diving trips can be arranged on the spot, but you are advised to book in advance, especially if you want to stay on Bunaken.

★★ There is accommodation to suit all tastes and pockets in Manado. On Bunaken island it is a choice of which homestay you prefer (there are plans to build a few small cottages, which will offer a greater level of comfort than the clean but very basic facilities provided by a homestay).

All diving equipment can be hired on the spot. Apart from insect repellent, sun block, and a sun hat, you are recommended to bring along a small supply of vinegar. This eases the effects of fire coral, which is difficult to avoid when under water.

lower part of the town, and, beyond it, receding into the distance, the Minahasa highlands.

In the boat with me were a Dutch couple who had already been on the island for several days and a very relaxed-looking German, Detlief, who was going to Bunaken to learn to dive. Ahead we could see the village of Bunaken on the shore at one end of the island; or rather we could see its huge church, white, like cake icing, in the sunshine. The boat lurched on before turning in across the coral reef and coming to a rest in the shallows by a beach. Holding our luggage up high, we paddled ashore between grotesque mangrove roots, sending dozens of little crabs scuttling in all directions before they vanished abruptly into the wet sand. The beach, of seaweed and ochre sand, extended in a long shallow curve around the forest which, dense and limp, was barely stirred by the merest hint of a breeze.

ISLAND LIFE

Our accommodation, at Papa Boa's Homestay, was on the beach. It was very simple, consisting of a covered eating area, which was the social centre of this part of the island, and a number of thatched huts on stilts containing beds with mosquito nets and a basic bathroom fitted out with a barrel of water and a ladle. It was clean, functional and rather attractively in tune with its surroundings.

I sat talking to Detlief while we waited for Christiane, the leading light of Froggie Divers, one of the principal dive operations in Manado. At about four that afternoon she arrived to deliver all her charges back to the homestay (Froggie Divers have their headquarters a short boat ride along the beach). Christiane, a chain-smoking dynamo, had a look at my diving record and, no doubt shrewdly assessing my capabilities, informed me that I would be "buddying up" with someone called Angus. Mentally

picturing a Scotsman, I realized I had misheard the name only when I was introduced to a young Dane called Anders, one of Christiane's charges who was learning to become a divemaster.

Soon there were others at the table, a mix of nationalities, ages, and backgrounds, all there just for the diving and the way of life that goes with it. Sorin was an American, coincidentally of Scandinavian extraction, who had recently quit his "headhunter" job in Singapore, while Mark and Clare, South Africans who had been working in London, were making their way home on an extended holiday through Asia and Australia. From where I stood, they fell into the Mad Divers category, completely fearless and willing to try anything. Mark told me about a dive off the South African coast during which he went into a cave, only to find his way out was barred by a large shark…

And there were several divers from the Netherlands, a Briton who had lived for many years in Taiwan, and a German family, including two young children, resident in Singapore. Dinner, taken by the yellow light of hurricane lamps (the electricity supply, which depended on a local generator, was erratic), consisted of a barracuda, its gaping mouth revealing a row of razor teeth and its blue scales burnt to a dark indigo.

REBELLION

Languid though Manado may seem today, in 1958 it was a different story. The people of northern Sulawesi had always been closer than other Indonesians to the Dutch colonists, a fact that led them to join in a rebellion against the government of President Sukarno, the centres of the uprising being Sumatra and North Sulawesi. Failure was followed by severe reprisals: in February of 1958 Manado was bombed by the Indonesian airforce and recaptured the following June.

LEFT *The best snorkelling in Indonesia is to be had off Manado*
BELOW *Village boys show off their catch*

ABOVE *A typical beach-front guest house and restaurant on Bunaken Island*

S U L A W E S I

COELACANTH—AN ANCESTOR OF OURS?

It is hard to believe, looking at fish, that one is perhaps looking at a distant relative. The fins of most fish consist of a series of flexible rays linked to bones within the body, but in some fish, including the coelacanth, first rediscovered off South Africa in 1938 and discovered in Indonesian waters off Manado in 1997, each fin has an internal bone structure that resembles a primitive hand. Such fish were common during the Devonian period, 400 million years ago, and it may well be that the first land vertebrates were descended from them. It is thought that they crawled out of the water on their fins and gradually adapted to the new environment, developing lungs and evolving to resemble newts. From newts came reptiles and then birds and mammals. The coelacanth, which grows to about 1.6m (5 feet), is the closest living relative of the earliest land vertebrates and is almost identical to fossils that date back 140 million years.

A SWEEPING CURRENT

The next day, after breakfast of fruit and bread and jam, tea or coffee, taken to the sound of cockcrow, the Froggie Divers fleet arrived, each boat already stocked with oxygen tanks and all the necessary equipment. Anders and I were diving with Karl-Heinz and Rocky, a local man from Sulawesi and one of Christiane's divemasters.

At Bunaken the coral reef extends several hundred metres from the beach. After a short ride, the boat anchored close to where it comes to an end. We donned our suits and fell in. The first few seconds are always a rather disconcerting experience, with the rush of water and bubbles around your head and the sound of your own breath amplified in the mask. Then you bob around on the surface until everyone is ready, the signal is given, the buoyancy vests are deflated, and you start to sink into the blue depths, remembering to "equalize" by pinching the nostrils and blowing gently through them until your ears pop. At the same time, you are trying to breathe as evenly as possible, yet exhaling with controlled restraint, like a car idling at traffic lights.

Pretty soon though, as your eyes become accustomed to the surroundings, everything comes into focus—darting slivers of colour, the outline of larger shapes at the limits of visibility,

and the coral garden that is the mighty reef wall.

Anders, I discovered, was a highly concerned "buddy," who never left my side, physically keeping me upright by hanging on to my arm and always ready to step in, or rather fin in, in the event of any problem. As it happened, his presence was more than welcome, because the current was astoundingly powerful, accelerating without warning to sweep us along at a terrifying rate, at the very limits of our control. We had somehow to harness the current and use it to our advantage. Since Anders could not speak to me, he had to do his best to convey how to cope by means of gesture and example, as the coral wall zipped past us like a fast-forwarded film. It was all we could do to note what we were seeing; but from time to time we managed to hook a finger on to a rock, hovering in order to look around us at the coral itself.

CREATURES GREAT AND SMALL

One of the most interesting aspects of the wall diving at Bunaken was the "macro" life, that is to say the smaller creatures like the iridescent nudibranches (something like sea snails) that lurk in crevices in the coral. Also thriving in the coral are red and orange encrusting sponges, anemones, seawhips, Spanish dancers, basket and tube sponges, and Christmas tree worms. We also saw innumerable electric blue dottybacks, a slender trumpet fish, and a massive puffer fish. Bunaken's other myriad marine species include stingrays, manta rays, barracuda, groupers and snappers, the brightly coloured parrot fish and clownfish, the giant Napoleon wrasse and harmless reef sharks, blue ribbon eels and sea snakes, turtles and dolphins.

I succeeded in staying down for over an hour, my best performance as far as air conservation went by a long, long way. But the others were far more skilled than me and we had to wait a further half an hour for them, after which we headed for Froggie Divers headquarters for lunch. Here too, everything was very simply laid out, with a large open-sided restaurant area, a storage hut for equipment, and bungalow-style living quarters.

There was, however, a reassuring air of meticulousness that was clearly a reflection of Christiane's thorough approach to her work. After our lunch of giant trevally fish we spent some time poring over books illustrating the region's fish and then, when sufficient time had elapsed for our bodies to have recovered from the morning's dive, it was back out to the reef wall. There are various charts to be consulted in order to work out how much rest is required between dives. The formula is based on the depth reached on the first, and successive, dives, and the time spent at those depths. It is very important to be as accurate as possible since underwater pressure can do damage that only becomes apparent afterwards.

THAT CURRENT AGAIN

The current was not now as violent as it had been in the morning, but it was still powerful enough to warrant care and attention. This time, however, I was in a better position to cope with it. Anders had warned me that he would not be quite as attached to me as he had been during the morning's dive; but on the other hand he had told me in advance how to best make use of the circumstances.

Thus, although we were again challenged by the current, it was not so much of a struggle. In a pleasant, dreamy way, we coasted along, following the unscrolling of a long and colourful parchment. From time to time I would still manage to lose control, getting stung by pink fire coral or scraping against a rock, but on the whole, the experience was an altogether more relaxed one.

I learned not to react to adversity by flailing my arms to regain my balance— this serves only to expend energy uselessly. Scuba-diving, after all, is not a natural activity for human beings. It is not surprising that instinct tells you to do what you would if you were on dry land, which is often the opposite of what is best when under water. It was only there at Bunaken that I realized that the basic open-water diving qualification was really only the beginning of a longer process.

THE BALD MALEO BIRD

If you see a bald bird about the size of a domestic hen, with black and white plumage, then you have come across the Maleo bird, unique to Sulawesi. The reason for its hairless pate is much debated. One theory is that it helps prevent overheating while foraging on broiling beaches. The Maleo is one of only a few birds in the world that do not incubate their eggs using body heat. Instead, they use the heat of the baking sand, or hot earth near volcanoes, or hot springs—of which there are many in Sulawesi. Holes are dug in the earth or sand and the eggs are buried. After the incubation period, the young bird struggles upwards for several days in order to emerge into the open air.

BELOW A picture-postcard sunset on Manado
LEFT and RIGHT Bunaken offers the best snorkelling in Indonesia: its coral reef still teems with amazingly colourful life, but divers must always be aware of how easily damaged it is

PARTY TIME

That evening there was to be a party at Froggie Divers HQ, in honour of a couple of employees who had recently been married. We piled into a boat for the ride across; on the way, phosphorescent plankton twinkled in the wake. There was palm wine to drink, dark and sweet and strong, and a band that played on, and on.

It started off well with guitars, a bass (improvised from an old tea chest) and bottle and spoon; and some very poignant Polynesian-style songs. As drink was taken, the renditions become rather more ragged but the music kept on course. The only hiccup came when a man from the local village, a surfeit of palm wine having imbued him with great powers of self-confidence, insisted on taking over the bass, plucking at the strings with frenzied gusto in the mistaken belief that he was playing in time and tune. The others gamely and tolerantly played along. Late in the evening all of us had to dance the *pato-pato*, a long and involved affair that exuberantly, if obscurely, tells the story of the sunrise.

Throughout all of this Christiane, a wiry 60-year-old, speaks of the complexities and rewards of living in Indonesia. It would be invidious to go into too much detail, but suffice it to say that the path to prosperity, even the

TIPS FOR WALL DIVING

There is a particular technique for wall—or drift—diving. The first and most basic rule is to stay close to the wall. This goes counter to a natural instinct to keep one's distance, for fear of collision, but the truth is that your body, by adopting the correct posture, merely rides with the current a few inches from the wall. By swimming too far back from the wall, on the other hand, there is a risk of being swept out to sea. The most practical position is the most stream-lined one that also enables you to maintain balance, with arms clasped across the chest and knees drawn up a little, like a cramped Egyptian mummy.

path to a normal existence, is uphill all the way if you are a foreigner. Every single institution appears to be against you but, as she pointed out, the only way forward was to work within the system. By dint of great determination and absence of egoism, Christiane had gained the respect of her Indonesian colleagues.

Between all of them, and against the odds, they ran an excellent operation with the accent on safety and on reef conservation, as well as sheer enjoyment. They were confident for the future—new headquarters were to be built for Froggie, on the beach close to Papa Boa's, with a couple of bungalows for rent that will provide more comfortable accommodation—for those who require it—than a homestay.

After midnight we were escorted along the beach by the still enthusiastic musicians and boated home underneath a star-spangled equatorial sky. The submarine world opened up by diving had been a revelation but it was still good, sometimes, to enjoy the mysteries above.

A VISIT TO LAKE TONDANO

If you have time, it is worthwhile taking a short trip from Manado about 40km (25 miles) south to Lake Tondano. It is pretty large—about 15km (9 miles) north to south—and requires a couple of hours to make the journey round it by car. Since the lake is located several hundred metres above sea level, the climate here is much pleasanter than on the coast. The villages around the lake, with their imposing churches, have character but are free of squalor and poverty, while the scenery, though unmistakably tropical, has the cool beauty of the Italian lakes. Here and there, restaurants offer fish freshly taken from the lake.

GOING IT ALONE

INTERNAL TRAVEL

By air Bunaken can be reached only from Manado, the port on the northern tip of Sulawesi. The easiest way of getting to Manado is by air. From Jakarta there are daily services on Garuda, the Indonesian national airline (journey time 90 minutes). There are also daily flights to and from many of the other major cities in Indonesia, including Ujung Pandang, in the south of Sulawesi, and Ambon, Denpasar, Gorontalo, Palu, and Ternate either on Garuda or on one of the other Indonesian airlines, Bouraq and Merpati. There are also flights available to Biak, Jayapura, Poso, Luwuk and Sorong.

A few international flights operate in and out of Manado. Silk Air, the regional carrier of Singapore Airlines, operates flights at least twice a week to Singapore. Bouraq operates a weekly flight to Davao, the port on the southern Philippine island of Mindanao.

By bus Manado's main long-distance bus terminal, Malalayeng, is located well outside town, roughly a 30-minute journey by *bemo* (the local minibus or 'jeepney' transport). From there it is possible to take buses to Gorontalo (250km/156 miles to the southwest) and onward to south and central Sulawesi.

By boat You can also get to Manado by boat. Manado's main port, Bitung, is 55km (34 miles) from Manado, on the opposite, western side of the peninsula. Pelni (the state shipping line) runs fortnightly loop services to various ports in Sulawesi, as well as to Jakarta and to Surabaya. There is also a weekly service (normally a Tuesday, journey time 35 hours) to Davao in the Philippines and various services to Balikpapan in Kalimantan (Indonesian Borneo). There are also a number of services from Manado itself, and from Singkil (1.5km/1 mile to the north), to various ports on Sulawesi and to Ambon and the Talaud Islands. These boats differ one from the other but in general offer four cabin classes and economy, or deck, class. To give some idea of prices, first class will cost about $380 on a Pelni from Jakarta to Bitung. Journey time is 4 days.

GETTING TO BUNAKEN FROM MANADO

To get to Bunaken from Manado is a boat journey of about 40 minutes. If you intend to stay on the island you should arrange accommodation in advance from Manado—the Smiling Hostel is probably the best place to do that. A transfer to the island can then be arranged at the same time. Otherwise there is a daily service to Bunaken Village, which will not be convenient if your accommodation is in a homestay further along the coast.

ORGANIZING A DIVE

Froggie Divers (see Contacts) are based on Bunaken. Other outfits (for example Barracuda) also offer dive packages to Bunaken. Neither is the cheapest operation in the area, but it is as well to note that cheap diving does not necessarily mean good, or, more importantly, safe diving.

WHEN TO GO

The temperature varies little through the year. The monsoons have become unpredictable, but the drier months tend to be August and September, the wettest December–February.

HEALTH MATTERS

- ❏ Take anti-malaria tablets.
- ❏ Use mosquito repellent and coils.
- ❏ Wear trousers and long-sleeved shirts at night.
- ❏ Bring a basic health kit.
- ❏ Drink bottled water.
- ❏ Arrange full medical insurance before departure.
- ❏ At least a month before leaving home, check up on vaccinations.

ESSENTIALS

If you are staying on Bunaken, you should bring your own towels, soap, and other toiletries, as well as a torch (and a spare battery), which will be useful when the electricity fails. There is a small shop on the beach, but you cannot depend on it having, for example, the size or type of battery you need. In addition, bring any relevant diving qualification certificate, swimming costume, and flip-flops or equivalent.

25 AMONG THE WRECKS OF CORON 248–256

24 MEETING THE T'BOLI PEOPLE 236–247

PHILIPPINES

The Philippines, a widely spread group of islands (the northernmost lie at a similar latitude to Hong Kong, the southernmost not far from Borneo) are surprisingly little visited. For adventurers this is a great bonus, for it is here, perhaps more than in many places in the region, that you can find large areas of unspoilt natural beauty inhabited by peoples whose friendliness is one of the country's most attractive attributes. The capital, Manila, is a sprawling traffic-ridden metropolis of extremes of poverty and wealth. Beyond it, however, is a world of charm and fascination. The Philippines were for long the playthings of the various Western colonial powers, but the external influences have been mostly Spanish and American. The Spanish influence is most evident in the faces of the people, whilst the American influence is felt through a surprisingly sophisticated familiarity with technology. At the same time, very old-fashioned infatuations with religion, music, corruption, and good-natured resignation are part of daily life.

Lake Sebu on the island of Mindanao in the Philippines

PHILIPPINES

Meeting the T'boli People

by Christopher Knowles

After a flight from Manila to the island of Mindanao in the far south of the Philippines, I went by jeep to Lake Sebu for a swim in one of the most beautiful inland waters in the country. Here, I met the delightful T'boli people, who in their ancestral domain cling to their traditional way of life.

 The trip to Lake Sebu is not difficult (unless undertaken by public transport) and once you are there it is easy to wander around at will, enjoying the atmosphere. The walk in the jungle is not long but can be tiring because of the heat and terrain.

 Accommodation in General Santos is plentiful at all levels. At Lake Sebu the choice is much more limited but there is at least one so-called resort hotel with acceptable facilities. In the future it may be possible to arrange a stay with a T'boli family but that does not appear possible as yet. The climate at Lake Sebu is cooler than on the plain, but it is still hot and the weather is unpredictable.

 Be prepared for rain, take a swimming costume and also, for walking in the jungle, good boots with a firm grip. Insect repellent will be useful and be aware that in the jungle there are creatures that can give very unpleasant bites. Long trousers and socks are recommended.

It was early in the morning but the waiting room at Manila's domestic terminal was crowded. Without warning, everybody seated around me rose to their feet and started speaking aloud. They were intoning the Lord's Prayer, echoing the words of a priest, kneeling at the front of the room dressed in full church regalia. Prayers at an airport are probably a good idea, but they were especially apt just then, in the Philippines, as the national airline had been declared bankrupt only the week before. Fortunately, that catastrophe did not appear to have interfered unduly with the flight schedule.

Few foreigners go to General Santos, a city on the southernmost Philippine island of **Mindanao**. I was the only one in a half-full plane—which carried, as far as I am aware, a unique form of in-flight entertainment: video cameras had been installed in the plane's fuselage so that passengers could watch take-off and landing. Once we were above the clouds, the plot became rather opaque but the opening and closing sequences were spectacular.

At General Santos airport I was met by "Boy" Santiago, who, in the frontier atmosphere of this compara-tively new town, overlooked by a 2,000-m (6,000-foot) extinct volcano, seemed to have fingers in any number of pies, including a restaurant and a bowling alley. In a country like the Philippines, where uncertainty is a way of life, it probably makes perfect sense to have a number of strings to one's bow.

General Santos, named after a revolutionary hero, is a port that special-izes in tuna for the Japanese market. Overflowing with restaurants and banks, it exudes a businesslike confidence, even at a time of economic gloom throughout the region.

KIDNAPPERS' PARADISE

After a lunch of *sashimi* at a local Japanese-style restaurant, Boy and I boarded a jeep for the journey to Lake Sebu, located in the hills to the north of the city. We set off on a long, busy high-way across the plain at the base of the volcano, passing through a succession of hectic little towns whose streets were packed with pedicabs and jeepneys. All of these buses-converted-from-jeeps, gaudily painted and trimmed in gleaming chrome, had passengers extruding from the interior and plastered over every scrap of space on the exterior. Behind the towns are fields of asparagus and pineapple, two crops that flourish in the fertile volcanic soil, as well as coconut groves and banana plantations.

Most striking is the Philippine love affair with both religion and firearms. Every conceivable Christian sect has its church, chapel, or meeting room in these towns, and there are any number of Christ the King Funeral Homes—hardly surprising, perhaps, when in local restaurants you see signs proclaiming "Guns For Sale" next to an advertisement for lunchtime specials.

After a while we stopped at a stall to buy some fresh fruit before turning off on to about 20km (12 miles) of pitted dirt track for Lake Sebu, climbing through increasingly lush vegetation and emerald green paddy fields. Huts of straw and bamboo, built on stilts or piles, became more in evidence as, over a wide stretch of forest, we could look back across the plain towards the sea.

We passed a sign welcoming us to the domain of the T'boli and soon, below us, there was a smaller, sister lake to Lake Sebu, marked out with fishing nets. A short way beyond it, at an altitude of some 600m (2,000 feet) above sea level, was Lake Sebu itself, encircled by high hills covered in bamboo forest and farm terraces. For a moment, coming upon this place of exquisite tranquillity and quiet beauty seemed to me nothing less than the chance discovery of an overlooked paradise.

ANCESTRAL DOMAIN

We turned sharply down another dirt track, following a sign to Punta Isla, a hotel perched on a promontory overlooking the olive waters of Lake Sebu. Opposite it, in the centre of the lake, was a palm-edged island. The shore of the lake was dotted with T'boli houses

TROUBLED TIMES

Every few kilometres along the road from General Santos to Lake Sebu there are military checkpoints, unmanned, I was relieved to notice, and seemingly out of use for the time being. Throughout the early 1990s, Mindanao acquired a dangerous reputation for kidnapping, mostly of foreigners (usually wealthy and of Philippino extraction) by militant Islamic groups. I was told that any kidnappings now take place in the eastern part of the island, while the latest newspaper reports hint that the leader of the terrorists has agreed to negotiate with the new government.

on stilts. Dug-out canoes glided here and there as men attended to fishing nets, and a little steamer did the rounds of the shoreline. In fact truly, here, old met new. The resort hotel was simple (the bedrooms had bamboo four-posters and bright red embroidered coverlets) but indisputably modern, with most conveniences available (even if the sink in the bathroom had no drainage pipe). Yet just a short stroll took you out of the hotel compound into the bamboo-and-straw world of the T'boli.

Only a few hundred metres away, a woman was working at her loom on the upper floor of her stilted bamboo house. I was invited in and removed my shoes, to find her sitting at a homemade loom, her feet stretched out to a sort of pedal (that keeps the warp taut). The pattern she was weaving was the product of her betel-nut induced dreams, and the colours, mostly black and red, the result of natural dyes extracted from leaf and tree bark fibre. She would sit there every day for several weeks to finish the 10-m (33-foot) bolt of cloth. Some of it might be used by local people, but much of it would end up for sale in General Santos. Surrounded by her basket of betel nuts, her gongs, and the other

ABOVE A traditional T'boli home built on stilts of bamboo and straw. Many are very close to the modern Punta Isla resort on Lake Sebu (below)
RIGHT Fishing in one of the streams that feeds Lake Sebu

musical instruments that many families seem to have here, not to mention her traditional bonnet (which at first I took to be a lampshade), she seemed to be blissfully unaware of the meaning of boredom. Further on, there was a brassmaker at work in a foundry right beneath his home. He was one of four men in the area renowned for bell-making—a skill that has been passed down through the generations after centuries of trading with the Muslims on the plain below.

Although there are a few loosely congregated villages, traditionally the T'boli live in houses built apart from each other. The houses, called *gunu bong*, are about 15m (50 feet) long and 10m (35 feet) wide, and stand on bamboo posts about 2m (6 feet) high. Whilst, in common with people all over the world, young T'boli have taken to jeans, many T'boli, especially the women, continue to wear their decorative jewellery (including a sort of necklace that extends from ear to ear, arching under the chin) and colourful turbans, called *kayabs*. Thursdays and Saturdays, when the T'boli who live in the jungle, a little further up in the hills, come down to the market, are the best days to see them in traditional clothes.

NIGHT DRAWS IN

At the hotel, meanwhile, Boy has found the two T'boli women who are to be my guides, Oyo and GingGing. There was some discussion as to what we might do over the next couple of days, and a warning from them that it can be very cold around the lake at night. There was also a rumour of an incident at the waterfall I was to visit the next day—it was not quite clear what form the incident took, but there was clearly still a little nervousness abroad, a hangover from the activities of terrorist groups.

In the evening, as darkness fell and the crickets and cicadas started up, a boy astride a water buffalo after a hard day in the fields let the animal forage at the side of the track, just outside the hotel. Fires flared into life, producing a homely, orange glow in the huts we saw earlier on the far side of the lake. A machine gun was left slung across the counter in the small hotel shop. A basket on a wire whipped to and fro between the dining room and the lakeside kitchen, transporting plates of freshly grilled fish, while dogs, cats, and ducks scavenged busily. Fishing eagles hovered and glided over the fish farms amid spiralling terns, while kingfishers darted, and little long-beaked yellow birds hopped among the branches. It had become a little cooler, but it was certainly not cold.

ONE MOTORBIKE, THREE PASSENGERS

In the morning I awoke to the whoopings and shriekings that is the dawn chorus of the jungle. Sometime after breakfast, with a rather endearing disregard for the time we had arranged, GingGing showed up. "Skylab is outside," she told me, casually. The beautifully named "Skylab" was an example of the standard mode of transport here (along with buffalo and horses)—a small motorbike which, by leaps of faith and imagination, advertised itself as having a capacity of five passengers. "Welcome

COCKFIGHTS

It may be unpalatable to Westerners, but cockfighting (*sabong*) is part of ordinary life in the Philippines. It takes place, usually on a Sunday or a public holiday in a wooden arena called the cockpit, and the fights may start early in the morning. The money men, or *kristos*, come into the ring before each fight to encourage the spectators to lay bets. They take all the bets there and then, and commit them to memory. Meanwhile, the birds, wearing sharp spurs and sorted into classes by weight, are being prepared for the fight, stoked up to inspire them into an aggressive frame of mind. The fight itself may last for only a few seconds, but a curious ritual prevails where the victor must peck the vanquished cock twice or the fight is declared a draw.

Aboard" was written on a sign at the back. So the three of us (GingGing, Benny the driver, and I), piled on to "Skylab," to head for one of seven waterfalls in the vicinity. Known as the **Second Falls**, it is the tallest.

After a mercifully short ride we turned off the road and came to a rest outside a house. "We walk from here," I was told, and after paying a toll to the householder, we started off down a muddy path overgrown with pink and blue flowers. The humid air was filled with a range of musky perfumes and every few metres clumps of massive bamboo, used as posterns in the building of traditional T'boli houses, sprouted from the banks.

We descended deeper into the jungle (for jungle is what it had become) and the path became stonier, steeper, and more slippery with every step. We could hear the sound of distant thunder. "Can you hear the falls?" "I can," I replied eagerly. "But we still have a long way to go," smiled GingGing sweetly.

A SWIM IN THE JUNGLE

She was right. It was very hot. A bamboo irrigation channel looked very inviting; but we passed it by, continuing our gradual descent. After some time we turned off down an impossible-looking mudslide, down which we slithered, trying unsuccessfully to avoid thorny tendrils, towards a cloud of vapour. "You have taken the wrong path," somebody shouted down, but it was too late now. I removed my shoes and flung them to the bottom, as suggested by GingGing, in the hope of gaining a firmer grip by using my toes. Somehow we made it to the bottom without serious injury and followed a grassy and then stony path along the banks of a frisky river towards the falls.

As is the way with these things, it was all worth it. For, there in the middle of the forest was a steep, horseshoe-shaped cliff, fully 90m (300 feet) high, and down it a river plunged in torrential white tresses. The beauty of it was that the water did not drop directly into the pool, but rather, it fell behind a stone curtain close to the base and, with the full force of its cascade blunted, sent up diaphanous folds of vapour. So by scrambling over rocks and boulders and by straddling the fast current that occurs where the pool narrows to become a river again, we were able to swim in the pool almost beneath the falls themselves, without being knocked unconscious by the torrent. With the heat, and the exertion of shinning down the hillside, the cool water was very welcome, but the real joy came from the exhilaration of bathing in amongst the bamboo and palm trees, to the crash of the tumbling water, while a short way downstream, by a bridge made out of bamboo, a local woman collected shellfish. Tarzan, I thought, eat your heart out.

The way back was a little easier—firstly because we found the correct path, secondly because going uphill made it easier to obtain a grip. By now my shoes were back on my feet, which was fortunate since I only just avoided stepping on a 15-mm (6-inch) coiled centipede with a shiny black carapace and wriggling red legs, which, Benny told me, was highly poisonous. We rested outside a little cluster of huts where a large sow was suckling her litter of squealing pigs and a man on a buffalo passed by dragging a huge trunk of bamboo.

MATINÉE PERFORMANCE

Back on "Skylab," we bumped our way higher into the hills to visit more villages and to see other T'boli weavers at work, using different patterns and materials. Up there, there was no electricity and the unchanging daily life of harvesting and preparing for market, with horse-loads of sacks and bundles of banana leaf fibre, was much in evidence. It was

INSPECTING THE CATCH

Watching the local fishing boats landing their catch at the port is unexpectedly fascinating. The multicoloured boats, with their outriggers, jostle for space and anchor opposite a large, open-sided shed where the fish wholesalers have their weighing machines and tables. As the fish, mostly tuna, are brought up from the holds, they are flung into the filthy water beside the boats. Local men—some not much more than boys—dive in and heave the fish on to their shoulders, as a stream of purple blood pours from their mouths, and walk unsteadily up the steps to have them weighed. Then the fish are lined up on a slab for inspection, as if they were maturing cheeses. A tube is inserted into the flesh and withdrawn to be sniffed and scrutinized by representatives of the big buyers. Gory though it is, all the colour and activity, together with the great heat, the sea, and the coconut palms, is quite mesmerizing.

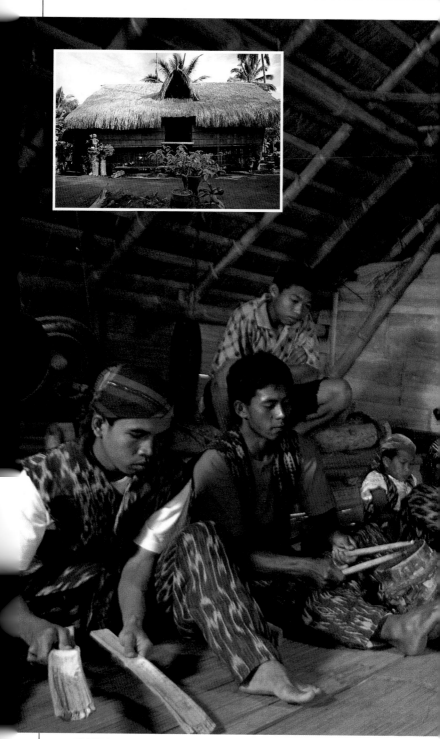

*ABOVE Our guide GingGing performs a
traditional mating dance*

INSET ABOVE A T'boli longhouse

all very placid, although according to GingGing the occasional battle still took place between villages over matters of land. As we started our descent, I could see wonderful views from the back of "Skylab" across the forest back to Lake Sebu, a picture, no doubt illusory, of idyllic tropical life.

Lunch was at GingGing and Oyo's home village of **Hellabong** and we took it in the tribal house, the local equivalent of a village hall. Fish and rice, which we ate with our fingers from large, glossy banana leaves, was followed by local coffee. And then it was time for some music and dance, still performed as a gesture of welcome in an area where there are but few tourists.

The whole neighbourhood, young and old, seemed to be involved. First, the instruments were introduced (drums, brass gongs, mouth harp, flute, bamboo lute, and a log tuned to a satisfactory resonance, beaten with great gusto by an elderly woman). Then, a selection of dances was performed by the younger girls (including GingGing), wearing their traditional costume of long woven skirts, blouses, belts with strings of bells, and ornamental combs in their hair.

Each dance was preceded by a ceremonial touch of the drum by the dancers involved, and ended in the same way. There was a dance for harvest, in which a scarf is swayed to simulate the gathering of fruit, and a dance to celebrate marriage (during which GingGing is unwillingly persuaded to swivel her hips before the guests). The boys then performed an endearingly friendly warrior dance, followed by a monkey dance. For this, some of the younger children were dressed as baby monkeys, and attached themselves to adult monkeys, played by older boys. They did as monkeys do to great merriment, until the whole performance dissolved into general hilarity. At the end everyone joined in the rendition of traditional songs, including one of prayer for the return of their ancestral lands, a plea

happily redundant since the government intervened to prevent them from losing all their land.

Looking through the straw blinds of the house down to Lake Sebu, which, as the fount of their prosperity, is of almost supernatural significance to the T'boli, it was easy to understand the importance of the song that has now become an anthem of thanks.

THE ONE THAT GOT AWAY

The next morning we were to go fishing on Lake Sebu in a traditional dug-out canoe. Oyo, her son Jayjay, GingGing, and Benny (who must still have been feeling cold, since he was wearing a balaclava) bowled up on "Skylab" with the usual cheerful disregard for time-keeping, and we went down to the lakeside to find a canoe whilst Oyo created a trio of bamboo fishing lines.

In these canoes you have to keep dead still to prevent them from capsizing, so the four of us clambered in with particular care. Sitting perched on the stern, for all the world as if it were her daily work, Oyo, who it transpired was heavily pregnant, paddled us out through the shallows, keeping to the shade provided by lakeside trees.

Eventually, however, we were forced into the broiling sunshine (which brings out a strong, fishy smell from the bottom of the canoe) to head towards fishing nets, and scattered among them, a marine

---

TERRITORIAL RIGHTS

There are about 60,000 T'boli people living in their ancestral area, the Tiruray Highlands, centred around Lake Sebu. The T'boli are one of three tribes, among the 60 or so throughout the Philippines, that have won back from the government the right to occupy their ancestral territory (hence the signs announcing our entry to the T'boli domain).

garden of gorgeously delicate open-cupped lotus. As we nudged through them, looking for a suitable point to stop, someone noticed that we had no bait. We tried to break out of the lotus stranglehold but found ourselves beached on a bed of purple flowers. We all disembarked to heave the canoe on to firmer ground, from where it was a short saunter up a slope to someone's house, where we begged for some worms.

Back in the canoe, the fish were not biting. An old man wearing an Ubo hat (something like a Mongol hat, worn by a neighbouring tribe) paddled up to us and, with a betel-nut smile, asked for a peso. Much of the fish farming is in the hands of absent owners, and many of the T'boli still earn their living by fishing the traditional way, earning perhaps 20 pesos for six or seven fish. We continued to sit patiently—there were several nibbles at the line but no takers. So it was back to the hotel for lunch of something caught by more successful anglers.

GingGing, Oyo, and Benny took their leave. T'boli culture appeared to be in good hands, if they were typical representatives. So far, the T'boli seem to have achieved a good balance between traditional and modern life. Whether it can continue remains to be seen.

That afternoon the jeep returned to take me back to General Santos. Roy, the driver, wanted to know if I would require the services of a bodyguard while I was in the city. Despite the recent history of the area, this seemed unnecessarily melodramatic, and I declined the offer. And as I strolled around the city centre that evening there was no sign of anything out of the ordinary—a few bars doing desultory business and any number of little stalls selling cheap food.

In the waiting room at General Santos airport, the assembled passengers were treated to an instruction video on loading containers on to aeroplanes. It seems an odd choice, yet a large part of the audience seems strangely absorbed by it. It is only as it comes to an end, and a couple of dozen people stand and leave the room, that all becomes clear to me—they are airport employees, and the waiting room doubles as a classroom.

MINDANAO'S NOBLE EAGLE

There are several national parks on Mindanao, the second largest island of the Philippines (the largest is Luzon). Among them, perhaps the most important is Mount Apo National Park, which lies to the northeast of General Santos. It was established in 1936 to protect the highest mountain in the Philippines, Mount Apo, which rises to a height of 2,954m (9,691 feet) and is an active volcano. Although it looks as if its peak is covered in snow, what you see is actually a thick white sulphur crust.

The park is highly characteristic of the forested volcanic regions of Mindanao, and has some spectacular scenery. It is also well known for its wildlife, and for one creature in particular—the Philippine monkey-eating eagle or haribon (*Pithecophaga jefferyi*), referred to as "the air's noblest flier" by American aviator Charles Lindbergh. There are very few examples—perhaps only a hundred or so—remaining of this beautiful bird, but a breeding programme appears to have saved it from extinction. At Malagos, which is about 36km (22 miles) northwest of Davao, is the Philippine Eagle Nature Centre (also known as Eagle Camp). Here, in handsome botanical gardens, are examples of a number of rare Philippine animals, including several of the few surviving Philippine eagles, which have been bred with some success here.

GOING IT ALONE

INTERNAL TRAVEL

The city best located for access to Lake Sebu is General Santos, in the deep south of Mindanao.

By air There are regular flights to General Santos from Manila (Philippine Airlines and Air Philippines). There are also flights to General Santos from Cebu City on Cebu Island, and from Iloilo City on Panay Island. Davao, the fastest-growing city in the Philippines after Manila, lies on the coast to the north-east of General Santos and is served by air from Manila and Cebu. Zamboanga, at the tip of the peninsula on the west coast of Mindanao, also has flights from Cebu and Manila.

In theory there is an air service from Manado in Sulawesi, Indonesia, to Davao, operated by Air Bouraq, but people seem to have little confidence in this airline. There are also flights from Kuala Lumpur.

By bus From Manila there are buses to Davao. These air-conditioned buses leave twice a day and the journey time (including ferries from Surigao to Liloan and San Isidro to Matnog) is around 40 hours.

By boat One of the best ways to savour the atmosphere of the South Seas is to travel by boat. There is a service to General Santos from Davao every Monday; the journey time is about 9 hours. There is also a service from Zamboanga on Wednesdays and Thursdays, the voyage

LEFT A T'boli fisherman makes his way across Lake Sebu in a dug-out canoe

lasting some 12 hours.

Pelni Lines operates a fortnightly boat service between Davao and Bitung or Manado in Sulawesi, which also calls at Ujang Pandang and Denpasar (Bali). There is also a weekly service between Bitung and General Santos.

WHEN TO GO

The Philippines are subject to typhoons—to avoid them it is best to travel between mid-December and mid-May. However, Mindanao is less affected than the areas to the north but the wet season here lasts from April to September, although it is not as severe as in other parts of the country. Avoid travelling on religious holidays—everybody is on the move.

PLANNING

Reaching Lake Sebu from General Santos takes about 3 hours by car. Although it would be possible to get there by public transport, it could well involve several hours on the roof of a jeepney and any number of changes along the way. It would be better to arrange in advance a car and driver, which are not expensive by Western standards.

Since there is not much in the way of accommodation at Lake Sebu, it would be advisable to book in advance. Similarly, in order to obtain a T'boli guide (without whom it might be difficult to establish contact with local people around Lake Sebu), it would be sensible to make arrangements beforehand through Symbiosis in London or through "Boy" Santiago in General Santos (see Contacts).

WHAT TO TAKE

- ❑ Waterproof jacket.
- ❑ Swimwear.
- ❑ Insect repellent.
- ❑ Walking boots.
- ❑ Light, long trousers, socks and long-sleeved shirt.
- ❑ Spare batteries and film.
- ❑ Water bottle.

HEALTH MATTERS

- ❑ Take anti-malaria tablets.
- ❑ Use mosquito repellent and coils.
- ❑ Wear long trousers and long-sleeved shirts at night.
- ❑ Bring a basic health kit.
- ❑ Drink bottled water.
- ❑ Arrange comprehensive medical insurance before departure.
- ❑ At least a month before leaving home, check with your doctor what vaccinations are needed.

SENSIBLE PRECAUTIONS

Mindanao has been off the beaten track to foreigners because of political problems. The main threat (kidnapping by terrorists of the Moro National Liberation Front, who have been fighting for an autonomous Muslim state on the island) seems to have receded almost completely, but all visitors are strongly urged to verify the latest situation with either the Foreign Office or its equivalent, or with the embassy in Manila.

Among the Wrecks of Coron

by Christopher Knowles

On a remote island to the west of Manila I went diving among the coral-encrusted remains of a Japanese flotilla sunk by the American air force during World War II. There were no skeletons, nor any treasure—just a strange excitement at finding myself in these eerie surroundings.

Manila never changes. Overcrowded, noisy, polluted, yet filled with optimistic, smiling, and sunny-natured rogues, it is not a beautiful city but, as a pullulating hub, it has its appeal. At any event, the quickest route to Coron, a small port on the island of Busuanga, is via Manila.

The flight from Manila to Busuanga is an adventure in itself. It is operated by an outfit called Air Ads Inc., who work out of a small hangar at the domestic airport (which shares runways with the international airport). Passengers filter into the tiny waiting-room, where we all sit watching the traffic news on local television. Eventually we are checked in and weighed together with hand luggage. Then we are called to the plane.

We walk out through the hangar, between a cluster of helicopters, towards an ancient biplane. Just for a moment it seems possible…but we continue past it to a fairly modern Britten-Norman Islander, on an apron outside. The pilot and co-pilot introduce themselves to the eight of us and give us a short briefing, after which we climb aboard according to an arrangement based on weight distribution. It is a pretty tight squeeze, and once the engines start, noisy enough to preclude conversation, but there is the advantage of being able to see everything that goes on, both in and out of the plane.

After rising above the congested rush-hour traffic of Manila, we swing round and head westwards to the coast. Soon we are passing small islands of

3 To go wreck diving you need to have an open-water diving qualification already (see pages 66–73). To get the most out of the experience, however, you are advised to gain an additional diving certificate in wreck diving, as without this you cannot enter the interiors of the wrecks.

The sea kayaking is strenuous only if you are paddling against the tide. Life vests are provided, but of course you should be able to swim.

★★ Accommodation on Busuanga varies from the simple but splendid Kubo Sa Nagat, built on stilts in the middle of a bay, to several lodges and cottages in Coron itself. There are also lodges and more luxurious accommodation elsewhere along the coast.

 All equipment is available through Discovery Divers (see Contacts).

coral, with their haloes of dazzling sand and waters in warm, inviting shades of blue, shielded by wisps of stripling clouds. The piloting is impressive, and every effort is made to avoid the dense, piled cloud that brings turbulence.

LANDING IN BUSUANGA

After 1 hour, 20 minutes we start to descend, heading towards the green hills of **Busuanga**. Busuanga is in fact one of the Calamian Islands, west of Mindoro and Manila, just north of the larger island of Palawan, which separates the Sulu and South China Seas. We make a right turn and there, along a valley bottom, is the island's airport, a strip of dirt and a shed. Beyond the dirt strip is a length of concrete which, I am told later, was going to be the new runway. Short of money, however, the powers that be abandoned the project, leaving Busuanga with nothing but a shorter strip of dirt.

The terminal is a hut and a couple of straw cottages. Not a lot is happening inside—a knot of passengers awaiting the return flight, a few dogs asleep on a table, and a couple of roosters strutting around them. A man called Goudie introduces himself to me (I had no idea who he was at the time, but he turned out to be the manager of the hotel where I was staying for the following two nights). Transport to Coron is by jeepney (a cross between a Land Rover and a fairground ride); but we have to wait for the return flight to board so that Air Ads personnel can return to town with us.

THE ROAD TO CORON

The road out of the airport is like a wide farm track, surprisingly firm except for a couple of patches where the surface, made soggy by rain and traffic, has subsided into troughs and furrows. There is a long wait for a vehicle to extricate itself from the mud, during which much cheerful barracking prevails. We pass streams and meadows that could almost be in rural England, were it not for the heat and the shambling local cattle with their eyes like marbles, their pendulous dewlaps, and their long rabbit ears.

After 45 minutes we arrive in **Coron**, with its little houses and gardens, and its seaside houses built on stilts. Beyond the harbour, dissected by precarious bamboo walkways and jetties, against which bob brightly coloured boats, is a distant range of hills which, in the grey light of that day, recede in misty shades of charcoal grey, like Chinese paintings.

Goudie leads me along one of the jetties to meet Gunter, who runs Discovery Divers. He is a young German who has lived here for seven years and, like many operators in this part of the world—where traditional forms of communication are frequently unreliable—he obtains much of his business through the Internet. He introduces me to

Yushie, a Japanese girl who is to be my divemaster and then I am measured up for the dives the following day.

BY OUTRIGGER TO MY HOTEL

In the meantime Goudie has had the transportation to the hotel brought to the jetty—a large white outrigger. Having agreed that Yushie will pick me up at nine the next morning, we climb aboard and pole out through the shallows to the centre of the bay. As a wind strikes up, bringing a driving rain, it becomes obvious why the time I have chosen to come—early October—is not the most popular among divers.

Half an hour later the boat turns into a sheltered stretch of water. In the middle of the bay is a sprawling wooden palace, built entirely on stilts. Originally the private house of a wealthy Manila man, it has been turned into the Kubo Sa Nagat hotel. Simple (made largely of local hardwood and bamboo) but

WRECK DIVING

With a basic open-water scuba diving qualification it is possible to go wreck diving but not, strictly speaking, to view the interiors of the wrecks. For this the novice diver should really undertake a specialist course in order to understand the particular hazards associated with this type of diving. It can be seriously disorientating to enter, for example, the hold of a wrecked ship. It may be large and dark inside and the single entrance, that seemed so obvious from the outside, can quickly appear to vanish in murky water. There is also the danger of snagging your equipment on jagged and sharp surfaces. Both can be dealt with quickly after the right instruction, which is recommended in order to obtain the best from the experience.

AFTER LUNCH EXERCISE

After lunch, we take some exercise, in the form of sea kayaking. Goudie (whose real name turns out to be Godofredo) is the one charged with taking me out on the high seas. The hotel is located in a sort of seawater lake, a large expanse of sea water protected and almost completely enclosed by mangrove swamp and jungle-clad hills. The water therefore, though tidal, is not much prone to roughness (even in choppy conditions it is apparently possible to kayak without any problem), although violent squalls can on occasion arise with unexpected rapidity.

Goudie climbs into a blue kayak; mine is bright pink. The kayaks, their shape adapted to the sort of conditions likely to be encountered along ocean coastlines, are made of a moulded plastic: getting in and out of them requires care to prevent them capsizing but once you are inside, balance is easy to maintain. We are to head across to the other

well thought-out, it has clean rooms, communal washing facilities (no hot water—but that is largely superfluous in this climate), and solar electricity. There is a lovely dining room built to funnel in the breeze coming in off the forest across the bay, an open-sided hall that also boasts a dartboard and, among the rafters, a single image of the Virgin Mary standing on a cloud.

There are six bedrooms, providing beds for 19 guests. On this occasion, however, there is just me. Immediately, I am served wonderful lunch of freshly caught fish (lapu-lapu, or garoupa) with beans and sweet, stubby bananas.

side of the bay and then find a creek to paddle up. The crossing is unexpectedly hard work, but it is only when we arrive at the other side that I understand why my shoulders are in such pain—we have been paddling against both wind and a

ABOVE Check-in, arrivals, and departures: Busuanga airport on the island of Coron
LEFT Room to let: this island getaway is built on stilts, like many local homes
BELOW A jeepney, the local taxi-cum-jeep form of transport, takes passengers from the airport to the town of Coron

receding tide. This also means that as we approach the shore of the bay the kayaks (which are very light) start to scrape the silty, root-encrusted bottom. Still, we keep going for a while, paddling up and down the shore looking for the entrance to the creek. Goudie, being lighter than me, is able to continue further, but pretty shortly we are both forced out of the kayaks and into heaving them towards the creek entrance, with the soft silt enveloping our naked feet, the soles of which are pricked by the stubbly mangrove roots.

Our plight amuses the occupants of a passing outrigger, children who yell out a laughing "halloo" to us, followed by a chorus of "I love you" (which throws an interesting light on their school English lessons). There are stingrays and swordfish in these waters, but Goudie assures me that the vibrations from our splashing feet will send them wriggling away.

UP THE CREEK

In front of us, fishermen are dragging their nets through the water in the search for shrimps. A few wading birds skitter away. Dragonflies hover and drive on by. We enter the creek and the water becomes deeper again. Of course we are still fighting the current and the only noise in the still, humid air is of our plunging paddles. From both banks, rows of mangrove roots dip their manifold limbs into the muddy water. Sometimes we can hear a popping noise like cracking wood—monkeys are in here somewhere but we cannot see them. A mosquito occasionally whines at one's ear. Birds dart across us from time to time.

After half an hour or so the current is too much, and we turn around, anticipating with pleasure the inevitable result—a lazy return journey to the mouth of the creek. We crack off at a fair rate, happy to lie back and let the river take us where it will. Our silence makes the birds more venturesome—there is a sapphire flash as a kingfisher makes a low run before me.

When we reach the mouth, the tide continues to take us out for a while but before long we are once again forced out of the kayaks. But, this time, once we have climbed back in, the receding tide and a following breeze carry us very gently towards the hotel. There follow 45 minutes of bliss as we bob across the water, the ruffled wavelets lapping with sweet little thuds against the kayak. In a small fishing settlement somewhere on the shore, a dog bays like a wolf.

In the evening, there is a blast of tropical rain to drown the distant purr of returning fishing boats. I watch the silent acrobatics of a tern as the forest exhales its steam and a flock of large geese-like birds flap over the forest and head for home. Soon there is complete silence except for the repeated murmurings of someone practising English. Sleep comes easily against a background of the chuck-chuck noise of wide-eyed lizards and the sound of restless water beneath my bedroom floor.

WRECK DIVING

At nine the following morning, after my vast breakfast of eight waffles with maple syrup, four fried corned beef cakes, and a fried egg, Yushie arrives on a pretty white ship with bright red outriggers. Lunch is loaded on board, and so are three of the girls from the hotel, who are in charge of all the cooking. "Hospitality girls!" Yushie joked. Yushie, from Sapporo, in Hokkaido, Japan, has, after several years of travelling, found herself in Coron, where she has been taken on by Discovery Divers. An expert diver, she speaks pretty good English, and, most valuable of all for the novice, is calm and helpful.

With Dentom at the helm, we head out westards along the south coast of Busuanga, making for **Concepcion**, where the first wreck lies. The journey, passing beneath perpendicular cliffs and high, green granite hills, whose foundations are gradually being eaten away by the sea, takes about an hour. Here and there pearl fisheries are marked out with buoys and from time to time brightly coloured outriggers slip by. We pass solitary thatched huts on stilts at the shoreline. Despite the season, the weather is warm and sunny, the sea sapphire blue.

We arrive above the wreck. Marked by a buoy, it lies in open water, in the middle of a bay. It is the *Taiei Maru*, one of eight Japanese freighters sunk by American dive-bombers on the night of September 24, 1944.

THE DIVE

There is a considerable running tide, and having donned my gear and jumped in I find it difficult to reach Yushie, who awaits me, as per instructions, clinging on to the buoy rope. Eventually this comic floater succeeds in reaching the rope, and in deflating his buoyancy vest, and we make our way down to the wreck. Before long, within five or six metres, the murk clears and there she is, a greenish, coral-encrusted hulk of

WORLD WAR II ACTION

Until September 24, 1944, the Japanese navy had felt secure in these inlets and coves close to the shoreline near Coron, where the water was deep. Furthermore, American carriers were operating far away, to the east of the Philippines, and the air space over the country was dominated by the Japanese air force. The American air force thought otherwise, and a low-level, maximum range attack was organized. Some 15 Japanese armed cargo vessels were anchored in the area of Concepcion and Tangat, including an armed naval escort vessel and some of Japan's last large tankers. Ten of these ships were sunk and only three American planes were lost. One plane crew was killed, but two others escaped to the island and were later rescued by Filipino resistance fighters.

rotting metal; so encrusted, in fact, that only the artificial lines of her design distinguish her from the ocean floor.

We pass open hatches and then take a watery stroll along one of the decks before taking our turn at look-out from the bridge. We tour around the whole thing, the current now sweeping us along its bows, which are breaking up and separating from the rest of the ship. It is impossible not to think of this ship sitting on the surface almost exactly 54 years ago, confident that an American attack was not even a remote possibility.

Now this ghost is the home, appropriately enough, of giant angel fish, as well as puffer fish, nudibranches and, in the shadow of the ship's mast, we spot a beautiful lion fish in all its splendour, hovering just above a section of rusty girder, its mane of spiky fins quivering in the current.

Once back on board our own ship, we sail back on ourselves and anchor near a coral reef. Inevitably, lunch is huge—two types of rice, chicken, and mutton together in a soy sauce, and two types of fish, including a tuna steak. Then some snorkelling in the clear water with acres of bright, spiky coral, before going to deeper water and the prospect, this time, of the smaller *Olympia Maru*, which lies on her side.

Although the tide is weaker here, the water is very murky indeed and the ship visible only from close quarters. In a way this heightens the interest and mystery of the experience and we do as before, only on this occasion we go right inside the wreck, into the cargo hold, and out through an enormous hole in the side (made, apparently, by Filipinos, in order to lever out the engine, which managed to survive the raid).

A giant tuna fish slides past us and we note a scorpion fish, well camouflaged in its barnacle and algae surroundings. And then up again, to put away the gear, lie in the sun, and enjoy a beer from the ice box before a roughish, exhilarating journey home across the open bays.

SOLITAIRE

That evening a sudden squall sweeps across the bay. After yet another gargantuan meal, we sit, Goudie and I, alone in the hall, playing solitaire on my computer. It must present a strange scene, as the storm rages about us in the darkness, and, beneath the light of a single light bulb, a delighted Goudie giggles at the discovery of a plastic "mouse" with the power to move one-dimensional playing cards. His happiness knows no bounds when he succeeds in getting all his cards out at the first attempt.

The inevitable early start the next morning takes me back to Coron, back to the bustling little port with its slightly down-at-heel atmosphere, accentuated by the sight of a seemingly disused flying boat stuck in the water. Gunter has told me that some visitors arrive in Coron expecting a coral-island paradise. In fact, Busuanga, with its warm water, its craggy bays and coves, and its wrecks, has a different appeal, a grander and wilder aspect that brings to mind the intrigues of the novels of Joseph Conrad. At the same time, there is a cheerfulness about the place that is immensely appealing. I am sorry to leave the island without having become better acquainted.

The flight home is a little rougher than the outward one. Next to me is a young Pole who sits enraptured at the adventure of being in such a tiny aeroplane flying across a sea sprinkled with gem-like coral islands. For myself, I am less enamoured with the thrills of small aircraft, exhilarating though the flight is in its low-level skim across the Sulu Sea. Once back on the mainland, it is not long before the sprawl of Metro Manila looms up. There is, I have to admit, something somehow satisfying about our bobbing descent to the firmly man-made rectangle of Manila airport's runway, and the bouncy landing that follows, in the wake of a huge commercial airliner. But give me a good dirt airstrip every time.

RIGHT A lion fish, with mane quivering, joins the divers in the Black Island wreck superstructure (also LEFT)
ABOVE LEFT The wreck of a fishing boat in shallow water near the entrance to Barracuda Lake, Coron Island

GOING IT ALONE

INTERNAL TRAVEL

By air Unless you are already in the area, the quickest way of getting to Busuanga is by air from Manila. The daily flight, by small turboprop aircraft operated by Air Ads Inc. (see Contacts), from Manila's domestic airport, takes about 1½ hours. Check-in is early in the morning but remember that Manila's streets can be choked with traffic at almost any hour. It is possible to check luggage in but there is very little space for much in the way of hand luggage. Pacific Airways also fly to Busuanga from Palawan, using an even smaller craft.

The drive from Busuanga's tiny YKR Airport to Coron town (not to be confused with the island of the same name) is a further half hour or more (depending on the state of the road)— a jeepney will be at the airport to transport flight passengers to the town for a few pesos. There is also another small airport just behind Coron—there are a limited number of flights to and from it operated by Pacific Airways.

By boat For travellers already in the area, Coron

is served by boat from the neighbouring island of Culion. There are early morning services from Culion every Tuesday, Thursday, and Sunday, with return services every Monday, Wednesday, and Saturday. The journey takes about 2 hours.

Further south is the largest island in the area, Palawan. From Taytay, the old capital of Palawan (worth visiting for its ruined 17th-century Spanish fort), there is a service to Coron by large outrigger boat every Wednesday and Saturday at 8am. The journey takes about 8 hours, although in the event of heavy seas the boat may anchor overnight at Linapacan island before continuing to Coron.

WHEN TO GO

Wreck divers come to Coron at almost any time of year but the best period is from April to July. The least good is from mid-September to mid-October.

PLANNING

There is a range of accommodation available in Coron and you should have no difficulty in finding inexpensive lodgings in one of the several cottages to be

found along the main street or on piles over the water. If you choose to stay in Kubo Sa Nagat, or one of the other hotels along the coast, you should try to book in advance. This may best be done by contacting Asiaventure Services in Manila (see Contacts). When booking, it is also possible to arrange a transfer from the airport or from Coron itself. Many of these places have kayaks for hire so that you can explore the Busuanga coastline.

DIVING COURSES

Discovery Divers (see Contacts) offer all sorts of packages to cater to every taste and ability. You can do your open-water course through them for around $270 or, if you already have your open-water qualification, become a wreck diver for around $180. The company also offers dive packages (to include accommodation, full board, and two dives) from $69 per person per day.

WHAT TO TAKE

❏ Swimming costume.
❏ Open-water (and wreck) diving qualification certificate if you have already it.
❏ Flip-flops or equivalent.
❏ Torch and spare battery.

HEALTH MATTERS

❏ Take anti-malaria tablets.
❏ Use mosquito repellent and coils.
❏ Wear trousers and long-sleeved shirts at night.
❏ Bring a basic health kit
❏ Drink bottled water.
❏ Arrange full medical insurance before departure.
❏ At least a month before leaving home, check with your doctor what vaccinations are needed.

THE NAME GAME

It is easy to become confused by the many similar names to be found on these islands. Busuanga is the name of the island off which the wrecks lie, but on the island itself you will also find two small towns called Busuanga—Old Busuanga in the northwest of the island and New Busuanga to the north of it. Coron is a town on the south coast of Busuanga, which is in fact part of the Calamian Islands, but is often bracketed with Palawan, the very much larger island to the south.

INTRODUCTION

C ontained in the first section of these "Blue Pages" are lists of selected contacts relevant to the 25 adventures related on pages 20–256. Because the adventures are personal accounts, the information provided here will reflect each author's own experience, and therefore details will vary accordingly, both in content and in the amount of information provided. Operators, guides, hire facilities, and other services mentioned in the adventures will appear here in more detail. This contacts section also complements the Activities A–Z in the second part of these "Blue Pages."

Below is some general information to help you plan your own adventures. Remember that some of the contacts are in remote places, so be sure to call or write before setting out. Also, none of the companies have been vetted by the publishers in any way and, although they have been used by our writers, there is no guarantee that any company will still be run by the same people or with the same proficiency.

INTERNATIONAL DIALLING CODES

The telephone and fax numbers given in this section of the book begin with the area code. When dialling from outside the country, prefix this number with the international access code of the country you are in (this is given below for the U.K. and the U.S.A.), followed by the country code (as below). For instance, to call Jakarta, in Indonesia: dial 00 from the U.K., or 011 from the U.S.A., then 62 (the country code for Indonesia), followed by 21 (the area code for Jakarta) and the number of the company or person you are calling.

INTERNATIONAL NETWORK ACCESS CODES

For calls from the U.K. 00
For calls from the U.S.A. 011

COUNTRY CODES

Cambodia 855
Indonesia 62
Laos 856
Malaysia 60
Myanmar (Burma) 95
Philippines 63
Singapore 65
Thailand 66
Vietnam 84

EMBASSIES AND CONSULATES

BRITISH EMBASSIES
Cambodia
British Embassy
29 Street 75
Phnom Penh
Cambodia
☎ (23) 427124
Fax: (23) 427125

Indonesia
British Embassy
Jalan M H Thamrin 75
Jakarta 10310
Indonesia
(21) 315 6264
(21) 314 1824

Malaysia
British High Commision
Commercial Section
185 Jalan Ampang
50450 Kuala Lumpur
☎ (3) 248-2122
Fax: (3) 248-0880

Myanmar (Burma)
British Embassy
Commercial Section
80 Strand Rd. (Box no. 38)
Yangon (Rangoon)
☎ (1) 295300
Fax: (1) 295306

Philippines
British Embassy
Floors 15-17 LV Locsin Bldg

6752 Ayala Avenue
Cor Makati Ave.
1226 Makati (P.O. Box 2927 MCPO)
☎ (2) 816-7116
Fax: (2) 819-7206

Singapore
British High Commission
Tanglin Rd.
Singapore 247919
☎ (65) 473-9333
Fax: (65) 475-2320

Thailand
British Embassy
Wireless Rd.
Bangkok 10330
☎ (2) 253-0191
Fax: (2) 255-8619

Vietnam
British Embassy
16 Pho Ly Thuong
Kiet
Ha Noi
☎ (4) 8252349
Fax: (4) 82657557

AMERICAN EMBASSIES
Cambodia
American Embassy
27 Street Angphanouvong
#240
Phnom Penh
Box P
APO AP 96546
☎ (23) 426436/38
Fax: (23) 426437

Indonesia

American Embassy
Jalan Medan Merdeka
Selatan 5
Box 1, Jakarta
APO AP 96520
☎ (21) 360-360
Fax: (21) 386-2259

Laos

American Embassy
Rue Bartholonie, B.P. 114
Vientiane
AMEMB Box V
APO AP 96546
☎ (21) 212-581
Fax: (21) 212-581

Malaysia

American Embassy
376 Jalan Tun Razak
PO Box 10035
50700 Kuala Lumpur
APO AP 96535-8152
☎ (3) 248-9011
Fax: (3) 242-2207

Myanmar (Burma)

American Embassy
581 Merchant St.
Yangon (Rangoon)
AMEMB Box B
APO AP 96546
☎ (1) 530151

Philippines

American Embassy
1201 Roxas Blvd.
Manila
APO AP 96440
☎ (2) 818 2684
Fax: (2) 523 1001
Telex: 722 27366 AME PH

Commercial Office
395 Senator Gil J. Puyat Ave.

Makita, Metro Manila
☎ (2) 890-9717
Fax: (2) 895-3028

Singapore

American Embassy
30 Hill St.
Singapore 0617
FPO AP 96534
☎ (65) 338-0251
Fax: (65) 338-4550

Thailand

American Embassy
95 Wireless Rd.
Bangkok
APO AP 96546
☎ (2) 252-5040
Fax: (2) 254-2990

Commercial Office & Library
3rd Floor,
Diethelm Towers Bldg
Tower A, 93/1 Wireless Rd.
10330 Bangkok
☎ (2) 255-4365/66/67
Fax: (2) 255-2915

OTHER INFORMATION

There are a number of companies who specialize in travel for particular purposes such as education or for more mature travellers. The companies below specialize in different areas:

Myths and Mountains

976 Tee Court
Incline Village
NV 89451
U.S.A.
☎ (800) 670-Myth or (0702) 832-5454
Fax: (0702) 832-4454
email: travel@mythsandmountains.com

Myths and Mountains is an educational adventure travel company specializing in group, custom, and non-profit organization trips to Southeast Asia, including Vietnam, Laos, Cambodia, and Myanmar. Established for ten years, the company offers educational studies of a country's history and heritage. Itineraries focus on themes such as culture and craft, religion, and the environment.

ElderTreks

597 Markham St.
Toronto
Ontario
Canada M6G 2L7
☎ (0416) 588-5000
Fax: (0416)588-9839 or 1-800-741-7956
email:
eldertreks@eldertreks.com
Eldertreks is dedicated exclusively to adventure holidays for people aged 50 and over. They offer trips to Laos, Cambodia, and Vietnam s well as more mainstream Southeast Asian countries. All trips involve walking.

Wexas International

45-49 Brompton ROad
Knightsbridge
London SW3 1DE
U.K.
☎ (020) 7581 8761
Fax: (020) 7838 0837
email: bluecard@wexas.com
Wexas aim to provide the excitement of an adventure holiday with the security of a pre-booked tour. They offer safaries, treks, and expeditions with themes ranging from cultural to wildlife. Destinations include Cambodia, Laos, Vietnam, and Malaysia.

ACCOMMODATION PRICES

Hotels listed in the Contacts and A-Z sections have been split into three price categories. Some parts of the world are generally cheaper than others but a rough guide is as follows:

Expensive = over $85
Moderate = $40–$85
Budget = under $40

A Trek to the Northern Hill Tribes
PAGES 20–29

OPERATORS
CHARLIE'S TOURS AND TREKKING
Moo 4
Rangsiyanun Rd.
Pai District 58130
Mae Hong Son
Thailand
This is a small, local operator run by Charlie Keereekhamsuk, a former Chiang Mai guide.

EAST–WEST SIAM LTD.
Building One, 11th Floor
99 Wittayu Rd.
Pathumwan
Bangkok 10330
Thailand
☎ (2) 256-6153
Fax: (2) 256-6665/256-7172
email: songyot@east-west-siam.com
Since it was founded in 1984, East–West Siam has pioneered the concept of "low density, high quality" tourism. It owns the charming Lisu Lodge (see under Accommodation) and offers adventure treks to hill tribes, as well as cycling trips, elephant safaris, and river rafting.

THAI ADVENTURE
13 Moo 4
Rangsiyanun Rd.
Pai District 58130
Mae Hong Son
Thailand
☎ (53) 699274/699111
Fax: (53) 699111
email: raftad@loxinfo.co.th
Established almost ten years ago by Frenchman Guy Gorias, Thai Adventure specializes in whitewater rafting in state-of-the-art rubber boats in Pai/Mae Hong Son (Jul–Dec). They also arrange trips that combine hilltribe trekking, mountain biking, and elephant riding.

TRACK OF THE TIGER TOURS
P.O. Box 3
Mae Ai
Chiang Mai 50280
Thailand
☎ (53) 459328
Fax: (53) 459329
email: tiger@loxinfo.co.th;
website: www.track-of-the-tiger.com
Established in 1987 by Shane Beary, the company operates its own "soft" adventure tours out of the delightful Mae Kok River Lodge in Tha Ton (see under Accommodation, below). Activities on offer include hilltribe trekking, rafting, elephant riding, and mountain biking.

INFORMATION
TOURIST AUTHORITY OF THAILAND (TAT)
105/1 Chiang Mai-Lamphun Rd.
Amphoe
Muang
Chiang Mai 5000
Thailand
☎ (53) 248604/248607
Fax: (53) 248602

ACCOMMODATION
The best way to arrange a stay in a hilltribe village is through one of the tour operators in Pai, Mae Hong Son, Chiang Mai, or Chiang Rai. Just turning up in a village is not recommended.

Lisu Lodge $$
Contact East–West Siam (in Bangkok):
Building One, 11th Floor
99 Wittayu Rd.
Pathumwan
Bangkok 10330
☎ (2) 256-6153
Fax: (2) 256-6665/256-7172
email: songyot@east-west-siam.com
Designed in traditional hilltribe style and modified for comfort, the Lisu Lodge, which lies 50km (30 miles) from Chiang Mai, offers hilltribe trekking, mountain biking, white-water rafting and elephant safaris. It can accommodate up to 12 people at one time.

Rim Pai Cottage $
17 Moo 3
Wiang Tai
Pai District 58130
Mae Hong Son
☎ (53) 699133
These are pleasant cottages on the banks of the Pai River, not far from the market.

Mountain Blue Guest House $
Chaisongkhram Rd
Pai District 58130
Mae Hong Son
The simple wooden bungalows here are popular with backpackers.

Mae Kok River Lodge $$
P.O. Box 3
Mae Ai
Chiang Mai 50280
☎ 66-53-459328
Fax: 66-53-459329
email: tiger@loxinfo.co.th
This is a delightful river lodge that offers a range of treks and tours out of this lodge in Tha Ton, 180km (110 miles) north of Chiang Mai.

A MOTORBIKING ODYSSEY
PAGES 30–39

OPERATORS
NORTH SIAM ROAD RUNNERS
P.O. Box 3
Mae Ai
Chiang Mai 50280
Thailand
☎ (53) 459328
Fax: (53) 459329
Set up by the intrepid Ed, this company organizes 5–12-day motorbike tours of northern Thailand using classic Royal Enfield 500cc bikes. Customized tours throughout the area can also be arranged on request.

SIAM BIKE TRAVEL CO. LTD
P.O. Box Prah Singh Box 71
50200 Chiang Mai
☎:(53) 409533
Fax: (53) 409534
email: siambike@asiaplus.com
website: http://asiaplus.com/siambike
This company organizes motorcycle and jeep tours (both standard and custom-made) in Thailand, Myanmar (Burma), and Laos. They will also arrange visas, conecting flights, and accommodation at every stage.

TRACK OF THE TIGER TOURS
P.O. Box 3
Mae Ai
Chiang Mai 50280
☎ (53) 459328
Fax: (53) 459329
email: tiger@loxinfo.co.th
website: www.track-of-the-tiger.com
For details see above. Can also put you in contact with North Siam Adventure Tours (above).

INFORMATION
TOURIST AUTHORITY OF THAILAND (TAT)
105/1 Chiang Mai-Lamphun Rd.
Amphoe
Muang
Chiang Mai 5000
Thailand
☎ (53) 248604/248607
Fax: (53) 248605

MOTORBIKE RENTAL
DANG BIKE HIRE
23 Kotchasarn Rd.
Chiang Mai
☎ (53) 271524
This outfit offers a range of well-maintained trail bikes and guarantees that if you break down anywhere in northern Thailand, it will provide immediate exchange or repair of your motorbike.

J.K. BIG BIKE
74/2 Chaiyapoom Rd. (opposite Somphet Market)
Chiang Mai
☎ (53) 251830
Find dirt and road bikes for hire here.

POP SERVICE
51 Kotchasarn Rd.
Chiang Mai
☎ (53) 276014/206747
Small Honda Dream motorcycles can be rented by the day.

ACCOMMODATION
River View Lodge $$
25 Charoen Prathet Rd.
Soi 2
Chiang Mai
☎ (53) 271101
Fax: (53) 279019

This is a small but pleasant lodge with adequate facilities and fine views over the River Ping

Once Upon A Time $$
385/2 Charoen Prathet Rd.
Chiang Mai
☎ (53) 274932
Fax: (53) 2338493
Beautiful northern teak houses on the banks of the River Ping with rooms with four-poster beds.

Mae Kok River Lodge $$
P.O. Box 3
Mae Ai
Chiang Mai 50280
☎ (53) 459328
Fax: (53) 459329
email: tiger@loxinfo.co.th
A delightful river lodge offering a range of treks and tours out of this lodge at Tha Ton, 180km (112 miles) north of Chiang Mai.

Saen Poo Hotel $$
Chiang Mai
☎ (53) 717300
Fax: (53) 711372
This is centrally located and offers a full range of amenities.

Boonbundan Guest House $/$$
1005/13 Jet Yot Rd.
 Chiang Rai
☎ (53) 717040
Fax: (53) 712914
Set in a walled compound, this guest house has a wide range of rooms and bungalows, and a leafy garden.

Rim Pai Cottage $
17 Moo 3
Wiang Tai
Pai District 58130
Mae Hong Son
☎ (53) 699103
Pleasant cottages on the banks of the Pai River within easy walking distance of the market.

Baiyoke Chalet Hotel $$
90 Khunlum Praphat Rd.
☎ (53) 611486
Fax: (53) 611533
Centrally located with standard rooms

Sang Tong Huts $
Mae Hong Son
Beautiful secluded huts, a short distance to the west of town.

KAYAKING AND CLIMBING AT PHANG NGA PAGES 40–49

OPERATORS
EAST–WEST SIAM LTD.
119 Ratutit 200 Years Rd.
Patong Khatu
Phuket
☎ (076) 340912/341209;
Fax: (076) 341188;
email philippe@samart.co.th;
website: www.east-west.com
Local office of East–West (see p259). In Phuket they offer trips on their stylish, traditional Chinese junk.

PHRA NANG DIVERS
P.O. Box 54
Krabi 81000
☎/**Fax** (075) 637064;
email: pndivers@loxinfo.co.th
This PADI-approved school offers diving courses and live-aboard sea safaris.

PRA-NANG ROCK CLIMBERS
P.O. Box 15
Krabi 81000
☎/**Fax:** (1) 4646358
Fax: (75) 612914
These half-day climbing courses include instruction and hire of such equipment as harnesses, shoes, quickdraws, figures of eight, belay devices, rope, and chalk bags. They have a supply of good route guidebooks for intermediate and advanced climbers.

SANTANA
6 Sawatdirak Rd.
Patong Beach
Phuket
☎ (076) 294220
Fax: (076) 340300
website: www.santanaphuket.com
Offers 1- to 3-day combined jungle-

trekking and canoe trips around Ao Phang
Nga and Khao Sok National Park.

Sayan Tour
Phang Nga Bay
☎ (076) 430348
Sayan runs reasonably priced trips
around the bay.

Sea Canoe
367/4 Yaowarat Rd.
Phuket 83000
☎ (076) 212252
Fax: (076) 212172
email: info@seacanoe.com;
website: http://seacanoe.com
Offers 1- to 6-day expeditions. The longer
trips are for experienced canoeists and
involve paddling about 10–15 km
(9 miles) a day.

Symbiosis Expedition Planning
Christopher Gow Enterprises Ltd.
5 St. John's Hill
London SW11 1TH
U.K.
☎ (020) 7924 5906
Fax: (020) 7924 5907
email: info@symbiosis-travel.co.uk
website: www.symbiosis-travel.co.uk
British-based adventure travel company
that are experts in adventure planning
throughout Southeast Asia. They organize "soft" adventure trips in
northeastern and northern Thailand.

Tex Climbing
Jana Travel Tour
143 Utarakit Rd.
Krabi
☎/Fax: (075) 631509;
email: tex@thaibiz.com
Half-day climbing courses with Tex
include instruction and hire of equipment
such as harnesses, shoes, quickdraws,
figures of eight, belay devices, rope, and
chalk bags, e.t.c.

Information
Phuket International Airport
☎ (076) 327230/4
There is an information counter at the
airport where you can pick up a free copy
of the A-O-A Phuket map and make hotel
reservations. Taxi and tour services are
also available.

Tourist Authority of Thailand (T.A.T.)
73–75 Phuket Rd.
Phuket 83000
☎ (076) 212213 / 211036
Fax: (076) 313582
T.A.T. will arrange air-conditioned
minibus trips to Phang Nga and Krabi.
Longtail boats depart regularly for
Railay Beach—the main centre for rock-
climbing.

Cycling in Isaan
Pages 50–57

Operators
Bike & Travel
802/756 River Park
Moo 12
Kookot
Lamlookka
Pratumthani 12130
Thailand
☎ 9900900/9900274
Fax: 9900374
Founded by the extremely affable
manager, Tanin Rittavirun, this is one of
the most highly recommended operators
of tailor-made cycle tours throughout
Thailand. Prices are very reasonable and
include cycle hire, food, accommodation,
and a support vehicle.

Diethelm Travel
Kian Gwan Building II
140/1 Wireless Rd.
Bangkok 10330
Thailand
☎ (662) 2559130 / 2559160 / 2559170
Fax: (662) 2560248;
email: dto@dto.co.th
Owned by Diethelm & Co., a Swiss trading company that has been active in
Thailand for 50 years, the company offers
a range of regular package tours out of
Bangkok to Laos, Cambodia, Myanmar,
and Vietnam. They offers mountain-biking discovery trips to northern Thailand.

One World Bicycle Expeditions
356 Chaikong Rd.
Chiang Khan
Loei 42110
Thailand

☎/Fax: (66) 42821825
website: www.Bikethailand.com
Run by Torsak and Katie Murray, One World organizes customized mountain-biking tours of some of Isaan's most scenic countryside. Overnight stays are arranged in traditional Thai homes, and other cultural insights are provided.

SYMBIOSIS EXPEDITION PLANNING

Christopher Gow Enterprises Ltd.
205 St. John's Hill
London SW11 1TH
☎ 0171-9245906
Fax: 0171 9245907
email: info@symbiosis-travel.co.uk
website: www.symbiosis-travel.co.uk
Cycling tours of northeastern and northern Thailand For further details see p262.

CYCLE/MOTOBIKE RENTAL

MUT MEE GUEST HOUSE

1111/4 Kaeworawut Rd.
Nong Khai
Fax (a nearby bookshop, which takes messages): 042-460717
email: wasambe@loxinfo.co.th
Mut Mee has 12 mountain bikes for rent (you must leave a deposit). If you are travelling in high season make sure you arrange in advance.

NANA MOTOR

1160 Chaiyaporn Market
Meechai Rd.
Nong Khai
☎ (042) 411998
Nana rents out 100cc Honda Dream motorcycles. You will have to leave a deposit as well as your passport.

INFORMATION

TOURIST AUTHORITY OF THAILAND (NORTHEAST OFFICE)

16/5 Mukmontri Rd.
Udon Thani 41000
☎ (42) 325406/7
Fax: (42) 325408

ACCOMMODATION

Nong Khai Grand Thani $$$

589 Moo 5
Poanpisai Rd.
Nong Khai
☎ (42) 420033
Fax: (42) 412026

This is a luxury hotel with good amenities, a restaurant and a swimming pool.

Holiday Inn Mekong Royal $$$

222 Jomanee Rd.
Nong Khai
☎ (42) 420024
Fax: (42) 421280
The hotel has conference rooms, a restaurant, and a cocktail lounge.

Mut Mee Guest House $

1111/4 Kaeworawut Rd.
Nong Khai
Fax (a nearby bookshop, which takes messages): 042-460717
email: wasambe@loxinfo.co.th
This is a popular backpackers' haunt with pleasant situation on the river and good restaurant.

Tim's Guest House $

Si Chiang Mai
☎ (42) 451072
A simple guest house.

Sangkhom River Huts $

Sangkhom
The pleasant thatched bungalows overlook the river with good food.

Pak Chom Guest House $

Pak Chom
Simple bungalows overlook the river.

Zen Guest House $

126/2 Chai Khong Rd.
Soi 12
Chiang Khan
☎ (42) 821119
A traditional stilted, family-run guest house offering massage, herbal saunas, and bike rentals.

OTS Guest House $

Ban Pak Huay
OTS offers extremely basic bungalows and a communal dining area with fine views over the Heung River towards Laos.

Phu Luang Hotel $$

55 Charoenrat Rd.
Muang Loei
☎ 811532

Mediocre air-conditioned rooms, plus a coffee-shop and night club.

RIDING THE E&O EXPRESS PAGES 58–65

OPERATORS
THE EASTERN & ORIENTAL EXPRESS
Beach Road
32–01/03 Shaw Towers
Singapore 189702
☎ 3923500
Overseas bookings:
U.K. ☎ (0171) 8055100
U.S.A. ☎ toll free 0/524-2420
Australia ☎ (3) 969 99766
Guests can book for the following routes, in either direction:
Singapore–Bangkok, Bangkok–Chiang Mai, Singapore–Butterworth. The fare includes all meals, complimentary tea and coffee, and excursions to the River Kwai and Penang.

GETTING THERE
CHANGI AIRPORT SINGAPORE
☎ 5421122
At the tip of the island, some 20km (12 miles) east of the city, Changi has a full range of excellent facilities.

INFORMATION
SINGAPORE TOURIST PROMOTION BOARD
2–34 Raffles Hotel Arcade
North Bridge Rd.
Singapore
☎ 3341335

ACCOMMODATION
Albert Court Hotel $$
180 Albert St.
Singapore
☎ 3393939
Fax: 3393252
This moderately sized hotel, in a restored part of Singapore, is convenient for Little India, shopping, and nightlife.

Goodwood Park Hotel $$
22 Scotts Rd.
Singapore
☎ 7377411
Fax: 7328558
A colonial-style hotel with new rooms, two swimming pools and full facilities..

Raffles Hotel $$$
1 Beach Rd.
Singapore
☎ 3371886
Fax: 3397650
Oversea bookings:
U.K. ☎ (0800) 282124
U.S.A ☎ 800/525-4800/1-800/232-1886
Australia ☎ (2) 9548157
Singapore's famous colonial hotel, surronded by gardens, has the ambience of older times, with excellent service and cuisine. The Tiffin lunch buffet is a must, as is a Singapore Sling in the Long Bar.

The Oriental $$$
48 Oriental Ave.
Bangkok
☎ (2) 2360400
Fax: (2) 2361939
This hotel exudes graciousness and charm, harking back to the Thailand of old. The Thai/Italian/ barbeque buffet dinner on the Sunset Terrace overlooking the Chao Phraya is not to be missed.

The Sheraton Royal Orchid Hotel $$$
2 Captain Bush Lane
Bangkok
☎ (2) 2660123
Fax: 2368320
A bustling, large riverside hotel close to the tourist sites, with very good cuisine. Try the speciality Thai restaurant.

Sol Twin Towers $$
88 New Rama VI Rd.
Bangkok
☎ (2) 2169555
Fax: (2) 216 9544
This is a large hotel situated between major tourist and shopping sites and adjacent to the airport expressway.

LEARNING TO DIVE IN PHUKET PAGES 66–73

OPERATORS
SYMBIOSIS EXPEDITION PLANNING
Christopher Gow Enterprises Ltd.
205 St. John's Hill
London SW11 1TH
U.K.
☎ (020) 7924 5906
Fax: (020) 7924 5907
email: info@symbiosis-travel.co.uk
website: www.symbiosis-travel.co.uk
For further details see page 262.

DIVING
THE PHUKET ISLAND ACCESS
website:
www.phuketcom.co.th/diving/guide.htm
This useful site has links to a range of local dive centres, as well as photographs of marinelife.

DIVESAFE ASIA
113/16 Song Roi Phi Rd.
Patong Beach
Phuket
☎ (076) 342518
Registers and approves diving outfits and runs Phuket's only decompression chamber.

FANTASEA DIVERS
219 Rat-U-thit 200 Year Rd.
P.O. Box 20
Patong Beach
Phuket 83150
☎ (076) 340088
Fax: (076) 340309
email: info@fantasea.net;
website: www.fanatsea.net
This long-established 5-Star PADI Dive Centre has an excellent reputation. It offers the full range of training courses and day trips to destinations, including Phi Phi and Rajah Islands. It also offers live-aboard cruises from 4–10 days to sites in Myanmar and Thailand, including the Similan Islands and Mergui Archipelago.

MARINA DIVERS
Marina Cottage,
P.O. Box 143
Kata-Karon Beach
Phuket 83000
☎ (076) 330272
Fax: (076) 330516
email: nour@iname.com
A large 5-Star PADI Instructor Development Centre, which also offers day trips to Ko Phi Phi, the Rajah Islands, and Shark Point, plus live-aboard trips to the Similan and Surin islands.

SANTANA
6 Sawadeerack Rd.
Patong Beach, Phuket 83150
☎ (076) 294220
Fax: (076) 340360
email: santanap@loxinfo.co.th
Established in 1979, Sanatana is one of the longest-running dive operations in Patong. It offers a full range of diving courses, day trips and 3- to 7-day cruises in the Andaman Sea, as well as sea-kayaking tours in Phang Nga Bay.

SOUTH EAST ASIA DIVERS
116/7 Thaweewong Rd.
Patong Beach
Phuket 83150
☎ (076) 292079
Fax: (076) 342530
email: info@phuketdive.net
website: www.phuketdive.net
A respected 5-Star Dive Centre offering all the usual courses and day trips. Its air-conditioned Seraph schooner, dating from 1906, is a particularly handsome vessel in which to cruise around Ko Phi Phi, the Rajah Islands, and Shark Point. There are also branches at Le Meridien and Kata Thani Beach resorts.

OTHER ADVENTURES ON PHUKET
TROPICAL TRAILS
☎ (076) 263239 or 01-607-0475
They organize mountain bike tours, jungle walks, and elephant hill treks in three different areas of the island. If you want to take off on your own, you can rent a 21-speed American Trek or Haro mountain bike, with helmet, lock, water bottle, and a Phuket trail map.

SIAM SAFARI
☎ (076)383172
Fax:(076) 280107
email: ecearth@samart,co.th
These people run first-rate eco-nature tours, including 30-minute elephant treks, mountain biking, walking trails, and inflatable canoe tours through the mangrove swamps.

THE TRAVEL COMPANY
70/85 Ratutit Road
Patong Beach
☎ (076) 340232
Fax: (076) 340292
email: travelco@loxinfo.co.th
The company can arrange mountain biking, walking, canoeing through mangrove swamps, and several half-day and one-day adventure safaris around the island using small four-wheel-drive vehicles. These can be combined with elephant treks. Longer trips to the forests and waterfalls of Phang Nga and to the Khao Sok National Park, both north of Phuket, are also available.

GETTING THERE
PHUKET INTERNATIONAL AIRPORT
☎ (076) 327230/4
Located 11km (7 miles) north of Phuket Town. It has a information counter where you can pick up a free copy of the A-O-A Phuket map and make hotel reservations. Taxi and tour services also available.

INFORMATION
Phuket **website:** www.phuket.net
email: info@phuket.net
or: info@phuket.com

TOURIST AUTHORITY OF THAILAND
73–75 Phuket Rd.
Phuket 83000
☎ (076) 212213/211036
Fax: (076) 313582

CAR RENTAL
VIA RENT-A-CAR
189/6 Rat-U-Thit Rd.
Patong Beach
83150 Phuket
☎ (076) 76341 660/340 007
Fax: (076) 341661

ACCOMMODATION
The main accommodation area is Patong, but quieter, less touristy areas include Karon, Kata, or even Phuket town, which makes up for its lack of sand with the island's best shopping and some original Sino-Portugese architecture. Rates across Phuket zoom up in the high season (Nov–Apr) and go through the roof over Christmas and New Year, when you'll need to book well in advance.

The Boathouse $$$
Kata Beach
Phuket 83100
☎ (076) 330 015
Fax: (076) 330 561
email: theboathouse@phuket.ksc.co.th;
website: www.theboathousephuket.com
A delightful, traditional hotel on one of the prettiest beaches in Phuket. The Boathouse Wine & Grill serves good, but pricey Thai and European cuisine. The hotel also runs a 2-day Thai cookery course that includes lunch and a set of traditional Thai recipes.

Expat Hotel $
89/14 Rat-U-thit Rd
Patong
☎ (076) 342143
Fax: (076) 340300
In the heart of Patong's bar district, this basic hotel has a 1950s feel. Its low-rise buildings are ranged around a small pool. There is a bar and restaurant attached.

Sea, Sun, Sand Guesthouse $
64/27 Soi Kepsup
Thaiwiwong Rd.
Patong
☎/Fax: (076) 343047
Less than a minute's walk from the beach, in a quiet location, this clean and spacious (for Patong) hotel has simply furnished rooms with hot showers, and friendly service.

FOOD AND DRINK
The Boathouse
Kata Beach
Phuket 83100
☎ (076) 330 015
Fax: (076) 330 561
email: theboathouse@phuket.ksc.co.th

website: www.theboathousephuket.com
Set on one of the prettiest beaches in
Phuket, the Boathouse Wine & Grill
serves good, but pricey Thai and
European cuisine. The hotel also runs a
2-day Thai cookery course that includes
lunch and a set of traditional Thai
recipes.

Baan Rim Pa
100/7 Kalim Beach Rd.
Patong
☎ (076) 340789
On a hill overlooking the beach from the
north end of Patong, this pricey, alfresco
restaurant is one of the best places for
traditional Thai food. Other fusion-style
dishes are available, all are served in
beautiful surroundings.

Pizzadelic
Beach Rd., between Bangla Road and
Banana Disco
Pizzadelic serves crispy, inexpensive
pizza and reasonably priced drinks, but
the real attraction is the internet café
at the back.

Sabai Sabai
Soi Post Office
Always packed, this no-frills, good-value
café serves tasty local and Western
dishes.

STEAMING UP
TO MANDALAY
PAGES 74–81

OPERATORS
THE EASTERN & ORIENTAL EXPRESS
Beach Road
32–01/03, Shaw Towers
Singapore 189702
☎ 3923500
Overseas:
U.K. ☎ (020) 7805 5100
U.S.A. ☎ 0800/524-2420
Australia ☎ (3) 96999766
The luxury ship *The Road to Mandalay*
runs a series of 3–4-night tours on the
Ayeyarwady River between Bagan and
Mandalay in Myanmar. Several times dur-
ing the season, an additional trip is run

between Mandalay and the ancient city of
Pyi (or Prome) lasting 8 or 6 nights. Tours
start in Bangkok, Yangon, Mandalay, or
Bagan. The company also has offices in
Myanmar, Japan, and throughout Europe.

BARANI CRUISE AND TRADING GROUP
10 Thazin Rd.
Ahlone Township
Yangon
Myanmar
☎ (1) 223104/225377 / 220949
Fax: (1) 223104
This company charters the *Irrawaddy
Princess* and the *Irrawaddy Princess 2*,
both less luxurious than *The Road to
Mandalay*. They cruise the Ayeyarwady
River between Bagan and Mandalay, and
Yangon and Mandalay.

INSIGHT MYANMAR TOURISM COMPANY
85/87 Thein Phyu Rd.
Botataung Township
Yangon
☎ (1) 29778
Fax: (1) 295599
The company handles all travel arrangements in Myanmar—tours, English-
speaking guides, reservations, and cars.

GETTING THERE
YANGON INTERNATIONAL AIRPORT
☎ (1) 662811
Hotel desks just outside the main arrival
area can arrange buses or taxis into
Yangon.

INFORMATION
MYANMAR TRAVELS AND TOURS
77/91 Sule Pagoda Rd.
Yangon
☎ (1) 78376/75328
Fax: (1) 89588

ACCOMMODATION
Yangon Savoy Hotel $$$
129 Dharmmazedi Rd.
Yangon
☎ (1) 526289/526298/526305
Fax: (1) 524891/2
This is a beautifully restored old colonial
hotel with excellent facilities and great
charm.

Inya Lake Hotel $$$

37 Kaba Aba Pagoda Rd., Yangon
☎ (1) 662857/9
Fax: (1) 665537
A large hotel on the shores of Inya Lake, popular with tour groups. Its facilities are good.

Sedona Hotel $$$

Kaba Aye Pagoda Rd.
Yangon
☎ (1) 666900/666959
Fax: (1) 666567
Large, new hotel located between the airport and the town, facing Inya Lake.

Yuzana Garden Hotel $$

44 Signal Pagoda Rd.
Yangon
☎ (1) 240989 / 248944
Fax: (1) 240074
The renovated colonial building has large rooms and a garden. Discounts are available.

Bagan Hotel, Old Bagan $$

☎ (62) 70311/2
Fax: (62) 70313
This stylish hotel, built in local materials, is close to the museum and the main sites.

Thante Hotel, Old Bagan $$

☎ (62) 70144
Fax: (62) 70143
Less stylish than the Bagan Hotel, but very comfortable, with balcony rooms overlooking the Ayeyarwady River and good food.

Sedona Hotel $$$

26th and 66th St.
Mandalay
☎ (2) 36488. In U.K. ☎ (0171) 4314045
Fax: (2) 36499
A large, comfortable hotel overlooking the Palace, with full facilities and helpful staff.

Mandalay Swan Hotel $$

No. 44B 26th St.
Mandalay
☎ (2) 31591/31601
Fax: (2) 35677
An older, comfortable hotel, next door to Sedona, with good facilities and friendly, helpful staff.

SMOOTH SAILING IN HA LONG BAY PAGES 84–91

OPERATORS

For a trip to Ha Long Bay it remains much easier to follow a tour than to go alone. Trips to Cat Ba Island, however, can be managed without a tour company although it is still far simpler to take a tour. Non verbal communication has its limits. While many companies offer tours to Halong Bay, only one company is offering sea canoeing.

Buffalo Tours

11 Hang Muoi
Ha Noi
☎ (4) 828 0702
Fax: (4) 826 9370
email: buffalo@netnam.org.vn
or bwt@netnam.org.vn
The professionally run company has 40 US-made sea canoes. Trips range from 1- night to 7-nights, or can be tailored to individual requirements. The guides speak good English.

GETTING THERE

NOI BAI AIRPORT, HA NOI

☎ (04) 8271513; (04) 8268522
35km (22 miles) north of the city.

INFORMATION

VIETNAM TOURISM

30A Ly Thuong Kiet St.
☎ (04) 8255552

ACCOMMODATION

Heritage Hotel $$$

88 Ha Long St.
Ha Long
☎ 84 33 846 888
Fax: 84 33 846 999
A 3-star hotel with plenty of facilities.

Vuon Dao Hotel $$

Ha Long Rd.
Baie Chai Beach
Ha Long
☎ 84 33 846 455
Fax: 84 33846 287

Family Hotel & Restaurant $
Cat Ba Island
☎ 84 31 888231
One of the bigger hotels in town, facing the bay with a competent manager and good food.

Van Anh Hotel $
Cat Ba Island
☎ 31 888 201
Fax: 31 888 325
Rooms have TV and telephone and hot water. Located next door to the Family Hotel overlooking the bay. It is popular and well run. James, the manager is an ex-teacher who speaks excellent English and can assist as a guide as well as organise trips on the island.

Gieng Ngoc 1 $
☎ 31 888 286
This is a new hotel overlooking the bay.

Ngoc Mai Hotel $
Vuon Dao St.
Ha Long
☎84 33 846 123

NORTHWEST VIETNAM
BY JEEP
PAGES 92–99

OPERATORS
BUFFALO TOURS
11 Hang Muoi
Ha Noi
☎ (4) 828 0702
Fax: (4) 826 9370
email: buffalo@netnam.org.vn
or bwt@netnam.org.vn
This is professionally run, young Vietnamese company. The guides speak good English. They offer Russian jeeps or Land Cruisers with a driver.

THE HANOI YOUTH TOURIST COMPANY
Kim Café, 135 Hang Bac
Hoan Kiem District
☎ (4) 9281378/8266901
email: kimcafe@hn.vnn.vn
The company offers a very flexible itinerary at competitive rates. Guests can

stay overnight in minority villages or small town hotels (or combine the two). It also offers treks to minority villages. Tours, in Russian jeeps or Land Cruisers, with a driver. Pay extra for guides.

GETTING THERE
NOI BAI AIRPORT, HA NOI
☎ (04) 8271513; (04) 8268522
The airport is 35km (22 miles) north of the city.

INFORMATION
VIETNAM TOURISM
30A Ly Thuong Kiet St.
Ha Noi
☎ (04) 8255552

ACCOMMODATION
Sofitel Metropole Hotel $$$
15 Ngo Quyen St.
Ha Noi
☎ (4) 8266919
Fax: (4) 826 6920
A gracious, renovated old French colonial hotel, perfectly located in the middle of colonial Ha Noi. Excellent facilities, service, and food. This is a good place to recover from the hardships of a trip.

Prince Hotel $$
88 Hang Bac
Ha Noi
☎ (4) 9260150
Fax: (4) 9260149
A new hotel with pleasant rooms equipped with phone, satellite TV, hot-water bath, and fridge.

Victoria Hotel $$/$$$
Sa Pa Town
Lao Cai
☎ (20) 871522
Fax: (20) 871539
Sa Pa's international hotel, within walking distance of the market. Log fires, French food and wine, and its own upmarket train carriage from Ha Noi to Sa Pa. Very comfortable. There are great views of Vietnam's highest mountain Mount Fansipan, when the weather allows.

Tam Duong Hotel $
Phong Tho
☎ (23) 875288

There is no need to book ahead for this budget hotel.

Airport Guest House $$
Dien Bien Phu
☎ (23) 824908
Clean rooms in a functional hotel.

Beach Lossom Guest House $$
Son La
☎ (22) 853823
Fax: (22) 853823
Unsophisticated

FOOD AND DRINK
The Lien Tuoi
27 Hoang Cong Chat St.
Dien Bien Phu
☎ (23) 824919
An excellent variety of traditional Vietnamese food.

Dien Bien Phu Airport Hotel
Cau Moi St.
☎ (84) 23825052
Used by several tour companies; offers good Vietnamese food.

Airport Guesthouse
☎ (23) 824908
(See Accommodation)

NAM OU RIVER VOYAGE
PAGES 100–10

OPERATORS
DIETHELM TRAVEL
Kian Gwan Building II
140/1 Wireless Rd.
Bangkok 10330
Thailand
☎ (2) 2559130/2559160/2559170
Fax: (2) 2560248/9;
email: dto@dto.co.th
Arrenges trips on the Nam Ou River. For further details see page 262

MEKONG LAND
LM International
399/6 Soi Thonglor 21
Sukhumvit 55
Bangkok 10110
Thailand.

☎ (2) 3810881
Fax: (2) 3917212
email: mekongld@mekongland.com
Mekong Land organizes 2-day/1-night luxury cruise from Houei Xai to Luang Prabang on the Mekong River. The company plans to start trips on the Nam Ou River.

SODETOUR
114 quai Fa-Ngum B.P 70
Vientiane
Laos
☎ 21213478/218433
Fax: 21216313
This is the best-known operator in Laos. Offers a combination of excellent adventure tours and tailor-made trips, including the journey up the Nam Ou River. You are advised to make reservations in advance.

SYMBIOSIS EXPEDITION PLANNING
Christopher Gow Enterprises Ltd.
205 St. John's Hill
London SW11 1TH
U.K.
☎ (020) 7924 5906
Fax: (020) 7924 5907
email: info@symbiosis-travel.co.uk
website: www.symbiosis-travel.co.uk
Arrnges trips on the Nam Ou River. For further details see page 262

ACCOMMODATION
Phou Vao Hotel $$$
P.O. Box 50
Luang Prabang
☎ 71212194
Fax: 71212534
The best Luang Prabang has to offer; swimming pool, tropical gardens, magnificent rooms, and a fine restaurant; situated on the edge of town.

Villa Santi $$/$$$
Sisavangvong
Luang Prabang
☎/**Fax:** 212267
A charming century-old royal mansion has been renovated as a 25-room hotel. Central location.

Khem Khan Guest House $
Nam Khan Rd.
Luang Prabang

The rooms are ordinary but it's in a fine situation, on the Nam Khan River.

Phongsali Hotel $
Phongsali
Basic rooms with communal showers and wash room. The best in hotel in town.

Auberge du Temple $$
184/1 Ban Khounta,
Vientiane
☎/Fax: 214844
Delightful converted villa on the outskirts of town.

Le Parasol Blanc $$
263 Sibounheuang Rd.
Vientiane
☎ (856) 216091
Fax: (856) 215444
The pleasant air-conditioned rooms are set around a swimming pool and restaurant.

SLOWBOAT ON THE MEKONG
PAGES 110–17

OPERATORS
MEKONG LAND
LM International
399/6 Soi Thonglor 21
Sukhumvit 55
Bangkok 10110
Thailand.
☎ (2) 3810881
Fax: (2) 3917212
email: mekongld@mekongland.com
Operator of the *Vat Phou* 3-day cruise from Pakse to Don Khong Island (round trip). Reservations should be made well in advance.

SODETOUR
No. 11 Road
Pakse
Laos
☎ (31) 212122
Fax (31) 212765
email: sodeloa@samart.co.th
The local branch of Sodetour (see page 270). They arrange trips both around Champassak and throughout the country.

You are advised to make reservations in advance.

SYMBIOSIS EXPEDITION PLANNING
Christopher Gow Enterprises Ltd.
205 St. John's Hill
London SW11 1TH
U.K.
☎ (020) 7924 5906
Fax: (020) 7924 5907
email: info@symbiosis-travel.co.uk
website: www.symbiosis-travel.co.uk
For further details dee page 262.

INFORMATION
OFFICE OF TOURISM CHAMPASSAK
No. 11 Road
Pakse
Laos
☎ (31) 212021

ACCOMMODATION
Champassak Palace Hotel $$/$$$
No. 13 Road
P.O. Box 718
Pakse
☎:(31) 212263
Fax:(31) 212781
The best Pakse has to offer, this hotel resembles a Christmas cake, with satellite T.V., travel centre, fitness room, and panoramic views.

Salachampa Hotel $$
No. 10 Road
Pakse
☎ (31) 212273
An old, restored French villa, but the upkeep is poor and rooms are overpriced

Sala Wat Phou $$
Champassak,
Pakse
☎ (31) 212725
The best place to stay if you want to be close to Wat Phu.

Auberge Sala Don Khong $$
Muang Khong,
Don Khong Island
Beautiful old teak house with a balcony overlooking the river; bicycles for rent.
Reservations - see Sodetur above

CAMBODIA'S ANGKOR WAT PAGES 120-9

OPERATORS

DIETHELM TRAVEL
Kian Gwan Building II
140/1 Wireless Rd.
Bangkok 10330
Thailand
☎ (2) 2559130/2559160/2559170
Fax: (2) 2560248/9
email: dto@dto.co.th
For details see page 262.

EAST–WEST TRAVEL (CAMBODIA)
No. 182A, St. 208
Sangkat Boeung Rang
Khand Daun Penh
Phnom Penh
☎ (23) 427118/426189
Fax: (23) 426189
email: eastwest@bigpond.com.kh
A division of East–West Siam, see page 259.

INFORMATION

GENERAL DIRECTORATE OF TOURISM
Monivong Boulevard
Phnom Penh
☎ (23) 25607

PHNOM PENH TOURISM
313 Sisawath Quay
☎ (23) 723949 / 725349

ACCOMMODATION
Angkor Villa $$
Siem Reap
☎ (15) 916048
Designed and owned by a French architect, these delightful raised bungalows linked by walkways around a central restaurant offer the perfect retreat after days of sightseeing.

Apsara Angkor Guest House $
No. 279, 6 St.
Siem Reap
☎ (15) 630125/963476
Fax: (15) 380025
A simple and pleasant guest house with a patio and restaurant.

Sofitel Cambodiana $$$
313 Sisowath Quay
Phnom Penh
☎ (23) 426288
Fax: (23) 426392
The classiest hotel in Phnom Penh, with swimming pool, tennis courts, and two restaurants.

Renakse $$
Opposite the Royal Palace
Phnom Penh
☎ (23) 722457/(23) 26036
Fax: (23) 426100
A delightful, rambling French colonial building with old, creaking rooms and a perfect location.

EXPLORING THE BOLOVENS PLATEAU PAGES 130-137

OPERATORS

SODETOUR
No. 11 Road
Pakse
Laos
☎ (31) 212122
Fax (31) 212765
For further details see page 270. You are advised to make reservations in advance.

INTER-LAO TOURISME
No. 13 Road
Pakse
Laos
☎ (31) 212226

SYMBIOSIS EXPEDITION PLANNING
Christopher Gow Enterprises Ltd.
205 St. John's Hill
London SW11 1TH
U.K.
☎ (020) 7924 5906
Fax: (020) 7924 5907
email: info@symbiosis-travel.co.uk
website: www.symbiosis-travel.co.uk
For further details see page 262.

INFORMATION
OFFICE OF TOURISM CHAMPASSAK
No. 11 Road
Pakse
Laos
☎ (31) 212021

ACCOMMODATION
Champassak Palace Hotel $$/$$$
No. 13 Road
P.O. Box 718
Pakse
☎ (31) 212263
Fax: (31) 21277880
The best Pakse has to offer, this hotel
resembles a Christmas cake, with
satellite T.V., travel centre, fitness room,
and panoramic views.

Salachampa Hotel $$
No. 10 Road
Pakse
☎ (31) 212273
This is an old, restored French villa, but
the upkeep is poor and the rooms are
overpriced.

Tad Lo Resort $$
Simple (but overpriced) bungalows in
beautiful setting on the river. You are
strongly advised to book in advance, especially during the peak season, when they
are often full. Book through Sodetour in
Pakse (see under Operators).

Sekong Hotel $
Sekong
The only hotel in town has basic rooms
and a restaurant.

Tavivan Guest House $
Attapu
Pleasant little guest house with a quiet
balcony and close to the river. Good
restaurant

Souk Somphone Guest House $
Attapu
Simple rooms in the middle of town.

MALAYSIA'S JUNGLE RAILWAY PAGES 140–147

OPERATORS
KOTA BAHARU TOURIST INFORMATION CENTRE
Jalan Sultan Ibrahim
Kota Baharu
☎ 9 748 5534
Fax: 9 748 6652
Guide Roselan Hanafiah can arrange
tours and homestay programmes in the
area.

TAMAN NEGARA RESORT
The Parks and Wildlife Department
office, next to the resort's shop, will book
boat rides, fishing huts, and camping
grounds. Guides can be hired here, and
guided walks, starting at 8:30pm every
night, can be arranged for groups of up to
ten people.

THE FAMILY RESTAURANT
This floating restaurant, immediately
west of the shuttle boat across the
Tembeling River, arranges several
activities, including night safaris along
the river, an exploration of Gua Telinga
(Bat Cave) and a visit to an Orang Asli
village, and river tubing. It also organizes
twice daily, return boat trips to Kuala
Tembeling.

GETTING THERE
KUALA LUMPUR INTERNATIONAL AIRPORT
KLIA, the main gateway to Malaysia, is at
Sepang, 33km (20 miles south of Kuala
Lumpur. Buses and taxis connect with
the city.

INFORMATION
MATIC (Malaysian Tourist Information
Complex)
109 Jalan Ampang
Kuala Lumpur
☎ 3 242 3929
Jalan Pesiaran Putra
Housed in a handsome colonial-era villa,
KL's main tourist office has plenty of
information on the city, including local

accommodation, but also can give advice on all areas of the country and make bookings for the national parks, including Taman Negara. Cultural shows, lasting 45 minutes, are held here on Tue, Sat, Sun, at 3:30pm. Office open daily 9am–6pm.

KOTA BAHARU TOURIST INFORMATION CENTRE
Jalan Sultan Ibrahim
Kota Baharu
☎ 9 748 5534
Fax: 9 748 6652
This is where to find guide Roselan Hanafiah, who can arrange tours and homestay programmes in the area

HOTEL SRI EMAS, JERANTUT
Briefing sessions on how to get to Taman Negara, where to stay, and what to do in the park are held here nightly at 8pm. Bookings can be made here for the activities organized by the Family Restaurant, on the Tembeling River (see under Operators, above)

TAMAN NEGARA RESORT
There is an information desk at the resort's front office. Within the grounds is a library and interpretative centre, which screens a 45-minute video on the park's attractions twice daily.

ACCOMMODATION
Kuala Lumpur
BACKPACKERS TRAVELLERS LODGE $
1st floor, 158 Jalan Tun H.S. Lee
Kuala Lumpur
☎ (3) 201 0889
Fax: (3) 238 1128
It's basic, but one of the better budget accommodation options in KL, in the heart of Chinatown and run by extremely friendly people who keep the place scrupulously clean. No curfew, videos shown nightly and a good source of information on what's going on. The hotel also runs Travellers email Centre at Rm 6, 3F, Wisma Kwong Siew, 147–149 Jalan Tun H.S. Lee.

COLISEUM $$$
98 Jalan TAR
Kuala Lumpur
☎ (3) 292 6270

Savour the brooding atmosphere at this old-style Chinese hotel, complete with heavy wooden furniture and giant fans in the rooms. There is a convivial bar (a former watering hole of plantation owners) and legendary steakhouse downstairs.

ISTANA $$$
73 Jalan Raja Chulan
☎ (3) 241 9988
Fax: (3) 244 0111; Tollfree 1800-883380,
email: hotel_istana@histana.po.my
website: http://www.smi-hotels.com.sg
This is one of KL's premier luxury hotels with a ideal position in the Golden Triangle area. Spacious, comfortable roomsand a full range of facilities, including a wide range of restaurants, a sumptous lobby lounge, pool, fitness centre, and tennis and squash courts.

THE LODGE HOTEL $$
Jalan Sultan Ismail
Kuala Lupur
☎ (3) 242 0122
Fax: (3) 241 6819
On the corner, opposite the Istana, this hotel is a fine mid-range choice. The cheaper rooms are in the annex and don't have TVs. There is also a 24-hour café, swimming pool, and a branch of the Indiam Muslim restaurant Hameeds.

RADISSON PLAZA HOTEL $$$
138 Jalan Ampang
Kuala Lumpur
☎ (3) 466 8866
Fax (3) 466 9966
email: rphkl@po.jaring.my
Within minutes' walk to the Suria KLCC shopping centre and Petronas Twin Towers (world's tallest building), this ultra-stylish new hotel has well-appointed rooms and some chic restaurants, a pool, jacuzzi, and a gym.

Kota Baharu
DIAMOND PUTERI HOTEL $$$
Jalan Post Office Lama
Kota Baharu
☎ (9) 743 9988
Fax: (9) 743 8388
email dp@adorna.po.my
web site http://www.diamond-puteri.com
This a high-class hotel with a good position on the waterfront. Facilities include a

classy Chinese restaurant and Western restaurant with a terrace overlooking the river. There is also has a pool and gym.

MENORA GUEST HOUSE $
3338d Jalan Sultanah Zainab
Kota Baharu
☎ (9) 748 1669.
One of the best of the many budget options in KB, this is run by the friendly Chua family. Ask for one of the pleasant penthouse rooms opening on to the roof garden. The alfresco shower only adds to the experience.

SAFAR INN $$
Kota Baharu
Jalan Hilir Kota
☎ (9) 747 8000
Fax: (9) 747 9000
This is a fine mid-range hotel in an excellent location, close by Kota Baharu's The rooms are nicely furnished and the rates include breakfast.

Jerantut and Taman Negara
HOTEL SRI EMAS $
Bangunan Muip
Jalan Besar
27000 Jerantut
☎ (9) 266 4499
Fax: (9) 266 4801
In a central location, near the shops, with a range of rooms, including dormitories, and some with air-conditioning. Nothing fancy, but very friendly and helpful people. Lots of information on how to get into the park and what to do there. There is a good café next door, with satellite TV to help pass the hours if you're waiting for a late night train. The same family run Hotel Jerantut, 100m east on Jalan Besar

TAMAN NEGARA RESORT $/$$/$$$
Kuala Tehan
☎ (9)-266 3500 / 266 2200
Fax: (9) 266 1500
KL Sales Office:
2nd floor, Hotel Istana
Jalan Raja Chulan
Kuala Lumpur
☎ (3) 245 5585 **Fax:** (3) 45 5430
Within the park boundaries, the resort's twin-bed chalets with air conditioning and en-suite bathrooms are the best accommodation you'll find, and if you

really want to push the boat out there are even more luxurious chalet suites and bungalows. The standard guesthouse rooms in the brick buildings at the far east end of the resort are less good value, but the hostel, with eight people to a room in bunk beds including mosquito nets, is worth considering as a budget option. Facilities include a restaurant and café (see below), and the recreation office runs a number of short trips around the park. There is also a campsite (bring your own gear or rent).

NUSA CAMP $
Reservations in Jerantu:
☎ (9) 266 2369
Fax: (9) 266 4369
In Kuala Lumpur at MATIC:
☎ (3) 262 7682 **Fax:** (3) 262 7682.
Some 2km further east along the Tembeling River from Kuala Tahan, on the opposite bank from the park, this is a more basic jungle resort with a choice of accommodation between Malay-style chalets, simple A-frame huts, four-bed dorm rooms, and a camping ground. There is also a cafeteria. Good if you're looking for a quieter jungle experience than at the increasingly busy Kuala Tahan, but the downside is that you'll have to take boats to get into the park.

SHOREA MOTEL $/$$
(formerly known as Ekoton Chalet)
Lot 1010
Kuala Tahan
☎/**Fax:** (9) 266 9897; cell-phone: 010-988 8932.
This is the best accommodation option in Kuala Tahan. The concrete chalets each have small verandas, air conditioning, and attached bathrooms, and there's a choice of air-conditioned and fan-cooled dormitory rooms. At the time of writing, they were building an attached café.

FOOD AND DRINK
Kuala Lumpur
COLISEUM CAFÉ
98 Jalan TAR
☎ (3) 292 6270
If you're after colonial ambience, the sizzling steaks and aged waiters in this hotel restaurant are hard to beat.

LE COQ D'OR
121 Jalan Ampang
☎ (3) 242-9732
The restaurant serves a mix of Malay, European and Chinese dishes in the faded grandeur of an old Chinese tycoon's mansion.

BON TON
7 Jalan Kia Peng
☎ (3) 241 3611
Eastern and Western cuisine is fused into delicious hybrids and served along with an excellent selection of fine wines in an imaginatively renovated bungalow.

CARCOSA SERI NEGARA
☎ (3) 282 7888
For real self-indulgence, eat at this former residence of the British Governor of the Malay States, now KL's most exclusive hotel. High tea here is an exercise in sweet decadence (and very reasonably priced), while the Sunday lunch eat-all-you-like curry "tiffin" is legendary.

SERI ANGKASA
☎ (3) 208 5055
For fine Malay dining with a view try this smart revolving restaurant atop the Menara KL. Bookings essential

CEYLON HILL
The up and coming inner city area has several places to head for, including the laid-back bar **Long Island Iced Tea House** (15 Changkat Bukit Bintang, ☎ 3 243 9089) with pool tables, good value food, including tandoori suppers and cheese and paté, and long happy hours; the more stylish and expensive **Little Havana** (2&4 Lorong Sahabat, ☎ 3 244 7170), complete with that essential for a trendy Southeast Asian restaurant: the cigar room; **Le Maschere** (16 Jalan Changkat Bukit Bintang, ☎ 3 244 6395), a pizza and pasta joint with bags of flair.

CHINATOWN
This district of Kuala Lumpur also under-going something of a rennaissance with the nostalgic **Old China Company Café and Restauran**t (Jalan Traffic Polis), serving classic Straits Chinese dishes in the former guild hall of the Selangor and Federal Territory Laundry Association.

Next door the ultra-modern **Kafe Halo** showcases local pop bands and singers.

BANGSAR
You might also consider hopping in a cab and heading for Bangsar, KL's trendiest suburb, jammed packed with a wide range of restaurants and bars, as well as an excellent open-air hawkers centre.

Kota Baharu
QING LANG
Jalan Zainal Abidin
Especially worth seeking outif you're vegetarian, since it serves spicy meat-free, tofu-based Chinese cuisine. The café is air-conditioned, another bonus.
The first floor of the **Central Market** has plenty of cafés serving freshly cooked local dishes, including seafood curries and sal-ads, during the day. The throbbing **night market**, in the car park opposite Central Market from 6:30pm to midnight, is the best place for dinner. Try the *ayam per-cik*, barbecued chicken doused in a delicious coconut sauce and *nasi kerabu*—rice in a range of colours (including purple, blue, and green) served with condiments such as toasted coconut, bean sprouts, spicy onions, , boiled eggs, dried fish and pickled garlic. The form is to buy from the stalls and then sit at any of the surrounding tables where you can order drinks and other individually cooked dishes. Water jugs on the tables are for rinsing hands after eating; if you prefer to use cutlery, ask at the stalls serving drinks.

Taman Negara Resort
The best place to eat in the resort is the **Tahan Restaurant**. The buffet dinners, including a good range of local and Western dishes and salads, are worth splashing out on. This is the only place you can buy alcohol in Kuala Tahan. Better value for breakfast and lunch is the self-service **Teresek Cafeteria** at the east end of the resort. Most visitors will cross the Kuala Tahan, to eat at one of the much cheaper, five floating restaurants on the river. They all serve more or less the same menu of noodle and rice dishes. The most popular option is the **Family Restaurant**. On Wednesday evenings, there's a night market along the main road into Kuala Tahan that's worth a browse.

ISLAND-HOPPING AROUND LANGKAWI PAGES 148–157

OPERATORS
DYNAMITE CRUISES
Awana Hotel Marina, Langkawi
P.O. Box 78
Kuah 07000
Langkawi
☎ (12) 4886933 **Fax:** (4) 9651411
email: dynamite@tm.net.my
Full-day trips run by New Zealander Lin Ronald on an 18-m (60-foot) sailing ship, *Dynamo Hum*, starting from Porto Malai marina. Includes buffet lunch with drinks. Also on offer are seasonal trips around the mangrove forests and rocky inlets on Langkawi's northeast coast—weather permitting.

FUTURISTIC ENTERPRISE (JURGEN ZIMMERER)
62 Hatiah Villa
B.K. Merang/Kedawang
0700 Pulau
Langkawi
☎ (4) 9554744
This small, friendly operation offers jungle tours and mangrove trips to north and northeast parts of Langkawi.

SYMBIOSIS EXPEDITION PLANNING
Christopher Gow Enterprises Ltd.
205 St. John's Hill
London SW11 1TH
U.K.
☎ (020) 7924 5906
Fax: (020) 7924 5907
email: info@symbiosis-travel.co.uk
website: www.symbiosis-travel.co.uk
For further details see page 262.

WILDLIFE LANGKAWI
Irshad Mobarak
☎ (18) 8402060 **Fax:** (4) 9652295
The company organizes wildlife walks around The Datai (see under Accommodation), coastal nature safaris from Tanjung Rhu into the mangrove forest, and bird-watching trips to Gunung Raya.

GETTING THERE
KUALA LUMPUR INTERNATIONAL AIRPORT
KLIA, the main gateway to Malaysia, is at Sepang, 33km (20 miles south of Kuala Lumpur) Buses and taxis connect with the city.

LANGKAWI AIRPORT
☎ (4) 9551311
On the west side of the island, the airport has a tourist information desk where you can pick up maps of the island.

CAR/MOTORBIKE RENTAL
Car hire is available at the ferry jetty and at local hotels (see Accommodation for details). Motorbike rental shops abound in the beach resort of Pantai Cenang. Be sure to check the bike fully and give it a test ride before handing over your cash.

INFORMATION
MATIC (Malaysian Tourist Information Complex)
109 Jalan Ampang
Kuala Lumpur
☎ 3 242 3929
Jalan Pesiaran Putra
For further details see page 274.

LANGKAWI TOURIST INFORMATION CENTRE
Jalan Pesiaran Putra
07000 Kuah
Langkawi
☎ (4) 9667789
Fax: (4) 9667889

ACCOMMODATION
Kuala Lumpur
BACKPACKERS TRAVELLERS LODGE $
1st floor, 158 Jalan Tun H.S. Lee
Kuala Lumpur
☎ (3) 201 0889 **Fax:** (3) 238 1128
It's basic, but one of the better budget accommodation options in KL, in the heart of Chinatown and run by extremely friendly people who keep the place scrupulously clean. No curfew, videos shown nightly and a good source of information on what's going on. The hotel also runs Travellers email Centre at Rm 6, 3F, Wisma Kwong Siew, 147–149 Jalan Tun H.S. Lee.

COLISEUM £$$

98 Jalan TAR
Kuala Lumpur
☎ (3) 292 6270
Savour the brooding atmosphere at this old-style Chinese hotel, complete with heavy wooden furniture and giant fans in the rooms. Stay here, and you're handily placed for both the convivial bar (a former watering hole of plantation owners) and legendary steakhouse downstairs.

ISTANA $$$

73 Jalan Raja Chulan
☎ (3) 241 9988
Fax: (3) 244 0111; Tollfree 1800-883380,
email: hotel_istana@histana.po.my
website: http://www.smi-hotels.com.sg
This is one of KL's premier luxury hotels with a ideal position in the Golden Triangle area. Spacious, comfortable rooms and a full range of facilities, including a wide range of restaurants, a sumptous lobby lounge, pool, fitness centre, and tennis and squash courts.

THE LODGE HOTEL $$

Jalan Sultan Ismail
Kuala Lupur
☎ (3) 242 0122 **Fax:** (3) 241 6819
On the corner, opposite the Istana, this good value hotel is a fine mid-range choice. The cheaper rooms are in the annex and don't have TVs.There is also a 24-hour café, swimming pool, and a branch of the Indian Muslim restaurant Hameeds.

RADISSON PLAZA HOTEL $$$

138 Jalan Ampang
Kuala Lumpur
☎ (3) 466 8866
Fax (3) 466 9966
email: rphkl@po.jaring.my
Within minutes' walk to the Suria KLCC shopping centre and Petronas Twin Towers (world's tallest building), this ultra-stylish new hotel has well-appointed rooms and some chic restaurants and bars, as well as a pool, jacuzzi, and gym.

Langkawi

THE ANDAMAN $$

Jalan Teluk Datai
07000 Langkawi
☎ (4) 9591088
Fax: (4) 9591168
email: anda@po.jaring.my
The more family-friendly of the two hotels that share the exclusive Pantai Datai beach. Vastly impressive lobby and elegant rooms are complemented by a fine choice of restaurants and a pool surrounded by jungle. Plenty of non-motorized watersports and a resident naturalist on hand for jungle treks.

BON TON AT THE BEACH $$

Lot 1047
Pantai Cenang
☎ (4) 9553643
Fax: (4) 9556790
email: nmmm@tm.my.com
Not only is this one of the best restaurants and craft shops on the island, it's also possible to stay in one of the eight charmingly renovated *kampung* (village) houses on the same compound, each individually decorated with local furniture and crafts. Some have verandas with hammocks, others bathrooms open to the sky. The company also has a luxury motor yacht for hire.

THE DATAI $$$

Jalan Teluk Datai
07000 Langkawi
☎ (4) 9592500 **Fax:** (4) 9592600
The ultimate in luxury, this exclusive hotel is one of the best in all Malaysia.

THE PELANGI BEACH RESORT $$$

Pantai Cenang
07000 Langkawi
☎ (4) 9551001
Fax: (0) 9551122
email: pbrl@tm.net.my
Grand-dame of Langkawi's luxury hotels, with a friendly atmosphere, comfortable rooms, and an excellent range of facilities including pools, watersports, a gym, shops, and a business centre.

FOOD AND DRINK
Kuala Lumpur
COLISEUM CAFÉ
98 Jalan TAR
☎ (3) 292 6270
If you're after colonial ambience, the sizzling steaks and aged waiters in this hotel restaurant are hard to beat.

LE COQ D'OR
121 Jalan Ampang
☎ (3) 242-9732
The restaurant serves a mix of Malay, European and Chinese dishes in the faded grandeur of an old Chinese tycoon's mansion.

BON TON
7 Jalan Kia Peng
☎ (3) 241 3611
Eastern and Western cuisine is fused into delicious hybrids and served along with an excellent selection of fine wines in an imaginatively renovated bungalow.

CARCOSA SERI NEGARA
☎ (3) 282 7888
For real self-indulgence, eat at this former residence of the British Governor of the Malay States, now KL's most exclusive hotel. High tea here is an exercise in sweet decadence (and very reasonably priced), while the Sunday lunch eat-all-you-like curry "tiffin" is legendary.

SERI ANGKASA
☎ (3) 208 5055
For fine Malay dining with a view try this smart revolving restaurant atop the Menara KL. Bookings essential.

CEYLON HILL
For details of good places to eat in this up and coming inner city area see page 276. There will no doubt be even more since the time of writing.

CHINATOWN
This district of Kuala Lumpur also undergoing something of a renaissance. For further details of restaurants and cafés see page 276.

BANGSAR
You might also consider hopping in a cab and heading for Bangsar, KL's trendiest suburb, jammed packed with a wide range of restaurants and bars, as well as an excellent open-air hawkers centre.

Langkawi
The best place to eat on Langkawi is around **Pantai Cenang**.

Air Hangat Village
☎ (04) 9591357
This lacklustre hot springs park 16km (10 miles) north of Kuah is worth visiting in the evening for its Malaysian buffet dinners and dance performance (not on a Tuesday). Both Barn Thai and Air Hangat Village offer return transport to the islands hotels.

Barn Thai
A pricey Thai restaurant and jazz club 10km north of Kuah; worth visting for its nearly 2-km (1¼ mile) walkway through the mangrove forests.

Bon Ton at the Beach
Lot 1047
Pantai Cenang
☎ (4) 9553643
Fax: (4) 9556790
email: nmmm@tm.my.com
A beautifully designed restaurant with attached crafts shop. See also under Accommodation.

The Breakfast Bar
On the main Pantain Cenang drag; serves excellent roti chanai.

Charlie's Place
Situated next to the yacht club on the ferry jetty in Kuah, this laid-back contemporary bar and restaurant serves Western dishes.

Warung Kopi
On the main road leading up to Bon Ton, this is the locals' preferred pit stop for cooling ice teas, coffee and cake, or nasi goreng around lunchtime.

RACING DOG RIVER RAPIDS
PAGES 160–169

OPERATORS
P.T. O'LEARY'S INDONESIA ADVENTURE HOLIDAYS
Jalan Armada 1
Medan 20217
Sumatra
Indonesia
☎ (61) 742425
Fax: (61) 719005
email: olearys@indosat.met.id
website:
www.indopro.com/indonesia_adventures
Run by genial Irishman Daniel O'Leary, this agency offers a wide range of fun adventure packages around Sumatra and can put together tailor-made itineraries. Trips include a 2-day Wampu River excursion, a 5-day river safari along the Alas River, and two nights on the Asahan from Lake Toba. Also offered are scuba diving in Pulau Weh, surfing off Pulau Asu, Pulau Nias, and Pulau Lhoknga, and a 14-day treck up Gunung Leuser.

PACTO LTD.
P.O. Box 1267
Jalan Brigjen Katamso 35
Medan 20151
Sumatra,
Indonesia
☎ (61) 510081
Fax: (61) 555820/513669
email: pactomes@indosat.met.id
website: www.pacto.com
Long-established and reliable tour operators who arrange upmarket trekking and rafting trips. Examples include a 6-day trip into the Gurah Rain Forest, in the heart of Gunung Leuser National Park, via Brastagi and 5-day rafting safaris on the Alas River.

TOBALI TOURS AND TRAVEL SERVICE
Jalan Kapt. Muslim 111
Komp. Tata Plaza B-59
Medan
Sumatra
Indonesia
☎/**Fax:** (61) 856770

Runs a variety of budget tours to Bukit Lawang, Brastagi, and Lake Toba, but their best services are the daily air-conditioned mini-buses, which link all the above places and include stops at other tourist attractions along the way. In Brastagi, the service operates out of the Raymond Steakhouse (49 Jalan Veteran) and there are also offices in Bukit Lawang and Prapat on Lake Toba.

INFORMATION
BUKIT LAWANG TOURIST OFFICE
Buses pull up here. The office has leaflets and information on guides and trekking, and the visitor centre has daily displays on the park and local natural history, including a 55-minute video "Orangutans, Orphans of the Forest" screened Mon., Wed., and Fri. evening. It also sells books.

ACCOMMODATION
Even the most expensive accommodation Simon Richmond sampled in Sumatra was less than about $7 a night, so the classifications in this section are relative to each other.

Bukit Kubu Hotel $$/$$$
Jalan Sempurna 2
Brastagi
☎ (628) 20832
Set in lovely grounds about 1km (½ mile) out of town. Modern cottages surround the main building, which is a run-down colonial gem.. Check out the rooms for cleanliness before booking in.

International Sibayak $$$
Jalan Merdeka
Brastagi
☎ (628) 91301 **Fax:** (628) 91307
Large upmarket hotel a short walk north of the fruit market. Comfortable rooms, with a good range of facilities, but lacking in character.

Sibayak Multinational $/$$
Jalan Perndidikan 93
Brastagi
☎ (628) 91031
Pleasant guest house with hot-water showers in the large rooms and a nice garden setting. Good location if you're planning on climbing Mount Sibayak since it's near the start of the trail,

although this also puts it a fair distance from centre of town.

Wisma Sibayak $
Jalan Udara 1
Brastagi
☎ (028) 91683
Fine travellers' hangout with a range of simply furnished budget rooms, a dormitory, and a café. Screens CNN and videos, and sells local guidebooks and maps.

Jungle Inn $
Bukit Lawang
At the far western end of the village, near the Orangutan Rehabilitation Station. This is a deservedly popular guest house, with a range of imaginatively designed rooms, some overlooking the river. Friendly service and a fine café.

Pongo Resort $$$
Bukit Lawang
☎ (645) 542574
Fax: (645) 549327
This is the only accommodation within Gunung Leuser National Park boundaries that gives guests unlimited access to the Orangutan Rehabilitation Station. It consists of fan-cooled, wooden chalets in a charming setting. Rates include breakfast and park permits.

Rindu Alam Hotel $$$
P.O. Box 20774
Bukit Lawang
☎ (61) 545015
The most upmarket accommodation in Bukit Lawang, but the roomy chalets are disappointingly made from concrete. At the far east end of the village.

Wisma Bukit Lawang Cottages $/$$
Bukit Lawang
One of the better operations in the heart of the village, with an elevated position on the southern flank of the Bohorok River. Wide range of attractive, good value accommodation.

FOOD AND DRINK
Raymond Steakhouse
Jalan Veteran 49, Brastagi
Good range of Western and local dishes, as well as some yummy homemade cakes.

Villa Flores
Jalan Veteran, Brastagi
At the southern end of the main road, this small restaurant, decorated with Batik prints is a gem. Chef Seth, a British guy, and his Indonesian wife, churn out miraculous pizzas, salads, and other Mediterranean-style dishes from a tiny kitchen. Beers also available.

Both the Jungle Inn and Bukit Lawang Cottages (see under Accommodation, above) have cafés attached, which serve a wide range of well-cooked visitors' favourites, as well as local dishes. For a change, try the Bamboo Pizzeria, which serves excellent pizza made in a real pizza oven, pasta, and salads.

Bagus Bay Homestay $
Tuk Tuk
Samosir
☎ (645) 41481
This is a popular option, but you get what you pay for with the cheapest rooms, which are grubby. There's a good atmosphere in the restaurant, where videos are screened, and there's a billiards table. It's also the only place to be on Saturday night, when the lively Batak singing and dancing show has the house on its feet and visitors snapping up the cassette tapes.

Carolina's $$$
Tuk Tuk
Samosir
☎ (645) 41520
Fax (645) 41521
Lovely accommodation, with the most delightful and best-kept Batak-style cottages on the island, not to mention a beautiful vista across Lake Toba and a fine swimming area. The only minus is the rather bland food.

Samosir Cottages $$
Tuk Tuk
Samosir
☎ (645) 41050
On the northern headland of the peninsula. The rooms are well kept and good value. The café is a convivial spot to eat and drink, and it hosts traditional dance performances at 7:30pm, Wed., Sat.

Tabo Cottages $$
Tuk Tuk
Samosir
☎ (645) 41614
Only a few rooms but bags of charm and set in a quiet plot with access to the water. The excellent restaurant and bakery are a bonus. At the time of visiting, it offered the only public Internet connection on Samosir, but the rates charged are high since calls are routed via Medan.

Yogyakarta
☎ (274) 373031
Fax: (274) 382202
A beautiful hotel of character with pool, and good food and location.

Vogels Hostel $/$$
Jalan Astamulya 76, Mount Merapi
☎ (274) 95208
A clean hostel with a dormitory, double rooms, and bungalows.

THE GREAT BOROBUDUR
PAGES 170–177

OPERATORS
PARAMITA TOURS
Ambarrukmo Palace Hotel
Yogyakarta
☎ (274) 566488 ext. 7142
Fax: (274) 563283
Contact Roswitha

SYMBIOSIS EXPEDITION PLANNING
Christopher Gow Enterprises Ltd.
205 St. John's Hill
London SW11 1TH
U.K.
☎ (020) 7924 5906
Fax: (020)7 924 590
email: info@symbiosis-travel.co.uk
website: www.symbiosis-travel.co.uk
A British-based adventure travel company that has a special interest in organizing trips to Southeast Asia.

GETTING THERE
YOGYAKARTA AIRPORT
☎ (274) 563706
Situated about 20 minutes' drive from the centre of town. There are plenty of taxis, and car hire also available from Bali Car Rental.

INFORMATION
TOURIST INFORMATION OFFICE
Jalan Malioboro 16
Yogyakarta
☎ (274) 66000
Open Mon.–Sat 8am–8pm.

ACCOMMODATION
Jogya Village Inn $$
Jalan Menukan 5

LIVING WITH THE IBAN
PAGES 180–187

OPERATORS
BORNEO ADVENTURE
55 Main Bazaar
93000 Kuching
☎ (82) 245175
Fax: (82) 422626
email: bakch@po.jaring.my
web site: www.borneoadventure.com
A commendable operation, which lives up to its mission statement of providing sustainable, nature-based tourism. The company have been running tours to Nanga Sumpa since 1987. The typical tour lasts 3 days/2 nights. It's possible to arrange extensions, staying in the company's jungle huts further upriver from the longhouse. Also offers longhouse trips along the Baleh River, a tributary of the Batang Rajang River.

BORNEO EXPLORATION
76 Wayang St
93000 Kuching
☎ (82) 252137
Fax: (82) 252526
email: bett56@hotmail.com
website: http://members.tripod.com/~borneoexplorer/
A favourite choice of backpackers, run by the enterprising Chris Kon, who'll try to put together groups so as to bring down the cost of individual travel. The 4-day/3-night trip is to the Skandis longhouse on the Lemanak River, where there is a guesthouse for visitors. One night is also spent in the jungle. Also offers 5- and 6-day programmes, involving longer jungle treks and different longhouses.

SYMBIOSIS EXPEDITION PLANNING

Christopher Gow Enterprises Ltd.
205 St. John's Hill
London SW11 1TH
U.K.
☎ (020) 7924 5906
Fax: (020) 7924 5907
email: info@symbiosis-travel.co.uk
website: www.symbiosis-travel.co.uk
For further details see page 262.

GETTING THERE

KUCHING INTERNATIONAL AIRPORT
☎ (82) 454242
Fax: (82) 454523
Located 11km south of the city.

INFORMATION

VISITORS INFORMATION CENTRE,
Padang Merdeka
Kuching
SarawakTel: (82) 410944/410942
Fax: (82) 256301
email sarawak@po.jaring.my;
website: www.sarawaktourism.com
This is run by Sarawak Tourism Board. It
shows daily video shows at 10am and
3pm, and handles bookings for the
National Parks, issuing visitor permits
and arranging accommodation for Bako,
Gunung Gading, Kubah.

SARAWAK TOURIST ASSOCIATION (S.T.A.)
Main Bazaar (on the waterfront side)
Kuching
Sarawak
☎ (82) 240620
Fax: (82) 427151
Both this and the Visitors Information
Centre (see above) provide copies of *The
Official Kuching Guide*, by Wayne
Tarman & Mike Reed (free), a handy,
annually updated and fully comprehen-
sive overview of what's going on in and
around the city.

ACCOMMODATION

Kuching Hilton International $$$
Jalan Tunku Abdul Rahman
P.O. Box 2396
93748 Kuching
☎ (82) 248200
Fax: (82) 428984
email: sales@hilton.co

A top-class hotel, on the Kuching waterfront, with comfortable, large rooms;
some floors are designated non-smoking.
Facilities include several excellent
restaurants, a pool, fitness centre, and
internet café.

Merdeka Plaza Hotel & Suites $$$
Jalan Tun Abang Haji Openg
P.O. Box A298
93000 Kuching
☎ (82) 258000
Fax: (82) 425400
email: mpalace@po.jaring.my Kuching's
newest luxury hotel, close by the
Sarawak Museum and overlooking
Padang Merdeka, has an opulent foyer,
but the rooms are on the small side.
There is a pool and fitness centre.

Telang Usan Hotel $$
Jalan Ban Hock
P.O. Box 1579
93732 Kuching
☎ (82) 415588
Fax: (82) 425316
email: tusan@po.jaring.my
Kuching's best mid-range hotel, owned
and run by locals, has a handy, quiet location, pleasant rooms, and excellent
service.

B & B Inn $
30–1 Jalan Tabuan (next to the Borneo
Hotel)
☎ (82) 237366
Run by the friendly Mr. Goh, this is the
top choice for backpackers, with a central
location, clean rooms, and simple breakfast included in the rates.

Batang Ai (Iban longhouses)
The best way to arrange to stay in a longhouse is via one of the tour operators in
Kuching (see above). Just pitching up at
one of the jetties in the hope that an offer
of accommodation might be forthcoming
is not recommended.

The Hilton International Batang Ai Longhouse Resort $$
Jalan Tunku Abdul Rahman
P.O. Box 2396 93748
Kuching
☎ (83) 584388

Fax: (83) 584399

The hotel commands a spectacular view over the reservoir created by the hydro-electric dam. Built is a longhouse architectural style with a pool, nature walk, mini library, and a decent restaurant. The hotel has a range of environmentally friendly policies, a resident naturalist on hand to answer guests' questions and conduct tours, and was a key force in the ban on polluting motorized watersports on the reservoir.

FOOD AND DRINK

A la Carte Food Centre
Temple St./Wayang St.
Kuching
Air-conditioned food court in the basement of Star car park complex. Popular with a younger crowd, it serves the full range of hawker specialities.

Denis' Place
80 Main Bazaar
This is a cheerfully painted, laid-back Western-style café, serving up a fair range of dishes, including sandwiches and other light snacks.

Life Café
108 Ewe Hai St.
☎ (82) 411754
This charming Chinese teashop serves some delicious vegetarian food and a fine range of drinks in a relaxed atmosphere.

See Good
Ban Hock Rd.
☎ (82) 251397
Seafood is the speciality at this partly alfresco Chinese café. The fish in black bean sauce is excellent and it's worth going for some of the more unusual seafood dishes such as sea needles. Serves an impressive range of reasonably priced wines.

Top Spot Food Court
Jalan Bukit Mata
Kuching
Head to the roof of the car park for this open-air food court with a view, serving a wide range of dishes including noodles, satay, and claypot chicken.

ON THE HEADHUNTER'S TRAIL
PAGES 188–197

OPERATORS

BORNEO ADVENTURE
55 Main Bazaar
93000 Kuching
☎ (82) 245175
☎ in Miri: (85) 414935
Fax: (82) 422626
email: bakch@po.jaring.my
web site: www.borneoadventure.com
This is a commendable operation, which lives up to its mission statement of providing sustainable, nature-based tourism. It operates 2-day visit to the park, taking in the four show caves, 5-day packages to the Pinnacles and back with the option of continuing along the Headhunter's Trail to Limbang, and a 4-day hike up Gunung Mulu. Optional tours include a day-long adventure caving trip through Lagan's Cave, with all equipment provided, and rock climbing and abseiling trips. Also offer longer trips to the more remote Bario area.

BORNEO EXPLORATION
76 Wayang St.
93000 Kuching
☎ (82) 252137
Fax: (82) 252526
email: bett56@hotmail.com;
website:http://members.tripod.com/~borneoexplorer/
This is a favourite choice of backpackers, run by the enterprising Chris Kon, who'll try to put together groups so as to bring down the cost of individual travel. It offers round trips to the Pinnacles and a 5-day/4-night trip on the Headhunter's Trail.

ENDAYANG ENTERPRISE
2nd floor, Judson Clinic
171a Jalan Brooke
Miri
☎ (85) 438741 **Fax:** (85) 438740
email: endaya@pd.jaring.m
Run by Thomas Ngang, a Berawan, this operator specializes in cheaper deals for independent travellers around the park.

SYMBIOSIS EXPEDITION PLANNING

Christopher Gow Enterprises Ltd.
205 St. John's Hill
London SW11 1TH
U.K.
☎ (020)7924 5906
Fax: (020) 7924 5907
email: info@symbiosis-travel.co.uk
website: www.symbiosis-travel.co.uk
For further details see page 262.

MULU ADVENTURE

☎ (85) 423969
Fax: (85) 437886
email: muluadv@kc.com.my
website:
http://www.kc.com.my/borneo/sarawak/travel/madv/index.html
This tour operator offers a range of packages, including sightseeing and shopping as well as adventure tours in Sarawak (including Kuching, Miri, Mulu), Sabah, Brunei, and Kalimantan.

TROPICAL ADVENTURES

228 Jalan Maju, Miri
☎ (85) 419337
A large agency, which apart from offering the standard range of trips into Mulu, also has treks along the Baram River and up in the Kelabit Highlands.

GETTING THERE

The air strip at Gunung Mulu is a few minutes upstream from the park HQ. A regular boat service runs to the park. Flights are available from Miri Airport, ☎ (85) 421620.

INFORMATION
KUCHING TOURIST OFFICE

Padang Merdeka
Kuching
☎ (82) 410 944
Fax: (82) 256301
Provides guides and permits to Gunung Mulu National Park. You can also book accommodation in the park from here.

MIRI TOURIST OFFICE

Lot 452
Jalan Melayu
98000 Miri
☎ (85) 434181
Fax: (85) 434179
The office issues permits to Gunung Mulu National Park. It will also provide a guide and book accommodation in the park.

ACCOMMODATION

There's little reason to hang around Miri, the main gateway to Gunung Mulu National Park, unless you've missed the last flight of the day. If you do get stuck, try:

Rihga Royal Hotel $$$

Jalan Temenggong Datuk Oyong Lawai
98000 Miri
☎ (85) 421121
Fax (85) 421099
website:
http://asiatravel.com/rihgaroyal/hotel.html
This top of the range resort-style hotel, set in pleasant gardens, has a large pool and fine range of other facilities.

Telang Usan Hotel $$

Lot 2431 Block 1
2.5km Airport Rd.
98000 Miri
☎ (85) 411433 **Fax:** (85) 419078
email: tusan@po.jaring.my
Good value, run by friendly local people.

Gunung Mulu National Park

The National Parks and Wildlife Office (see Kuching and Miri Tourist Offices for details) offer several budget accommodation options in and around the park. Next to the park headquarters are modern, simply furnished four-bed chalets, as well as dormitory accommodation. The accommodation is even better at the Kuala Mentawai Ranger Post, at the northern extremity of the park, for the same prices. Camping charges on the way up Gunung Mulu or along the Headhunter's Trail are covered by the park fees.

Endayang Inn $

☎ (85) 438740
One of the better options among the basic inns along the Melinau River.

Royal Mulu Resort $$$

Sungai Melinau
Mulu
☎ (85) 421122/420780
Fax: 421088
website: http://

asiatravel.com/royalmulu/resort.htlm
A short drive from both Mulu airport and the park headquarters. The resort offers the park's only luxury accommodation. Designed to blend with the surrounding jungle, it incorporates chalet-style rooms linked by raised wooden walkways. Staff are pleasant, and there's a pool, a small shop stocking essentials, snacks, and souvenirs. Look out also for the resident hornbill, the only bird to hang around after a fallen tree cut through the netting on the resort's aviary.

FOOD AND DRINK
Royal Mulu Resort
Sungai Melinau
Mulu
☎ (85) 421122/420780
Fax:421088
website: http://
asiatravel.com/royalmulu/resort.htm
The food is patchy but there is a reasonable selection of wines

Sipan Bar
Next to the bridge across the Melinau River to the park headquarters, this is a good spot to chill out after a trek over a cold beer.

Tradmu Café
Next to the park headquarters' chalets, the café serves a short menu of noodle and rice dishes and soft drinks.

THE CORAL WALL OF SPIDAN
PAGES 198–207

OPERATORS
BORNEO DIVERS
Lot 401–412, 4th Floor
Wisma
Sabah
☎ 222226
Fax: 221550
 email: bdivers@po.jaring.my
A highly respected, PADI-accredited iving school, which offers trips to Sipadan and has equipment for hire.

PULAU SIPADAN RESORT
484 Block P
Bandar Sabindo
Pulau Sipadan
Sabah
☎ 765200
Fax: 763575
One of the operators working on the island of Sipadan intself.

SIPADAN DIVE CENTRE
A1103, 10th Floor
Wisma Merdeka
Jin Tun Razak
Kota Kinabalu
Sabah
☎ 240584
Fax: 240415
Another Sipadan operator.

GETTING THERE
Kota Kinabalu International Airport
88618 Kota Kinabalu
Sabah
Malaysia
☎ (88) 238555
Fax: (88) 219081
Situated 6km (3 miles) from town, the airport is served by regular bus and minibus services, and taxis are available.

INFORMATION
TOURISM MALAYSIA SABAH
Wing On Bldg.
Jin Sagunting
Kota Kinabalu
Sabah
☎ (88) 211698

CAR HIRE
Avis
Hyatt Kinabalu Hotel
Jin Datuk Salleh Bldg.
Kota Kinabalu
Sabah
☎ (88) 428577

ACCOMMODATION
Accommodation in Sipadan is included in the diving packages, as are all meals.

CLIMBING MOUNT KINABALU
PAGES 208-215

OPERATORS
BORNEO DIVERS
Lot 401–412, 4th Floor
Wisma
Sabah
☎ 222226
Fax: 221550
email: bdivers@po.jaring.my
The company arranges guides and
accommodation for climbing Mount
Kinabalu, as well as being a highly
respected PADI- accredited diving
school.

SABAH NATIONAL PARKS OFFICE
Block K
Sinsuran Kompleks
Jalan Tun Fuad Stephens
Kota Kinabalu
Sabah
☎ (88) 211585
The offaice can arrange bookings and
guides for expeditions to Mount
Kinabalu.

INFORMATION
TOURISM MALAYSIA SABAH
Wing On Bldg.
Jln Sagunting
Kota Kinabalu
Sabah
☎ (88) 211698

CAR HIRE
Avis
Hyatt Kinabalu Hotel
Jln Datuk Salleh Bldg.
Kota Kinabalu
Sabah
☎ (88) 428577

ACCOMMODATION
Hotel Holiday $/$$
Penampang Road
88300 Kota Kinabalu
Sabah
☎ (88) 712311
Fax: (88) 717866

email: borneo-online.com.my/hotel/holi-
daypark
Modest, comfortable hotel in quiet suburb.

Shangri-La Tanjung Aru Resort $$$
Tanjung Aru
☎ 225800
Fax: 244871
email: borneo-online.com.my/shangri-la
500 room modern complex with pool and
all facilities.

FOOD AND DRINK
Restoran Ali
Segama Complex
Kota Kinabalu
Opposite the Hyatt Hotel, this serves
good-value, traditional Malay food.

THE TARSIERS OF TANGKOKO
PAGES 216-223

OPERATORS
SYMBIOSIS EXPEDITION PLANNING
Christopher Gow Enterprises Ltd.
205 St. John's Hill
London SW11 1TH
U.K.
☎ (020) 7924 5906
Fax: (020) 7924 5907
email: info@symbiosis-travel.co.uk
website: www.symbiosis-travel.co.uk
For further details see page 262.

GETTING THERE
Sam Ratulangi Airport
Manado
☎ (431) 60864
Situated 13 km (8 miles) from the city.

PELNI
Jalan Sam Ratulangi 7
☎ (431) 62844
The state shipping line runs boats from
Bitung, Manado's main port, to various
desinations in Sulawesi, and to Jakarta,
and Surabaya.

INFORMATION
North Sulawesi Tourist Office
Jalan 17 Augustus
Manado
☎ (431) 64299

ACCOMMODATION
Ranger Homestay, Batuputih $
This is one of five homes.
Accommodation here can be arranged
through Smiling Hostel or Froggie Divers
(see under Manado's Coral Paradise,
below). Food is available.

MANADO'S CORAL PARADISE
PAGES 224–233

OPERATORS
BARRACUDA DIVE CLUB
Jalan Sam Ratulangi 61
Molas
Manado
☎ (431) 854288
Fax: (431) 864848
Offers dive packages to Bunaken, and runs
a dive resort about 8km (5 miles) from
town, with accommodation and tuition.

FROGGIES DIVERS
Tongkaing
Kec. Molas
Manado
Sulawesi
☎ (431) 821152
Fax: (431) 859375
email: blume@manado.wasantra.net.id
Contact Peter Blume
website: www.divefroggies.com
PADI courses run. Mainly shallow dives
and snorkelling. Deep dives by arrange-
ment.

SYMBIOSIS EXPEDITION PLANNING
Christopher Gow Enterprises Ltd.
205 St. John's Hill
London SW11 1TH
U.K.
☎ (020) 7924 5906
Fax: (020) 7924 5907
email: info@symbiosis-travel.co.uk
website: www.symbiosis-travel.co.uk
For further information see page 262.

GETTING THERE
SAM RATULANGI AIRPORT, MANADO
☎ (431) 60864
Situated 13 km (8 miles) from the city.

PELNI
Jalan Sam Ratulangi 7
☎ (431) 62844
The state shipping line runs boats from
Bitung, Manado's main port, to various
destinations in Sulawesi, and to Jakarta,
and Surabaya.

INFORMATION
NORTH SULAWESI TOURIST OFFICE
Jalan 17 Augustus
Manado
☎ (431) 64299

ACCOMMODATION
Smiling Hostel $
Jalan Rumambi no. 7
Pasar Ikan Tua
Manado
☎ (431) 868463
Simple accommodation but adequate.

Papa Boa's Homestay $
Bunaken
Simple accommodation with mosquito
nets and barrel of water. Food is available, especially fresh fish. Contact
through Smiling Hostel (see above).

Happy Flower Homestay $/$$
Tomohon
Desa Kakaskasen II.
☎ (431) 352787
A homestay where food is available.

MEETING THE T'BOLI PEOPLE
PAGES 236–457

OPERATORS
ASIAVENTURE SERVICES LTD.
Manila Pavilion Hotel
Room 501
United Nations Ave.
Ermita
Manila 1000
☎ (2) 5237007 **Fax:** (2) 5251811
email: asiaventure@ibm.net

SYMBIOSIS EXPEDITION PLANNING
Christopher Gow Enterprises Ltd.
205 St. John's Hill
London SW11 1TH
U.K.
☎ (020) 7924 5906
Fax: (020) 7924 5907
email: info@symbiosis-travel.co.uk
website: www.symbiosis-travel.co.uk
Symbiosis can arrange local T'boli guides
in advance of your trip. For further information see page 262.

T'BOLI TRIBE TREKKING
Fiesta sa Barrio
J. Catolico Senior Ave.
9500 General Santos
Philippines
☎ (83) 5522512
Fax: (83) 5527221
Contact Fernando "Boy" Santiago to
arrange a local guide who will introduce
you to the T'boli people.

GETTING THERE
GENERAL SANTOS CITY AIRPORT
☎ (83) 5531042
The airport is a 20-minute taxi ride from
the city centre.

PELNI LINES
☎ (82) 2211346
Fax: (82) 2218348
A weekly boat service operates between
Bitung in Sulawesi and General Santos.
There is also a fortnightly service
between Davao and Bitung or Manado.

ACCOMMODATION
Hotel Sansu $$
Pioneer Ave.
General Santos
☎ (83) 5527219
Fax: (83) 5527221
A hotel of reasonable quality with a cen-
tral location and air conditioning.

Punta Isla Resort $/$$
Lake Sebu
The resort overlooks the lake, with
charming if simple rooms. Serves
good fish.

AMONG THE WRECKS OF CORON
PAGES 248–256

OPERATORS
ASIAVENTURE SERVICES LTD.
Manila Pavilion Hotel
Room 501
United Nations Ave.
Ermita
Manila 1000
☎ (2) 5237007
Fax: (2) 5251811
email: asiaventure@ibm.net

DISCOVERY DIVERS
5316 Barangay 5
Coron
Palawan
☎ (32) 6817745
Fax: (32) 6456616
email: Ddivers@vasia.com
Contact Gunter Bernert to arrange your
complete diving package, including all
equipment.

SYMBIOSIS EXPEDITION PLANNING
Christopher Gow Enterprises Ltd.
205 St. John's Hill
London SW11 1TH
U.K.
☎ (020) 7924 5906
Fax: (020) 7924 5907
email: info@symbiosis-travel.co.uk
website: www.symbiosis-travel.co.uk
For further details see page 262.

GETTING THERE
AIR ADS INC.
☎ (2) 8333264
Daily flights operate from Manila to the
small airstrip outside Coron.

ACCOMMODATION
Kubo Sa Dagat $/$$
Coron
Palawan
No telephone
Built on stilts in the middle of a bay, 30
minutes' boat ride from Coron.

ACTIVITIES A–Z

INTRODUCTION

This book has, we hope, whetted your appetite for adventure, and the Activities A–Z is intended to supply a useful, if not comprehensive, list of as many adventurous activities as the authors could discover within an area.

The activities vary from volunteer work, cultural, and language opportunities to really intrepid sports. Most of the experiences call for interaction with local people and many are directly connected to ecotourism—where strict controls are applied to guarantee the benefits to the environment and to minimize the damage caused by the impact of increasing numbers of visitors to sensitive areas.

We have supplied the names and addresses of organizations that can help the traveller to achieve these challenging pastimes, but they have not been inspected or vetted by us in any way. The entries in the A–Z are in addition to those under the Contacts section. Even where the authors have used a company to organize their own trip, this is no guarantee that any company is still run by the same people or to the same degree of efficiency.

Bear in mind that many of the regions covered can be volatile both climatically and politically. Weigh up all the factors first, get a feel for your chosen destination, and let us guide you towards the outfits that can help.

BIRD-WATCHING

Southeast Asia is a bird-watcher's paradise, with a diversity of species rivalled only by Amazonia. The region's national parks provide excellent trekking and boating trips for keen ornithologists and have plenty of information for those going it alone. Binoculars are a must—7X magnification will be adequate. If you plan to take photographs, remember that a camera permit may be required. Light, long-sleeved clothing will help to keep insects at bay. Try to keep the colours of your clothes as inconspicuous as possible. If you are going it alone, take a compass and map.

Teman Negara National Park, Malaysia

This spectacular national park on the peninsula is thought to be the oldest in Malaysia and is home to a truly splendid array of birds, including black-thighed falconet, masked finfoot, buffy fish-owl, and nine species of kingfisher.

Teman Negara

A87, Jalan Teluk Sisek
25000 Kuantan
Pahang
Malaysia
☎ (09) 5555808
Fax: (09) 5555828
Staff at the park HQ will help plan your itinerary and there are regular informa-

tion slide shows. Bookings for boat trips and hides can also be made. Hostel and chalet accommodation is available, and there are some floating restaurants across the river from HQ.

SPKG Tours Sdn Bhd

16, LKNP Building
Bandar Baru
27000 Raub
Malaysia
☎ (09) 2662369
Fax: (09) 2664369
This company specializes in river safaris, and tours include transport and accommodation.

Khao Yai National Park, Thailand

The country's oldest national park, Khao Yai boasts up to 1,000 species of bird. Of particular interest are the immense great and wreathed hornbills. A December/January visit will be enriched by species native to Siberia and China wintering in Thailand. There is no longer accommodation in the park, but the HQ can provide information and maps for day trips.

Khao Yai Garden Lodge

Hong Ahan Ying Yong
135 Thanon Thannarat (St. 2090)
Km 7, 30130 Pak Chong
Thailand
☎ (044) 313567
Fax: (044) 312143
The German owner of this comfortable

lodge on the edge of the park organizes tailor-made, special interest tours to Khao Yai.

Friends of Nature

133/21 Rachaprarope Rd.
Rachatavee
Bangkok 10400
Thailand
☎ (02) 64244268
Fax: (02) 6424428
email: foneco@hotmail.com
This outfit was formed in 1993 and operates birding tours with particular emphasis on protecting the environment.

Field Guides Incorporated

P.O. Box 160723
Austin
TX 78716-0723
U.S.A.
☎ 512/327-4953 or 800/728-4953 (toll-free)
Fax: 512/327-9231
The company employs one of the foremost ornithologists in the country as a tour guide. It can arrange travel from the U.S.A. and will also arrange trips to Vietnam and Malaysia.

MERGUI ARCHIPELAGO, MYANMAR

This chain of more than 800 uninhabited islands is home to many exotic species, including hornbill, parrots, and eagles.

In Depth Adventures

In Thailand (September–April)
☎ (076) 383 105
Fax: (076) 383 106
In USA (May–August)
☎ (0707) 443 1755
Fax: (0707) 844 8574
email: indepth@loxinfo.co.th
website: http://www.indepthadv.com
Trained and experienced conservationists lead tours that can be customized to make birdwatching on land or sea either the main focus or integrated into other activities.

TANGKOKO BATUANGAS, INDONESIA

Home to 17 per cent of the world's species, Indonesia is a birdwatching mecca. And Tangkoko, one of the most impressive nature reserves in Indonesia, boasts the world's densest population of hornbills. The park is accessible by jeep or taxi from Girian, on the main Manado–Bitung road. Permits can be got at the PHPA/KSDA office in Manado or at the entrance in Batuputih, where guides are also available. There are four basic homestays in Batuputih near the park entrance: Mama Ros, Londa Linda, Ranger, and Tarsius. Inside the reserve there is the Cagar Alam Homestay.

Kungkungan Bay Resort

P.O. Box 16
Bitung 95500
North Sulawesi
☎ (0438) 30300 **Fax:** (0438) 31400
email: kbresort@mdo.mega.net.id
This holiday resort, 30km (19 miles) from the park, offers day trips in air-conditioned vehicles.

CAVING

Southeast Asia has some magnificent caves, many of which are tourist attractions. Some contain religious artefacts. Aside from the more accessible caves, there are vast underground complexes that should be tackled only by experienced cavers or with guides. Take a sturdy pair of firm-grip boots and a torch. Tour guides should provide helmets and lamps if necessary.

NIAH CAVES, NIAH NATIONAL PARK, SARAWAK, MALAYSIA

The oldest human remains in Southeast Asia were discovered in the spectacular Great Cave at Niah. The cave, thought to be one of the largest in the world is also home to bats and swiftlets—the latter providing the ingredients for the delicacy, bird's nest soup. The nearby Painted Cave served as an ancient burial site. There is a path inside the caves, but a torch is still essential.

Miri Tourist Office

Lot 452, Jalan Melayu
98000 Miri
Sarawak
Malyasia
☎ (085) 434181 **Fax:** (085) 434179
The office supplies permits and guides,

and arranges accommodation for Niah National Park.

Mulu Adventure Sdn Bhd
Lot 230, First Floor
Beautiful Jade Centre
P.O. Box 1586
98008 Miri
Sarawak
Malaysia
☎ (085) 437885
Fax: (085) 437886
Mulu Adventure offers 1- to 3-day trips to the caves and park, with an overnightstay in an Iban longhouse.

MULU NATIONAL PARK, SARAWAK

This park is renowned for its labyrinth of underground caves, including the Sarawak Chamber and the 51km (32 miles) long Clearwater cave. The more spectacular Clearwater and Wind caves can be reached only by boat.

Outer Edge Expeditions
45500 Pontiac Trail
Walled Lake
MI 48390-4036
U.S.A.
☎ (0248) 624 140 or (0800) 322 5235
Fax: (0248) 624 6744
email: adventure@outer-edge.com
website: www.outer-edge.com
This company specializes in small, group expeditions, allowing personal service and trip flexibility. A proportion of the profits go to local conservation projects. As well as trips to the "tourist" caves they offer "wild" caving, off the beaten track. Whitewater rafting and trekking are also on offer.

SAGADA CAVES, BONTOC, PHILIPPINES

This quiet town is noted for its burial caves and hanging coffins, suspended on the rocks according to ancient Igorot tribe burial customs. Casual visitors can visit the Lumiang and Sugong caves with ease and without a guide. More experience, strong light, and a guide are needed for the Sumaging and Latipan caves. Hire a guide from the Sagada Environmental Guides Association at the Tourist Information Centre.

Interesiland Travel and Tours Inc.
Suite 12
Manila Midtown Arcade
M. Adriatico St.
Ermita
Manila
Philippines
Postal Address: C.P.O. Box 4058 Manila
☎ (0632) 5238720/21/22/23
Fax: (0632) 5224795
This operator organizes day trips to Sagada and handles tours all over the Philippines.

PHONG NA CAVE, DONG HOI, VIETNAM

There are thousands of metres of tunnels and rivers in this huge complex. Some of the grottoes are lined with spectacular stalactites and stalagmites and were used as Buddhist sanctuaries in the 9th and 10th centuries. The journey through the caves is made by boat and on foot. Hire a guide at the Dong Hoi tourist office.

Nomad Travel Planners
3200 W. 88th no. 1
Anchorage
Alaska 99502
U.S.A.
☎ 907/243-0313/346-3622
Fax: 907/243-0333/346-3622
website: www.nomad-travel.com/contact.htm
Nomad operates 3-day trips, leaving from Hue on the east coast and staying in luxury hotels in Dong Hoi. It also offers a full-day boat trip through the caves.

CONSERVATION TOURS

Conservation tours use paying volunteers to assist in a variety of projects, from monitoring endangered species to archaeological excavations. As well as providing a worthwhile service to the local community, these tours are a great way to learn new skills. Some projects particularly welcome volunteers with specific areas of expertise such as carpentry or environmental science. All require a good level of fitness, a positive attitude and the ability to work as a team. Some tours also expect you to help with the cooking and cleaning.

Accommodation can be basic, so be prepared to live without hot water, flushing toilets, and showers. Note that the projects mentioned below are subject to change.

DONSOL, SORSOGON, PHILIPPINES
Whale Shark Monitoring

Only "discovered" in May 1998, the colony of whale sharks that bask in the Pacific ocean along the coastline of this fishing village is thought to be one of the largest in the world. But, despite an inter-national ban, the sharks (or *butanding* as they are known locally) are under threat from poachers. Local operators, in conjunction with WWF Philippines, recruit volunteers to help monitor and interact with the sharks. This involves swimming, rather than diving. Non-swimmers can help by recording data on the boat.

Worldwide Fund for Nature (Philippines)
☎ 4333220/2
Fax: 4263927
email: KKp@mozcom.com
Various conservation projects are orga-nized locally. Contact for further information.

Karina Escudero
c/o Mayon International Hotel
Legaspi
Makati
Philippines
☎ (02) 8935198/8188290
email: karina@artbridges.com
Karina Escuardo is involved in building a register of the sharks and coordinating the project in conjunction with the local community. Comfortable accommodation is provided at the Mayon International.

Reefside Diving, Sorsogon
c/o Rico Estrellado or Ramir Aglicup
☎ (056) 211 275
email: koriks@hotmail.com
Both the above are local operators working in conjunction with the project and will take conservationists out on shark-tracking trips. Register with the Donsol Municipal Tourism Council in the visitors' centre on Donsol Pier, who will hand out research packs.

NAKHON RATCHASIMA PROVINCE, THAILAND
Iron Age Excavation

Join an archaeological dig in rural Thailand to help piece together the origins of the Angkor empire. You will use hand tools to excavate and search for artefacts, which must then be processed at the adjacent field lab. Previous excavation experience is not needed as Earthwatch will provide on the job training.

Earthwatch
680 Mt. Auburn St.
P.O. Box 9104
Watertown
MA 02272-9104
U.S.A.
☎ 800/776-0188 **Fax:** 0617/926-8532

57 Woodstock Road
57 Woodstock Rd.
Oxford OX2 6HJ, U.K.
☎ (01865) 311600 **Fax:** (01865) 311383
This international non-profit making organization recruits people to help scientists gather data and communicate information on a variety of conservation projects. There are around 150 projects running worldwide at any one time.

KALIMANTAN, BORNEO
Marine conservation

Deforestation and damaging fishing methods mean that Southeast Asia's coral reefs and marinelife are under threat. Volunteers work closely with local communities in establishing marine conservation camps. Although the Borneo tour requires experienced divers only, no experience is necessary for other locations in the region. Scuba diving courses and marine biology training are offered free of charge.

Coral Cay Conservation
154, Clapham Park Rd.
London SW4 7DE
U.K.
☎ (020) 7498 6248 **Fax:** (020) 7498 8447
email: ccc@coralcay-org
Winners of the Tourism for Tomorrow and International Marine Environmental awards, this company offers marine conservation tours to the Philippines,

Indonesia, Borneo, and other regions worldwide. No experience necessary for most trips. Free scuba diving courses.

CRUISING

The fragmented landmass of Southeast Asia lends itself well to exploration by boat. There are thousands of islands, basking in the warm waters of the Indian and Pacific Oceans. Boat tours are the perfect way to try other activities such as diving, fishing, snorkelling, or exploring the jungle-clad islands. Vessels range from small basic boats to traditional luxury schooners. The smaller boats tend to offer sleeping on deck or camping accommodation, while the deluxe versions have en-suite, air-conditioned cabins. Take extra care with sun-protection, as sea breezes can disguise the early stages of sunburn.

TIOMAN ISLAND, MALAYSIA

On the east coast of peninsular Malaysia, Tioman and its surrounding islands are a snorkeller's paradise, with abundant sparkling white beaches, coral reefs, and other exciting marinelife. There are good jungle treks to be had on Pulau Sibu, and the extinct volcano island of Pulau Tinggi is worth a visit.

Sulawesi Charters

Sea Consortium Pte Ltd.
11 Duxton Hill
Singapore 089595
☎ 3223204
Fax: 2270168
email (bookings):
sulawesi@seacon.com.sg
email (skipper): jony@sezcon.com.sg
website: www.seacon.com.sg/sulawesi
The traditional Indonesian boat the *Sulawesi* also offers trips around the Indonesian Riau archipelago, just south of Singapore, and the remote Anambas archipelago.

NUSA TENGGARA, INDONESIA

This chain of islands just east of Bali boasts a rich diversity of culture and nature. Boat trips take in the spectacular volcanic lakes of Flores, the prehistoric dragons of Komodo, and the stone tombs of Sumba.

Song Line Cruises of Indonesia

P.T. Pinisi Duta Bahari
Jalan Danau Tambingan no. 64
Sanur
Bali
Indonesia
☎ (0361) 286992/287119
Fax: (0361) 286985
email: info@songlinecruises.com
website: www.songlinecruises.com/
These are luxury cruises in traditional Indonesian schooners. The company also has dive boats for private hire.

International Expeditions

One Environs Park
Helena
AL 35080
U.S.A.
☎ 800 633 4734 (toll free)
email: nature@ietravel.com/intexp
website: www.ietravel.com/intexp
Expeditions depart monthly on the tall-ship *Adelaar* from March to October. They work with the International Rhino Foundation through the IRF/Indonesia Government Sumatran Rhino Sanctuary in Way Kambas, donating $100 per passenger.

Explore Worldwide

1 Frederick St.
Aldershot
Hampshire
GU11 1LQ
U.K.
☎ (01252) 319448
Fax: (01252) 343170
email: info@explore.co.uk
This company specializes in small group exploratory trips and offers a 15-day "seatrek" to the region in a traditional schooner. Cruises generally take place overnight allowing optimum time to snorkel, swim, and explore during the day.

PALAWAN, PHILIPPINES

The 1,768 islands of Palawan are among the cleanest and greenest in the Philippines. Pristine beaches, under-ground rivers, and dramatic rock formations, such as the El Nido marble cliffs, make this an impressive and unusual cruise destination.

Palawan Tourist Travel & Tours Agency (P.T.T.T.A.)

Rizal Ave.
Puerto Princesa City
Palawan
Philippines
☎ (048) 4333877 **Fax:** (048) 4333554
email: cocoloco@pal-onl.com
or pedzi@pal-onl.com
This is the only agency that offers sea-camping tours around El Nido and Sulu. Three meals a day; tent or resort accommodation; fishing and snorkelling gear are provided.

CYCLING

Cycling enables you to cover a lot of ground in a short time while making a minimal impact on the environment. It is an excellent way to explore the region's spectacular, varied, and reasonably flat countryside. Although many tour companies include good-quality bikes in the package, hire cycles from local shops are often not suitable for long distances, so if you are going it alone it is better to bring your own. Bikes can travel by plane, but your airline may want you to dismantle at least some of it for easier carriage; check first. It is essential to take a comprehensive repair kit, as spares can be hard to find. The poor quality of some roads in the region makes mountain bikes preferable, and for off-road cycling they are essential.

THE RIAU ISLANDS, INDONESIA

The complete absence of traffic makes this archipelago of tiny islands off the east coast of Sumatra perfect for cycling. The local tour operator uses boats as a base from which to explore this beautiful wilderness. Although there are no roads, cycle tracks make most of the terrain pleasantly manageable. There are more challenging routes for the very fit and the very keen.

Riau Island Adventures

c/o PT Bahari Riau Tualang
Blok D no. 10
Komplex Batam Plaza
Nagoya
Batam
Indonesia

☎ (778) 452434/(811) 702203
email: iabookings@post1.com
This company caters for the complete novice as well as the committed enthusiast. It rents out good-quality mountain bikes.

NORTHERN THAILAND

Cycling is an excellent way to explore this diverse and spectacular landscape. Follow little-used trails to remote villages, explore the famous Chiang Dao caves, and freewheel alongside the Mae Kok River. There are some fairly steep climbs, so you should be moderately fit.

The Wild Planet

No. 9 Thonglor Soi 25
Sukhumvit Rd.
Prakanong
10110 Bangkok
☎ (02) 712 8748 / 712 6880
Fax: (02) 712 8188
email: info@wild-planet.co.th
Experienced Western or Thai cyclists with first aid qualifications lead groups of 6 to 12 people. More difficult routes for experienced cyclists can be arranged. American-designed, 21-speed mountain bikes are provided, as is a support vehicle, which non-cyclists are invited to enjoy a relaxing tour.

Contact Travel & Adventure

420/3 Chiangmailand Rd.
Changklan
Chiangmai 50100
Thailand
☎ (053) 277178 **Fax:** (053) 204104
email: adventure@thailine.com
The company offers moderately difficult tours covering from 15 to 60km (10 to 30 miles) a day. A back up vehicle is always available.

PHUKET, THAILAND

The steep hills on Phuket make this a bit of a tough route. But for the very fit Kao Sok National Park with its abundant wildlife is a couple of days' cycle away and well worth a visit.

Asian Adventures

Checkmark Enterprise Co. Ltd.
231 Rat-U-Thit
200 Pee Rd.

Patong Beach
Phuket 83150
Thailand
☎/Fax: (076) 342798
email: info@asian-adventures.com
This trip for adventurous and experienced cyclists starts with a tour of the island and then continues on a round trip taking in Kao Sok National Park and Krabi.

Ha Noi–Saigon, Vietnam

The reasonably flat terrain and good quality of the major road makes cycling an excellent way to view the spectacular and varied countryside of Vietnam. And you'll be going native—everyone in Vietnam cycles, although traffic around major cities can get pretty hectic. Tour operators offer 9- to 12-day trips with support vehicles and trains to help you on your way.

Exodus
9 Weir Rd.
London SW12 OLT
U.K.
☎ (0181) 675 5550
Fax: (0181) 673 0779
email: sales@exodustravels.co.uk
Reasonable fitness is required for these expeditions. Expect to travel 50–120km (30–75 miles) a day. Exodus provides a back-up vehicle and employs local guides.

Butterfield and Robinson
70 Bond St.
Toronto
Ontario
Canada M5B 1X3
☎ 416/864-1354
Fax: 416/864-0541
email: info@butterfield.com
website: www.butterfield.com
The company offers a 10-day/10-night trip with support vehicle and baggage transportation. Expect to cycle 40–48km (25–30 miles) per day. Most meals and sightseeing tours are included in the price.

Eastern Bali, Indonesia

From the lush greenery of Ubud to the pristine beaches of Tulamben, eastern Bali offers cultural and scenic variety.

Good roads make the terrain relatively easy, but the slopes of Gunur Catur make for a challenging ride.

Sobek
Jalan Tirta Ening no. 9
By Pass Ngurah Rai
Sanur
Bali
Indonesia
☎ (0361) 287059
Fax: (0361) 289448
Sobek provides good-quality mountain bikes for day trips.

Backroads Travel
801 Cedar St.
Berkeley
CA 947100
U.S.A.
☎ 510/527-1555
Fax: 510/547-1444
website: www.backroads.com
The company organizes a moderately easy 10-day trip starting in Ubud, taking in Lovina, Baturiti, Tulamben, and Candi Dasa, and finishing up at Denpasar airport. Luxury accommodation and dining is provided.

DIVING

With clear, warm waters and abundant marinelife, dive resorts are plentiful and cheap in Southeast Asia. However, not all of them are reputable. Make sure your dive centre is PADI (Professional Association of Diving Instructors), NAUI (National Association of Underwater Instructors), or BSAC (British Sub-Aqua Club) approved. You can then choose between a shore-based or a live-aboard (boat-based) trip. Some resorts are qualified to teach diving, but note that this involves extensive written as well as practical testing. Consider completing at least the theory part of the course at home, before setting off.

Sangihe-Talaud Archipelago, Indonesia

The waters surrounding this chain of 40 volcanic islands off the northeast peninsula of Sulawesi are among the deepest in the world. Their remote location ensures that the plentiful marinelife survives relatively unscathed.

South East Asia Liveaboards Co. Ltd.

225 Rat-U-Thit 200 Year Rd.
Patong
Phuket 83150
Thailand
☎ (076) 340406/340932
Fax: (076) 340 86
email: info@sealiveaboards.com
SEAL were the first operators to charter Sangihe-Talud. They also run tours to Mergui Archipelago (Myanmar), Similan Islands (Thailand), and Andaman Islands (India). The company boasts three live-aboard yachts, a PADI 5-Star Centre, and BSAC International School status.

Aquatours

Charter House
26 Claremont Rd.
Surbiton
Surrey KT6 4QU
U.K.
☎ (0181) 2558050
Fax: (0181) 2558052
email: arnie@aquatours.com
Aquatours arranges tailor-made tours to any destination in the world, including flights and accommodation. Sulawesi and Malaysia are specialities.

Koh Samui, Thailand

Thailand's third largest island has many stretches of scenic coastline and numerous beautiful white beaches. The calm waters in the northeast of the island are ideal for swimming and watersports.

Abyss Dive Center

129/1 M.1 Maenam
Koh Samui
☎ (077) 247 038
This small Dutch-managed dive centre provides top-quality diving instruction, with full diver insurance. To ensure that each student receives personal attention, no more than four students are instructed at one time (although there is flexibility with larger family/friend groups).

BOHOL, PHILIPPINES

In the heart of the Visayas, Bohol and its surrounding islands offer some spectacular diving with visibility up to 30m (100 feet). Expect to see black coral forest, giant turtles, and hammerhead sharks, as well as the region's usual huge variety of fish.

Dive Buddies Philippines

Manila Tour Center
L&S Building
1414 Roxas Blvd.
Manila
Philippines
☎ (0632) 5219168/5219169
Fax: (0632) 5219170
email: offices@divephil.com

Makati Office:

Makati Dive Center
G/F Robelle Mansion
877 J.P. Rizal St.
Makati
Philippines
☎ (0632) 8997388
Fax: (0632) 8997393
This long-established company offers trips to accredited dive resorts all over the country, including El Nido, Cebu, and Batangas. It also runs a dive school and a "dive buddy" directory to team up solitary divers.

Seven Skies

South China Sea, Indonesia
This 98,000-tonne wreck, which sank following an explosion in 1967, now forms a giant artificial reef, covered in a stunning array of soft corals. Home to barracuda, trevally, batfish, and visited by mantas and whale sharks, this is one of Asia's top wreck dives.

MV Empress

14 Hyde Park Gate
Seletar Airbase
Singapore 799543
☎ 482 5354
Fax: 745 3265
email: diver@pacific.net.sg
website: www.swiftech.com.sg/~vidar
This comfortable live-aboard offers dives from Ujung Pandang, Sulawesi, and the islands east of Bali. Courses in marine biology/photography by pre-arrangement. Sleeps 15. BSAC approved.

DRIVING

Touring by car is a good way to see large portions of a country quickly and in comfort. Car rental is now relatively easy in the region, and many companies offer guided tours with the option of a driver. In the less developed countries you will have difficulty renting a car without a driver. Four-wheel-drive (4WD) tours can mean anything from a simple sight-seeing trip, to harsh off-road driving involving overnight camping. Always check the brakes, tyres, and general roadworthiness of your vehicle before you set off.

LOMBOK, BALI

The unspoilt splendour of this island in the Nusa Tenggara chain, just east of Bali, is best explored by four-wheel-drive. The relatively undeveloped infrastructure means there are plenty of off-road tracks for the adventurous driver, many running through terraced ricefields.

The Novotel Lombok Mandalika Resort

Pantai Putri Nyale
Pujut
Lombok Tengah
Nusa Tenggara Barat
Lombok
Indonesia
☎ (0370) 653333 **Fax:** (0370) 653555
email: novotellombok@bali-paradise.com
Full-day, guided tours in self-drive jeeps run to Kaliantan, Telukmanuk, and Garuda. Some of the tours are combined with "soft" trekking.

CENTRAL HIGHLANDS, VIETNAM

This spectacular mountain region in the heart of Vietnam boasts many waterfalls, rivers, and lakes. It has a pleasantly cool climate and is home to many tribespeople or Montagnards.

Green Bamboo Travel

42 Nha Chung St.
Ha Noi
Vietnam
☎ (0844) 8268752 / 8286504 / 8249179
Fax: (0844) 8264949

website: www.vietnamonline.com/green-bamboo/adventur.html
Custom-made 4WD tours with guides and driver in northern and central Vietnam.

MALAY PENINSULA

Although the roads are generally good in this area, the off-road conditions can be challenging. Four-wheel-drive is an excellent way to explore the varied landscape, which incorporates ancient rain forest and a spectacular coastline.

Wexas International

45–49 Brompton Rd.
Knightsbridge
London SW3 1DE
U.K.
☎ (020) 7581 8761
Fax: (020) 7838 0837
email: bluecard@wexas.com
This well-established, experienced company provides a large range of air-conditioned, fully licensed, and insured cars with cassette radios via a reputable local company. They also help plan routes and make hotel reservations along the way. They do not have four-wheel-drive vehicles.

Mud Trekker

No. 42, SS24/1
Taman Megah
Petaling Jaya
Selangor 47301
Malaysia
☎/**Fax:** (03) 7054284
email: mudtrekker@geocities.com
Mud Trekker runs small, friendly overnight camping tours with an emphasis on preserving the environment. The trips can be tailor-made.

FISHING

Crystal-clear waters and abundant marinelife make for excellent sea angling. Expect a wide variety of game fish, including sailfish, wahoo, and tuna. Some companies run boat trips with fishing as an option, which may be of interest to those travelling with a non-fishing partner (see Cruising). But for serious anglers, a better option may be speciality operators with expert staff and sophisticated, wide-ranging fishing techniques.

Day and overnight trips are usually on offer—the latter involving accommodation on board or camping. Check that your operator has radio contact and sufficient safety equipment.

SIMILAN ISLANDS, THAILAND

This marine national park in the Andaman Sea consists of nine jungle-clad islands 90km (55 miles) northwest of Phuket. Expect catches of sailfish, wahoo, giant trevally, dogtooth tuna, and tenggiri. Night-fishing for sharks is also available. The popper casting for giant trevally early in the morning is also excellent.

Andaman Hooker Sport Fishing Charter

6/6 Soi Suki Moo 9
Tambool Chalong
A. Muang
Phuket 83130
Thailand
☎/**Fax:** (076) 282 036
Mobile: (01) 979 7011
email andamanhooker@phuket.com
Andaman Hooker offer 1–5-day year-round charters with equipment, baits, food, and soft drinks. The boat carries an English-speaking crew of three. The company supports "catch and release" of all billfish.

Blue Water Anglers Co. Ltd.

35/7 Sakidej Rd.
Amphur Muang
Phuket 83000
Thailand
☎ (076) 391287 **Fax:** (076) 391342
The enthusiastic staff are knowledgeable in a wide range of fishing techniques. The company offesr live-aboard trips from 2 to 7 days to Thailand and Myanmar.

Siam Exclusive Tours

Building One, 11th Floor
99 Wireless Rd.
Bangkok 10330
Thailand
☎ (02) 2566153/5
Fax: (02) 2566665
This company offers a choice of three purpose-built sports fishers with comfortable accommodation for private charter.

SOUTHERN BALI, INDONESIA

The warm waters of the Indian ocean that surround Bali's southern coast are rich in tuna, wahoo, and mai mai. There is also the opportunity to spot dolphins.

Bali Deep Blue

J1. By Pass Ngurah Rai
Blanjong-Sanur
Denpasar 80238
Bali
Indonesia
☎ (0361) 289308 **Fax:** (0361) 287872
Runs deep-sea fishing day trips around the southeast coast of Bali in a traditional outrigger.

MERGUI ARCHIPELAGO, MYANMAR

Burmese waters have not been heavily commercially fished and yield large quantities of black marlin, sailfish, king mackerel, tuna, and wahoo. Huge snappers and groupers offer action for the bottom fisherman.

Blue Water Anglers Co. Ltd.

35/7 Sakidej Rd.
Amphur Muang
Phuket 83000
Thailand
☎ (076) 391287 **Fax:** (076) 391342
The enthusiastic staff are knowledgeable in a wide range of fishing techniques. Offer live-aboard trips from 2 to 7 days to Thailand and Myanmar.

HANG-GLIDING/ PARAGLIDING

This is the closest humans get to flying, and the sheer exhilaration of it is addictive. The aim is to locate air currents and steer the craft accordingly. Beginners will stay close to the ridge, while more experienced gliders have the option of flying cross-country. It's a fantastic way to see the countryside, and Southeast Asia's varied landscape makes for superb bird's-eye views. Some companies provide lessons, but you may get more out of your holiday if you qualify before you set off. Of the two, paragliding is the simpler to learn and the equipment is easily transportable. Hang-gliding gear, however, is more robust in difficult conditions.

NOEN KRAPOK MOUNTAIN, BANCHANG, RAYONG, THAILAND

There are two locations on this mountain in southern Thailand that can be used for flying throughout the year. The take-off point on the eastern part of the mountain is about 80m (262 feet) above sea level and suitable for beginners. The southern take-off point is for pilots with some experience and affords beautiful views of the Banchang Sea.

Suwat Hannarong S.E.T. Sky Sport School

66/34 Eastern Star Plaza, M.3
T. Pala, Banchang
Rayong 21130
Thailand
☎ (038) 880161
Fax: (038) 880439
email: setthai@infonews.co.th
The comprehensive course covers flying equipment, safety, rules and regulations, environment, weather conditions, and a field lesson. Visits can be arranged to other locations in Thailand, including Poo Ruer, Loei, and Promthep Cape, Phuket.

ULU WATU, BALI

Soar above the coastline from these towering cliffs and view the spectacular Ulu Watu temple from the sky. The best time to go is June–September.

Bali Adventure Tours

Adventure House
J1. By Pass Ngurah Rai
Pesanggaran
Bali
☎ (0361) 721480
Fax: (0361) 721481
email: baliadventuretours@bali-paradise.com
Fly with a fully trained instructor on a 20-minute tandem flight. The cost of the tour includes hotel transfers, tandem pilot, a 20-minute flight, and insurance.

TOBA LAKE, NORTH SUMATRA

The hills surrounding Toba Lake provide a good take-off point for gliding over one of the largest lakes in Indonesia, with spectacular views of waterfalls.

Anten Wisata

Ir.H. Juandra no. 5
Bekasi 17141
Indonesia
☎ (021) 8841915
Fax: (021) 7970924
email: anwisata@cbn.net.id
http://flieg.com/indonesia
This German-run company also organizes paragliding and hang-gliding tours to Maninjau, West Sumatra. Tours and lessons are in German. Hang-gliding Association Pilot Licence-approved. Provides free transport from the airport.

JUNGLE TOURS

This section caters to those who want to visit the region's spectacular rain forest without the strain of a hard trek or a particular focus, such as wildlife-watching. Wear long sleeves and trousers to protect against insects, and always carry water with you. Jungle boots protect against leeches, which can surface after a rainstorm. If you are going it alone, take a trail map and compass.

UJUNG KULON NATIONAL PARK, JAVA, INDONESIA

This is the last lowland tropical rain forest in Java, home of the endangered Javan rhino. Track animals and watch birds in the grazing ground. You can escape the heat of the jungle by snorkelling and swimming along the pristine coast.

Adventure Indonesia

Bumi Serpong Damai Estate
Sector 1–3
Block BK 32
Tangerang 15310
Jakarta Barat, Indonesia
☎ (021) 5383222/5384352
Fax: (021) 5384352
email: green@idola.net.id
website: www.adventureindonesia
Dedicated and experienced guides run exploratory tours lasting 4–7 days.

KHAO SOK NATIONAL PARK, THAILAND

Half way between Phuket and Surat Thani, this spectacular rain forest boasts a huge diversity of flora, including the

Rafflesia, famous for its giant flowers. Wildlife is also abundant, with gaur, banteng, serow, Malayan tapir, and sunbear still roaming the remoter park areas. Small numbers of elephants, tigers and leopards also survive. There is very basic accommodation in the form of treehouses and lodges inside the park.

South Nature Travel
P.O. Box 267
Phuket
Thailand 83000
☎/Fax: (076) 234201
Operates 2-day tours with accommodation in jungle lodges. Emphasis on conservation. Can organize tailor-made trekking tours.

BAKO NATIONAL PARK, MALAYSIA
This beautiful area contains 27sq km (10 square miles) of unspoilt rain forest. It is home to the rare proboscis monkey, and boasts exotic flora such as pitcher plants and wild orchids.

Sarawak Tourist Information Centre
Lot 31
Jalan Masjid
93400 Kuching
Sarawak
Malaysia
☎ (082) 410944
Fax: (082) 256301
Provide permits and guides to the park.

Active Travel
email: irene@activeco.co.nz
website: www.activecp.co.nz
Specialists in travel to the area. Offer a longboat trip along South China Sea to the park. Also run a jungle survival school, giving travellers a chance to live in a longhouse community with the Iban people and immerse themselves in their ancient way of life.

KAYAKING/ CANOEING

The warm waters and beautiful coastline of Southeast Asia are perfect for canoeing. Sea-kayaking can mean anything from paddling gently around a calm bay to battling through waves to explore remote sea caves. For the more adventurous trips navigational and paddling skills are essential, as are a knowledge of winds and tides. Operators usually provide lessons for novice paddlers. PFDs (personal flotation devices), spray jackets, and helmets should also be provided. Wear synthetic, easy-dry clothes and protect your feet with sandals or trainers.

MERGUI ARCHIPELAGO, MYANMAR
This scattering of tiny islands, covering 16,000sq km (10,000 square miles), boasts a rich diversity of wildlife, including tigers, rhinos, parrots, and sea eagles. The islands, which were closed to the public for 50 years until January 1997, are solely inhabited by the Moken, a tribe of sea gypsies whose way of life has changed little for generations.

South East Asia Liveaboards Co.
225 Rat-U-Thit 200 Year Rd.
Patong
Phuket 83150
Thailand
☎ (076) 340406/340932
Fax: (086) 340586
email: kayak@sealiveaboards.com
SEAL runs a guided 6-day/7-night sea safari, with back-up radio vehicles and double kayaks for novices.

Maluku Adventures
P.O. Box 7625
Menlo Park
San Francisco
CA 94026-7625
U.S.A.
☎ 415/731-2560; 800/566-2585 (toll free in U.S.A. only) **Fax:** 415/731-2579
email: Maluku@maluku.com
This company has been operating since 1991, and designs package tours to suit beginners or advanced paddlers.

CORÓN, PHILIPPINES
This limestone island off the coast of Busuanga is home to an indigenous population who have little communication with the outside world. Its coastline boasts towering cliffs, mangrove swamp inlets, and coral-filled crystal clear waters.

Worldwide Escapes, LLC

3450 Sacramento St., no. 439
San Francisco
CA 94118
U.S.A.
☎ 415/351-1957; 800/958-8524 (toll free)
Fax: 415/351-1958
Specializes in short adventure trips for
business travellers. The trips are
weighted towards novice canoers.

Sea Canoe

367/4 Yaowarat Road
Phuket 83000
Thailand
☎ (076) 212252
Fax: (076) 212172
In U.S.A.: ☎ 800/444-1043; **Fax:** 888/824-5621
In U.K.: ☎/**Fax:** (020) 7691 9348
In Australia: ☎/**Fax:** 02 94750196
email: webinfo@seacanoe.com
This is the foremost canoeing outfit in
Southeast Asia. Local guides have access
to relatively untouched areas. It also
offers trips to Thailand, Vietnam, and
Laos.

Nusa Dua, Bali

This is an exclusive resort tucked away in
the south of Bali. The beautiful coastline,
which boasts the towering Ulu Watu
cliffs, makes for pleasant, rather than
adventurous, paddling.

Club Med

P.O. Box 7
Lot 6, Nusa Dua
Bali
Indonesia
☎ (0361) 771521 **Fax:** (0361) 771835
This luxury resort offers the use of kayaks
as part of its holiday package. Day passes
enable you to use the resort's facilities,
including all water sports. But there is no
instruction.

Kwai Noi, Thailand

The Kwai Noi River in the Kanchanaburi
area of Thailand is ideal for beginners
who want to practice a bit before embarking on white-water trips. The river winds
its way through the Sai Yok Yai National
Park past beautiful waterfalls to the
Khmer ruins of Prasat Muang Sing.

The Wild Planet

No. 9 Thonglor Soi 25
Sukhumvit Rd.
Prakanong
10110 Bangkok
☎ (02) 712 8748 / 712 6880
Fax: (02) 712 8188
email: info@wild-planet.co.th
Fully trained instructors provide tours
varying in length and difficulty, from historical trips of the River Kwai to
white-water adventures down the Mhae
Kong. All tours are accompanied by a
support vehicle or raft.

Ha Long Bay, Vietnam

The 3,000 islands dotted around the
emerald waters of Ha Long Bay are perfect for exploration by kayak. Visit
innumerable limestone caves, grottoes,
and beaches in this spectacular region
east of Ha Noi.

Global Spectrum

1901 Pennsylvania Ave.
NW St. 204
Washington, DC 20006
U.S.A.
☎ (202) 293-2065 or 1-800-419-4446
Fax: (202) 296-0815
email: info@vietnamspecialists.com
Global Spectrum started in 1992 as cul-
tural exchange between the U.S.A. and
Vietnam. They provide a
backpacking/kayaking adventure down
the Mekong Delta and around Ha Long
Bay with expert guides.

Vietnam Sea Kayaking

Asian Adventures
Checkmark Enterprise Co. Ltd.
231 Rat-U-Thit 200 Pee Rd.
Patong Beach
Phuket 83150
Thailand
☎/**Fax:** (076) 342798
email: info@asian-adventures.com"
The company offers a 10-day trip
designed for experienced sea kayakers
who want to explore the complexities of
Ha Long Bay. The tours are offered from
May to October.

MOTORCYCLE TOURS

Aside from the exhilaration, motorcycle touring has many practical advantages. It gives you the freedom to see a country at your own leisure and is a great way to beat sluggish local transport systems and rough terrain. But it can also be extremely dangerous, and many foreigners are injured or killed each year. Always wear a helmet and protective clothes. Some companies offer all-inclusive tours with guides, but there are also motorcycle hire places in most big towns. Before renting a bike, take it for a test run and check tyres, lights, horn, brakes, and handling before you commit yourself. Bike theft is rife in the region, so make sure you take a good lock and chain.

PENINSULAR MALAYSIA

The thick rain forest of Taman Negara, the cool air of Fraser's Hill, and the spectacular western coastline make this stretch of land between Thailand and Singapore wonderfully diverse. The roads are good and sparsely populated, and offer a relatively easy ride.

Asian Motorbike Adventures

1st floor, no. 2, Jalan Tuaran
88767 Kota Kinabalu
Sabah
Malaysia
☎ (088) 438223 **Fax:** (088) 439268
email: ama_reed@hotmail.com
website: www.asianbiketour.com
Founder Reed Resnikoff has been riding motorcycles around Thailand, Laos, Malaysia and Myanmar (Borneo) for 10 years. His tours are designed to fit comfortably within a two-week holiday.

29–32 Jalan Desa

Taman Desa 58100
Kuala Lumpur
Malaysia
☎ 3 7831879 **Fax:** 3 7831897
Round-trips start at Kuala Lumpur. The price includes back-up vehicle, bikes, comfortable mid-range accommodation, food, non-alcoholic drinks, and fuel. Also trips to Laos, Golden Triangle, and southern Thailand. Offers tips on how to cope with local traffic.

MEKONG RIVER, LAOS

The rough terrain in Laos means that this is a tour only for very experienced riders, with guides. The riding is mainly off-road and can be extremely tough. But the rewards are manifold—Laos is still relatively untouched by Western influences and much of the country is covered in lush rain forest. Tours along the Mekong are a great way to access jungle roads.

Siam Bike Travel Company

P.O. Prah Singh Box 71
50200 Chiang Mai
Thailand
Fax: (053) 409534
email: siambike@asiaplus.com
The bikes range from 125cc to 750cc. A back-up vehicle is supplied, with mechanic and room for passengers. Riders who can't take the pace are shipped back to Thailand via the Mekong. Prices include bike, fuel, hotels, visa, guides, and ferry trips. The company also offers tours to Thailand and Myanmar.

NORTH VIETNAM HIGHLANDS

Drive through the cool mountainous region west and north of Ha Noi, gazing down on amazing valleys and meeting local montagnards (hill tribes). If you are going it alone you may need to arrange permits and guides for areas near the Chinese border that are considered militarily sensitive. The situation is changing all the time, so check with the tourist office in Ha Noi.

Green Bamboo Travel

42 Nha Chung St.
Ha Noi
Vietnam
☎ (084) 8268752/8286504/8249179
Fax: (084) 8264949
Provides 5- to 6-day trail bike tours, covering around 550km (342 miles). Also hires out 125cc motorbikes at a daily rate for independent travellers.

MOUNTAINEERING

With one notable exception, mountains in Southeast Asia are relatively gentle and take no more than 3 days to climb. Gentle, however, doesn't mean boring—

scaling the region's cool, volcanic slopes as the sun rises can be a breathtaking experience. And there are still dangers involved. Hypothermia and altitude sickness, for instance, are real and life-threatening possibilities. Make sure you have adequate clothing, including good walking shoes; check with your tour operator for guidelines. Novice climbers should never venture alone without a guide, and a map and compass (and the ability to use them) are essential.

GUNUNG KERINCI

It is a 2-day climb to the summit of this active volcano—at 3,805m (12,480 feet), the highest peak in Sumatra There is a camp at 3,000m (9,800 feet), where most climbers spend the night. Although the paths are clearly marked, it is sensible to climb with a guide.

Down Under Adventure
12727 NE 20th St.
Suite 5
Bellevue
WA 98005
☎ (0800) 788-6685 or (0425) 895-0895
Fax: (0425) 895-8929
email: info@duatravel.com
Down Under Adventures specializes in adventure holidays in Southeast Asia and the South Pacific. All staff are from or have lived in the area. They offer an 8-day trek to the mountain including white-water rafting on the Batan Berangin River, as well as biking, hiking, and sea-kayaking trips.

PUNCAK JAYA, IRIAN JAYA, INDONESIA

The snowcapped peak of Puncak Jaya (known locally as Carstensz Pyramid) is the highest in the region (5,029m/16,499 feet) and towers majestically above the rain forest. This is a tough climb, for experienced mountain-climbers only, requiring harness, ropes, and other specialist equipment. You will need to buy a *surat jalan*, or permit, from a police station in Jayapura, Sentani, or Biak. Note that the political situation in this region is highly sensitive and until recently foreigners were barred from the mountain. Check the situation before setting off.

Adventure Indonesia
Bumi Serpong Damai Estate
Sector 1–3
Block BK 32
Tangerang 15310
Jakarta Barat
Indonesia
☎ (021) 538 222, 5384352
Fax: (021) 5384352
email: info@adventureindonesia.com
The company's expert guides led the first Indonesian team to climb Mount Everest. It is a 2-day jungle trek to reach base camp, so you must be in good condition. Can arrange tailor-made trekking and climbing tours in Irian Jaya.

MOUNT APO, DAVAO, PHILIPPINES

No specialist equipment is needed for the relatively gentle climb up this active volcano, the Philippine's highest peak, at 2,954m (9,692 feet). Expect to see hot springs, waterfalls, and maybe the rare Philippine eagle on your way to the top. March to May is the best time to visit.

Tourist Office
Magsaysay Park
Santa Ana Wharf
Davao
☎ (082) 2216798
The office can arrange guides and offer advice for the climb.

GUNUNG RINJANI, LOMBOK, INDONESIA

Lombok is dominated by this mountain—the third highest in Indonesia, at 3,726m (12,224 feet). It is a challenging 3-day climb, but the large green lake, the hot springs, and the magnificent view from the huge crater more than make up for it. Guides are recommended.

Express Tours and Travel
Jalan Adi Sucipto no. 10
Mataram 83125
Lombok Island NTB
Indonesia
☎ (0370) 22688 **Fax:** (0370) 35968
email: express@lombokisland.com
English-speaking guides from this outfit run 4-day camping and fishing tours up the mountain.

ARC Journeys
102 Stanley Rd.
Cambridge CB5 8LB
U.K.
☎ (01223) 779200
Fax: (020) 7681 3175
email: Arc@travelarc.com
website: www.travelarc.com
ABC run volcano and beaches tours—a
winning combination of hard climbing
and sunbathing. Areas covered include
Mt. Kerinci and Mt. Kinabalu.

RAFTING

Southeast Asia has several dramatic
descents suitable for the adrenaline-
pumping sport of white-water rafting.
The difficulty of the descent can be
gauged by the international river grading:
Class 1 (slow-moving water) to Class 5
(ultimate whiteknuckle ride). Class 6 is
not considered safe for commercial use.
Rafting falls into two types: paddle
rafting, in which passengers paddle
themselves while being steered by a
guide, and oar boat rafting, where the
rowers carry the rest as passengers.
Check that the company provides life
jackets and helmets, and that the staff
have completed a rescue training course.

ALAS RIVER, GUNUNG LEUSER NATIONAL PARK, INDONESIA
The upper part of the river offers adventurous class 3 rafting, while further
downstream it is more peaceful—giving
you an opportunity to observe the park's
abundant wildlife. In the dry season elephants visit the river to drink.

Indonesia Adventure Holidays
P.T. Olearys
Jalan Armada no. 1
Medan 20217
Indonesia
☎ (061) 742425 / 741040
Fax: (061) 719005
This company offers a 5-day river safari
with an emphasis on conservation. The
energetic can combine the tour with a
trekking trip.

ASAHAN RIVER, SUMATRA, INDONESIA
This fast-flowing but manageable river

(Class 3) drains into the Toba Lake in a
remote western corner of Sumatra. The
many waterfalls and lush vegetation
give this narrow canyon a magical
atmosphere. The trip involves camping
at Parhitean, the start of the
commercial run.

Tracks Outdoor
Sdn Bhd, no. 91
Jalan SS2/74
47300 Petaling Jaya
Malaysia
☎ (03) 7778363
Fax: (03) 7778363
email: Tracks@mol.net.my
All guides are Swiftwater Rescue trained.
The company provides camping trips to
locations in Malaysia and Indonesia
covering Class 2–5 rivers. Taman Negara
National Park is one of the easier
descents.

Telom River, Malaysia
The Telom River (Class 3–5) starts high
up in the jungle-clad, butterfly-rich
mountains of Cameron Highlands, about
2,200m (7,200 feet) above sea level. As it
flows down, it is fed by other streams in
the Kuala Terla Valley. The descent offers
routes for all ability levels.

Tracks Outdoor Sdn Bhd
Sdn Bhd, no. 91
Jalan SS2/74
47300 Petaling Jaya
Malaysia
☎ (03) 7778363
Fax: (03) 7778363
email: Tracks@mol.net.my
All guides are Swiftwater Rescue trained.
The company provides camping trips to
locations in Malaysia and Indonesia
covering Class 2–5 rivers.

RIVER AYUNG, BALI, INDONESIA
Journey through brilliant jungle scenery
and cool, deep river gorges in this
relatively gentle, but still adrenaline-
pumping white-water descent. Class 2,
suitable for all the family.

Sobek Bina Utama
Jalan Tirta Ening no. 9
By Pass Ngurah Rai
Sanur Denpasar

Bali
Indonesia
☎ (0361) 287059 **Fax:** (0361) 289448
The guides here are Swiftwater Rescue
trained. Many of them represented
Indonesia in the 1993 World
Championships and today form the
Indonesian National team. The company
offers mainly day trips, rather than
camping tours.

Bali International Rafting

J1. By Pass Ngurah Rai no. 7
Padang Galak
Sanur Denpasar
Bali
Indonesia
☎ (0361) 281408 **Fax:** (0361) 281409
email: bir@topservice.com
Offers day packages to Telaga Waja, at
the foot of Gunung Agung. The package
includes air-conditioned transport to
and from hotel, equipment, highly
qualified guides, safety briefing, and
Balinese buffet.

SAIDAN RIVER, TANA TORAJA, SULAWESI, INDONESIA

Mountains and rice terraces tower over
this dramatic class 3–4 river descent. The
surrounding Torajan villages offer a fascinating insight into an ancient way of life.

Outer Edge Expeditions

45500 Pontiac Trail
Walled Lake
MI 48390-4036
USA
☎ (0248) 624 140 or (0800) 322 5235
Fax: (0248) 624 6744
email: adventure@outer-edge.com
The experienced guides offer a 14-day
tour that combines rafting with trekking
through this fascinating area.

SAILING

Deserted beaches and turquoise waters
are what sailing in Southeast Asia is all
about. Although conditions are relatively
safe, novice sailors should never attempt
to take out a boat unsupervised. If you
don't have your own boat, the best
places to hang out are marinas or yacht
clubs, some of which are open to non-
members. They lay on sailing lessons and
charter yachts, and you will meet other

sailing enthusiasts—some of whom may
be looking for extra crew members.

TAAL LAKE, PHILIPPINES

This is one of the most beautiful lakes in
the Philippines. It is also the site of the
Taal Volcano, which makes for many
interesting craters below the surface. No
motorized sports are allowed on the lake.

Taal Lake Yacht Club

Barrio Santa Maria
Talisay
Batangas
Philippines
☎ 0912-332-9550 (cellphone)
Head Office:
Corinthian Plaza
Paseo de Roxas
Makati
Philippines
☎ (02) 8113183 **Fax:** (02) 8113236
email: sailphi@i-manila.com.ph
Open to non-members, this prestigious
yet friendly club offers sailing lessons and
boat rentals. Kayaks and windsurfers are
also for hire. Free camping.

PHUKET, THAILAND

Phuket is the perfect base to explore
Myanmar (Borneo), Malaysia, and the
splendid national marine parks of the
Andaman Sea.

Asian Adventures

231 Rat-U-Thit 200 Pee Rd.
Patong Beach
Phuket 83150
Thailand
☎/**Fax:** (076) 342798
email: info@asian-adventures.com
Asian Adventures offers 1- to 2-week
bareboat charters in the Andaman Sea
and day trips around Phang Nga Bay.
Crew optional.

KUAH,LANGKAWI, MALAYSIA

This upmarket resort has excellent
facilities for sailors, plus waterfalls, hot
springs, and caves for the landlubber.

Langkawi Yacht Club Sdn Bhd

Kuah Jetty
Jalan Dato Syod Omar
07000 Kuah
Kedah
Malaysia

The club has a 44-berth capacity for visiting vessels and it is possible for non-members to charter yachts. Provides sailing courses, fishing trips, and diving equipment rental, and can also organize accommodation in the area.

Sail Asia Yacht Charters
35/7 Sakdidet Rd.
Amphur Muang,
Phuket 83000
Thailand
☎ (076)391287
Fax: (076) 391342
Handphone: 01-8914756
This company offers the Maraija—a comfortable, easy to sail 7-berth catamaran for bareboat charter. Fishing and snorkelling gear are included in the price.

SURFING

Idyllic beaches and sensational breaks have made Southeast Asia (particularly Indonesia) something of a surfing mecca. The best time to visit the region is in the dry winter months, from early June to October. Some companies include lessons and equipment hire as part of the package, but if you are going it alone get a reputable outfitter to advise you on suitable gear. Take two surfboards in case one breaks, as well as leg-ropes, helmet, and a light wetsuit, as some of the more remote regions will not have surf shops. Surfing can take a while to master, so it may be a good idea to take a few lessons before embarking on a trip.

PULAU ASU, SUMATRA, INDONESIA
These islands provide consistently high waves, which originate from giant, low pressure systems in the southern Indian Ocean. Only a short boat ride away is a break, which has been compared to Sunset Beach in Hawaii.

Indonesia Adventure Holidays
P.T. Olearys
Jalan Armada no. 1
Medan 20217
Indonesia
☎ (061) 742 425 / 741040
Fax: (061) 719005
This company provides small, eco-friendly tours to Sumatra. As well as

taking you to the best waves, they can organize inland activities such as mountain biking and trekking.

GRAJACAN (OR G-LAND), JAVA
G-Land is a legendary surfing break, on the southern most tip of Java, boasting perfect 2-m (6-foot) waves between May and November. Tiger Trails and 20/20s are quieter—although still impressive—breaks in the area.

G-Land Jungle-Beach-Village
Pt. Plenkung Indah Wisata
Andhika Plaza Building
Simpang Dukuh 38–40
Surabaya 60275
East Java
Indonesia
☎ (031) 5314752/5314753
Fax: (031) 5313073
email: g-land@rad.net.id
website: www.g-land.com/
Accommodation, restaurants, leisure facilities, surf guides, and transfer from hotels in Bali can all be arranged here.

World Surfaris Pty Ltd
86 Fuller St.
Windsor
Qld 4030
Australia
☎ (07) 38611163
Fax: (07) 38611165
email: bookings@worldsurfaris.com
website: www.worldsurfaris.com/html
This company offers package tours to G-land with the option of lessons. Discounts for non-surfing partners. Price includes transport from hotels in Bali.

SIARGAO, PHILIPPINES
The most popular spot on this remote island northeast of Mindanao is General Luna, which boasts Cloud 9, one of the world's top ten waves. As yet, there are no surf shops anywhere near the area, so bring extra leg-ropes and a repair kit.

Green Room Surf Camp
General Luna
Siargao
Philippines
☎ (032) 3401785/3405726
Fax: (032) 3405726
email: emmarcon@usa.net
This is the only surf camp on the beach

(to date). It can arrange packages from the U.S.A., Europe, and Australia.

Surf Schools International

P.O. Box 1525
Noosa Heads
Qld 4567
Australia
☎ (07) 54 749076 **Fax:** (07) 54 748433
In operation since 1991, this is a surf school rather than a travel company. Accommodation is organized but flights must be arranged locally.

MENTAWAI ISLANDS, INDONESIA

The remote location of this picturesque chain of islands off the mid-west coast of Sumatra has kept tourism at bay, but the situation is changing fast. The area offers impressive breaks for surfers who want to escape the crowds.

Good Sumateran Surf Charters

P.O. Box 266
Pacifica
CA 94044
U.S.A.
☎ 1-888-407-GOOD
Fax: (0751) 34265 (Indonesia)
The company offers cruises to Mentawai Islands in search of the best breaks, with an emphasis on conserving local environment. Surf guides available.

Waterways Travel

15145 Califa St.
Suite 1
Van Nuys
CA 91411
U.S.A.
☎ 800/928-3757 (toll free)
Fax: 818/376-0353
email: info@waterwaystravel.com
website: www.waterwaystravel.com
Waterways are agents for Good Sumateran Surf Charters (see above).

TREKKING

From dense, steamy jungle to cool hilltribe villages, Southeast Asia provides a huge variety of excellent trekking terrain. Anyone who can walk for 5–6 hours a day over a period of several days can go trekking, but routes vary greatly in degrees of difficulty, so check the level of fitness required before you set off. On average, expect to cover around 16km (10 miles) a day, so good-quality walking boots are obviously essential. You will be invited to stay in traditional houses, so look to your guide for advice on respecting local customs. Remember that thoughtless trekking can damage eco-systems, so do try to seek out an environmentally aware operator.

KELABIT HIGHLANDS, SARAWAK, MALAYSIAN BORNEO

The rain forest in this relatively unexplored area offers a fascinating diversity of culture. Trek through dense jungle to meet Borneo's last nomadic hunter-gatherer tribe, the Penan, and the Kelabit, characterized by their elaborate body tattoos.

Symbiosis Expedition Planning

Christopher Gow Enterprises Ltd.
205 St John's Hill
London SW11 1TH
U.K.
☎ (020) 7924 5906
Fax: (020) 7924 5907
email: info@symbiosis-travel.co.uk
website: www.symbiosis-travel.co.uk
The company offers small package or tailor-made tours in the region, with an emphasis on conserving local cultures.

Borneo Exploration Tours & Travel Sdn Bhd

76, Wayang St.
93000 Kuching
Sarawak
Malaysia
☎ (082) 252137/252526/410577 (outside office hours)
Fax: (082) 252526
Experienced guides offer tailor-made tours to the region.

BALIEM VALLEY, IRIAN JAYA, INDONESIA

Spectacular scenery coupled with the fiercely traditional culture of the Dani people makes this a truly memorable trip. The treks are for the more adventurous trekker as the routes can be arduous. You must have a *surat jalan* (permit) to visit the region—obtainable in Biak, Jaya Pura, and Sentani. Travel agencies based in nearby Wamena can advise you on local guides.

Asia Transpacific Journeys

P.O. Box 1279
Boulder
CO 80306
U.S.A.
☎ 800/642-2742 (toll free)
Fax: 303/443-7078
email: travel@southeastasia.com
website: www.southeastasia.com
The company offers a rigorous tour for very fit adventurers, involving swamp and jungle trekking and overnight stays in tree houses. It specializes in adventure tours to the region.

Chandra Nusantara Tours and Travel

Jalan Trikora 17
Wamena
Irian Jaya
Indonesia
☎ (0969) 31293
This local company is very knowledgeable about the native tribespeople, and offers fascinating, non-exploitative tours.

Outer Edge Expeditions

45500 Pontiac Trail
Walled Lake
MI 48390-4036
U.S.A.
☎ (0248) 624 140 or (0800) 322 5235
Fax: (0248) 624 6744
email: adventure@outer-edge.com
With this company, which specializes in personalized tours, you can visit tribal people living as they have for centuries and make minimum impact on the environment. Irian Jaya trips run for 15 days with 2–6 guests.

LUZON AND MINDORA, PHILIPPINES

Visit ancient tribes who retain pre-Christian beliefs and marvel at the spectacular rice terraces of the Ifugao people, carved to have minimum impact on the environment. Irian Jaya trips run for 15 days with 2–6 guests.

NORTHERN THAILAND

Northern Thailand has a lot to offer the serious trekker (it is home to traditional hill tribes and much of the country's indigenous wildlife), but be aware that some areas—notably Chiang Mai—have become overrun with tour operators, which means that trekking is no longer the unique experience it once was.

Asian Adventures

Checkmark Enterprise Co. Ltd.
231 Rat-U-Thit
200 Pee Rd.
Patong Beach
Phuket 83150
Thailand
☎/**Fax:** (076) 342798
email: info@asian-adventures.com
This company offers a challenging 15-day trek far from the tourist trails and into the heart of the mountains and jungles of north and the west Thailand, home to traditional hill tribes and much of the country's indigenous wildlife. This trip is ideal if you are very fit and looking for an off the beaten track experience

SA PA, VIETNAM

Escape from the tropical heat to trek through this beautiful, if chilly, valley (0°C/32°F in winter) on the Chinese border. Sa Pa and its surrounding mountains (nicknamed the Tonkinese Alps by the French) are home to traditional hill tribes, or Montagnards.

Global Spectrum

1901 Pennsylvania Ave.
NW Ste. 204
Washington DC 20006
U.S.A.
☎ (02) 293 2065 or 1 800 419 4446
Fax: (02) 296 0815
email: info@vietnamspecialists.com
Global Spectrum started in 1992 as cultural exchange between the U.S.A. and Vietnam. They offer a 10-day adventure in northern Vietnam, meeting indigenous people of the Thai, Hímong, and Zao hill tribes. It is a physically demanding programme, which involves living and working alongside villagers.

Green Bamboo Travel

42 Nha Chung St.
Ha Noi
Vietnam
☎ (084) 8268752/8286504/8249179
Fax: (084) 8264949
website: www.vietnamonline.com/green-bamboo/adventur.html

Established in 1990, Green Bamboo offers tours to remote mountain zones in north and central Vietnam, including Buon Ma Thuot, Cao Bang, and Bac Ha. Trips arranged on request only.

WILDLIFE-WATCHING

Southeast Asia shelters some of the most exotic creatures on earth—many of them endemic, including tigers, elephants, and the endangered Javan rhino. Sumatra and Borneo provide sanctuary for the endangered orangutan, while Komodo features the sinister and prehistoric Komodo dragons. When viewing wildlife, remember to move slowly and quietly in small groups and wear subdued clothing that blends in with the surroundings. Binoculars are a must for spotting wildlife in the jungle, but take a waterproof bag to keep equipment dry.

KOMODO NATIONAL PARK, INDONESIA

This small, volcanic island in the Nusa Tenggara chain offers a glimpse of the closest living relative to the dinosaur. The giant monitor lizards known as Komodo dragons (or *ora* to the locals) grow to 3.5m (12 feet) in length, and have been known to attack humans, although they usually prefer birds and small mammals. The dry season, May to October, is the best time to visit.

Grand Komodo Tours & Travel
P.O. Box 3477
Denpasar 80034
Bali
Indonesia
☎ (0361) 287166 **Fax:** (0361) 287165
Choose from scheduled and chartered tours to Komodo and other islands in the Nusa Tenggara chain. The company also runs live-aboard dive tours.

Smailing Tour
By Pass Ngurah Rai
Sanur Denpasar
Bali
Indonesia
☎ (0361) 288224 **Fax:** (0361) 288738
This large company is expert on all aspects of Indonesian travel and arranges day trips to Komodo.

TANJUNG PUTING, INDONESIA

This national park sits on a peninsula jutting out into the Java Sea and is one of the region's most important wildlife preservation areas. Its best-known inhabitants are the orangutan, which can be seen at the research base at Camp Leakey, but the park is also home to clouded leopards, civets, Malaysian sun bears, and 220 varieties of birds.

Mesra Tours
Samarinda
East Kalimantan
Indonesia
☎ (0541) 38787/32772
Fax: (0541) 35453/41017
email: mesratours@smd.mega.net.id
Mesra arrange jungle treks and boat rides through the park, with stops at Camp Leakey to view the orangutan. The accommodation is in park lodges.

Asia Transpacific Journeys
P.O. Box 1279
Boulder
CO 80306
U.S.A.
☎ 800/642-2742 (toll free)
Fax: 303/443-7078
email: travel@southeastasia.com
website: www.southeastasia.com
This operator arranges 4-day trips from Bali to the research centre at Camp Leakey, involving boating, hiking, swimming, canoeing, and birding.

SANDAKAN, SABAH, MALAYSIAN BORNEO

While there is not much to see in Sandakan itself, it is an ideal base for exploring the surrounding area's diversity of wildlife. Offshore is Turtle Islands National Park, where giant turtles come to lay eggs. The Sepilok Orangutan Rehabilitation Centre, which is also home to Sumatran rhinos, is 25km (15 miles) away. And sightings of proboscis monkeys and other wildlife are common along the Kinabatangan River.

Sabah Parks Office
9th Floor
Wisma Khoo Siak Chiew
Jalan Tiga
Sandakan

☎ (089) 273453
The office makes reservations to visit the Turtle Islands National Park and provides information about Sepilok Orangutan Centre.

Borneo Adventure
55 Main Bazaar
93000 Kuching
Sarawak
Malaysia
☎ (082) 245175/410569/415554
Fax: (082) 422626/234212
email: bakch@borneoadventure.com
website: www.borneoadventure.com
Runs all-inclusive tours to the area with a focus on wildlife.

WINDSURFING

Contrary to popular belief, you can learn to windsurf in a day or two—but it takes a lifetime to master the sport. As a novice, you will spend most of your time getting wet, so the tropical temperatures and clear waters of Southeast Asia make it perfect place to learn. Many resorts offer equipment hire and lessons, sometimes initially on a dry-land simulator. Beginners' boards are large, providing optimum balance, although smaller boards are more flexible. Generally speaking, December to March is the best time to visit, although Thailand's windy season lasts until September. There should be no need for a wetsuit, but bring a Lycra top for sun protection. It may also be a good idea to bring rubber booties to protect your feet against sea urchins. You should be able to swim at least 50m (55 yards).

PATTAYA, THAILAND
Pattaya, which means southwest wind, is Thailand's largest beach resort and home to the national windsurfing team. In summer, during the southwest monsoon, the wind is onshore. The best months are March/April and July/August. Most of the action takes place in Jomtien Beach, a 10-minute drive from Pattaya. The resort also hosts two major longboard events each year, in April/May and November/December.

Club Loong Chat
309/46 Moo 12
Nongprur
Banglamoong
Pattaya City
Chonburi
Thailand
☎ (01) 8219110 **Fax:** (02) 4336365
email: popw@loxinfo.co.th
Facilities include undercover board and sail storage, a grassy rigging area and rig-washing facilities. Board rental and lessons available.

BORACAY, PHILIPPINES
The surfing on this beautiful island off the coast of Panay is in a big lagoon, protected by a reef. Winds of 25 knots or more are quite common during the northeast monsoon (winter) season. The shallow water makes this a great spot for beginners.

Markus & Bernadette
Bulabog
Boracay Island
Philippines
☎/**Fax:** 36 2883876
This company provides lessons and full equipment hire. Slalom, wave, and beginners boards are all available. They operate from December to April.

BINTAN ISLAND, INDONESIA
This idyllic island is accessible from Singapore. The waters can be choppy, as the north side of the island is exposed to the full onslaught of the northeast monsoon coming in over the South China Sea. For experienced shortboard sailors the best season is from November to March. Longboards can be used the rest of the year.

Mana Mana Beach Resort
Eresindo Resorts Singapore Pte Ltd.
33 Liang Seah St. no. 01–01/02
Singapore 189054
☎ 3398878 **Fax:** 3397812
email: manamana@pacific.net.sg
The qualified coach uses simulators to get novices started and video analysis to improve the technique of experienced sailors. There is good quality equipment for hire.

GENERAL INDEX

A

Akha	20, 105, 108
Alak	133
animism	21, 217
archaeological digs	285

B

babirusa	222
Batak	161, 163, 168
batik	173
bats	44, 156, 188
bell-making	238
Bidayuh	180, 182
birdlife	
Borneo	196
Cambodia	124
Laos	104
Malaysia	155, 156
Philippines	245, 252
Sulawesi	221, 229
Thailand	42
bird's-nest soup	40
bird-watching	277, 290–1
black macaques	221–2
Black Zao	95
Bond, James	44
Buddhism	36, 48, 54, 108, 173
Bun Pha Wet	112
bus trips, Laos	132, 135–6

C

canoeing	
Philippines	244–5
Thailand	73
see also sea canoeing/ kayaking	
car/ car and driver rental	277, 286–7
Cambodia	129
Laos	137
Malaysia	157
see also jeep tours	
car hire	
Laos	137
Malaysia	157, 277
Vietnam	99
caves	
Borneo	188–9, 192, 193, 194

Laos	101–2
Malaysia	156
Thailand	28, 40–1, 44, 48, 56
Vietnam	89
caving	291–2
Borneo	188–9, 192, 193, 197
Malaysia	156
Thailand	48
chao ley *(sea gypsies)*	40, 41
Chinese junk trips	49
climate and seasons	
when to go	14–15
Borneo	187, 197, 207, 215
Cambodia	129
Java	177
Laos	109, 119, 137
Malaysia	147, 157
Myanmar (Burma)	81
Philippines	247, 256
Sulawesi	223, 233
Sumatra	169
Thailand	29, 39, 49, 57, 65,73
Vietnam	91, 99
climbing/rock climbing	284, 303–5
Borneo	189–90, 193, 197, 208–15, 284, 287
Java	175–6
Sulawesi	216–17
Sumatra	161, 168
Thailand	45–8, 49, 261
cloves	218
cockfighting	240
coelacanth	224, 228
coffee plantations	134
conservation tours	292–4
coracles	85
coral reefs	70, 153, 199, 201, 202–3, 224, 228–9, 231, 286
Cotton Blossom Festival	56
crafts	
Borneo	181, 185
Java	172, 173
Malaysia	149
Myanmar (Burma)	78, 80
Philippines	237–8
Thailand	25, 28
Vietnam	97
cruising	267–8, 286, 294–5

see also river cruising	
cultural performances	
Java	174
Malaysia	141
see also music and dance	
cultural tours	
Angkor Wat	120–9, 272
Borobudur	170–7, 282
Lao ethnic groups	133
northern Thai hill tribes	20–9, 259
puppetmakers and kitemakers	141
T'boli people	236–47, 280–1
see also longhouse tours	
cycling	295–6
Thailand	28, 50–7, 262–3

D

deforestation	136
dialling codes	257
diving	296–7
Borneo	198–207, 286
buddy system	207
Malaysia	153
Philippines	248–56, 281, 297
Sulawesi	224–33, 288
Thailand	49, 66–73, 265–6, 296–7
wall diving	205, 232
wreck diving	252–3, 289
dolphins	116
driving	298
see also car /car and driver rental; jeep tours	
drug trafficking	24, 36
drums, decorative	141
durian	134

E

eagles	42, 156, 245
Eastern & Oriental Express	58–65, 58–9
eco-nature tours/walks	
Borneo	200
Malaysia	143, 147, 152,153–5, 157
Thailand	73
see also jungle treks	

elephant rides/treks
  Laos   132–3
  Thailand   25–6, 73
elephants 22, 25, 131, 132–3
embassies and consulates
              257–8
ethnic minorities
  Laos   105, 133
  Malaysia   145
  Philippines   236–45
  Vietnam 92–3, 95–6, 97
etiquette
  Borneo   184, 185
  Thailand   21

F

festivals
  Laos   111–12, 114
  Thailand   39, 56, 68
fiddler crabs   43
fishing and fish farms
     156, 241, 245, 298–9
  Borneo   184–5
  Malaysia   145
  Philippines   245, 299
flora
  Borneo 196, 209, 212
  Laos   104
  Malaysia   153–4
  Sulawesi   220
  Thailand   24, 25
food and drink
  Borneo   181, 187
  Cambodia   128
  hygiene
    49, 109, 119, 128, 129
  Laos   101, 113, 133
  Myanmar (Burma) 76, 77
  tea, Burmese   76
  Thailand 25, 36, 52, 60
  Vietnam   85
four-wheel drive safaris,
  Thailand   73

G

gold-mining   143
goldleaf   80
gunu bong *(T'boli home)*
    238, 238, 242–3

H

hang-gliding/paragliding
       153, 299–300

headhunting   182, 192
health matters
  general   16–17
  Borneo 187, 197, 207, 215
  Cambodia   129
  Java   177
  Laos   109, 119, 137
  Malaysia   147, 157
  Myanmar (Burma)   81
  Philippines 247, 256
  Sulawesi   223, 233
  Sumatra   169
  Thailand 29, 39, 49, 57, 65
  Vietnam   91, 99
hill tribes
  Thailand   20–6, 37
  Vietnam   93
history
  Cambodia 122–4, 128
  Philippines   253
  Sulawesi   225
  Thailand   35
  Vietnam 85, 92, 96–7
  World War II 61–3, 253
Hmong 20, 92, 95–6, 98, 105
homestay programmes,
  Malaysia   147
hongs   41–2, 44
hot springs   215

I

Iban   180–5
indigo   95
inoculations
  Borneo 187, 197, 207, 215
  Cambodia   129
  Java   177
  Laos   109
  Malaysia   157
  Myanmar (Burma)   81
  Philippines 247, 256
  Sulawesi   223, 233
  Thailand   29, 49, 57
  Vietnam   99
island-hopping, Malaysia
       148–57, 271–2

J

jeep tours   298
  Vietnam 92–9, 269–70
jeepneys   249, 251
jungle treks   300–1
  Borneo   185,
  192–3, 194, 196,197, 282–6

Malaysia 144–6, 147, 273–4
night treks   146, 220
Philippines   240–1
Sulawesi   219–23
Sumatra   165, 169
Thailand   73

K

Karen   20, 21, 25, 26
karsts   41, 42–3, 85
Katou   133
Kayan   180
Kelabit   180
Kenyah   180, 190
Khao Phansaa   56
Khmer architecture 121
Khmer Rouge 123–4, 128
kidnapping   237, 247
kites   141
kayaking *see* sea
  canoeing/kayaking

L

Lahu 20, 21, 23, 24, 26–7
lao lao *(rice whisky)* 116–17
leeches   27–8
legends
  Malaysia 148, 149, 152
  Thailand 20–1, 36, 48
  Vietnam   89
Lisu   20
longhouses
  180–4, 185, 187, 196
longhouse tours, Borneo
  180–7, 196, 282–4. 284–6
longtail boat trips   49

M

macaques   45
Magha Puja   112
make-up, Burmese 77
malaria
  99, 109, 119, 129, 169
Maleo bird   229
mangroves   156
mangrove tours
  Malaysia   157
marine life
  Borneo 201–2, 204, 205
  Philippines   253
  Sulawesi 228–9, 231
  Thailand   68, 71, 72

markets
Cambodia	125–6
Java	172
Laos	105
Malaysia	140, 143
Sulawesi	218
Vietnam	93, 94–5

Melanau 180, 182
Mohammed, Dr Mahathir 148, 149
motorbiking 303–4
Malaysia	149, 157
Thailand	30–9, 260–1
Vietnam	89, 91

motorbike rental, Malaysia 157, 277
Mouhot, Henri 100, 101, 124
mountain-bike tours, Thailand 73
mountaineering *see* climbing/rock climbing
music and dance
Borneo	182, 185
Java	174, 174
Malaysia	141
Philippines	242–3, 244
Thailand	29
Vietnam	98

N

national parks
Malaysia	142–3, 143–6
Philippines	245
Sulawesi	219–22
Sumatra	165
Thailand	53
Vietnam	89–90

Ngan Kin Jeh 68
Nge 133

O

opium poppies 24, 105
Orang asli 145
Orang Ulu 180
orangutans 166–8, 166–7
orchids 24, 25, 104

P

packing tips
Borneo	197, 207, 215
Java	177
Laos	109, 137

Malaysia	157
Myanmar (Burma)	81
Philippines	247, 256
Sulawesi	223
Sumatra	169
Thailand	29, 39, 49, 65
Vietnam	99

Padang 37
palm oil 64, 144, 219
Penan 180
personal security
Cambodia	124, 125, 129
Laos	136
Myanmar (Burma)	81
Philippines	237, 247
Thailand	29, 56

phi *(spirits)* 37
Phi Ta Khon festival 56
Phou Noi 105
pitcher plants 209
Pla Buk 108
puppets 141
pythons 222

R

railway journeys
Malaysia	140–4, 147, 273–4
Thailand	58–65, 264

Rafflesia 209
river rafting 305–6
Sumatra	169, 305
Thailand	28
see also white-water rafting

Red Zao 92–3
registration (Laos) 109, 137
religion 237
see also animism; Buddhism
rhododendrons 212
rice 30, 54, 54–5, 155
river cruising
Laos	101, 110–19, 270–2
Myanmar (Burma)	74–81, 267–8

river journeys
Borneo	181–2, 184–5, 191
Cambodia	125–8
Laos	100–19, 134–5, 271–2
Malaysia	140–1, 147
slowboats	109
speedboats	109

Road to Mandalay 74–80
rubber plantations 64, 144

S

safety	16–17
sailing	306–7

sea canoeing/kayaking 277–9, 301–2
Philippines	250–2
Thailand	40–5, 49, 261–2, 268–9
Vietnam	84–91, 268

Sea Dyaks *see* Iban
snorkelling
Borneo	206
Malaysia	153

stilt houses 152, 237, 238, 250
see also longhouses
strangler fig 153–4
surfing 307–8
swiftlets' nests 40–1, 43

T

Ta-oy	133
T'ai	97
tarsiers	220, 287–8
T'boli	236–45, 288–289
telephones	257

temples
Cambodia	120–8, 123
Java	172–4
Laos	101, 106, 108, 112–14, 117, 118–19
Thailand	32, 33, 36, 37, 38, 48, 54

tin-mining 64, 143
tops, spinning 141
travel, internal
Borneo	187, 197, 207, 215
Cambodia	129
Java	177
Laos	109, 119, 137
Malaysia	147, 157
Myanmar (Burma)	81
Philippines	247, 256
Sulawesi	223, 233
Sumatra	169
Thailand	29, 39, 49, 57, 65, 73
Vietnam	91, 99

travellers' tips
Borneo	187
Laos	137
Myanmar (Burma)	81
Thailand	21, 37, 57

Vietnam 88, 99
trekking 296–7, 308–10
  Thailand 20–9, 295–60
  see also jungle treks
tuak *(rice spirit)* 187, 196
tuk-tuks 50

V

Vegetarian Festival 68
Vietnam War 97, 134, 136
Vietnamese language 91
volcanoes
  161, 162, 176, 216–17, 220

W

waruga tombs 217, 218–19
waterfalls
  Laos 101, 116, 132, 136

Malaysia 149
Philippines 240, 241
when to go 14–15
white-water rafting 305–7
  Malaysia 146
  Sumatra 160, 164–5, 280–1
  Thailand 28
wildlife
  Borneo 188, 191, 196, 200
  Laos 104, 108
  Malaysia 145,
    146, 149, 152, 154–5, 156
  Sulawesi 220, 221–2
  Sumatra 165–8
  Thailand 44, 45
  Vietnam 90
  see also birdlife
wildlife-watching 310–11
  bird-watching 290–1
  conservation tours 292–4

Sulawesi 220–2, 287–8
Sumatra 166–8, 169
  see also eco-nature
    tours/walks; jungle treks
windsurfing 311
World War II 61–3, 253

X

Xouei 133

Y

Yao 20

GAZETTEER

A

Akha	34
Alas River	164, 305
Ambarita	168
Angkor Thom	121
Angkor Wat	120–9, 122–3, 126
Annamite Mountains	113
Ao Phang Nga	40, 41, 42–3, 44
Ao Pra-Nang	45, 48
Ao Thalan	44
Asahan River	164, 305
Attapu	130, 135–6, 137
Ava	79–80
Ava Bridge	79
Ayeyarwady River	74, 78, 80, 81
Ayung River	305

B

Ba Cat Island	85, 88
Baan Hin Taek	36
Baan Kien Tang Le	133
Baan Meung Phen	24
Baan Pa Mon Nai	24
Baan Paou	117
Baan Tad Soon	133
Bagan	74–7, 75
Baie Chai	84
Bako National Park	301
Bali	296, 298–9
Baliem Valley	305, 308–9
Ban Boun	113
Ban Don	102
Ban Hat Sa	105
Ban Noi	117
Ban Pak Huay	55, 56
Ban Pak Kud	136
Ban Ruammit	36
Ban Thoed Thai	36
Ban Yo	108
Bangkok	59, 61
Bantei Srei	121, 124–5
Baphuon Temple	124
Barracuda Point	206
Barusjahe	161
Bat Cave	44
Batang Ai	180

Batang Ai National Park	182, 184
Batang Ai Reservoir	181
Batang Rajang River	187
Batuputih	217, 219, 222
Bayon Temple	121–2
Belawan	169
Big Lagoon	44
Bintan Island	311
Bitung	223, 233
Blangkerjeren	168
Bohol	297
Bohorok River	168, 169
Bolovens Plateau	116, 130–7
Book Village	153
Bontoc	292
Bor Sang	32
Boracay	311
Borneo	179, 180–215
Borobudur	170–7, 170–1, 175
Brastagi	160, 161, 169
Brunei	179
Buddha's Footprint	48
Bukit Lawang	160, 165, 166, 169
Bukit Teresek	144
Bunaken	224–33, 227, 230–1
Burma *see* Myanmar	
Burma Banks	73
Burma Railway ("Death" Railway)	61–2
Busuanga	248–9, 256
Butterworth	63

C

Calamian Islands	248
Cambodia	83
Casuarina Bay	156
Cat Ba Bay	89
Cat Ba Island	85, 86, 89, 91
Cat Ba National Park	85, 89–90, 91
Cave Lod	28, 37
Cave of Tales	156
Cave of Wonders	89
Champassak	112
Chiang Dao	33
Chiang Khan	54–5, 57

Chiang Khong	111
Chiang Mai	20, 29, 32, 39
Chiang Rai	20, 29, 36, 39
Chinese Cave	195
Chom Thong	38
Chong Kham Lake	37
Clearwater Cave	189, 192, 197
Concepcion	252
Coral Garden	206
Corón	248–56, 250–1, 301
Culion	256

D

Dabong	143
Dansai	56
Dau Go Cave	89
Davao	247, 304
de Castries' Bunker	96
Deer Cave	188, 197
Delok River	181
Diamond Cave	48
Dien Bien Phu	96–7, 98
Dog River	160, 164–5
Doi Ang Khang	33
Doi Inthanon National Park	38
Doi Tung	36
Dokan	161
Dolok	168
Don Khong Island	111, 113
Dong Hoi	292
Dong Trieu	84
Donsol	285

E

East Railay	45, 46–7, 48

F

Fairy Cave	194
Four Thousand Islands	113
Friendship Bridge	52

G

G-Land (Grajacan)	307
Galleria Perdana	149
Gemas	140
General Santos	236, 245, 247
Georgetown, Penang	63
Golden City Temple	101

Golden Triangle 36
Grotte des Merveilles 89
Gua Cherita 156
Gua Kelawar 156
Gua Musang 143
Gunung Api 189, 193
Gunung Kinabalu Park 208–15
Gunung Kerinci 304
Gunung Leuser National Park 165–6, 305
Gunung Mat Cincang 153, 157
Gunung Mulu 189–90, 197
Gunung Mulu National Park 188–97, 190–1
Gunung Raya 155, 157
Gunung Rinjani 304
Gunung Tahan 144

H

Ha Long Bay 84–91, 302
Hai Phong 90
Ha Noi 296
Hat Ham Par Nag 48
Headhunter's Trail 189, 192, 194, 197
Hellabong 244
Heung River 56
Hin Mu Sang 73
Ho Chi Minh Trail 136
Hong Yai 44

I

Isaan 50–7
Island of the Big Lion 152
Irian Jaya 308–9

J

Jakarta 170
'James Bond Island' 44, 46–7
Java 159, 170–7, 307
Jelawang Country Park 143
Jerantut 141, 143, 147
Johor Baru 64
Jong Khneas 125

K

Kachanaburi 62, 62–3
Kachanaburi Allied War Cemetery 62–3
Kaeng Kut Khu Rapids 54

Kalimantan 179, 182, 293
Kaliurang 175
Kampung Kijang 141
Kelabit Highlands 308
Kelantan River 140–1
Kenong Rimba State Park 143
Ketambe 169
Khao Sok National Park 73, 300
Khao Yai National Park 290
Khong Hai Mountains 114, 116
Khong Phapheng Falls 114, 116
Khun Yuam 38
Kilim River 156
Killing Fields of Choeung Ek 128
Kinabatangan River 298
Kisap River 156
Ko Hong 41
Ko Khao Ping Kan 43, 44, 46–7
Ko Phi Phi 73
Ko Racha Yai 73
Ko Rajah Noi 73
Ko Samui 67, 297
Ko Similan 73
Ko Surin Islands 73
Ko Tao 67
Ko Tapu 43
Ko Thalu 40
Ko Yao Noi 44
Kok River valley 33, 34–5
Komodo National Park 300
Kompong Chnang 128
Kong River 134–5
Korat Plateau 50
Kota Baharu 140, 141, 143, 147
Kota Kinabalu 200, 207, 208, 211, 215
Krabi 45
Krung Thep *see* Bangkok
Kuah 148, 152, 154–5, 306
Kuala Kenian 145
Kuala Kerai 142–3
Kuala Lipis 143
Kuala Lumpur 64, 65, 140, 198, 200
Kuala Perkai 145
Kuala Tahan 144

Kuala Terikan 96
Kuching 180–1, 187
Kungkungan Bay Resort 284
Kutacane 165, 169
Kwa Noi River 302
Kwuang Sy Waterfalls 101

L

Laban Rata Resthouse 212
Lachau 181
Laem Phrao 41
Laem Pra-Nang 45
Lahu 34
Lai Chau 95
Lake Kawar 160
Lake Sebu 236, 237, 238, 239, 244, 246, 247
Lake Toba 168, 290
Lake Tondano 232
Langkawi 148–57, 306
Lang's Cave 189, 197
Lao Cai 92
Laos 83, 100–19, 303
Lata Berkoh 145
Lemanak River 187
Limbang 197
Limbang River 196
Lingga 161
Lisu 34
Little Switzerland 33
Loei 56
Lombok 298–304
Long Berar 192
Low's Peak 213
Luang Prabang 100–1, 106–7, 109, 111
Lubang China 196
Luzon 245, 309

M

Mae Cham 38
Mae Hong Son 28, 29, 37–8
Mae Malai 24
Mae Salong 34, 35–6
Mae Sariang 33
Mae Surin National Park 38
Mae Taeng 33
Mai Chau 97–8
Maiden Grotto 89
Makam Mahsuri 152
Malagos 245

GAZETTEER

Malaysia 64, 138–57, 198, 200, 303
Mamutik Island 200, 207
Mana Mana Beach Resort 299
Manado 216, 218, 222, 223, 224, 230–1, 233
Manado Tua 224
Mandalay 80
Manila 235, 236, 248, 254, 256
Marudi 197
Medalam River 196
Medan 160, 169
Mekong River 101, 110–19, 110–11, 114–15, 303
Melinau Gorge 193–4
Melinau River 191–2
Mentawai Islands 308
Mergui Archipelago 73, 291, 299, 301
Mindanao 236, 245, 247
Mindora 309
Minglazedi 77
Mingun Village 80
Miri 197
Mount Apo National Park 245, 293
Mount Belirang 168
Mount Fang Xi Pang 92, 93
Mount Fou Fa 105
Mount Kinabulu 200, 208–15, 210, 214
Mount Lokon 216–17
Mount Mahawu 220
Mount Merapi 174, 176
Mount Phousi 101
Mount Sibayak 161, 162, 169
Mount Sinabung 160, 161, 169
Muang Khua 104
Muang Loei 56
Muang Noi 103, 104
Mulu National Park 292
Museum of Genocide, Phnom Penh 128
Myanmar (Burma) 19, 74–81

N

Nakhon Ratchasima Province 293
Nam Ou River 100–9

Nam Phak River 104
Nam Se River 112
Nanga Sumpa 181, 184, 185
National Museum of Arts, Phnom Penh 128
Niah National Park 291
Nias 169
Noen Krapok Mountain 300
Nong Khai 50, 51, 56
Nusa Dua 302
Nusa Tenggara 294

O

Orangutan Rehabilitation Centre, Bukit Lawang 166–8, 166–7, 169
Orangutan Rehabilitation Centre, Sepilok 298
Oriental Hotel, Bangkok 59
Oudomxay 105
Oum Muang 117, 118

P

Pa Mon Nok 21, 23
Pagan see Bagan
Pai 20, 37
Pai River 23, 28
Pak Beng 101
Pak Chom 53, 57
Pak Ou Caves 101–2
Pakxe 111, 112, 114, 117, 119, 132, 137
Pakxong 136
Palawan 248, 256, 294
Panguruan 168
Pantai Cenang 149, 157
Pantai Datai 153
Pantai Kok 149
Patong 67
Pattaya 311
Penang 60, 63–4
Perbesi 161
Perhentian Islands 140
Petronas Towers, Kuala Lumpur 140
Phang Na 49
Phang Nga Bay 40, 42–3, 44, 46–7
Philippine Eagle Nature Centre 245

Philippines 234–56, 306–9
Phnom Bakheng 124
Phnom Penh 126, 128
Phong Na Cave 292
Phong Thô 93–4
Phongsali 105
Phu Kradung National Park 53, 56
Phu Reua National Park 53, 56
Phuket 49, 66–73, 70–1, 295, 306
Pimai 120
Pinnacles 189, 191, 193, 195, 197
Poipet 124
Poring Hot Springs 215
Pra-Nang Peninsula 45
Preah Khan 125
Princess Lagoon 48
Pulau Asu 307
Pulau Beras Besah 153, 157
Pulau Dangli 156
Pulau Dayang Bunting 152
Pulau Gasing 156
Pulau Gaya 200
Pulau Labuan 215
Pulau Langkawi 148, 150–1
Pulau Pasir 156
Pulau Payar 153
Pulau Singa Besar 152, 157
Pulau Tuba 148
Pulau Weh 169
Puncak Jaya 304

R

Raffles Hotel, Singapore 59
Railay 45
Rajah Islands 73
Rajah Yai 72
Riau Islands 295
Rih Tengah 163
River Kwai 61, 62, 62–3
Ronggurni Huta 168
Royal Palace, Phnom Penh 128
Rumah Bala Lasong 196

S

Sa Pa 92–3, 309
Sabah 179, 200, 310
Sagada Caves 292

Sagaing Hill   79, 80
Saidan River   306
Samosir   168
Sandakan   310
Sangihe-Talaud Archipelago
                               296
Sangkhom   53, 57
Santikhiri *see* Mae Salong
Sarawak   179,
            180–97, 301, 309
Sarawak Chamber   193
Sarawak Museum   180–1
Sawangan   217, 218–19
Second Falls   240
See Pan Done   113
Sekong   134, 137
Semangat Gunung   161
Semporna   204
Serian   181, 187
Seven Wells   149
Shark Point   73
Shwe Kyet Yet   79
Si Chiang Mai   52, 57
Siargao   307
Sidihoni Lake   168
Siem Reap   121, 124
Silver Pagoda   128
Simanindo   168
Similan Islands   68, 299
Singapore   58–9
Sipadan   198–207
Sisophon   124
Skrang River   187
So'n La   97
Soppong   28
Sorsogon   285
Sulawesi   179, 216–33, 306
Sumatra   159, 160–9,
               300, 305, 307

T

Ta Phrom   121, 124, 127
Taal Lake   307
Tad Hang Waterfall   133
Tad Lo   132, 137
Tad Phan   136
Tadlo   116
Tahan River   145, 146
Taiping   64
Tanah Merah   165
Tana Toraja   306

Tangkahan   169
Tangkoko National Park
                      216–23, 291
Tanjung Puting   310
Tanjung Rhu   156
Taski Dayang Bunting 152, 157
Taungthamon Lake   78–9
Tawau   207
Telaga Tujuh   149
Telom River   305
Teman Negara National Park
       142–3, 143–6, 146, 147, 290
Tembeling River   144, 145, 146
Terengganu   140
Terikan River   194, 196
Tha Bo   52
Tha Li   56
Tha Teng   134
Tha Thon   24
Tha Ton   33–4
Thailand   18–73
Tham Lawd   28, 37
Tham Paa Phu   56
Tham Pla   38
Than Thip Falls   53
Than Thong Waterfall   53
That Luang   108
Tiger Cave   192–3
Tiger Cave Temple   48
Tioman Island   294
Toba Lake   300
Tomohon   216
Tomok   168
Tonkinese Alps   92, 93
Tonle Sab Lake   125–6
Tonlé Sab River   128
Tuk Tuk   168
Tumpat   140
Tuol Sleng Museum, Phnom
Penh   128
Turtle Cave   206
Turtle Islands National Park
                           298

U

Udom Xai   108
Ujung Kulon National Park 300
Ulu Watu   300

V

Vientiane   108, 109
Vietnam   83, 84–99,
               298, 303, 309

W

Wakaf Bharu   141
Wampu River   160, 164–5
Wat Chom Si   101
Wat Chom Thong   113–14
Wat Chong Kham   37
Wat Chong Klang   37
Wat Doi Suthep   32
Wat Hat Pratum   52
Wat Hin Maek Peng   53
Wat Kaek   50
Wat Mahathat   54–5
Wat Mai   101
Wat Ngam Muang   36
Wat Ongtu   108
Wat Phnom Penh   128
Wat Phou Ngoy   117
Wat Phra Kaeo   36
Wat Phra That Doi Kong Mu
                            38
Wat Phra That Doi Tung   36
Wat Phu   111, 112–13, 119
Wat Po Chai   50, 52
Wat Pra Bhat   54
Wat Sisakhet   108
Wat Tha Ton   33, 35
Wat Tham Sua   48
Wat Xieng Thong   101, 106
West Railay   45
Western Baray Reservoir   124
Wet Rice Island   153
Wind Cave   189, 192, 194, 197

X

Xe Xet River   132

Y

Yogyakarta   171-2, 177
Young Lady Cave   192

Z

Zamboanga   247

ACKNOWLEDGEMENTS

Ben Davies would like to thank the following: Chris Gow at Symbiosis Expedition Planning; Dawn Ellis, Laurent Desmazier at Mekong Land; Sia Souk at Sodi Tour in Vientiane; Cristina Landazabal, Francis Middlehurst and Charles Coleman.

Jill Gocher would like to warmly thank Myra French at the Singapore office of Eastern & Oriental Express as well as train manager Christopher Byatt for his help and wonderful repetoire of stories. The Oriental Hotel in Bangkok and the folk at Buffalo Tours in Hanoi also deserve special thanks. Also thank you to everone concerned who helped to make the adventures memorable and enjoyable.

Christopher Knowles would like to thank all those who contributed to the success of the journeys that he undertook, organizers and fellow travellers alike. Most are mentioned in the text—without exception they made my 'adventures' enormous fun. In addition, I would like to thank Lescek of Voyages Jules Verne, London for organizing some of the air tickets and Symbiosis Expedition Planning, London for planning and arranging a seemingly impossible itinerary.

Abbreviations for terms appearing below: (t) top; (b) bottom; (l) left; (r) right; (c) centre.

Cover acknowledgements

Front cover (t): NHPA (John Shaw)
Front cover main picture: Tony Stone Images
Front cover (b): Bruce Coleman Collection
Spine: NHPA (John Shaw)
Back cover (t): Image Bank
Back cover (ct): Steve Watkins
Back cover (cb): AA Photo Library/Jim Holmes
Back cover (br): Bruce Coleman Collection
Inside flaps: (t) AA Photo Library/Ben Davies; (ct): AA Photo Library/Jill Gocher; (cb): AA Photo Library/Jill Gocher; (b): Fiona Dunlop

---

The Automobile Association wishes to thank the following photographers and libraries for their assistance in the preparation of this book.
Axiom(Jim Holmes) 87(b), 90, 211(t), 211(c); **Ben Davies** 42/3, 42, 114, 119;
James Davis Travel Photography 127; **Fiona Dunlop** 170/1, 175, 183, 222;
Jill Gocher 14/15, 182(t), 186(t), 190/1, 190, 194(t), 194(b), 195, 210, 211(b), 214(t), 214(b), 223, 226, 227(b), 230/1, 231; **Robert Harding Picture Library** 46/7, 71(t), 71(b), 146, 154/5, 250; **Jack Jackson** 67(t), 67(b), 199, 202/3, 254(t), 254(b), 255; **Patrick Lucero** 234/5, 238(t), 238(b), 239, 242/3, 242, 246, 251, 250/1; **Malaysia Tourism Promotion Board** 186(b); **Simon Richmond** 14(b), 46, 47, 142, 151, 158/9, 162, 178/9, 191.

The remaining photographs are held in the Association's own photo library (AA PHOTO LIBRARY) and were taken by the following photographers:
Dirk Buwalda 167, 174, 218, 218/9, 227(t), 230; **Ben Davies** 2/3, 15(t), 15(cl), 15(cr), 19, 22, 23(t), 23(b), 27, 30, 31, 34, 34/5, 35, 38, 54, 54/5, 55, 102(t), 102(b), 103, 106/7, 106, 107, 110/1, 110, 114/5, 118, 122/3, 122, 123, 126(t), 126(b), 131, 134/5, 135, 159;
Jill Gocher 15(b), 58/9, 58, 59, 75(t), 75(b), 78, 78/9, 82/3, 87(t), 90/1, 94, 95, 98(t), 98(tr), 163(t), 163(b), 166, 166/7; **Nick Hanna** 3, 7, 143, 155, 182(b), 198, 203(t), 203(b), 206;
Jim Holmes 14(t), 86, 94/5, 98(b); **Ken Paterson** 138/9, 139, 142/3, 150/1, 150, 154;
Rick Strange 6/7, 18/9, 26/7, 26, 43, 50, 51, 62/3, 66, 70/1.

SOUTHEAST ASIA

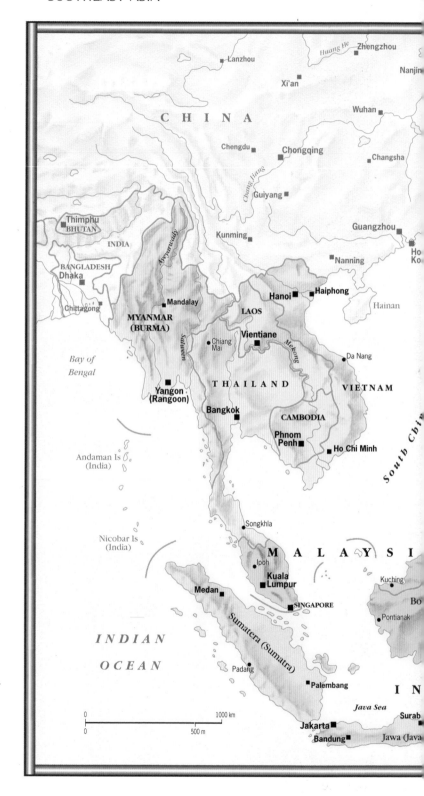

CHINA

Lanzhou
Xi'an
Wuhan
Zhengzhou
Nanjin
Chengdu
Chongqing
Changsha
Guiyang
Thimphu
BHUTAN
Guangzhou
Kunming
INDIA
Nanning
Ho
Ko
BANGLADESH
Dhaka
Hainan
Chittagong
Mandalay
Hanoi
Haiphong
MYANMAR
(BURMA)
LAOS
Chiang
Mai
Vientiane
Bay of
Bengal
Da Nang
THAILAND
VIETNAM
Yangon
(Rangoon)
Bangkok
CAMBODIA
Andaman Is
(India)
Phnom
Penh
Ho Chi Minh
South Chi
Nicobar Is
(India)
Songkhla
MALAYSI
Ipoh
Kuching
Kuala
Lumpur
Bo
Medan
SINGAPORE
Pontianak
INDIAN
OCEAN
Padang
Palembang
I N
Java Sea
Jakarta
Surab
Bandung
Jawa (Java

Ayeyarwady
Chang Jiang
Salween
Mekong
Huang He
Sumatera (Sumatra)

0   1000 km
0   500 m